Psyche Reborn

D1158536

Photo of H.D. by Man Ray

Psyche Reborn

THE EMERGENCE OF H.D.

Susan Stanford Friedman

Indiana University Press Bloomington

First Midland Book Edition 1987

Copyright © 1981 by Susan Stanford Friedman

All rights reserved

No part of this book may be reproduced or utilized in any form
or by any means, electronic or mechanical, including photocopying
and recording, or by any information storage and retrieval system,
without permission in writing from the publisher. The Association
of American University Presses' Resolution on Permissions constitutes
the only exception to this prohibition.

Manufactured in the United States of America

Library of Congress Cataloging in Publication Data

Friedman, Susan Stanford.
Psyche reborn.
Includes bibliographical references and index.
1. Doolittle, Hilda, 1886-1961.   2. Poets, American—
20th century—Biography.   3. Psychoanalysis and literature.   4. Occultism in literature.   I. Title.
PS3507.0726Z66   1981   811'.52   [B]   80-8378
cl. ISBN 0-253-37826-5   AACR1
pa. ISBN 0-253-20449-6

2   3   4   5   6   91   90   89   88   87

For the guardians of my beginnings,
with love and respect,
Anne Thompson Stanford and Ralph Stanford

Contents

Preface   ix

Acknowledgments   xvi

Introduction   1

PART I: H.D. and Psychoanalytic Tradition

1   Freud as Guardian of Beginnings:
     Biographical Roots of Psychoanalytic Influence   17
2   Hieroglyphic Voices:
     The Unconscious and Psychoanalytic Modes of Translation   50.
3   Delphi of the Mind:
     The Unconscious as Muse and Prophet   70
4   "Transcendental Issues":
     Artist and Scientist in Debate   87
5   "The Professor Was Not Always Right":
     Woman and Man in Conflict   121

PART II: H.D. and Religious Tradition

6   Initiations:
     Biographical Roots of Occult Influence   157
7   "Companions of the Flame":
     Syncretist Mythmaking in the Crucible of War   207
8   "Born of One Mother":
     Re-Vision of Patriarchal Tradition   229
9   Poetics of Conflict and Transcendence:
     Kabbalah and the Search for Wholeness   273

Notes   297

Index   325

PREFACE

THIS BOOK is about the making of a great artist, about the process of influence that led to the development of a major twentieth-century writer whose works unfortunately still require considerable introduction because of their relative neglect in the annals and anthologies of literary history. H.D.'s interactions with the artistic, intellectual, and political currents of her era led her from the confines of the perfect imagist poem to the creative maturity evident in such brilliant modernistic works as *Tribute to Freud*, the *Trilogy*, and *Helen in Egypt*. Despite the frequently expressed view that H.D.'s art was too fragile for the harsh, modern world, H.D. squarely confronted the central questions of the century and experimented with new forms that could reflect the modernist despair and quest for alternative meanings. Her lifelong revolt against a traditional feminine destiny, however, set her apart from the literary mainstream and led her ultimately to a woman-centered mythmaking and radical re-vision of the patriarchal foundations of western culture.

Psyche Reborn argues that H.D.'s experience as an analysand with Sigmund Freud and her exploration of esoteric tradition provided her with an interrelated framework of quest that nourished the explosion of a new kind of poetry and prose during the forties and fifties. The book also examines H.D.'s interactions with psychoanalysis and esoteric religion as a particularly clear instance of a larger debate in modern thought between scientific and artistic modes of creating meanings. Her sessions with Freud and the extraordinary reflections on them in her tribute constitute a dramatic dialogue between artist and scientist, mythmaker and rationalist, woman and man. This confrontation of opposites and H.D.'s search for transcendence provide the organizational framework for *Psyche Reborn*.

Part I examines H.D.'s explorations with Freud, assesses his impact on her poetic development, identifies the sources of her disagreement with Freud, and places her evaluation of Freud's contributions within the context of scholarly debates on psychoanalysis. Chapter 1 is an account of her experiences with psychoanalysis. Chapter 2 considers the significance of Freud's theories about the dream-work and the unconscious for H.D.'s search for a translation of the hieroglyphics of the psyche. Chapter 3 questions the impact of Freud's hypothesis about the common origins of religion and art in the unconscious on the development of the prophetic voice in her quest poetry. Chapter 4 examines their opposing conceptions of reality as the crucial dialogue that led to H.D.'s modernist mythmaking. Chapter 5 demonstrates how H.D. used aspects of Freud's theories about women and his diagnosis of her "symptoms" to overturn his misogyny and develop an authentic female voice.

Part II examines H.D.'s involvement in a syncretist religious tradition that incorporated the occult and esoteric mysticism. It defines the nature of her interest, explores her redefinitions of that tradition, and shows how basic hermetic concepts influence both her artistic vision and aesthetic forms. Chapter 6 is an extensive biographical account of her involvement in occult phenomena, numerology, Tarot, astrology, spiritualism, and the Kabbalah. Chapter 7 considers the dialectical nature of her modernist mythmaking as she both reflected and transformed esoteric tradition. Chapter 8 examines the significance of the Goddess in the evolution of her re-vision of patriarchal traditions. Finally, chapter 9 describes her poetic search for transcendence of polarities under the guiding inspiration of the Kabbalah.

In *Psyche Reborn*, I have integrated several types of critical methodologies because no one approach is sufficient for an exploration of the multiple dimensions of H.D.'s life and work. As biography, the book presents information taken from her journals and letters to establish the basic outlines of her life. As critical biography, it focuses extensively on the significance of her experiences as a woman and her interest in psychoanalytic and religious tradition for her artistic development. As a specific study of influence, it examines both the ideas and the dialectical process of influence. As a history of ideas, it explores the larger debates between art and science, religion and science, woman and man implicit in H.D.'s interactions with Freud. As textual criticism, it examines H.D.'s development of aesthetic forms characteristic of modernism and incorporates explication of her prose memoirs

and the difficult poetry of the forties and fifties into the larger arguments of the book. And finally, as feminist criticism, it shows how
H.D.'s perspective as a woman mediated the influence of patriarchal
traditions and led to a poetry centered on woman as both authentic
symbol and questor. It has been my intention that this multifaceted
study of H.D.'s life and work will serve as both catalyst and context
for future scholarship on specific aspects of her complex canon.

Psyche Reborn represents the final emergence of H.D. from the
critical cage of imagism to which she has largely been confined by
literary history. Her reputation as the perfect imagist and "publicity
girl" for the Greeks has rationalized the inclusion of one or two short
poems in poetry anthologies and the relative absence of serious critical
attention to her complex spiritual and philosophic explorations in a
number of genres. I say *final emergence* because this book rests with
gratitude upon the thoughtful studies of her work that have appeared
with increasing frequency in recent years. A growing community of
H.D. scholars has recognized the accuracy of Hugh Kenner's statement that identification of H.D. as an imagist poet is "as though five
of the shortest pieces in 'Harmonium' were to stand for the life's
work of Wallace Stevens."

This liberation of H.D. from the imagist label, however, is inextricably connected with her emergence from the phallic criticism
that has plagued her woman-centered mythmaking to a frequently
greater degree than it has other women writers. Her psychoanalysis
with Freud as well as her extensive self-revelations in memoir and
poem left her particularly vulnerable to the excesses of psychoanalytic
criticism. The double standard of literary criticism that subtly evalu-
ates a work of art in terms of the gender of its creator operated to
intensify the celebration of H.D.'s traditionally "feminine" lyric and
the dismissal of her adaptation of the "masculine" modes of epic
quest and philosophic symbolism. More than any other factor, however, the nature of her work itself destined her critical reputation to
the distortions of a phallic criticism whose presuppositions hindered
any comprehensive illumination of her vision. H.D.'s art is a profound
exploration of the situation of the woman as writer, lover, and seeker
of redemptive realities in a male-dominated world that is perpetually
at war. It represents the extraordinary achievement of a woman who
immersed herself in the androcentric traditions of literature, psychoanalysis, and religion and transformed them so that they could pro-

vide the framework for authentic female quest. The foundation of her art was the metamorphosis of culture. *Psyche Reborn* rests implicitly on the assumption that the critical re-vision her work demands must begin with this foundation as the illuminating context of the multiple dimensions of her life and work.

In a sense, then, *Psyche Reborn* is a beginning, one that recognizes the ultimately collaborative nature of knowledge and intends to provide the initial catalyst to the proliferation of different inquiries, even conflicting perspectives on H.D.'s achievement. Not only does her work justify such expansion of research, but the manuscript collections of her papers combined with her extensive canon of published work provide an unusually rich store of material. Her close friend and literary executor, the late Norman Holmes Pearson, is largely responsible for the wealth of materials recently becoming available to scholars. He urged her to send him letters, diaries, notebooks, and manuscripts, promising a home for them in the Collection of American Literature, Beinecke Rare Book and Manuscript Library at Yale University. In their correspondence his steady encouragement and advice aided greatly in the completion of such manuscripts as *Selected Poems of H.D.*, *Helen in Egypt*, *Tribute to Freud*, and *End to Torment*. He furthermore asked her to detail and reflect upon major events in her life and the processes by which she shaped them into art. His efforts resulted in a collection of manuscripts at Beinecke Library that encourage extensive research on the interrelations between her life and her work. His bequest to Beinecke included the unpublished manuscripts for three romans à clef, five novels, three memoirs, five journals (including records of dreams), one epic poem, and a great deal of miscellaneous prose, poetry, and notes on her reading. In addition, manuscripts of much of her published work are part of the collection, including both handwritten and typed copies with H.D.'s own revisions. Many of these materials are as yet uncatalogued, and I am greatly indebted to H.D.'s daughter, Perdita Schaffner, and to Donald Gallup, Curator of the Collection of American Literature, for allowing me to read these illuminating materials.

Pearson's bequest to Beinecke also included extensive correspondence he had collected between H.D. and some forty people, including many who were extremely important to both her life and her art. While I was writing the book, I was fortunately able to read some of this rich material: H.D.'s letters to Viola Jordan (catalogued under

Jordan), Ezra Pound, Kenneth Macpherson, Brigit Patmore, Walter Schmideberg, Robert Herring, and Gretchen Wolle Baker; and letters to H.D. from Pound, Sylvia Beach, Dorothy Richardson, Denise Levertov, and Vita Sackville-West. Because of the stipulations of Pearson's will, I was *not* able to see H.D.'s letters to Bryher, Pearson, or Richard Aldington; nor did I have access to correspondence from Aldington, Pearson, Bryher, or Macpherson to H.D.

While *Psyche Reborn* was in production, however, this important collection of letters was opened to scholars. During the summer of 1980, I was able to read parts of the voluminous correspondence between H.D., Aldington, and Bryher. Although I was unable to integrate all that I read into my book, I was pleased to see that what I read confirmed the arguments I had made and in many cases contained evidence that is much stronger than I was able to provide from available manuscripts and published materials. In certain instances, I have been able to insert relevant quotations and footnotes to the most significant letters. In particular, Aldington's extraordinary letters to H.D. from France in 1918 and 1919 confirm not only the essential accuracy of her portrayals of the dissolution of her marriage, but also exhibit the pattern of rejection and betrayal that I have argued was essential to H.D.'s palimpsests of disaster. H.D.'s even more extraordinary letters to Bryher in 1933 and 1934 while she was in analysis with Freud provide strong evidence in support of my arguments on Freud's "diagnosis" of her "symptoms" and H.D.'s interpretations of her breakdowns, sexuality, and fascination with the occult. At the same time, these letters indicate another layer of complexity in H.D.'s explorations of her sexuality and her identity as a woman. I am currently at work on a project that incorporates this dimension of H.D.'s life and work.

With the generous permission of Perdita Schaffner and Beinecke Library, I have quoted extensively from H.D.'s unpublished papers not only because they provide vivid evidence of her development, but also as a service to those who cannot use Beinecke's important collection. Although I have corrected H.D.'s occasional typing errors, I have left her idiosyncratic spelling as it appears in the manuscripts because I believe she would have wished it to remain as written. Aldington used to correct her spelling with great concern lest she appear less "perfect" than she was. She in turn wrote angrily to Bryher about Aldington's "psychotic" attitude toward her spelling.

The emergence of *Psyche Reborn* from the chrysalis of my own life would have been impossible without the presence of an environment of people and ideas to nurture it. To name the most significant will indicate a process of influence in itself, one that demonstrates the intersections of the personal and the professional, the past and the present, the emotional and the intellectual, the text and the context in the emergence of a scholarly book. I am indebted in the broadest sense to the moment in history when I came into professional maturity. The rebirth of feminism has given urgent purpose to my interest in literature and criticism, a vital paradigm for exploring my interests in revolutionary ways, and a community of women who have both enriched my understanding and absorbed what I have written. The Women's Studies Program at the University of Wisconsin-Madison epitomizes for me both the change in higher education and the opportunity I have had for meaningful work and relation. Individuals whose help over the years has made it possible for me to take advantage of the historical moment include: my parents, Anne Thompson Stanford and Ralph Stanford, whose love and ambition for all their daughters gave me the inner strength, conviction, and passion to pursue the life I wanted regardless of the prejudice I have faced; my life-partner, Edward Friedman, who has always taken for granted the significance of my work and whose help has covered the spectrum from profound respect to blunt criticism, careful reading of chapters, and leaving me to the quiet of my study; my daughters, Ruth Jennifer Friedman and JoAnna Stanford Friedman, whose pride in their mother supports my work and whose needs provide my opportunities for play; my teachers at Lake Forest High School, Swarthmore College, and the University of Wisconsin, Mary Thorne-Thomsen, Frank Townsend, Martin Otswald, Helen North, Thomas Blackburn, David Cowden, L.S. Dembo, Cyrena Pondrom, and Walter Rideout—all of whom taught me to think and to value what I thought. Most especially, I must single out Larry Dembo, my mentor and thesis advisor. His exciting work in epistemology and poetry, his introduction of H.D. to me, and our lengthy debates were the foundation of my work on H.D.

The scholarship of the many people who have written about H.D. constitutes an influence that I want to acknowledge; whether I have agreed or disagreed with, amplified or seemed to ignore their work, the writings of people like Rachel Blau DuPlessis, Norman Holmes Pearson, L.S. Dembo, Kenneth Fields, Robert Duncan, Susan Gubar,

Lucy Freibert, Albert Gelpi, Vincent Quinn, Norman Holland, Linda Welshimer Wagner, Joseph Riddel, Charlotte Mandel, Toni McNaron (and others) have stimulated my own thinking. My debt is also enormous to those who have read the various manuscripts of this book (or articles related to it) and offered their much-needed encouragement, questions, and tough criticism, including especially Perdita Schaffner, Rachel Blau DuPlessis, Norman Holmes Pearson, Adrienne Rich, Elaine Marks, Gloria Bowles, Walter Rideout, Michael Hinden, Phillip Herring, Annis Pratt, Silvia Dobson, Barbara Guest, and Biddy Martin. DuPlessis, in particular, provided the criticisms that forced me to pull the manuscript into its final form. Without the able assistance of Donald Gallup and the staff at Beinecke Library, this book would have little of the richness that manuscript research makes possible. I am grateful for their help. Cindy Townsend, Jane Renneberg, Karen Wick, and Laurel Curtis have done the essential, but hidden, labor of manuscript preparation, and I have deeply appreciated the speed and accuracy with which they have transformed scribbles on yellow paper into a finished manuscript. And finally, I want to thank my close friends (they know who they are) whose caring is my daily support that keeps the professional and personal sides of my life afloat.

ACKNOWLEDGMENTS

Quotations from the Hilda Doolittle papers and the photograph of H.D. taken by Man Ray are reprinted by permission of Perdita Schaffner and the Collection of American Literature, Beinecke Rare Book and Manuscript Library, Yale University.

The quotation from Ernest Jones, *The Life and Works of Sigmund Freud,* edited and abridged by Lionel Trilling and Steven Marcus, copyright © 1961 by Basic Books Publishing Co., Inc., is reprinted by permission of Basic Books.

Materials from *Tribute to Freud* by H.D., © 1956, 1974 by Norman Holmes Pearson, were reprinted by permission of David R. Godine, Publisher, Inc.

Extracts from the following works by H.D., *Helen in Egypt,* © 1961 by Norman Holmes Pearson, *Trilogy,* copyright 1944, 1945, 1946 by Oxford University, *Hermetic Definition,* © 1958, 1959, 1961, 1969, 1972 by Norman Holmes Pearson, and *Selected Poems,* copyright 1925, 1953, © 1957 by Norman Holmes Pearson, were reprinted by permission of New Directions.

Psyche Reborn

Introduction

HILDA DOOLITTLE's emergence on the pages of *Poetry* magazine in 1913 as "H.D., Imagiste" heralded the beginnings of a writer whose canon spans half a century and the genres of poetry, fiction, memoir, essay, drama, and translation. This achievement was firmly rooted in H.D.'s central participation in the imagist movement, a short-lived moment in literary history, but one whose experiments changed the course of modern poetry with its concept of the "image" and its advocacy of vers libre. Settled in London after 1912, H.D. was particularly close to her old friend Ezra Pound and the British poet Richard Aldington, whom she married in 1913. With their encouragement, she began to write what she called her "first authentic verse" in the midst of a cross-cultural ferment that mingled the ideas of Henri Bergson and T.E. Hulme with the poetic forms of Japanese haiku, Greek lyrics, French symbolists, and the troubadours of medieval Provence.[1]

Despite H.D.'s decision to make her home with the London community of English and expatriate American artists, her roots were distinctly American. Born in Bethlehem, Pennsylvania in 1886, H.D. spent her earliest years in the tight-knit Moravian community of her mother's extended family. When her father became director of the Flower Observatory at the University of Pennsylvania in 1892, the family moved to Upper Darby where she attended a Friends school and then nearby Bryn Mawr College. Her intellectual and artistic awakenings, however, had their source in personal interactions rather than the classroom. As a young woman, she shared her enthusiasm for literature with her half-brother Eric, with friends like William Carlos Williams and Frances Josepha Gregg, and most intensely with

Pound, to whom she was briefly engaged. With Pound, she exchanged books; they read together and wrote poems for each other. To Gregg, she wrote her first published poems modeled on the Theocritus translations Pound had given her. Her earliest attempts at verse and her brief experiment with bohemian living in New York's Greenwich Village, however, left her fundamentally unsatisfied. In 1911, she sailed for Europe with Gregg and found the creative stimulation and support she required to begin her artistic career in the avant-garde milieu of London.[2]

Sea Garden, published in 1916, was the poetic culmination of her early apprenticeship in London, and it won for her the reputation of being the best of the imagist poets. Her poems avoided the vague moralizing and sentimental mythologizing that the imagists deplored in much of the "cosmic" poetry of the late nineteenth century. They were crisp, precise, and absolutely without excess. The imagist emphasis on hard, classical lines, however, did not mean that the poems were without emotion. Most imagist poems rely heavily on precisely delineated objects from nature to embody subjective experience. But as poems like "Heat" and "Oread" demonstrate vividly, H.D.'s imagist poetry was not a form of nature poetry adapted to the modern world. The essence of the imagist task was to locate the "image" that incarnated an "intellectual and emotional complex in an instant of time"—or, to use T.S. Eliot's later term, the "objective correlative" of subjective experience.[3] In *Sea Garden*, H.D. fulfilled that task by rendering intense passions and perceptions in images that originated in her visits to Cornwall and her American childhood: in particular the harsh, northern seacoasts of Cornwall and Maine, the uncultivated fields and woods she roamed near her home in Upper Darby, and the flowers of the garden planted by her grandmother and enlarged by her mother. The mythological personae that appear in many of her poems did not represent an escapist attempt to return to ancient Greece, but rather served as personal metaphors or masks that allowed her to distance intense emotion sufficiently for artistic expression.

H.D.'s ability to fulfill the aesthetic demands of imagist doctrine has been well recognized. Less frequently understood, her contribution to the major shift in modern poetry was organizational as well as aesthetic. She, along with Amy Lowell, helped to insure the continuation of the imagist community after Pound's efforts to retain sole editorial power split the original group in 1915. As editor of *The*

Egoist from 1915–1917, H.D. encouraged poets to write and helped them find an audience during the difficult war years.[4] But H.D.'s efforts to keep alive the poetic visions of her soldier-husband, Richard Aldington, and the other members of their artistic community were doomed by the violence and meaninglessness of the First World War. Her leadership role as both poet and editor dissolved amidst the personal and societal pressures of the times. Her emergence at the very center of the London avant-garde gave way to what she called the loss of "the early companions of my first writing-period in London, you might say of my 'success,' small and rather specialized as it was."[5]

Bid Me to Live (*A Madrigal*), her roman à clef, tells the story of the intersecting personal and cultural catastrophes that ended her "specialized" success. Aldington's affair with Dorothy Yorke and the dissolution of her marriage, the deaths of her brother and father, the loss of D.H. Lawrence's friendship, and her own grave illness during the last stage of her pregnancy merged with the general destruction of war to break apart the relatively secure world of imagist compatriots. The war did more than strain personal relationships, however. It produced the historical conditions that made the intensely aesthetic world of imagism inadequate and gave enormous impetus to the growth of modernism. The hysteria of mindless patriotism and the omnipresence of death in a trench war for inches and feet of blasted territory created the necessity for a different kind of art, one that could record the fragmentation of culture and begin the quest for new meanings. Since the First World War was the result of the gradual disintegration of European civilization, it did not by itself cause the despair, confusion, and sense of loss characteristic of the modernist perspective. But it did reinforce and confirm for a whole generation of educated Europeans and Americans what a few isolated voices like James Joyce in *Dubliners*, T.S. Eliot in "The Love Song of J. Alfred Prufrock," and G.B. Shaw in *Heartbreak House* had said before the war. The war embodied the violent decay of the old order; its meaninglessness challenged western belief in the superiority of its religions, institutions, sciences, and technologies.

The dissolution of symbolic systems unveiled as grand illusions impelled a literature centered on quest, art whose forms and themes were consistent with the search for new patterns of meaning. The bitter events of history forced H.D. and her writing companions to emerge from the limited perfection of imagism. With its emphasis on the poem as the instantaneous visual incarnation of an "emotional and intellectual complex," imagism could not explain the violence of war and the fragmentation of belief systems. Its disdain for philosophies and cosmologies as well as its demand for brevity left both form and content of the imagist poem inadequate before the historical imperatives for a literature based on the search for living mythologies. Imagism had begun as a philosophy of art, but it evolved into a craft that could be incorporated into the larger explorations of modernist literature. H.D.'s reflections in an interview with the *New Haven Register* in 1956 are a perceptive commentary on the significance of imagism in the development of modern poetry. She emphasized to the reporter that "the term [imagist] cannot be applied to describe her work since World War I." Imagism, she said, was "something that was important for poets learning their craft early in this century. It is still important to any poet learning his craft. But after learning his craft, the poet will find his true direction, as I hope I have." H.D. described "her early work as 'a little sapling,' which in the intervening years, 'has grown down into the depths and upwards in many directions.' Her poetry, she said, quoting from a poem from her 'Rosemary in Avon,' 'is growing within the grave—Spreading to heaven.' "[6]

In the postwar years, artists went beyond the earlier imagist breakthrough and turned increasingly to the archetypes of quest in mythological and literary traditions for models of search. Although Ezra Pound, in his "Hugh Selwyn Mauberley," was perhaps the only poet of the London literary circle to denounce the emptiness of formalism in the face of historical realities, his abandonment of aestheticism for the structures of epic quest in *The Cantos* paralleled the development of many other modernist writers. Eliot stopped writing poetic tableaux like "Preludes" and entered on a mythological path through "the waste land" and ultimately on to religious conversion and his *Four Quartets*. Williams increasingly devoted his energy and vision to *Paterson*, his epic poem about an American poet-hero, who sought union with the goddess of the park and the absolute reality of things within the ordering "ideas" of the poet. Expanding on his early search for the life force, Lawrence journeyed to the powerful cultures of so-called primitive peoples and explored the energy of the unconscious of all people in his rejection of mechanized, industrialized, and rationalistic modern society. Joyce, somewhat on the fringe of the imagist movement in any case, extended the forms of the realist novel to in-

corporate mythic patterns, past traditions, and subjective consciousness or even unconsciousness as the structures of everyday life in the
modern world. Outside the imagist circle, but in the modernist mainstream, W.B. Yeats developed his early interest in myth into the
mysticism of occult traditions and the idiosyncracies of his symbolic
systems. Hart Crane's vision of the modern city and the bridge that
lends a myth to God incorporated legends of the American past and
relied on an archetypal mythology to transform the demonic technology of the modern age into the apocalyptic expression of divinity.
H.D.'s development from imagist to epic art places her squarely in the
center of this modernist mainstream. Her work shares with all of these
writers the fundamental spirit of quest given shape by myth and
mythic consciousness, by religious vision or experience, and by a new
synthesis of fragmented traditions.

H.D. did not, however, find the direction that led to her mature
art with the immediacy of compatriots like Pound and Williams. While
The Cantos and *Paterson* began to take shape in the twenties, H.D.'s
route to a modernist perspective and aesthetic was more indirect and
included considerable experimentation with a variety of genres and
even art forms as she attempted to find her "true direction." Recovery
from the personal collapse that followed Aldington's desertion, her
own near-death from the influenza of 1919, and the birth of her
daughter, Perdita, was slow. She herself credited her return to life to
the devotion of her new friend Bryher, a very wealthy and rebellious
young woman who found in H.D. the validation for her own desire
to reject a feminine destiny and become a writer. Their friendship
deepened into an intense relationship that remained a permanent anchor for H.D. till her death in 1961. Born Winifred Ellerman in 1894,
Bryher legally adopted her pseudonym as her name, thereby declaring
a symbolic independence from her demanding family, ruled by Sir
John Ellerman, the shipping magnate. Bryher and H.D. lived together
throughout the twenties, thirties, and early forties in an enduring relationship that coincided with Bryher's marriages to Robert McAlmon
and Kenneth Macpherson as well as H.D.'s affairs with a number of
people. As H.D. wrote in her poem dedicating the novel *Palimpsest* to
Bryher, *"when all the others, blighted, reel and fall, / your star, steel-
set, keeps lone and frigid trist / to freighted ships baffled in wind and
blast."*[7]

In 1920, the two women traveled alone to Greece and later, in

1923, to Egypt, where they toured the newly discovered tomb of King Tut. Throughout the decade and into the next, their travels and residences crisscrossed Europe—predominantly London, Berlin, Paris, Vienna, and Switzerland. Their own commitment to writing led them to immersion in the intellectual and aesthetic currents of the avant-garde in the years between the two world wars. Fascination with film, the newest of the art forms, took them to Hollywood where they quickly became disillusioned with commercialized movies. But back in Europe, involvement with film critic and director Kenneth Macpherson restored their belief in the aesthetic potential of film. H.D. wrote for their film journal *Close-Up* and acted in three of Macpherson's films.[8]

H.D.'s artistic efforts during the twenties were extensive although the results were uneven and often left in draft form. Sharing with Bryher a great admiration for their friend Dorothy Richardson's *Pilgrimage*, H.D. experimented with her own technique of interior monologue in her two published novels, *Palimpsest* (1926) and *Hedylus* (1928) and a number of shorter prose works like "Moose Island" and "Narthex." All of them prose masks for her own life, primarily her marriage to Aldington, these autobiographical fictions disturbed many of the readers who had admired "H.D., Imagiste." Her "specialized" success as an imagist created narrow expectations for her new work that inhibited her desire to expand into new forms and subjects. As she wrote to her friend Viola Jordan, the confinement of her reputation was frustrating and required a rebellious spirit to break through: "I am bringing out a volume of prose, semi-private in Paris. No one really much likes my prose but I can't be held up by what the critics think H.D. ought to be like. . . . I have a purple sex story (though highly spiritualized) about a Greek girl in Rome which I like but people don't think 'worthy' quite of H.D. I say WHO is H.D.? They all think they know more about what and why she should or should not be or do than I."[9] In actuality, her desire to develop a new "H.D." involved fiction to a greater extent than her critics imagined. She left in manuscript form three thinly disguised autobiographical novels about her relationships with Gregg, Pound, Aldington, Bryher, Lawrence, and others of the imagist and postwar circles. An unpublished historical novel, *Pilate's Wife*, was begun in 1924, completed in 1934, and served in her mind as an answer to Lawrence's *The Man Who Died*.[10]

Interest in fiction did not lead H.D. to abandon poetry, however.

In *Hymen* (1922) and *Heliodora* (1924) she expanded the imagist gems of *Sea Garden* into more diffuse, exploratory correlatives for emotion. Her *Collected Poems* (1924) presented an overview of the poetic achievement begun in 1913, and, at the end of the decade, she brought out *Red Roses for Bronze* (1931). Her work on translations from Greek lyrics and verse drama in *Hippolytus Temporizes* (1927) as a source of influence on her own poetry paralleled the pattern of Pound's work. By the end of the twenties, H.D. did not appear to be in search of her "true direction." She had worked enormously hard at a variety of manuscripts—"I sit at my typewriter until I drop," she wrote to Jordan; "I have in some way, to justify my existence, and then it is also a pure 'trade' with me now. It is my 'job' " (10 January 1926). Some two decades of writing and publication had established H.D. in the public domain of literature. But this achievement reached an aesthetic dead end in the thirties. With the rise of fascism and the imminence of a second catastrophic war, H.D. wrote far less regularly and published little in any genre. She did translate and publish Euripides' *Ion* with her own commentary (1937), work that Pearson said was very important to her later development. She did write a few short stories and a group of nine loosely connected poems, apparently intended for a small volume called *The Dead Priestess Speaks*. But none of the short stories were published, and only parts of a few poems appeared in little magazines such as *Life and Letters Today*. The unfinished volume, with its multiple drafts and various tables of contents, testifies that H.D. seemed to have lost that certain sense of direction, that sure inner knowledge of "WHO H.D. is" or should be. A letter from Sigmund Freud in 1934 extends his sympathy for the fact that "you do not yet work" and thereby suggests that H.D. was quite concerned about the artistic blockage that characterized the thirties for her (*T.F.*, p. 192).

The violence of war jolted H.D. out of a decade of relative latency. The Blitz transformed London into "a city of ruin, a world ruined, it might seem, almost past redemption," she wrote in *Tribute to Freud* (p. 84). Destruction, paradoxically, brought in Pearson's words, "an astonishing revitalization" for her. Forced by the crucible of war to find a poetic voice and vision that confronted historical reality, H.D. began once again to write with the rapid intensity of inspiration. The Second World War functioned for her much as the First World War had for writers like Pound. Her sense of destiny as poet-prophet in the modernist apocalypse was certain and took on various forms of quest in *The Gift, Tribute to Freud,* and most importantly in her epic, *Trilogy,* composed of three volumes published as she wrote them: *The Walls Do Not Fall* (1944), *Tribute to the Angels* (1945), and *The Flowering of the Rod* (1946).[11] In the *Trilogy,* which can serve as both primer and profound expression of the modernist spirit, H.D. sought to discover or create through the "Word" some ordering pattern that could redeem the surrounding ruin. She herself reflected on the change the *Trilogy* represented: "This is not the 'crystalline' poetry that my early critics would insist on. It is no pillar of salt nor yet of hewn rock-crystal. It is the pillar of fire by night, the pillar of cloud by day."[12] The *Trilogy* is a record of quest, a search deep within the unconscious and throughout many mythological traditions for the knowledge of unity beneath division and destruction. In short, H.D. began to write the kind of "cosmic poetry" the imagists had sworn to abandon. "Resurrection is a sense of direction," H.D. wrote in the *Trilogy* (*T.,* p. 123). Her "rebirth" as a revitalized poet during the war gave her a sense of her "true direction" that led her with steady inspiration to produce the mature work written in the late forties and fifties: *By Avon River* (1949); *Helen in Egypt* (1961); *Winter Love* (1973); *Sagesse* (1973); *End to Torment* (1979); and *Hermetic Definition* (1973).[13]

Cosmic quest did not, however, lead H.D. to abandon imagist craft. Her later work bears a strong resemblance to imagist technique in the continued clarity and simplicity of her poetic line and the precise shape of her images. She continued to anchor the poem in the concrete world with images of flowers, rocks, insects, birds, and the seashore. The continuities between her imagist and epic work recall the way Pound's "super-positions" survived as small units within *The Cantos.* Similarly, the intensely personal emotion masked by mythological personae in poems like *Helen in Egypt* and *Winter Love* was present in her imagist lyric. Conversely, the seeds of later growth existed in the nearly animistic apprehension of nature in her imagist poetry, a continuity that her friend Robert Duncan explored in his partially completed "H.D. Book."[14] But her growth "into the depths and upwards" fundamentally transformed the function of both myth and subjective experience in her poetry. In the *Trilogy* and in all the poetry she wrote thereafter, the personal and the mythological are made to serve the needs of a religious and philosophical quest to explore basic humanistic questions about women and men, life and death, love and hate, destruction and renewal, war and peace, time and eternity.

With the benefit of hindsight made possible by the explosion of H.D.'s writing in the early forties, it is clear that the extensive experimentation of the twenties and the relative latency of the thirties were a sort of "incubation" period out of which the new H.D. emerged. Why did it take her twenty years to develop her own modernist voice when her writing companions of the First World War made the shift so much earlier? What, in fact, were the conditions of H.D.'s gradual metamorphosis? The clues to her development lie in her own images of self-exploration in *Tribute to Freud*.

Although this memoir revolves structurally around Freud, it reveals the framework of her search in the thirties for a regenerated and redirected artistic identity. As she had done even in her earliest imagist poetry, H.D. identified herself with a figure from mythological tradition to stimulate the unfolding reflections of memory and myth. For her persona, she chose Psyche, the mortal woman whose search for Eros has frequently been interpreted as the soul's quest for divine immortality. The name "Psyche" comes from the Greek word for "soul," often portrayed in Greek art as a butterfly that leaves the body at death. Psyche is the spirit that survives physical decay to be reunited with the divine. But in the story first told by Apuleius and later retold by countless poets, Psyche must undergo severe trials culminated by the archetypal descent to the underworld before she can rejoin Eros.

H.D. wove together these fragments of myth and imagery to create her own "legend" of metamorphosis, as she called it (*T.F.*, p. vii). The First World War and its subsequent personal and cultural consequences had constituted a kind of death for H.D., a descent to the underworld from which she had to emerge in a process of spiritual rebirth that was decades in the making. Repeatedly, she used imagery based on the life cycle of the butterfly to describe the journey of her soul from death to life. "Your psyche, your soul, can curl up and sleep like those white slugs" of a childhood memory, she wrote in *Tribute to Freud* (p. 31). After a period of living death, the soul begins its emergence as butterfly. In her autobiographical novel *Her*, H.D. recalled such a period in her life. Hermione is her persona, and "Her" is her nickname as she images her emergence from breakdown in the correlative of the butterfly leaving the cocoon: "A white butterfly that

hesitates a moment finds frost to break the wavering tenuous antennae. I put, so to speak, antennae out too early. I felt letting Her so
delicately protrude prenatal antennae from the husk of the thing called
Her, frost nip the delicate fibre of the star-fish edges of the thing I
clung to. I, Her, clung to the most tenuous of antennae. Mama, Eugenia that is, Carl Gart and Lillian were so many leaves wrapped
around the unborn butterfly."[15]

In the *Trilogy*, H.D. announced the rebirth of Psyche, the butterfly who emerges from the cocoon of near-death. Throughout the first
volume, the poet is the "industrious worm" who must "spin my own
shroud" to become one of the "latter-day twice-born" (*T.*, pp. 12–22).
In the second volume, Psyche emerges from the ruins of another war
in her vision of the "Lady," a woman carrying the blank pages of a
book yet to be written. She is a projection of the poet who has been
reborn: "she is Psyche, the butterfly / out of the cocoon" (*T.*, p. 103).

Psyche's "gestation" was gradual, unlike the transformations that
produced *The Cantos, Paterson,* and *The Waste Land* in the twenties.
Tribute to Freud once again points to a possible explanation for this.
A pervasive undercurrent in the book is the theme of her "difference":
her recognition of, desire for, and pride in multiple forms of "difference." What set H.D. apart most profoundly, however, was her
status as a woman writing in a predominantly male literary tradition.
As "fellow" imagist Amy Lowell wrote, "we're a queer lot / We wom-
en who write poetry. And when you think / How few of us there've
been it's queerer still."[16] Even as a woman in the male circle of
imagists and artists in London, H.D. was alone. Sappho's influence on
imagists no doubt helped to validate H.D.'s leadership role in the development of the modern lyric. But as historical forces fostered a
poetry of quest that borrowed from epic and heroic tradition, H.D.
became even more of an anomaly. Few women poets have ventured
into the masculine domain of quest literature—Mary Tighe in her
Psyche (1805) is one of the notable exceptions, but there is no evidence
that H.D. knew of this much-neglected writer. Archetypes of questors
in both literary and mythological tradition are overwhelmingly male:
figures like Perseus, Hercules, Jason, Theseus, Lancelot, Percival, and
Beowulf overshadow the travels and trials of Demeter, Isis, and Psyche. Indeed, cultural definitions of the heroic presume masculinity
while the complementary assumptions about the nature of the heroine
frequently presuppose feminine passivity and helplessness. Patriarchal

tradition held out little encouragement for H.D. to develop a woman-centered epic in which woman was the seeker and doer instead of the angelic or evil object of male quest. From this perspective, it is not so amazing that H.D.'s growth was more gradual than that of her fellow modernists. Rather, it is extraordinary that she ultimately managed to defy the dominant tradition entirely by creating woman heroes whose search for meaning bears so little resemblance to the stereo-typed female figures in the quest poetry written by men—the apoca-lyptic Pocahontas and the demonic prostitute in *The Bridge*, the fecund goddess in the park sought by the poet Paterson, the super-ficial women walking to and fro talking of Michelangelo. Not sur-prisingly, H.D.'s woman-identified questors spun a different web of meanings, ones that resurrected the life-giving female symbols and values which J.J. Bachofen had identified with the goddesses of ancient matriarchies.

The roots of H.D.'s emergence from the cocoon of the thirties lay in two sources of inspiration that seem antithetical, but which she ex-perienced as parallel forms of spiritual quest. Broadly defined, those inveterate foes science and religion took her "down into the depths and upwards in many directions," to quote from her own definition of growth. Her experience with psychoanalysis, highlighted by her sessions with Freud in 1933 and 1934, led her down into the depths of unconscious memory and dream. As modern "Door-Keeper" of the human psyche, Freud appeared to her like the Egyptian god Thoth, the "infinitely old symbol, weighing the soul, Psyche, in the Balance" (*T.F.*, p. 97). As the gentle guardian of self-exploration through psy-choanalysis, Freud watched over the "poor child, poor shivering and unprotected soul" (*T.F.*, p. 110). In his office H.D. sat wrapped in the "silver-grey rug" on his famous couch: "I have been caterpillar, worm, snug in the chrysalis" (*T.F.*, p. 177). Psychoanalysis took H.D. inward in a way that systematized and expanded on her early fascination for intense, subjective experience. In the unconscious decoded with Freud's help, H.D. found the wellsprings of inspiration. At the same time, this journey inward taught her to relate the personal to the universal. In the words of her friend Norman Holmes Pearson, Freud showed her the "relationship between the individual dream and the myth as the dream of the tribe."[17]

Esoteric tradition, including the many shapes of the occult, con-tained the "tribal myths" that reproduced her personal dreams on a cultural level. Complementing the impact of psychoanalysis, syncretist religious traditions led her out of her moment in history, took her through many cultures and eras, and revealed universal patterns underlying the shape-shifting forms of all experience. At the same time that such traditions as astrology, Tarot, and Kabbalah led her away from herself, they also turned her gaze inward. All these forms of the occult insisted that spiritual reality cannot be learned through reason alone. Intuitional, visionary, and experiential apprehension of spiritual reality is essential. With Freud's help in decoding her dreams and visions, H.D. found the spiritual and philosophical underpinnings of a chaotic and violent world.

With the war as her catalyst, H.D. wove the science and religion of the psyche together to produce an art that was both deeply personal and broadly based in religious traditions that are the legacy of time. The impact of Freud and of esoteric religion was enormous, both personally and aesthetically. Both influences permeate her mature work and form the context in which it can be most fully comprehended.

To research the parallels in H.D.'s work with psychoanalytic or occult tradition, however, would result in a superficial understanding of their significance for her development. Influence is not a process that flows in one direction as the active transmission of ideas into the passive receptacle of the artist's mind. Whether or not we accept Harold Bloom's hypothesis that the anxiety of influence reenacts the Oedipal family romance, the process of influence must surely be recognized as fluid and personal, dialectical and never static. It operates as a creative collaboration in which the artist interacts with her or his sources and ultimately transforms them to serve the requirements of individual vision. This dynamic quality in the process of influence is clearly delineated in H.D.'s case, particularly in her interactions with Freud. Their relationship was a complex emotional and intellectual dialogue in which their disagreements did as much as their agreements to focus Psyche's quest. Especially because she left a record of that dialogue, their collaboration serves as a virtual paradigm of working influence. Because Freud's impact on twentieth-century art has been so enormous, H.D.'s creative transformation of his theories can serve as a superbly outlined case study of his influence on literary artists.

The interplay of their two creative minds, however, points to the paradoxical nature of Freud's influence on H.D. and other modern artists. She described Freud as the "guardian of all beginnings," but she also reminded herself repeatedly that "the Professor was not always right" (*T.F.*, p. 18). She wrote, "About the greater transcendental issues, we never argued. But there was an argument implicit in our very bones" (*T.F.*, p. 13). As much as agreement, her opposition to his ideas vitalized his influence. His impact on H.D. and other artists was dependent upon their ability to revise fundamental assumptions in his work. Freud considered himself a man of science, his methods empirical, and psychoanalysis the extension of scientific method to the psyche. He celebrated reason over passion and belief, and looked forward to a future when the infantile consolations of religion would be replaced by the rational power of "logos." His conception of reality was unreservedly materialist, and his vision of human history had its roots in Enlightenment assumptions of progress from savagery to civilization. In contrast, H.D. and others influenced by Freud were disillusioned with the limited truths of rationalism and the destructive horrors of technological progress. They celebrated intuition, the vision of dreams, and the "primitive" myths still living in the human psyche and recorded in tradition.

On another level, H.D.'s very survival as a woman artist required her to confront Freud's misogyny if she were to continue in the traditionally male roles of questor and poet. Consistent with his reliance on the status quo as the touchstone for ultimate reality, Freud believed that psychological sex differences and related sex roles were innately determined. His theories of psychosexual development became "scientific" arguments for the inferiority of women and therefore rationalizations for inequality. H.D. sought inspiration from one of the greatest legitimizers of patriarchy. Her success as a woman depended upon conflict.

Mutual warmth and respect characterized their relationship, as both their letters and *Tribute to Freud* attest. But in another sense, their sessions together represent a prototypical confrontation between the polarities that permeate the modern world: man against woman, science versus religion, fact versus faith, objective versus subjective reality, reason versus intuition, the rational versus the irrational. H.D. and Freud dramatically personified the intellectual oppositions of the age. Their "argument," played out in his office at Berggasse 19 and in the pages of H.D.'s memoir, is a microcosm of vital twentieth-century debate.

H.D.'s response to the confrontation was fundamentally dialectical. To serve the needs of spiritual quest, she developed aspects of Freud's thought until they became antithetical to his own perspectives. Freud, she wrote, was "midwife to the soul" (*T.F.*, p. 116). But, once reborn, Psyche emerged with a voice distinctly her own. Once having clarified the poles of opposition, her search for synthesis led to a transcendence of their differences in a vision that incorporated the whole. This transformation of Freudian theory simultaneously served as the basis of her mature art and as a brilliant reevaluation of Freud's significance for the twentieth century. Long before theorists like Norman O. Brown and Herbert Marcuse reinterpreted Freud's thought, H.D. reflected on the man who survived in her memories and in his books until she found the artist within the scientist, a prophet within the apostate, and the woman within the man.

Part I
H.D. and Psychoanalytic Tradition

I

Freud as Guardian of Beginnings

BIOGRAPHICAL ROOTS OF PSYCHOANALYTIC INFLUENCE

PSYCHOANALYSIS SERVED H.D. as a dimension of quest that allowed her to confront and transform the intersecting personal and historical disasters of her century. As "midwife to the soul," Sigmund Freud greeted Psyche at the threshold of inner exploration and acted as her "guardian of all 'beginnings' " (*T.F.*, pp. 97, 106, 116). "I seized on the unexpected chance of working with Professor Freud," she wrote, because "I wanted to dig down and dig out, root out my personal weeds, strengthen my purpose, reaffirm my beliefs, canalize my energies" (*T.F.*, p. 91). H.D.'s work with the Professor was the central point around which a forty-year involvement with psychoanalysis revolved. Freud's role as guardian of beginnings in 1933 and 1934 was greatly reinforced by H.D.'s previous and subsequent exposure to psychoanalysis. Her friendships with proponents of Freud's new science, her extensive reading in the psychoanalytic literature, her experiences with other psychoanalysts, and most importantly her reflections on Freud in her memoirs and notebooks, laid the foundation for his impact. Examination of these sources greatly illuminates Freud's significance for the transformation of H.D.'s art.

H.D.'s earliest acquaintance with psychoanalysis probably began in the home of her friend Frances Josepha Gregg sometime before they left for Europe in 1911. In *Her*, the autobiographical novel dealing with the years 1909 and 1910, H.D. wrote that Gregg had given her some psychoanalytic books in German. Since she had difficulty with the language, Gregg's uncle translated sections for the two friends.[1]

While there is no evidence that H.D. pursued this early interest in Freud during the imagist heyday in London, her exposure to psychoanalysis was renewed during the postwar years and greatly expanded as the twenties progressed. Bryher was an early advocate, even financial supporter, of psychoanalysis, and subscribed regularly to the *Psychoanalytical Journal*. "You could not have escaped Freud in the literary world of the early twenties," Bryher wrote: "Freud! All literary London discovered Freud about 1920 . . . the theories were the great subject of conversation wherever one went at that date. To me Freud is literary England . . . after the first war. People did not always agree but he was always taken in the utmost seriousness."[2] Bryher explained, however, that reading psychoanalysis was inadequate as a source of illumination: "You don't read psychoanalysis, you experience it." Determined to "try out the theories," Bryher began her analysis in 1928 with Hanns Sachs, one of the "original 'Seven' " around Freud. She regarded herself and her fellow analysands as "pioneers" engaged in making early "discoveries on the seas of the human mind."[3]

By the late twenties, H.D. could hardly have escaped almost daily involvement with psychoanalysis; Bryher's enthusiasm was leading her to plan a future as an analyst, and the two women were attending many lectures on psychoanalysis and anthropology in Berlin. H.D. did not, however, agree to Bryher's plea that she enter analysis herself until 1931. From April to July of that year, H.D. had twenty-four sessions at Tavistock Square, Bloomsbury, with her friend, the analyst Mary Chadwick. This early experience proved unsatisfactory, apparently for a number of reasons. H.D. felt that Chadwick "could not follow the workings of my creative mind," and she was moreover inhibited from speaking freely because Chadwick was a member of H.D.'s immediate circle, the artists and intellectuals clustered around the production of the film journal *Close-Up*. H.D. also wrote Macpherson that she was unable to make the "transference" with Chadwick, nor, for that matter, was she able to do so with her next analyst, Hanns Sachs. At Bryher's instigation, H.D. had at least three sessions with Sachs during the winter of 1931–1932.[4] He suggested that she work directly with Freud and wrote a letter of introduction for her (*T.F.*, pp. 91, 97). Bryher made the final arrangements with Freud and, in the process, struck up a warm friendship with him, Anna Freud, and a number of Freud's immediate associates. During the year before H.D. actually saw Freud, she began "intensive reading" of psychoanalytic journals and books, including many works by Freud. A letter to her American friend Viola Jordan attests to the new intensity of her interest: "I am keenly interested though never 'dabbled' in psycho-analysis when there was the first superficial post-war wave of it. I read much now, however; and have had many revelations, find it terrifically absorbing" (6 January 1933).[5]

Bryher's library, however, was only the preparation, not the substitution, for the extended experience of analysis itself. In March of 1933 H.D. went to Vienna, where she saw Freud five days a week for three or four months. Letters among the three—Bryher, Macpherson, and H.D.—indicate that both H.D. and Freud were exhilarated by the sessions. H.D. wrote Macpherson after two weeks with Freud that analysis "just IS too, too wonderful and simple and beautiful and dear." Contrasting Freud with Chadwick and Sachs, she was delighted to find that she had "made irrevocably the 'transference.'" Her early impressions of Freud not only demonstrate the power of her immediate attachment, but also present an infrequently observed aspect of the great man:

> I wish he had a thousand lives and arms and brains ... the world is literally his "child." He is so impersonal and tender. . . . Freud is simply Jesus-Christ after the resurrection, he has that wistful ghost look of someone who has been right past the door of the tomb, and such tenderness with such humour, he just IS all that. I am sure he IS the absolute inheritor of all that eastern mystery and majic, just IS, in spite of his monumental work and all that, he is the real, the final healer. . . . Once in a while I drag out a dream, and he gets ME to interpret it (how marvelously a comment on Chaddie who told me in so many words, to keep right off the psycho-analytical grass.) Now and again we exchange a few comments on Yo-fi [Freud's dog] . . . who is pregnant. . . . He is small, fragile, as delicately put together as Bill [Bryher's pet monkey]. He is very sharp like a little adder when he wants to be, but has not been with me, except to show he CAN be. (14, 15 March 1933)

According to Bryher, Freud admired H.D. greatly and enjoyed their sessions enormously. On June 13, 1933, Bryher wrote to Macpherson that "Freud grumbles [to Bryher] he has no exciting patients par Kat [H.D.] and a Dutchman [Van de Leeuw];" and on June 14th, Bryher continued her report of Freud's comments on H.D.: "Then he went on to say that seldom if ever had he come into contact with a mind so fine, a spirit so pure, as that of our esteemed Kat and he hoped that after a summer rest, she would return to resume an analysis of months or weeks or even years as she so desired, and she would have preference always over all others. So Kat's tail is one spike of esteem" (13, 14 June 1933).

After the break in analysis during June 1933, H.D. did not return to work with Freud until the end of October, 1934. She saw him on a daily basis for five weeks until the ominous spread of Nazism cut their sessions short (*T.F.*, pp. 4, 91). They exchanged warm letters and occasional gifts during the rest of Freud's life, but H.D. saw him only once after their work ended (*T.F.*, pp. 11–12, 189–94). In subsequent years, H.D. continued their interaction in the aesthetic world of memoir and poem: first with her draft of "Writing on the Wall" in 1944; then with her portrait of Freud in the guise of Theseus in *Helen in Egypt* (1952–1956); and finally with her final preparation of *Tribute to Freud* in 1956.

While her analysis with Freud was clearly the most influential, her association with psychoanalysis did not end with him. In London, H.D. saw the British psychoanalyst Walter Schmideberg, a member of Freud's circle, for two years, 1936 and 1937. After the war Schmideberg and Bryher took the badly shattered H.D. to a residence sanatorium in Switzerland. At Küsnacht Klinik, where people went to convalesce from a wide variety of physical and mental ills, H.D. spent six months recuperating from her war shock, undoubtedly with the help of analysts.

Later, in 1953, she returned to Küsnacht for two operations, and during this second stay she met Erich Heydt, an analyst associated with Medard Boss's school of existential psychoanalysis in Zurich. As her friend, colleague, and analyst, Heydt remained close to H.D. for the remainder of her life. H.D. traveled frequently during the fifties, but she returned for considerable periods of time to her room at Küsnacht especially during the long recuperation period for her broken hip in 1956 and 1957. She wrote in an unpublished memoir, *Compassionate Friendship*, that Heydt treated her "as a colleague" with whom he could discuss his other patients. Rica, H.D.'s persona in an unpublished novel about the people at Küsnacht, is carefully distinguished from the other patients by her own self concept and by Heller's (Heydt's) treatment of her. H.D. did, however, consider her frequent "tea sessions" with Heydt as a form of analysis. With him, she worked through her intense feelings about Pound and the repressed emotion centered on the birth of her stillborn child in 1915. Heydt's importance to her is recreated in both her poetry and prose: he is the model for Paris in *Helen in Egypt*; he is the caring but often uncomprehending Germain in *Sagesse*; he is the steady support in *End to Torment*, H.D.'s memoir of Pound; and he is the "magic mirror" reflecting everyone's secret self in *Magic Mirror*.[6]

The biographical outline of H.D.'s involvement with psychoanalysis establishes its pervasive presence in her life, but reveals little in itself about her reasons for seeking analysis or her interpretations of its significance. These issues must be addressed if the impact of psychoanalysis on her art is to be understood. Fortunately, her tribute to the founder of psychoanalysis is not merely a memoir, a prose poem of praise to a famous man. *Tribute to Freud*, first drafted ten years after her analysis, is a series of reflections on her sessions that not only recreate many of their discussions, but also continue the process of analysis begun on the worn couch in Freud's office. Freud trained her to translate "the hieroglyph of the unconscious" by following his fundamental rule of analysis—free association (*T.F.*, p. 93). At her writing table ten years later, psychoanalytic technique became aesthetic structure as H.D. relied on her stream of associations to decipher her experience with Freud.[7] By allowing her impressions to "recall her" in a series of associationally linked memories, H.D. circled around her multiple reasons for seeking analysis, the direction it took under Freud's guidance, and her creative interaction with his ideas. *Tribute to Freud* is H.D.'s phenomenological memoir in which consciousness turns inward upon itself and memory to discover the essence of her experience with Freud and, by that token, fundamental truths about Freud himself.

H.D.'s tribute to her guide reveals strikingly how misleading it would be to view H.D.'s purpose in analysis in the early days of psychoanalysis through the perspective of what psychiatry has become in the present. The commonly perceived chasm between doctor and patient, expert and "mentally ill" person, was easily bridged in H.D.'s experience. She regarded herself as a "student" of psychoanalysis, in the same category as Dr. J.J. Van de Leeuw, the "eminent scholar," educator, and theosophist who saw Freud in the hour immediately preceding her own (*T.F.*, pp. 5, 18, 20): "The Professor had said in the beginning that he classed me in the same category as the Flying

Dutchman—we were students. I was a student, working under the direction of the greatest mind of this and of perhaps many succeeding generations" (*T.F.*, p. 18). Like Bryher, H.D. partially regarded analysis with Freud as a training in psychoanalysis that she could use to help other war-shocked people: "I had begun my preliminary research in order to fortify and equip myself to face war when it came, and to help in some subsidiary way, if my training were sufficient and my aptitudes suitable, with war-shocked and war-shattered people" (*T.F.*, p. 93).[8]

Her training as Freud's student increasingly gained direction until she regarded herself as one of his disciples by the end of analysis. Both she and Van de Leeuw would carry through with his ideas in a way quite different from the analysts who surrounded him, but one nonetheless important to his future place in history. After Van de Leeuw's unexpected death in an airplane accident, H.D. returned abruptly to Vienna in 1934 to tell Freud how "sorry" she was, how she had believed Van de Leeuw to be Freud's heir: "I felt all the time that he was the person who would apply, carry on the torch—carry on your ideas, but not in a stereotyped way. I felt that you and your work were especially bequeathed to him" (*T.F.*, p. 6). Freud responded that she had not come back to express sorrow, but to do what Van de Leeuw had failed to do: "You have come to take his place" (*T.F.*, p. 16). She would carry on the torch of Freud's ideas in her own way, as a poet rather than a theosophist, educator, or member of the Psycho-Analytic Association.

With *The Interpretation of Dreams*, Freud had begun his exploration of the unconscious realm by bringing his own dreams to the light of analysis. Like all his disciples, H.D. expected to undergo the experience of self-revelation rather than the memorization of his theories. Learning psychoanalysis was to be for H.D. a personal quest that would purify the past through catharsis and redirect the future through greater self-knowledge. This quest was not ultimately narcissistic, however. H.D.'s uneasiness, the "something that was beating in my brain," was not the neurotic maladjustment of a Greek naiad to modern times. It emerged out of the context of the times, out of the same despair and search for meaning that H.D.'s fellow artists were portraying in the modernist literature between the wars.

With the rise of Hitler, H.D. in particular was convinced there would be another world war. Her friends either told her she was being "morbid" or "deluged" her with brilliant political talk that nonetheless led nowhere (T.F., pp. 57–61). At least in part, H.D. went into analysis to fortify herself against the impending war. She wrote: "I did not specifically realize just what it was I wanted [from psychoanalysis], but I knew that I, like most of the people I knew, in England, America, and on the Continent of Europe, was drifting. We were drifting. Where? I did not know but at least I accepted the fact that we *were* drifting. At least, I knew this—I would (before the current of inevitable events swept me right into the main stream and so on to the cataract) stand aside, if I could (if it were not already too late), and take stock of my possessions" (T.F., p. 13).

A modern Thoreau, H.D. echoed his language of quest and determined to find in her experience of psychoanalysis what the transcendentalist found in his retreat to Walden Pond.[9] Thoreau's "retreat" was an active search, and in nature he found the symbols that embodied spirit. Similarly not escapist, H.D. captured the meaning of her "retreat" in a rich fusion of poetic, religious, and mythological traditions. Throughout her tribute, she established her analysis as spiritual quest through a deliberate choice of mythological language and image. Freud's designation of water as a dream symbol for birth perhaps helped to shape her account of spiritual rebirth, for water imagery and metaphors of journey down the great "river of life" permeate her descriptions of analysis.[10] At one point, she imaged the Self as a "narrow birch-bark canoe" which seeks the guidance of a hermit, who in his modern guise appears in the form of Sigmund Freud, scientist of the unknown: "The great forest of the unknown, the supernormal or supernatural, was all around and about us. With the current gathering force, I could at least pull in to the shallows before it was too late, take stock of my very modest possessions of mind and body, and ask the old Hermit who lives on the edge of this vast domain to talk to me, to tell me, if he would, how best to steer my course" (T.F., p. 13).

This medieval language of quest is fused with Goethe's poem "Kennst du das Land" as the perfect "*translation* of . . . our work together" (T.F., pp. 95, 108). Psychoanalysis is a new form of the dragon hunts of old. The "phobias" of the subterranean unconscious are the psychological dragons of Goethe's poem and mythological tradition: "And our very Phobia is here and the host of allied Phobias, the Dragon and its swarm of children, the Hydra-headed monster, . . . the old dragon-brood—or the ancient brood of the Dragon—lives in the caves. Like the Christian of the Puritan poet, John Bunyan, we must push on, through and past these perils" (T.F., p. 109). As H.D. journeyed over "the chasms or gulfs where the ancient dragon lives" (T.F., p. 111), she called on Freud to be her guardian. Freud became Goethe's "Beschützer," the newest transformation in a series of historical metamorphoses from ancient Egyptian, Greek, Roman, and finally Christian forms of the protector spirit.

H.D. occasionally referred to Freud as a great scientist, but more frequently she mythologized him, just as she did the whole process of analysis. While Freud might have chosen for himself the mask of Copernicus, Newton, or Darwin, H.D. saw him as a twentieth-century avatar of great artists, philosophers, prophets, and deities of wisdom. Similarly, her role as the "seeker" gained heroic proportions as she donned the masks of Moses, the Old Testament dreamer Joseph, Bunyan's hero Christian, Perseus the Gorgon-slayer, and Mercury during the analysis. Originating in the theosophical literature H.D. was reading, "seeker" is a term referring to the adept engaged in the process of spiritual quest.[11] H.D.'s choice of the word "seeker" is not a casual one, and its meaning underlines her essential purpose in her work with Freud (T.F., p. 20).

H.D.'s mythological metamorphoses of herself and Freud are central to the significance psychoanalysis was to have for her art in later years. Her allusions to heroes are not decorative, nor was their intent inordinate praise for Freud or egotistical self-glorification for herself. In her tribute, the "transference" does indeed "in all its glory stand unveiled," as Merrill Moore wrote in his introduction.[12] But Freud's mythic masks have little to do with transference because H.D. mythologized her own role as much as she did Freud's. Her purpose was to capture the essential meaning of her experience with Freud. In her view, her inner journey made with his guidance was a modern manifestation of the universal pattern of spiritual search. It served as the prototype for the processes of vision and artistic creation that followed.

Wearing the masks of Perseus, Moses, and Joseph in analysis with Freud, H.D. realized that she was something of an anomaly as a traditional questor. As a woman in a role usually played by men, she understood that she was transforming the traditionally passive role that women play in most quest literature. Norman Holland and Joseph Riddel have mistakenly argued that H.D. mythologized Freud and identified herself with male heroes as a way of acquiring the strength, objectivity, and completeness denied to women by nature. Riddel in particular connected these qualities with men and referred to H.D. as the "phallus-less self" suffering from an "ontological deprivation."[13] But H.D.'s mythological masks do not reflect her envy of the phallic self so much as they reflect the paucity of tradition. As analysand, she had to revise tradition to become a hero on her own terms. In a twentieth-century context, she would do as Perseus once did: slay the dragon within herself, the monster spawned by the fragmented modern world.

Significantly, H.D.'s only female mask in *Tribute to Freud* is Mignon, the girl who asks the questions in Goethe's lyric "Kennst du das Land." H.D. identified Mignon with Psyche and used the image of the small girl to render the contradictions of a woman questor trapped in male-centered literary and mythological traditions. Her story echoes the fairy tale of the "ugly duckling," and its relevance to her analysis and her art is greatly illuminated by information about her childhood:

> One of these souls was called Mignon, though its body did not fit it very well. It was small, *mignonne*, though it was not pretty, they said. It was a girl between two boys; but, ironically, it was wispy and mousy, while the boys were glowing and gold. It was not pretty, they said. Then they said it was pretty—but suddenly, it shot up like a weed. They said, surprised, 'She is really very pretty, but isn't it a pity she's so tall?' The soul was called Mignon but, clearly, it did not fit its body.
> But it found itself in a song. Only the tune is missing. (*T.F.*, pp. 106–107)

Childhood ambivalence toward her "golden" brothers and discomfort with her body is subtly interwoven with her questing personae in *Tribute to Freud*. Biographical sources help untangle the thread of associations. As the only surviving girl in a family with five boys, H.D. felt outside the family norm of sons. As a child, she learned that her baby sister Edith, her half-sister Alice, and her grandmother's daughter Fanny all died in infancy while every male child survived. "Why was it always a girl who died?" the child Hilda asked in *The Gift*.[14] Not quite "right" as the only daughter, she was also a "misfit" as a girl because her height was inappropriately unfeminine. In the Hirslanden Notebooks, she recorded a dream about her childhood schooldays illustrating this negative attitude toward her "difference": "I am a misfit. I am . . . too advanced in some ways, backward in others. I am either at the head of the school procession or at the tail, because I am so tall" (III, p. 4). H.D. identified strongly with her artist mother, but she felt her mother favored her older brother Gilbert and considered her only daughter "an odd duckling." Because she failed at math and wanted to go to art school, she was also a "disappointment" to her father, who had determined that his bright daughter would be a mathematician or a scientist like Marie Curie (Hirslanden II, pp. 26–27). Not a son and not the right kind of daughter for either parent, the child Hilda was caught in a bind of disapproval. Her "soul . . . did not fit its body," but the origin of this dissonance was not biological or "ontological deprivation." Rather, cultural norms and family expectations created a standard that made Mignon unacceptable. To sing her songs and find the missing tune, the adult H.D. could similarly be neither the stereotypically masculine questor of tradition nor the feminine object of quest. The ugly duckling grew up to be the gifted poet without substantial family encouragement for her art and without many female models in literary and mythological tradition with whom she could identify. Her mythopoetic transformation of her analysis with Freud is both a record of those contradictions and the avenue by which she transcended those constraints.

H.D.'s designation of herself as hero coincided completely with a recognition of the dangers of spiritual adventure. Her dedication of her tribute to "Sigmund Freud *blameless physician*" establishes his most important mythological form and indicates a final significant purpose she had in analysis. The "blameless physician" is Asklepios, the healing teacher of the gods in Greek mythology. As Asklepios, Freud was both her "Professor" and the guardian whose knowledge could cure. Psychoanalysis was "the science of the unravelling of the tangled skeins of the unconscious mind and the healing implicit in the process" (*T.F.*, p. 16), H.D. wrote. H.D. saw herself as Freud's student and disciple, but there was also a dimension of personal urgency in her analysis that was fused with her sense of spiritual adventure.

H.D. had had a series of breakdowns in the course of her life, and she hoped that the process of self-discovery would bring healing along with it. The Hirslanden Notebooks clarify somewhat the immediate causes and periods of breakdown, at least as she reflected on them during the fifties. She commented at one point, "Going over the years and checking up on the various breakdowns and collapses (including the two confinements) I can philosophize and find a reason, more or less, for each one" (II, p. 9).[15] Her references to breakdowns throughout the notebooks are fragmentary, but they center around a series of crisis periods in her life. The first, "a slight break-down," came during and immediately following her failure in math and withdrawal from Bryn Mawr College, to her father's great disappointment. The second crisis was the stillbirth of her child in 1915. While she did not in fact experience a collapse at this point, she believed that the repressed grief and shock conditioned later experiences, particularly since the stillbirth was connected in her mind with the sinking of the Lusitania and the violent mobs of London. In 1919, toward the end of her second pregnancy, a series of personal shocks converged with double pneumonia that almost killed her and the unborn child. News of her brother Gilbert's death in France and her father's death "from shock" immediately following combined with the dissolution of her marriage and brought her to a state of both physical and mental collapse. Visits from Pound and Aldington to the maternity hospital completed the process. Pound was apparently "pounding (*Pounding*)" away on her wall with his walking stick and telling her " 'my only real criticism is that this is not my child.' "[16] Aldington, she wrote Pound ten years later, had originally promised to take care of her and the baby, but one day he suddenly appeared with Dorothy Yorke at the hospital to threaten her into divorce: "I put down a lot of myself after Perdita's birth. I loved Richard very much and you know he threatened to use Perdita to divorce me and to have me locked up if I registered her as legitimate. This you see, was after he had said he would look after us, up to the point at least, of seeing me on my feet again. I was 'not on my feet' was literally 'dying.' I mean, anything in the way of a shock brings that back and I go to pieces ... that is why I kept away from you all."[17] H.D. credited her recovery to Bryher's support and vigilance. But during the healing process, she experienced a number of visionary hallucinations that she and her friends associated with her breakdown (*T.F.*, pp. 39–56, 153–63).

In 1934, the news of Van de Leeuw's sudden death brought on a recurrence of the 1919 breakdown because, she believed, she unconsciously associated him with her brother Gilbert. And finally, in 1946, in a state of extreme nervous fatigue from years of bombing, she suffered "a severe illness" when her companion in spiritualist séances,

Lord Hugh Dowding, suddenly repudiated her "messages" and abandoned their relationship. Her unpublished memoir, *The Sword Went
Out to Sea*, describes these séances in journalistic prose and then
moves rapidly into associational interior monologue to render the inner realm of madness. Predating the builders of bomb shelters in the
fifties, H.D. became convinced that the Third World War had begun,
that bombs were dropping in her garden, that tunnels crisscrossing
Europe were war zones, and that an atom bomb had been dropped on
St. Paul's Cathedral. Her personal hallucination is strikingly similar to
the widespread cultural terror of the Cold War decades. Her visions of
world war extended into temporary insanity not so much because they
were unreasonable as because of their capacity to render her helpless.
Under their influence, she was unable to distinguish between the potential dangers of the incoming atomic age and the external realities
of the moment. For six months, she stayed at Küsnacht Klinik, and
in her own words, "I didn't stay long in the bee-hive. I got well
there."[18]

In the Hirslanden Notebooks H.D. wrote with confidence about
her ability to find a reason for each collapse. Unfortunately, re-creation of those reasons must be fragmentary and speculative at this
point. But enough can be induced, I believe, to clarify the recurrent
themes of those breakdowns, particularly as H.D. understood them
and wrote them into her fiction and poetry. H.D. referred somewhat
casually to these periods of illness and their immediate cause: "And
the thing I primarily wanted to fight in the open, war, its cause and
effect, with its inevitable aftermath of neurotic breakdown and related
nerve disorders, was driven deeper. With the death-hand swastika
chalked on the pavement, leading to the Professor's very door, I must,
in all decency, calm as best I could my own personal Phobia, my own
personal little Dragon of war-terror" (*T.F.*, p. 94). H.D. never spoke
directly with Freud about her war phobia because her sensitivity to his
situation as a Jew in Austria during the rise of Nazism kept her silent.
But she did approach these periods of "neurotic breakdown and related nerve disorders" indirectly. In her later diaries, notebooks, and
poems, she indicated the principles she learned from Freud that helped
her confront the "Dragon of war-terror." Integrating Freud's concepts
of projection, repetition compulsion, repression, and trauma, H.D.
looked for the recurring patterns in her periods of personal disaster.
The emotions and actions of nervous breakdown, she believed, were

partially determined by the buried layers of preceding catastrophes projected onto the present. She frequently turned to the image of "palimpsest" to describe this process. "Palimpsest" means literally "scraped again" in Greek and refers in English to a tablet which is imperfectly erased and written upon many times. H.D. used the metaphor in *Palimpsest, Trilogy,* and a number of journals to express her concept of "superposition," the layering of similar events throughout time.[19] As she applied the metaphor to her own life, personal history became a series of "writings" inscribed on the same tablet. Each layer of time is erased to make way for the future, but the new is always determined in some way by the old. For H.D., the palimpsest of disaster involved the interconnected shock waves brought on by war, death, and betrayal in love. The presence of any one of these seemed to bring to the surface her previous experiences with all the others. For example, she reflected about the impact of World War II: "the past is literally blasted into consciousness with the Blitz in London" (Hirslanden III, p. 2). The Second World War released repressed memories of abandonment because the bombings of the First World War were intertwined with her personal loss in childbirth and marriage. As she viewed the dissolution of her marriage in *Bid Me to Live* (*A Madrigal*), Aldington went off to fight in the trenches in 1917 and returned home fundamentally altered by the war. To H.D., he appeared to have abandoned his poetic muse to become a toughened, insensitive "soldier." No longer her companion-lover, he seemed to be a conquering "Roman" whose military masculinity led him inevitably into an affair with the conventionally beautiful and feminine Dorothy Yorke. This betrayal coincided generally with the bombings of London, the news of her brother's and father's deaths, and her fears for the coming child. Her first baby died during premature labor brought on, H.D. believed, by her shock at hearing the news of the Lusitania (*T.F.,* p. 40). Rica, H.D.'s persona in *Magic Mirror,* links that shock and death with insensitivity on Aldington's part: "Rafe Ashton [Aldington] (though not so stated in Madrigal) destroyed the unborn, the child Amor, when a few days before it was due, he burst in upon Julia [H.D.] of that story, with 'don't you realize what this means? Don't you feel anything? *The Lusitania has gone down.*' "[20] War, death, masculine insensitivity and betrayal became completely interwoven in H.D.'s mind. When she projected her brother's image onto Van de Leeuw, his death in 1934 released the complex of emotions and events of 1919 from the caverns of the unconscious. When Hugh Dowding "repudiated" their spiritual companionship just after the bombing finally ceased, the war terrors repressed for nearly thirty years returned to cause another severe breakdown.[21] H.D. did not discover what she believed to be the essential pattern underlying the palimpsest of her life until the 1950s, but without doubt, part of her purpose in seeking Freud was the "healing implicit in the process" of self-discovery.

Self-exploration fed the sources and expressions of creativity for H.D. She understood and Freud confirmed for her that the palimpsests of shock and breakdown in her life profoundly affected her art. Although *Tribute to Freud* is silent on the subject, H.D.'s letters to Bryher while she was in analysis openly discuss the writer's block in 1933 and 1934. At first, she was reluctant to talk about herself as a writer with Freud and did not bring up the subject in a substantive way until she had been in analysis for about seven weeks. This silence apparently "amazed" Freud, who said he had "never known such 'modesty,' but I tell him it is something deeper, but we are to go in to that later."[22] They did thoroughly go into this subject a few weeks later. H.D. was reading *The Letters of D.H. Lawrence*, edited by Aldous Huxley, and this released a "flood of war memories." "All this has come up," H.D. wrote Bryher, and "made a violent purple-patch in my analysis, but I presume it is a good thing, as the past was alive and kicking under the débris" (11 May 1933). Freud seemed to have connected the repression of these memories with her loss of creative direction. His "cure" included a therapeutic writing of events without embellishment or distancing masks. H.D. wrote to Bryher, "Evidently I blocked the whole of the 'period' and if I can skeleton-in a vol. about it, it will break the clutch. . . .the 'cure' will be, I fear me, writing that damn vol. straight, as history, no frills as in Narthex, Palimp. and so on, just a straight narrative, then later, changing names and so on" (15 May 1933). Throughout the remaining weeks of her analysis with Freud, she continued to work on her "damn vol." and to some extent was pleased with the "cure." She wrote to Bryher, "I have been writing since I got up, so feel a little blurred. . . . the vol. writes itself, . . . I do feel I want to get it done and don't want to tempt providence. It will mean everything, but the more I like the vol., the less I like ps-a [psychoanalysis]. That, I suppose was sure to happen" (28 May 1933).

However, when H.D. returned to Freud after another breakdown in 1934, she was still having difficulty with her writing. The few short stories and poems of this period did not "write themselves," as so much of H.D.'s work did when her creative energies were focused in a clear direction. At one point during analysis, she begged Bryher not to ask her any more about her book: "PLEASE Fido, if you love me, and love my work, leave that to work its own will in its own way. I got out those four stories, by the sweat of my brow" (24 November 1934). The volume Freud wanted her to write became *Bid Me to Live* (*A Madrigal*), first drafted in 1939 after her divorce from Aldington became final. The "novel" is a straightforward re-creation of H.D.'s London circle in 1916–1919—without "frills," without Greek masks, with only the names changed "at the end." It centers on her response to rejections first by Aldington, then by Lawrence as they intersected with the historical horror of the First World War.[23] For two decades thereafter, H.D. wrote easily and continuously, with the rapidity and intensity of certain inspiration. Perhaps as Freud predicted, drafting *Bid Me to Live* helped to "break the clutch" that hindered the natural flow of her writing. The "healing implicit in the process" of analysis included not only the identification of destructive patterns in her relationships, but also the related repression of her creative drive.

H.D.'s dependence on Freud as healer and her admiration for him as professor operated within the context of the "woman question," as it was called in the late nineteenth century. H.D. was not only student and patient in her interactions with Freud, but she was also a *woman* who had been advised by Sachs to continue the work of self-exploration with a *man*, "preferably one superior" to herself (*T.F.*, p. 150). *Tribute to Freud* seldom addresses the significance of gender in their work directly, but their historical context, their knowledge of feminist issues, and H.D.'s fiction written prior to the thirties all demonstrate indirectly that her purpose in working with Freud inevitably incorporated a desire to understand herself as woman.

Neither Freud nor H.D. approached the subject of woman's nature, status, and potential in their work ignorant of the current debates on feminist issues. The historical period that formed the contextual backdrop for H.D.'s childhood and youth and for the bulk of Freud's innovative work included a highly visible and active women's movement. Feminism was as inescapably "in the air" around the turn of the century as psychoanalysis was to be a decade later. Contrary to its popular image, this movement was not simply suffragist in its orientation any more than the movement today could be fully characterized by the struggle to pass the Equal Rights Amendment in the United States. Feminists in the nineteenth century extensively explored most of the issues raised by the second wave of feminism: the historical and biological roots of women's oppression; the destructive economic, political, and legal aspects of sex roles and the institution of the family; the role of socialization and education in creating sex differences; the ideological functions of religion, philosophy, science, and art in defining women's nature negatively; male control of female sexuality and reproduction; and the intersections of racism and class oppression with sexism.[24]

However, more direct evidence for Freud's and H.D.'s acquaintance with at least some of these issues exists than simply their historical context. Ernest Jones's biography of Freud recounts how Freud translated into German four essays by John Stuart Mill to relieve the boredom of his year of military service as a medical student in 1879–1880.[25] Among the essays was that of Harriet Taylor Mill and John Stuart Mill *On the Subjection of Women*, a comprehensive treatise on the injustice perpetuated by culturally created sex differences. In a letter to a friend, Freud attacked the Mills' argument. His defense of sex roles and the status quo reveals how fully Freud had internalized the Victorian idealization of the pure, childlike lady and the dichotomy of public and private spheres along sex lines:

> In his [Mill's] whole presentation it never emerges that women are different beings—we will not say lesser, rather the opposite—from men. He finds the suppression of women an analogy to that of Negroes. Any girl, even without a suffrage or legal competence, whose hand a man kisses and for whose love he is prepared to dare all, could have set him right. It is really a stillborn thought to send women into the struggle for existence exactly as men. If, for instance, I imagined my gentle sweet girl as a competitor it would only end in my telling her, as I did seventeen months ago, that I am fond of her and that I implore her to withdraw from the strife into the calm uncompetitive activity of my home. It is possible that changes in upbringing may suppress all a woman's tender attributes, needful of protection and yet so victorious, and that she can then earn a livelihood like men. It is also possible that in such an event one would not be justified in mourning the passing away of the most delightful thing the world can offer us—our ideal of womanhood. I believe that all reforming action in law and education would break down in front of the fact that, long before the age at which a man can earn a position in society, Nature has deter-

mined woman's destiny through beauty, charm, and sweetness. Law and custom have much to give women that has been withheld from them, but the position of women will surely be what it is: in youth an adored darling and in mature years a loved wife.[26]

Freud placed women on a pedestal of "beauty, charm, and sweetness" upheld by discriminatory "law and custom." Biographical information about H.D.'s childhood and early years in London as well as an unpublished story she wrote when she was a young woman indicate that she understood the falsity of that pedestal and at least some of the major issues raised by the early feminists. Her father, H.D. told Norman Pearson, was a great sympathizer with the feminist demands to open options for women beyond the home. For H.D., his sympathy took the form of active encouragement for her to become the "new woman," one like Marie Curie, who would achieve great things in fields traditionally reserved for men. As in many father-daughter relationships, however, his attempt to help her with math resulted in her frustration, fear of disappointment or rejection, and paralysis—social scientists today call this complex of emotions "math anxiety" and recognize its predominance among girls and women. In *Magic Mirror*, H.D. referred explicitly to the tension between herself and her father concerning her failure to fulfill his mathematic and scientific ambitions for her: "My father wanted to help me with long-division. I felt stupid and helpless. The more he explained, the less I understood it."[27] The feared disappointment of her father became a reality when she failed math at Bryn Mawr College and "managed to have a slight breakdown." Her failure to please her father no doubt eroded her self-image considerably, but she did not rebel against her father's "modern" ambitions by fleeing into the security of a traditional female role. As Freud was quick to point out on the basis of her dreams, she recognized her "difference" and desired another form of greatness—"megalomania," he termed it (*T.F.*, p. 51). She would achieve in art what her father hoped she would accomplish in science.

An early short story titled "The Suffragette" deals explicitly with H.D.'s defiance of traditional norms for women and demonstrates her ability to translate a number of feminist issues into artistic form.[28] Perhaps echoing the Jamesian theme of American innocence acquiring knowledge in Europe, "The Suffragette" centers on the conversion experience of a naive American girl who meets a feminist in an English boardinghouse. The respectably middle-class young hero is ignorant, but curious, about the militant British suffragists. In the course of the story, she registers the significance of a boisterous man's laughing dismissal of feminism, talks with the dignified and articulate Miss Marston, and hears a story of job discrimination in the mills from the ragged girl Maggie. At first she declines Marston's invitation to go to a meeting, but by the end of the story she has changed her mind and become more sympathetic with the militancy of the British feminists. The story records a political awakening to women's issues and suggests the making of an activist. The story is brief, more of an imagist sketch than a narrative, and the conversion is not fully rendered. But much about the story demonstrates H.D.'s general familiarity with the "woman question" and even further a subtle comprehension of how the issue of suffrage is related to the general status of women in society.

The biographical core of this story is H.D.'s acquaintance with the well-known British feminist Dora Marsden and Marsden's connections with the imagist circle. Marsden had been part of the Pankhurst group that stoned Parliament, went to jail, and instigated the famous hunger strikes of 1911.[29] But later that year, Marsden decided that the suffragette movement was too narrow for her radical feminist demands. She left the movement to found and edit a theoretical journal, The Freewoman (1911–1912), that would explore a wide range of feminist issues, including the taboo subjects of female sexuality and homosexuality. In 1913, the journal changed its name to The New Freewoman and featured first Pound and then Aldington as literary editors. In 1914, the journal once again changed its title, this time to The Egoist, now edited by Harriet Shaw Weaver, a lifetime friend and supporter of Marsden as well as James Joyce. While Marsden no longer wanted editorial responsibility for the journal, she continued to publish a feminist theoretical essay as the lead article in each issue of The Egoist. Pound was openly uninterested in the political debates within the little magazine that he used as an outlet for the literary avant-garde. But Weaver, a friend of H.D.'s, continued to support the wide-ranging feminist vision of her friend. In the power struggle between the feminist theoreticians and the poets, it is not clear how much communication existed between them, or even whether they read each other's work. But H.D.'s unpublished story suggests that she had considerable knowledge about and sympathy with the woman who locked horns with Pound. Why H.D. never developed this form of explicit exploration of contemporary political issues in her art must be left to speculation at this point. Among the complex of personal and aesthetic reasons, the fact that her early artistic community in London was predominantly male might have discouraged further experimentation with explicitly feminist themes.

H.D. did, however, develop close relationships with two women who wrote directly about the difficulties creative women faced—Amy Lowell and Bryher. Like Marsden, Lowell faced Pound's demand for editorial control and explored issues of woman's nature in her own publications. Lowell's poem "The Sisters" creates a "family" of writers whose bond is established by sex, the "queer lot" of "women who write poetry." The cost of this effort, however, is a specifically female form of fragmentation—the double self torn between traditionally "masculine" aspirations and "feminine" circumstance: "I wonder what it is that makes us do it, / Singles us out to scribble down, man-wise, / The fragments of ourselves. Why are we / Already mother-creatures, double-bearing, / With matrices in body and in brain?"[30] Duality is also the organizing metaphor of Bryher's fascinating second novel, *Two Selves*, completed with H.D.'s help during the years the women traveled to California and Egypt. Using the poetics of imagism within a narrative structure, *Two Selves* is a continuation of *Development*, Bryher's autobiographical novel of a young girl growing up in upper middle class Victorian England. It explores the constraints and aspirations of a talented young woman who is continually frustrated by her family's denial of every request for "adventure." Her bitterness emerges out of the recognition that if she had been a boy, all her suggestions would have been enthusiastically encouraged: "If she had been a boy life would have lain at her feet."[31] Her "two selves" are a metaphoric representation of her surface capitulation to convention and her hidden resistence to it: "Two selves. Jammed against each other, disjointed and ill-fitting. An obedient Nancy with heavy plaits tied over two ears that answered 'yes, no, yes, no,' according as the the wind blew. A boy, a brain, that planned adventures and sought wisdom. Two personalities uneasy by their juxtaposition. As happy together as if a sharp sword were thrust into a golf bag for a sheath."[32]

The inner self that Bryher identifies as the "boy" grows up with the dream of freedom only to discover the realities of restriction, loneliness, and despair: " 'When I'm grown up I shall be free.' But there was no freedom. Only an invisible but actual clutch of circumstance that wove grey chains back and forth across her limbs and mind."[33] The discovery of her first real friend, H.D., springs the Victorian trap of feminine obligation. As a symbol of a new, integrated selfhood, her meeting with H.D. serves as the spiritual (and narrative) climax to the years of alienation and rebellion Bryher experienced in the face of traditional role expectations for women. Bryher's portrayal of a woman's rebellion against a male-dominated society is sophisticated in its perception and powerful in its anger. H.D.'s involvement in Bryher's writing of this novel establishes her familiarity with the ideas that Bryher explored on the "woman question." Like Lowell's poem, Bryher's novel was an important and immediate context for H.D.'s own understanding of her position as a woman artist.

In her perceptive book on the female poetic tradition, Suzanne Juhasz has articulated the conflict of identities imaged in Bryher's and Lowell's work. Juhasz's discussion helps to clarify the tensions in H.D.'s own situation that she must have brought to her sessions with Freud. The life and art of many women poets, Juhasz wrote, has been a "double-bind situation, one of conflict and strain." In a culture that has defined art as masculine creation and relationship as feminine creation, the woman poet has been caught between her desire to be an artist and her identity as a woman. Because cultural norms dictate a division between "woman" and "poet," the woman poet has faced an impossible choice between two separate identities. Juhasz wrote: "The conflict between her two 'selves' is an excruciating and irreconcilable civil war, when both sides are in fact the same person. If she is 'woman,' she must fail as 'poet'; 'poet,' she must fail as 'woman.' Yet she is not two people. She is a woman poet whose art is a response to, results from, her life."[34] H.D.'s novels, *Palimpsest* and *Bid Me to Live (A Madrigal)*, explore the "double bind" she felt as an artist and a woman in her relationships with men, particularly Aldington and Lawrence. Both novels painfully portray gifted women whose intellect and creativity make them sexually undesirable to men who ultimately reject them for stereotypically feminine and erotic women. For H.D.'s personae in these novels, success as a "poet" brings failure as a "woman," just as Juhasz has argued.[35] In the years before H.D. worked with Freud, her awareness of the woman artist's conflict with societal norms was well developed.

Awareness, however, never guarantees solution. If *Palimpsest* is an accurate reflection of H.D.'s general state of mind in the late twenties and early thirties about the conflict of identities she faced as a woman, she understood her victimization far better than she did the route to transcendence. Where Bryher thrived on rebellion, H.D. seems to have suffered with what she called her "difference." Where Bryher's memoirs reveal a pugnacious temperament, H.D.'s uncover a vulnerability painfully sensitive to rejection.

H.D.'s writing block in the thirties was at least partially the result of the vulnerability she felt as a woman in a man's world. While H.D.'s memoirs and journals never create a grandiose or egotistical artistic persona, they are relatively free of insecurity and quite matter-of-fact about her talents and commitment to art. She was indeed capable of making detached, even negative comments about her own work without doubting her authority as artist (*T.F.*, pp. 148–49). But her letters to Bryher in 1933 and 1934 demonstrate that the image of literary men, especially of those whom she loved, still haunted her and hindered her ability to write. Exploring the Lawrence memories and materials would, for example, help "my creative work. I think I will finally get this idea out of my head of being a back-number" (12 May 1933). Three days later she wrote Bryher, "I keep dreaming of literary men, Shaw, Cunninghame, Grahame, now Noel Coward and Lawrence himself, over and over. It is important as book means *penis* evidently and as a 'writer,' only, am I equal in uc-n [unconscious], in the right way with men. Most odd" (15 May 1933).

H.D.'s ambivalence toward "literary men," a theme she explored fully in *Hermetic Definition* and *End to Torment*, represented her own internalization of a masculine cultural tradition. But her identity as an artist was not the real center of her vulnerability. It was herself as woman, particularly as sexual being, that she questioned. Her journals, memoirs, and autobiographical novels portray a series of relationships with men in which she is, or at least feels, rejected. Pound, Aldington, Lawrence, Macpherson, and Dowding seem to have been the most important, with Aldington's affair with Dorothy Yorke as probably the most traumatic rejection for her. Each subsequent rejection by men seems to have triggered the pain and insecurity induced by Aldington's actions. This personal "palimpsest" of victimization is in part what H.D. referred to in one of her statements about why she went to see Freud: "I wanted to free myself of repetitive thoughts and experiences—my own and those of many of my contemporaries" (*T.F.*, p. 13).

Although the nature of her relationships varied greatly, H.D.'s feeling of inadequacy as a woman, especially as a sexual woman, was so central to the breakup of her marriage that her other experiences of rejection were probably colored by this insecurity. Aldington apparently told Yorke that H.D. could not bring him happiness because she "had no body."[36] In *Bid Me to Live*, Julia (H.D.'s persona) is afraid to have sex with her soldier husband because her doctor told her after the stillbirth of her baby that another childbirth would kill her. Her inability to tell her husband about her fear of pregnancy leaves him baffled at her avoidance of sex.[37] In *Palimpsest*, Hipparchia is the highly educated, exquisitely sensitive Greek slave and concubine of Marius, the Roman conqueror. While he cannot free himself of his fascination for her, he repeatedly tells himself that "Hipparchia . . . was no woman." She in turn "struggled against the warm smothering of his kisses" and experienced intercourse as an attack that left her passionless: "Plunge dagger into a gold lily. What more was she, had she in her most intimate encounters given him? You might as well plunge dagger into the cold and unresponsive flesh of some tall flower." (*P.*, pp. 6, 15). *End to Torment* explores some of the reasons for sexual inhibition—H.D. returns repeatedly to the image of being discovered while she and Pound were kissing (*E.T.T.*, pp. 12, 17–19, 54). A variety of sources, in other words, suggest that H.D.'s sexual relations with men were troubled—whatever the cause. Aldington thought her sexually cold, if not "frigid," and his affair with the beautiful Dorothy Yorke was tantamount to a rejection of H.D. as a woman. Aldington most likely viewed her sexual difficulties—whatever their exact nature or cause—as a symptom of psychological failure. His choice of a "feminine" woman who delighted in centering her life completely in her love for him may have reinforced the cultural stereotype of intellectual, gifted women as asexual, emotionally cold, and unfeminine. H.D.'s vulnerability as a woman arose out of her own internalization of these dominant cultural norms and Aldington's expression of them. Hipparchia in *Palimpsest* demonstrates the painful mixture of guilt, inadequacy, and anger that characterizes women trapped in the "double bind" Juhasz described.

The insecurity and fragmentation of identity H.D. experienced in her intense relationships with men is strikingly absent in her accounts of her relationships with two women: Frances Josepha Gregg, whom she met in Philadelphia after she left Bryn Mawr College, and Bryher, who was her close companion from 1919 to 1961. In H.D.'s notes on her early sessions with Freud, she linked the two women and used the word "infatuation" to describe her feelings about Gregg: "When I told the Professor that I had been infatuated with Frances Josepha and might have been happy with her, he said 'No—biologically, no.' For some reason, though I had been so happy with the Professor (Freud—*Freude* ["joy"]), my head hurt and I felt unnerved" (*T.F.*, p. 152). In an analysis of a dream about Gregg, H.D. concluded: "Bryher seems to appear, as she did in actual life, to take the place of Frances" (*T.F.*, p. 152). H.D. never used the word "lesbian" to define herself or her close friends either in *Tribute to Freud* or in any of the journals, manuscripts, or letters yet made available to scholars. But the conversation she recorded in "Advent" is a clear reference to the lesbian nature of her feelings toward Gregg and Bryher. By "lesbian" feelings I mean, simply, strong, erotic, love emotions directed toward women. Freud's negative reaction to biological fulfillment in lesbian sexuality appears to have given H.D. considerable pain. But in "Advent," as in her other public and private writings, H.D. did not explicitly define the "biological" or physical nature of her relationships with Gregg and Bryher. In three unpublished romans à clef, however, she explored the psychological aspects of her attraction and love for the two women, especially for Gregg. The novels, written during the twenties, follow the broad outlines of H.D.'s life from the time she dropped out of Bryn Mawr to the breakup of her marriage, the birth of her child, and the early years of her relationship with Bryher. They are *Paint It Today*, dated 1921; *Asphodel*, dated 1921–1922 and labeled "early edition of MADRIGAL, DESTROY," in H.D.'s hand; and *Her*, dated 1927, the most polished of the three.[38] All three are remarkable in the extent to which they explore H.D.'s wholehearted passion for Frances Gregg and her more ambivalent feelings toward first Pound and then Aldington. In contrast to her relationships with Pound and Aldington, her love for Gregg led her to affirm a womanhood that fused her self as artist and lover into a single, whole identity.

Her, the novel completed shortly after the publication of *Palimpsest*, reveals most fully this aspect of her identity which serves as an important context for her discussions with Freud. The story takes place in her family's suburban Philadelphia home in the year after she failed conic sections in math at Bryn Mawr. As the novel opens, Hilda's persona, Hermione Gart, nicknamed Her, is severely depressed by a double sense of failure—as a student and as a woman: "I am Hermione Gart, a failure. . . . I should have letters and letters, almost spelling things after my name, Her Gart, Scd., LiD, I am Her Gart, O.M., Old Maid precisely. . . . She only felt that she, a disappointment to her father, an odd duckling to her mother, [was] an importunate over-grown, unincarnated entity that had no place here," (*Her*, pp. 3, 9).[39] In the midst of her identity crisis, words such as " 'failure complex,' " " 'compensation reflex,' " and " 'arrested-development' " had "opened no door to her" (*Her*, p. 1).

Hermione's search to transcend her sense of inadequacy acts itself out in the conflict she feels in her relationships with George Lowdnes, the dashing young poet to whom she is engaged (Pound), and Fayne Rabb, the strange young woman whose intensity borders at time on psychic trance (Gregg). Both are considered "eccentric," but Eugenia Gart's (her mother) opposition to George yields to enthusiasm for her daughter's coming marriage. But as the marriage gains social approbation, Hermione's discomfort with George and her fascination with Fayne rapidly increase. To others, her marriage to the penniless, iconoclastic, brilliant poet who wears an inappropriate velvet jacket everywhere, represents a great risk and adventure. But to Hermione, the marriage comes to represent her capitulation to the socially accepted role of wife. As she walks in the woods with George, she feels she is playing a "role," as if she were Hermione in Shakespeare's *The Winter's Tale*. Social role and acting role overlap, both ultimately unreal: "Almost, almost Hermione was Hermione out of Shakespeare . . . but not quite" (*Her*, p. 90). Being George's fiancée is like "playing" that she is a grown-up: "She wanted George as a little girl wants to put hair up or to wear long skirts. She wanted George with some uncorrelated sector of Her Gart. She wanted George to define and to make definable a mirage. . . . Regarding him, very hot in the wood-path, Hermione became almost collegiate of the period, almost a person with hair up and with long skirts" (*Her*, pp. 84–85).

But instead of "defining" her, George blots her out. "The kisses of George smudged out her clear geometric thought. . . . Smudged out. I am smudged out" (*Her*, p. 100). Sex with George carries overtones of violence and humiliation as she increasingly feels they are playing scenes from a "bad novel":

> People are in things. I am in Her. George never understood me. Rising to her feet, knowing that he would not understand Her, she was drifted

toward the divan. George with a twist and deft knee movement had thrown her on the low couch. . . . Now more than ever she knew they were out of some bad novel. Sound of chiffon ripping and the twist and turn of Hermione under the stalwart thin young torso of George Lowdnes. Now more than ever thought made spiral, made concentric circle toward a darkened ceiling. The ceiling came down, down. . . . The ceiling was a sort of movable shutter like some horrible torture thing out of Poe's tales. . . . Walls were coming close to suffocate, to crush her ... "you've torn this chiffon sleeve thing horribly."

A twist, a turn. Men are not strong. Women are stronger. I am stronger. I turn and twist out of those iron arms because if he had held me, I would have been crushed by iron. Iron is in walls. (*Her*, pp. 231–32)

George's rough attack without regard for her feelings leaves her frightened, humiliated, and "smudged out." But his psychological attack, coming in the form of adoration, is even more threatening to her sense of self:

He wanted Her, but he wanted a Her that he called decorative. George wanted a Her out of the volumes on the floor, out of the two great volumes. He wanted Her from about the middle, the glorious flaming middle, the Great Painters (that came under Florence) section. George, regarding Her, was saying "you are so decorative." There was something stripped of decoration, something of somewhat painful angles that he would not recognize. George saying "choriamics of a forgotten Mellic" [about one of her poems] was flattering her, tribute such as some courtier might play to a queen who played at classicism; he did not proffer her the bare branch that was the strip of wild naked olive or the tenuous oleander. (*Her*, p. 230)

As Rachel Blau DuPlessis has argued, H.D. punned on Hermione's nickname in the syntactical position of sentence "object" to stress her "object" status within the conventions of heterosexual marriage.[40] George's "decorative object" she refuses finally to be: "I am Hermione Gart and will be Hermione Lowdnes . . . It wasn't right. People are in things, things are in people. I can't be called Lowdnes" (*Her*, pp. 232, 153–54). As his wife, she would be *his* poem, no longer a poet in her own right. In her fear of a marriage which would absorb her identity into "Lowdnes," she attempts to recover an image of herself: "Straight and strong like some girl athlete from Laconian hill slopes, straight and brave like the maiden Artemis" (*Her*, p. 235).

This hidden self matches that of her "twin," her ideal "sister," her "alter-ego"—Fayne Rabb. Before she meets Fayne, she yearns for a true "sister," one who "would run, would leap, would be concealed under the autumn sumac or lie shaken with hail and wind, lost on some Lacedomonian foot-hill. A sister would have companion hound, Hermione's the more lithe, the more regular in fleetness, her sister's heavier for whelping and more subtle and less of a rival in matter of speed, in manner of springing" (*Her*, p. 11). Images of freedom in the wild contrast with her feminine sister-in-law Minnie, whom she detests, and with the "soft," maternal figure of Eugenia, who is bound tightly by social convention. Hermione finds that spirit-sister in her relationship with Fayne. Her lasting image of Fayne as the boy huntress was set when she watched Fayne act in a play. As she recollects that image with Fayne at a later point, mutual erotic feelings rise to a crescendo without any threat of physical or psychological violence. With a woman, Her's ambivalence toward love and sexuality disappears:

> The mouth was straight now, the mouth of a boy-hunter. . . . Across the shoulders there was a strap holding arrows. Marble lifted from marble and showed a boy. "You might have been a huntress." . . . "I don't mean huntress like that—like that—I don't mean country clubs—not things like that. I mean a boy standing on bare rocks and stooping to take a stone from his strapped sandal." . . . "I mean you were so exactly right in that stage tunic. You were so exactly right as that Pygmalion." Her bent forward, face bent toward Her. A face bends towards me and a curtain opens. . . . Almost along the floor with its strip of carpet, almost across me I feel the fringe of some fantastic, wine-coloured parting curtains. Curtains part as I look into the eyes of Fayne Rabb. "And I—I'll make you breathe, my breathless statue." "Statue? You—you—you—*you* are the statue." Curtains fell, curtains parted, curtains filled the air with heavy swooping purple. Lips long since half kissed away. Curled lips long since half kissed away. (*Her*, pp. 217–18).

Mutual absorption does not threaten to objectify the Laconian girl athlete or the boy huntress. Syntactical balance underscores the identification of the lovers: "Her bent forward, face bent toward Her." Merging with her sister-image brings her first confident assertion of identity: "I know her. Her. I am Her. She is Her. Knowing her, I know Her. She is some amplification of myself like amoeba giving birth by breaking off, to amoeba. I am a sort of mother, a sort of sister to Her" (*Her*, p. 211). Where her nickname symbolized her object status in Her's relationship with George, it signals a liberating woman-identification in her relationship with Fayne: "I will not have her hurt. I will not have Her hurt. She is Her. I am Her. Her is Fayne. Fayne is Her. I will not let them hurt HER" (*Her*, p. 244). This identification of sisters, based in recognition of sameness and erotic desire, does not threaten her capacity to create; it inspires it. Unlike George, who compares Her to art objects in a book, Fayne understands that Her's writing is the essence of her identity, as inseparable from her as breathing. She tells Her that her writing "is the pulsing of a willow, the faint note of some Sicilian shepherd. Your writing is the thin flute holding you to eternity. Take away your flute and you remain, lost in a world of unreality [a world of] false, super-imposed standards" (*Her*, p. 215). With Fayne, the double bind of the woman writer does not exist. Nor does she experience the fragmentation of identity that Bryher expressed in *Two Selves* and Amy Lowell pointed to in "The Sisters." Lowell referred to women acting "manwise" when they wrote, and Bryher identified her hidden, free self as a "boy." H.D.'s lesbian lover-poet is thoroughly "woman-identified," to borrow a contemporary feminist concept. That is, Hermione discovers her creative center in her identity as *woman* through her love of her sister-image.[41]

The repeated refrain in *Her* is from Swinburne's "Itylus": *O sister my sister o singing swallow, the world's division divideth us*" (*Her*, p. 241). Its warning foreshadows the difficulties Fayne and Her face in their unconventional love. They are aware that the world would consider them "indecent." George for once agrees with Eugenia in declaring Fayne "unwholesome," and tries to scare Her out of her fascination by reminding her that in the old days she and Fayne would have been "burnt for witchcraft" (*Her*, pp. 219–20). Hermione understands that she and Fayne must redefine "decadence" and "innocence" just as she transforms the negative "circles" of conic sections into the "circles" of intimacy: "Her Gart saw rings and circles, the rings and circles that were the eyes of Fayne Rabb. . . . Her and Fayne Rabb were flung into a concentric intimacy, rings on rings that made a geometric circle toward a ceiling, that curved over them like ripples on a pond surface. . . . there were rings on rings of circles as if they had fallen into a deep well and were looking up ... 'long since half kissed away.' 'Isn't Swinburne decadent?' 'In what sense exactly decadent, Fayne?' 'O innocence, holy and untouched and most immoral. Innocence like thine is totally indecent' " (*Her*, p. 218).

In *Asphodel*, the first part of which is H.D.'s second attempt to explore her relationship with Frances Gregg, social convention divides the lovers. Hermione's passionate plea for Fayne to stay in London instead of returning to the States with her mother Clara synthesizes a number of themes developed in *Her*: lesbian love as an alternative to social convention; the lack of ambivalence, sexual or psychological, in her love for Fayne; the connections between her work and her love; the condemnation of the world. Fayne asks if they would live with Delia as a "screen"; Her responds:

> "We don't need to be screened. What have we done or could we do to need any apology or explanation. I am burning away that's all. The clear gem-like flame. I don't want you to miss it. I'm going to write, work. . . . I, Hermione, tell you I love you Fayne Rabb. Men and women will come and say I love you. I love you Hermione, you Fayne. Men will say I love you Hermione but will anyone ever say I love you Fayne as I say it?. . . . I don't want to be (as they say crudely) a boy. Nor do I want you to so be. I don't feel a girl. What is all this trash of Sappho? None of that seems real, to (in any way) matter. I see you. I feel you. My pulse runs swiftly. My brain reaches some height of delirium. Do people say it's indecent? Maybe it is. I can't hear now see anymore, people. Some are kind some aren't. . . . This thing that you allow to creep over you, to swamp you. . . . You aren't going to stay because you're afraid simply. . . . There is a door leading nowhere. That is that trip to Liverpool, the boat to New York. There is a door of cowardice and unattainment and of nullity." (*Asphodel*, p. 100)

H.D. did not call either *Her* or *Asphodel* "autobiography," and it would certainly be unjustified to equate either novel with the factual events of her life.[42] But since Hermione is admittedly a persona for H.D., the novels do work through concepts of womanhood, work, and love that probably characterize H.D. of the twenties. It is not surprising that *Her*, polished as it is, never got published, given the outraged reception Radclyffe Hall's *The Well of Loneliness* received in 1928. *Asphodel* was indeed a draft for *Bid Me to Live*, but the published novel completely eliminates the relationship with Fayne that is explored in such depth in *Asphodel*. Did H.D. suppress these books out of a pragmatic fear? Given a different cultural climate, would she have openly and explicitly identified herself as a lesbian? Or at least would she have called her relationships with Gregg and Bryher "lesbian"? Is the sexual identity expressed in these novels consistent with the women in the rest of her work—or consistent with what is known about H.D.'s later life? To go back to the question she asked Freud, would she have been happier, would she have felt less victimized (as she often felt with men), if she had lived with Frances Gregg—that is, lived a fully lesbian identity? If so, what impact did that have on her art? Does H.D.'s work, in short, belong squarely in the center of a lesbian literary tradition?

I do not believe that enough biographical information is available at this point to understand the nature of H.D.'s sexual identity, preference, and experience throughout her long life. Alongside *Her, Asphodel,* and her love poems for Bryher are the prose and poetic accounts of a love for men, different in kind but equal in intensity. Her epics of the fifties, like *Helen in Egypt* and *Vale Ave,* seem as profoundly heterosexual in their portraits of love between archetypal woman and man as *Asphodel* and *Her* are fundamentally lesbian in their exploration of erotic sister-love. Did H.D. change her orientation? Or is she best described as bisexual—loving fully, though differently, individuals of both sexes?

Complicating the difficulty of incomplete biographical information is the role potentially played by sexual inhibition, guilt, and practical considerations for safety. H.D. and Bryher both grew up in strict, Victorian homes that most likely produced an attitude toward sexuality which would have made sexual fulfillment of any kind difficult.[43] In a society as homophobic as our own, silence about sexual preference and the double life of the "closet" have frequently been the only safe options for women who would face a storm of abuse, prejudice, and outright discrimination if they spoke and lived openly as lesbians. Internalization of heterosexist norms further caused many lesbians to maintain the silence with each other, even with themselves—not daring to name and therefore legitimate their sexual identity.[44] Where H.D. fits in this spectrum of sexuality, inhibition, and silence is very difficult to determine.

Compounding the difficulties of ignorance is the current ambiguity of the labels "lesbian," "bisexual," and "heterosexual" in our culture in general and in the feminist movement more particularly. They are terms in the process of definition, especially the word "lesbian" which in the exhilaration of emergence from the "closet" has taken on a complex array of often inconsistent meanings with the result that effective discourse on the subject has become difficult and frequently highly charged. All three terms are variously used to describe specific sexual behavior at any point in time; inherent, lifelong sexual preference; socially conditioned sexual preference; erotic attraction and fantasy; sexual and/or psychological identity, including those whose behavior is at odds with their sense of self; and a political perspective, epistemology, and lifestyle. Within this complex of definitions, "lesbianism" has been inconsistently equated with everything from sexual intimacy between women, to female friendship and sisterhood, woman's creative center, woman-identification, and the epistemology of the oppressed who exist on the fringes of the patriarchy. When the meaning of words shifts so radically, the usefulness of labeling artists becomes questionable. Perhaps we need to invent more words to distinguish among all the physical, psychological, and political phenomena coexisting under the umbrella of "lesbianism."

The issue is ultimately an important one, however—both for a full comprehension of H.D.'s work and for the emerging scholarship on lesbian culture. If any artist has lesbian feelings or relationships in the context of a culture that defines lesbianism as "sick" or "deviant," that experience will inevitably play a profound role in her concept of her self as woman and its expression in her art. Furthermore, the discovery and exploration of the doubly hidden history of lesbian women and culture is of critical importance to a more comprehensive, less distorted understanding of the past and to the related emergence of authentic lesbian identities in the future. My objective is to avoid the obfuscating ambiguity of terminology without sacrificing discussion of the issue itself.

H.D.'s search for her identity as woman in both her life and her art went in both lesbian and heterosexual directions with great intensity. The biographical and artistic records of her life from 1910 to 1928 provide undeniable evidence of these dual dimensions. She brought the contexts of *both* experiences into her sessions with Freud: the insecurity and fragmentation she wrote about as a woman in relationships with men; the sense of wholeness and affirmation she wrote about as a woman in relationships with women. Freud knew about her insecurities as a woman before H.D. arrived in Vienna because he had read and been very interested in *Palimpsest* (T.F., p. 190). How much of the self recorded in *Her* and *Asphodel* H.D. allowed Freud to see is unclear from her own published accounts. But her letters to Bryher, written while she was in analysis, along with an unpublished poem about Freud demonstrate that she brought both her lesbian and heterosexual loves to their discussions for explanation. Freud apparently told her that, as she wrote to Bryher, "I am that all-but extinct phenomenon, the perfect bi-[sexual]." In "The Master," she made clear reference to her bisexuality:

I had two loves separate;
God who loves all mountains,
alone knew why
and understood
and told the old man
to explain

the impossible.

which he did.[45]

In the office of "the Master," then, H.D. fused the roles of woman, student, disciple, seeker, and patient into a united intellectual and emotional complex of experience. It would be a distortion of the whole to reduce that experience to any one of its significant parts. The healing catharsis of self-knowledge and understanding that she really began with Freud and that continued throughout her life gave her the power to transmute experience into art. To use one of her own images in the *Trilogy*, psychoanalysis was the "crucible" that allowed her to transform the personal and social chaos of the century into the vision of "spiritual realism" that dominates her later poetry (*T.F.*, pp. 71–75).

The most fruitful approach in determining the significance of psychoanalysis for H.D.'s development as an artist is one that uses H.D.'s own attitudes as the touchstone of analysis. The temptation to bypass H.D.'s multifaceted purposes and begin with an attempt to psychoanalyze her as a patient is indeed great. The gold mine of personal impressions recorded in her books, diaries, and dream accounts certainly provides the critic with more images from the unconscious and her free associations upon them than psychoanalytic critics usually have as they attempt to reconstruct the psychosexual development of artists. In his extensive work on H.D., Holland demonstrates the dangers of reductionistic distortion by focusing on what her written work might reveal about her oral, anal, phallic, and oedipal stages of development. Quoting Freud's theory that a woman's "strongest motive in coming for treatment was the hope that, after all, she might still obtain a male organ, the lack of which was so painful to her," Holland argued that H.D. sought to identify with the "phallic power" of Freud because "fusion with a man insures against deficiency."[46] Riddel similarly found in H.D.'s poetic use of myth and symbol her search for the "phallus . . . the signifier, the giver of meaning" and her recognition that she "suffocates" from her "feminine inwardness," "softness," "subjectivity," and "incompleteness."[47] Both critics use a crudely Freudian terminology to assert that the genesis of H.D.'s art was the longing to possess what any man has at birth.

Operating on the androcentric Freudian premise of female difference and consequent inferiority, Holland's and Riddel's reduction of H.D.'s search to penis envy is ridiculous at best and oppressive at worst. An exploration of H.D.'s psychology could more usefully speculate on the rich personal material suggesting that her mother's favoritism of her brother and her father's disappointment in a nonmathematical daughter caused psychic scars not easily healed. Perusal of her dream records reveals potentially significant clues to H.D.'s considerable fear, anger, and hurt concerning the victimization and powerlessness of women. One dream, for example, begins with H.D. sobbing, " 'My mother, my mother' " as she sees her mother lying passive, about to be raped. Another presents that favored brother trying to strangle her with a length of braided cord from a box of candy they are sharing.[48] Fear, awe, and competition with this brother are evident in *Tribute to Freud*, as well as the hurt she felt in her mother's favoritism toward Gilbert (*T.F.*, pp. 25–29, 33–34). H.D. might well be compared to Maggie Tulliver in George Eliot's *The Mill on the Floss*, the brilliant free spirit of a girl child who is gradually imprisoned in a feminine role as her rather dull brother gains in masculine honor and prestige. Perhaps H.D.'s brother served as her psychological double, living out the destiny she would have liked to have but could not because her family and society favored men and masculinity. His death caused two breakdowns, one direct in 1919, and the other indirect, through Van de Leeuw in 1934. But perhaps it also paved the way for her to "take his place," as Freud suggested (*T.F.*, p. 6). With him gone, she did not have to be Miriam, the patient sister; as in her "Princess" dream, she could herself be Moses, founder of a new religion (*T.F.*, pp. 37, 120).

While a feminist psychoanalytic perspective on H.D.'s dreams and reflections is indeed more enlightening than the androcentric approaches of Holland and Riddel, the assessment of Freud's impact on

H.D.'s life and art should not begin with a speculative attempt to re-create H.D.'s psychological development. Instead, the focus of analysis should begin with H.D.'s own ideas about what she learned from Freud. His theories and her experience with him were a tremendous catalyst in her poetic development. Analysis of that influence should emerge directly out of H.D.'s own attitudes toward and interpretations of psychoanalysis. Rather than beginning with speculation about her personal neurosis, we need to see Freud's influence as a collaboration, a dynamic interaction of two whole human beings. Within the framework of this critical approach, the central questions to be explored in subsequent chapters include the following: What Freudian theories appealed to H.D.? What ideas did she reject? What did she learn from Freud about her identity as an artist? What did Freud's theories about women do with H.D.'s vulnerability with men or with her search for a "sister"? Did he drive the wedge between woman and poet even deeper? Or did he help to heal the conflict of selves? Most importantly, how did H.D. transmute Freud's theories and their interactions into art?

Hieroglyphic Voices

THE UNCONSCIOUS AND PSYCHOANALYTIC
MODES OF TRANSLATION

FREUD TOLD H.D., " 'My discoveries are not primarily a heal-all. My discoveries are a basis for a very grave philosophy. There are very few who understand this, *there are very few who are capable of understanding this*' " (*T.F.*, p. 18). The beginnings of H.D.'s collaboration with Freud centered on her recognition of this "grave philosophy" based on his pioneering mapmaking of the unconscious. Ernest Jones, Freud's biographer, wrote in his definition of "what psychoanalysis really is" that "the essence of Freud's discovery is his exploration of the unconscious, a concept which before his work was an empty term."[1]

For centuries, the "unconscious" has been neither an unknown phenomenon nor an empty term to artists and mystics. As Freud himself was quick to say, they had already explored the special realm of mental activity that operates outside of ordinary consciousness. Today, the proliferation of psychological theories has been so great that Freud is commonly associated with the specific hypotheses of psychoanalysis while the controversial novelty of his fundamental premise is easily overlooked. Freud was the first to posit the existence of the unconscious in the language of science and to systematize knowledge of that realm into a comprehensive body of theory.

H.D. honored that achievement by stating that Freud was the first to open "the study of this vast, unexplored region," the first to draw the "shapes, lines, graphs, the *hieroglyph of the unconscious,*" (*T.F.,* p. 93). Freud's theories on the epistemology and language of the unconscious and his methods for translation had a deep impact on H.D.'s concept of the psyche and her related development of aesthetic image and structure. Understanding Freud's influence on H.D. therefore begins directly with his basic theories of the unconscious.

Freud called the unconscious "a special realm," connected to but distinct from the conscious mind. He frequently used spatial and chronological metaphors to emphasize the separation between conscious and unconscious functions. These two realms are like adjoining rooms with an official doorkeeper between them to control the flow of messages, he wrote at one point. Or, he said at another point, the mind is like the city of Rome, whose evolution is recorded in the succession of strata uncovered by archeologists. Just as the archeologist pieced together the fragments of an ancient vase, so the analyst sorted through the patient's dreams and fragmentary memories to re-create some forgotten or repressed event.[2]

H.D. echoed Freud's imagery by transforming the arrangement of his office into a reenactment of the human psyche. She likened Freud to the Roman god Janus, the guardian of doorways who faced two ways (*T.F.,* pp. 100, 102). Freud stood on the threshold of the psyche looking into the contrasting realms of consciousness and unconsciousness. As analyst, he led H.D. from his study to the semidarkened anteroom off the fourth wall (*T.F.,* p. 23). After outlining an elaborate map of Freud's office, H.D. looked beyond the space "left vacant by the wide-open double doors" to see "the room beyond," sometimes "very dark," sometimes in "broken light and shadow. . . . One may walk into that room, as the Professor invited me to do one day, to look at the things on his table" (*T.F.,* p. 23).

H.D.'s image is spatial: the unconscious is a room filled with treasures like the sacred art objects in Freud's collection. But "Old Janus was guardian of the seasons too, that time-sequence of the four quarters of the year" (*T.F.,* p. 100). And the "fourth dimension" is a temporal metaphor as well as a spatial one: "Past, present, future, these three—but there is another time-element, popularly called the fourth-dimensional. The room has four sides. There are four seasons to a year. This fourth dimension, though it appears variously disguised and under different subtitles, described and elaborately tabulated in the Professor's volumes—and still more elaborately detailed in the

compilations of his followers, disciples, and pseudo-disciples and im-
itators—is yet very simple. It is as simple and inevitable in the building of time-sequence as the fourth wall to a room" (*T.F.*, p. 23).

H.D.'s pun on "building" mixes metaphors to collapse the distinctions between space and time. The unconscious is a "time-element" as well as a "world" to be explored with Freud's guidance.
When Freud takes H.D. back into the little room off the fourth wall,
he helps her recapture the mysteries buried in time in addition to her
own psyche; the ancient art objects displayed on the table in the
tiny room simultaneously represent her individual soul and the past
of humankind. One of H.D.'s descriptions of her sessions with Freud
presents in microcosm the process and product of his influence:

> My imagination wandered at will; my dreams were revealing, and
> many of them drew on classical or Biblical symbolism. Thoughts were
> things, to be collected, collated, analyzed, shelved, or resolved. Frag-
> mentary ideas, apparently unrelated, were often found to be part of a
> special layer or stratum of thought and memory, therefore to belong
> together; these were sometimes skillfully pieced together like the
> exquisite Greek tear-jars and iridescent glass bowls and vases that
> gleamed in the dusk from the shelves of the cabinet that faced me
> where I stretched, propped up on the couch in the room in Berggasse
> 19, Wien IX. The dead were living in so far as they lived in memory
> or were recalled in dream (*T.F.*, p. 14).

In *The Interpretation of Dreams* and *A General Introduction to
Psychoanalysis*, Freud developed his theories on the epistemology and
language of this "realm" whose form of "knowing" and "speech" was
so profoundly different from that of the conscious mind. "The unconscious," he argued, "is a special realm, with its own desires and
modes of expression and peculiar mental mechanisms not elsewhere
operative." It is a nonrational realm whose "associative thought" contrasts with "conscious logical thought."[3] Visual images juxtaposed in
an associative sequence replace the logical progression of concepts. Allusion and analogy operate as nonempirical forms of persuasion rather
than the rhetoric of rational cause and effect. Tapestries of time in
which past, present, future, and fantasy form a single time element
substitute for the linear chronology based on distinctions. These attributes of the unconscious characterize what "might be called The

Kingdom of the Illogical" where "the governing laws of logic have no sway."[4]

H.D. never used the phrase "Kingdom of the Illogical," but she repeatedly emphasized that the unconscious has its own mode of perception, a nonrational form of knowing. She wrote that the unconscious represents "an unusual dimension, an unusual way to *think*" (*T.F.*, p. 47). Vivid dreams, startling fragments of childhood memory, and psychic hallucinations are "almost events out of time. . . . they are steps in the so-far superficially catalogued or built-up mechanism of supernormal, abnormal (or subnormal) states of mind. . . . when ordinary consciousness ceases to function for a time" (*T.F.*, p. 42). Like Freud, H.D. understood these events to be expressed in a visual language, the "hieroglyphics" of the unconscious mind (*T.F.*, pp. 36, 47, 56, 93). In this fourth-dimensional time element, the thread of associations running through the unconscious wove her past, present, future, and fantasy into one out-of-time tapestry: "The years went forward, then backward. The shuttle of the years ran a thread that wove my pattern into the Professor's. . . . It was a present that was in the past or a past that was in the future" (*T.F.*, p. 9).

Freud hypothesized that the dream is the primary voice of the unconscious, and he agreed with artists and prophets that the dream's seeming nonsense contained the keys to self-knowledge. Fantasies, day dreams, hallucinations, slips of the tongue, wit, "screen memories," and "neurotic symptoms" all paralleled the dream as obscure expressions of the unconscious and constituted a rich storehouse of secrets about the inner psyche.[5] In contrast to the direct and conceptual communications of the conscious mind, the language of the inner voice is indirect and visual. The dream is essentially unconscious thought in hieroglyphic form. Freud called the creator of the dream the "dream-work" and wrote that its task was "a translation of the dream-thoughts into a primitive mode of expression, analogous to hieroglyphics." The dream-work had to abandon words "in alphabetic characters in favour of hieroglyphics" and transform "thoughts into *visual images*," as if it had to "replace a political article in a newspaper by a series of illustrations."[6] The syntax of this visual language uses a variety of combinations to translate the "latent" thoughts of unconscious impulses into the "manifest" script of the dream. Allusion, condensation, displacement, punning, and symbolism are the predominant modes of the dream's expression. These nonrational modes of expression create pictographs in which every fragmentary image is weighted with significance and "over-determined" by a wealth of associations.[7]

The underlying premise of Freud's theory of the dream-work is that its indirect modes of expression serve "the purpose of concealment." The dream-work must obscure its message at the very moment of expression because the unconscious thoughts are morally repugnant to the superego, the psychic embodiment of cultural values. Such thoughts are usually safely censored from consciousness, but in the night world of the dream and the day world of fantasy, the doors of repression are opened partway. The ego or conscious self is under pressure from the unconscious whose desires seek release and the superego whose norms denounce those desires. The dream-work brings about a compromise by translating unconscious thoughts into often undecipherable hieroglyphics. The dream is a disguise that reveals at the same time it conceals.[8]

Freud believed that the objective of analysis was to pierce the disguise, undo the dream-work by decoding the hieroglyphs of the dream, and bring to consciousness the forbidden latent thoughts of the unconscious realm. This self-exploration is accomplished through the "fundamental rule of psychoanalytic technique": free association on dreams and memories. Freud taught his analysands to release their minds from the bonds of rational thought by allowing random associations to overwhelm consciousness. Consciousness must become receptive, and its processes as close to the nonconceptual mode of the unconcious as possible: "Your talk with me must differ in one respect from an ordinary conversation. Whereas usually you rightly try to keep the threads of your story together and to exclude all intruding associations and side-issues, so as not to wander too far from the point, here you must proceed differently. . . . So say whatever goes through your mind. Act as if you were sitting at the window of a railway train and describing to someone behind you the changing views you see outside."[9] Once these associational fragments have been restored to consciousness, the analyst and analysand could collaborate on a translation of their significance.

H.D.'s deconstruction of the unconscious and reconstruction of the self in Freud's office deeply influenced the aesthetic forms she developed after the renewal of her artistic inspiration in the forties and fifties. Freud's ideas did not revolutionize her own, for the roots of his influence lay in the general consistency of his theories with many of the literary perspectives of H.D.'s former artistic community. But his theory of unconscious language as a visual disguise shaped the transition of H.D.'s image from the objective correlative of imagism to the poetic craft of modernism. H.D. had already experimented extensively with interior monologue and associational structures in her fiction of the twenties. But Freud's translation of unconscious hieroglyphs provided her with a model of meditative quest that systematized the flow of associations and contributed to her development of an epic form based on reflection rather than action.

Many have noticed the striking similarity between the mechanisms of the dream-work and the devices of poetic form. Lionel Trilling, for example, argued that Freudian psychology, more than any other theory of "mental systems," has understood that poetic form is "indigenous" to the unconscious mind which is a "poetry-making organ."[10] Philip Rieff wrote: "All the terms—'distortion,' 'projection,' 'displacement,' 'condensation'—which Freud uses in interpreting psychological artifacts such as dreams, errors, art, myth, refer to this double level of truth. The 'work' of the imagination is to distort, complicate, individualize, and thereby conceal the potent sub-individual wishes and desires. Exactly the same adaptations to reality prevail in the special kind of symptomatic statement which is art."[11] Freud and his interpretors did not mean that art is achieved through "automatic writing"; the dream-work is not itself the artist. Rather the conscious craft of the poet is *analogous* to the techniques of the dream-work. The language of poetry, like the script of the dream, embodies thought in a nonconceptual, often visual form that conceals as it reveals.

This concept of poetic form is potentially stimulating to many types of poets. But it probably had a special relevance for H.D. because Freud's description of unconscious thought processes is particularly in tune with imagist aesthetics. The most striking parallel is the imagist and psychoanalytic emphasis on nonrational image. The dream-work thinks in pictures, never in concepts. It creates a "series of illustrations," a hieroglyphic language of images. Its "technique" or "representation" creates a "plastic, concrete piece of imagery" which substitutes for abstract thought.[12] Unlike the surrealists, the imagists never handed the pen over to the unconscious. But they advocated a visual mode of thought and expression to capture the fleeting essence of experience, a nonrational, nonconceptual mode of expression in an "image." The imagists made concrete pictures with words as they tried to avoid the abstractions of the "cosmic poet."[13] They believed that poetry is not a rational form of discourse. Its essence is suggestive, not definitive; its "argument" is visual, not logical; and its image or metaphor is neither mere ornament nor analogy. It is instead an emotion or idea incarnate, subject and object fused in the image. Pound wrote: "An 'Image' is that which presents an intellectual and emotional complex in an instant of time. I use the term 'complex' rather in the technical sense employed by the new psychologists such as Hart. . . . It is the presentation of such a 'complex' instantaneously which gives that sense of sudden liberation."[14]

A corollary to the concreteness of the image was the demand for absolute conciseness: "To use absolutely no word that does not contribute to the presentation."[15] Condensation of idea or emotion to bare representation in an image or series of images parallels Freud's theory that a dream is highly condensed or "over-determined." One picture-image in a dream can stand for a whole series of attitudes, associations, or memories just as one image in a poem suggests far more than it spells out explicitly.

One of H.D.'s earliest and best-known poems, "Oread," illustrates how the visual language of imagism parallels the mechanisms of the dream-work as Freud described them. This important similarity helps to establish how the poetic epistemology of imagism laid a foundation that made H.D. particularly receptive to psychoanalytic influence.

> Whirl up, sea—
> whirl your pointed pines,
> splash your great pines
> on our rocks,
> hurl your green over us,
> cover us with your pools of fir. (S.P., p. 26)

Since most imagist poems present images from nature, it is easy to assume that imagist poetry is about nature. But "Oread" and most of H.D.'s imagist poems are phenomenological in emphasis; they are poems about consciousness, not the world of objects external to consciousness. The center of "Oread," as the title indicates, is not the sea; it is instead the perceptions and emotions of an oread, a nymph of the mountains, as she regards the sea aroused in a whirling passion of intensity. Analogous to the manifest and latent content of the dream, the poem presents images of the sea in order to embody an "intellectual and emotional complex," which is the real subject of the poem.

The images that simultaneously obscure and reveal the emotions of the oread are not surrealist images emerging from the unconscious. "Oread" is a controlled poem, not the achievement of the dream-work. But the waves made of pine trees and the trees made of water have a quality analogous to the dream. The rational eye of the conscious mind would not see pine-tree waves, splashing pines, or "pools of fir." Such vision belongs to the "Kingdom of the Illogical." If H.D. were to report such dream-images to Freud, he might well have called them an illustration of "dream-distortion." Through "condensation," the poem presents a distortion of reality that suggests a whole range of interrelated ideas and emotions encoded in a few images. Decoding these condensed distortions would have to begin with the recognition that they result from a picture-making mode of thought, rather than an analytic mode. The poem significantly does not rely upon similes, which by definition remind the reader that the images only make comparisons, not equivalences. The speaker does not say that a rough sea looks *like* pointed trees; she *sees* tree-waves. Just as the dream-work gives the dreamer a visual representation of unconscious impulses, so the poem conjures an illustration of nonrational reality that conveys an "intellectual and emotional complex" in a highly condensed form.

"Condensation," Freud believed, also allowed the dream-work to express "contraries" and outright "contradictions" in a single dream-picture.[16] The condensation of imagist technique accomplishes just that fusion of opposites in "Oread." The poem's pronouns—"us" and "you"—establish the oppositions in the poem imaged in the land and the sea. The oread *is* the land and consequently identifies with the shore and addresses the waves as "you." As the spirit of the land, she understandably perceives her fluid opposite in her own terms: waves are pointed pines that whirl up, crash, and make pools of fir. This nonrational mode of thought gives motion, fury, and a watery stillness to the land; conversely, it gives stature and stability to the sea. But these images condense opposites into a contradictory whole; they simultaneously affirm and deny the division of land and sea.

The fusion of land and sea in "Oread" does not in itself explain

the emotional intensity of the poem. The parallel verbs of the poem—
"whirl," "crash," "hurl," and "cover"—create the oread's sensation
of being submerged in the violence and then stillness of the waves.
Robert Duncan wrote perceptively that many of H.D.'s "nature
poems" have a sexual dimension: they "betray in their troubled ardor
processes of psychological and even sexual identification. . . . [there is
a] poetic magic in which the natural environment and the sexual experience are fused."[17] The imagery and rhythm of "Oread" suggest
that Duncan is correct. The waves whirl up to become phallic pines
that crash down "on our rocks . . . over us." The poem ends on a
final note of protectiveness as the waves "cover us" in quiet pools.
The oread's commands throughout the poem emphasize that the sea
acts while the land is acted upon. H.D.'s images may be identifying a
traditional masculinity with the waves (movement; sexual assault) and
a traditional femininity with the land (passivity; sexual receptivity).
The action of the waves on the shore combined with the emotional
intensity suggest that the poem can be read as a correlative of sexual
experience or emotion. Since the synthesizing "logic" of the images
has already created a fusion of land and sea, the poem additionally
may be suggesting an androgynous identity for the oread. The experiential reality of the poem illustrates that externally opposite qualities such as active/passive or masculine/feminine coexist within a
single individual.

Freud's syntax of the dream-work includes the important technique he called "displacement," by which intense feelings are projected onto a relatively unimportant person or set of events.[18] In
"Oread," the oread's identity and sexual emotions are "displaced"
onto a natural event, the meeting of the land and sea on the shore-
line. More significantly, the poet's relationship to her speaker is analogous to the dream-work's displacement of emotion. The oread is a
persona for the poet herself as well as an anthropomorphic embodiment of the land. She is a personal metaphor whose experience gave
indirect, and therefore permissible, expression to the intense passion
that characterizes much of H.D.'s early poetry. To give form and
expression to her own experience, H.D. displaced her voice into that
of the oread and substituted the oread's emotion for her own. Norman
Holmes Pearson warned that H.D.'s use of Greek masks as a distancing device has all too often been ignored by her critics. He told his
interviewer, L S. Dembo: "When you said that she used Greek myth

to find her own identity, you hit upon an aspect of H.D.'s poetry which, rather surprisingly, has gone unrecognized. She has been so praised as a kind of Greek publicity girl that people have forgotten that she writes the most intensely personal poems using Greek myth as a metaphor."[19] The oread may be Greek, but the setting for "Oread" comes from a past not more remote than her visits to the Cornwall seacoast and her childhood summers on the shores of the Atlantic Ocean. The ultimate subject of the poem is the consciousness of the poet herself, the intellectual and emotional complex of perception that finds its clearest expression in the picture-making mode of imagist epistemology. H.D.'s poetic apprenticeship with imagism laid the groundwork for her rapid absorption of Freud's related theories of the encoding and decoding of the unconscious.

None of the imagist poets followed their prescriptive rules for poetic form throughout their poetic careers. But as H.D. said, imagism provided a "craft" or concept of form that they could use within the larger context of their later poetry.[20] For Pound, continuity between his imagist and epic forms is evident in the evolution of the brief image to the loosely connected sequence of ideograms. Chinese characters, originally pictographic in representation of meaning, influenced his concepts of correct poetic language, the image, and structure in his cantos. There is continuity also between the image-centered poem of H.D.'s early work and the imagistically rendered hieroglyphics of her epic poems. But H.D.'s work with Freud in translating the hieroglyphs of the unconscious ultimately created a psychoanalytic dimension in her later use of the image. She learned with Freud that the visual thought process upon which imagism depended could provide more than an image which safely expressed thoughts unsuitable for rational discourse. The visual voice of the unconscious also contained the clues to Psyche's identity, the inner mysteries of the self. Hieroglyphs of the unconscious were hieroglyphs of the self. After decoding the images of her dreams and fantasies with Freud, H.D.'s poetic use of the image frequently became a form of self-exploration.

Helen in Egypt, written from 1952 to 1956 and published just before H.D. died in 1961, epitomizes the impact of Freud's ideas on her development of aesthetic form. Unconventional in its handling of chronology, situation, and plot, however, the epic requires a brief outline of its major parts before an analysis of its forms can be undertaken. The epic, based on obscure variants of Greek myth, takes place shortly after the end of the Trojan War, and centers on the postwar destinies of Helen and Achilles. With a carefully balanced structure, the epic has three main parts: "Pallinode," composed of seven "Books"; "Leuké," also broken down into seven "Books"; and "Eidolon," consisting of six "Books." Each Book throughout the epic is made up of eight loosely connected poetic sequences introduced by a voice that reflects in prose on the subsequent stanzas. The locale, sequence of time, and "plot" of each major part are different. "Pallinode" begins with the prose voice reminding the reader of how Stesichorus was struck blind after he wrote a scathing ode against Helen as the cause of the Trojan War. He regained his sight only after he wrote a "Pallinode" that exonerated Helen by telling the story of how Zeus secretly transported her to Egypt, where she waited throughout the war, the epitome of the faithful wife, until Menelaus came to retrieve her. It was a phantom of Helen, not the real Helen, that walked the ramparts of Troy and coldly watched the city being destroyed for the sake of her husband's honor.[21] Like Stesichorus' Helen and Euripides' Helen, in *Helen in Egypt*, H.D.'s Helen is alone in Egypt, guarded in the tranquil corridors of the sacred Amen temple. But unlike the earlier, patient Helen praying for Menelaus' return, H.D.'s Helen wants to understand why Zeus brought her to Egypt, to clarify her relation to the hated phantom of Helen, and to recover the significance of fragmented memory.

In the action that sets the epic in motion, Helen's power draws the dead Achilles to her for the answers he might provide. Shipwrecked, lost, and limping from the fatal wound in his heel, Achilles shatters Helen's peace of certain innocence. When he recognizes the woman he used to watch in fascination and anger, he calls her "Hecate," "witch," and tries to strangle her. She appeals desperately to his mother Thetis, the goddess of the sea. The name of the goddess recalls Achilles to a former self that knew nothing of killing, and his violence turns to love (*H.E.*, pp. 15–17). The two lovers meet again to decipher their memories and the meaning of the past. For Helen, the main task is to answer the question, "Helena? who is she?" "Pallinode" is a love story of sorts. But before Achilles and Helen can be united on the island of Leuké, as the variant myth has it, Helen must discover who she is. In search of his own identity, Achilles leaves Egypt for Leuké. Thetis urges Helen to follow immediately, but she decides to remain alone to remember earlier selves.

"Leuké" and "Eidolon" are structured primarily by Helen's inner confrontation with the past. Narrative based on identifiable action is scanty and often like a dream sequence in its shifting time and locale.[22] As "Leuké" opens, a skiff brings Helen to the island, where she awakens not to Achilles, but to the memory of laughing joyfully with Paris (*H.E.*, p. 116). Space has become time as she remembers her "first rebellion," the joy of springtime love. The alchemy of her memory draws Paris to her and together they relive the years of the war in Troy. Paris tells Helen that they are now both dead, reminds her of her vows, and denounces Achilles—"I say he never loved you" (*H.E.*, p. 144). Helen refuses Paris' appeal, but cannot go to Achilles until she resolves the conflict of dual selves: "Helen Dendritis," the young Helen who loved Paris, and the older Helen of Egypt. "Who is Helena?" The old question is still with her and sends her "baffled" and "very tired" to the home of Theseus, her first lover. Now an old man, he kindly helps Helen sort through the past to reconcile her various fragmented selves.

"Eidolon" records Helen's slow process of synthesizing dual selves in the search for wholeness. As Helen wakes up to a new "dawn" uniting all oppositions, she is ready to join Achilles on Leuké. This union and the subsequent birth of their child, Euphorion, however, take place "off stage" and do not serve as the climax of the epic. Instead, the emphasis is on Helen's own sense of who she is. Helen, first repressing all memories of the past, has become Helen, at peace with a fully healed, conscious self.

In the epic, the "image" is as central to Helen's inner journey as it was to the instantaneous portrait of "an intellectual and emotional complex" in her imagist poetry. But in the epic, the aesthetic image has become psychological hieroglyph, the visual script "that concealed yet revealed" the enigma of the buried self (*H.E.*, p. 44). Before Achilles' appearance, Helen played the peaceful role of scribe and studied "this great temple's / indecipherable hieroglyph" (*H.E.*, p. 21). During her first electric meeting with Achilles, however, she learns with shock that she herself is the "living hieroglyph" that must be studied (*H.E.*, p. 23). She attempts to deny it, to remain satisfied that she can " 'read' the hare, the chick, the bee." But Achilles identifies her with the strange "night-bird" that hoots nearby. She reassures him, "I know the script, the shape of this bird is a letter, / they call it the hieroglyph . . . dedicate to Isis." With his sudden recognition of her identity, he condemns her as living hieroglyph: "for you were the ships burnt, / O cursèd, O envious Isis, / you—you—a vulture, a hieroglyph" (*H.E.*, pp. 13–14, 17). His attack forces Helen to question the "phantom theory" of Helen of Troy. Was she on the ramparts at Troy? Did she exchange the fatal glance with Achilles that caused him to neglect his ankle greave, as he claimed? Or did Zeus bring her innocent to Egypt? Helen treats Achilles with great ambivalence because his questions destroy the peace of easy innocence. She both draws him back with her magic and sends him away: "and do I care greatly / to keep him eternally? / I was happier alone, / why did I call him to me? / Must I forever look back?" (*H.E.*, p. 36). Helen "resists" his questions within the psychoanalytic sense of the term. The answers lie buried in repressed memory, hidden from her conscious self because she could not face the hatred of the Greeks and the resulting feelings of guilt. "Pallinode" begins in an affirmation that Helen was never in Troy and ends by pushing her deep into *the so far suppressed memory*" (*H.E.*, p. 109).

"Unraveling the tangled skeins" of her memories, Helen recovers fragments from her Spartan childhood, adolescence, marriage, and love affair. Through reflection, these thoughts begin to coalesce and become decipherable.

"Thoughts were things, to be collected, collated, analyzed" in *Tribute to Freud*; similarly in *Helen in Egypt*, the recovery of particular buried hieroglyphs leads to a translation of the general hieroglyph of self (*T.F.*, p. 14). "I am awake, no trance, / though I move as one in a dream," Helen says at one point (*H.E.*, p. 44). Her whole life, like a dream, is a visual enigma that she must learn to "read."

The last repressed memory to be recovered is the most painful, the moment she left her child, Hermione. The stark return of this memory vividly demonstrates how imagist craft renders the living hieroglyph emerging from the depths of the psyche. Helen is in Athens and a familiar fragrance triggers the picture of an earlier time:

> . . . —familiar fragrance,
> late roses, bruised apples,
>
> now I remember, I remember
> Paris before Egypt, Paris after;
> I remember all that went before,

Sparta; autumn? summer?
the fragrant bough? fruit ripening
on a wall? the ships at anchor?

I had all that, everything,
my Lord's devotion, my child
prattling of a bird-nest,

playing with my work-basket;
the reels rolled to the floor
and she did not stoop to pick up

the scattered spools but stared
with wide eyes in a white face,
at a stranger—and stared at her mother,

a stranger—that was all,
I placed my foot on the last step
of the marble water-stair

and never looked back;
how could I remember all that?
Zeus, our-father was merciful. (*H.E.*, pp. 227–28)

The craft of H.D.'s imagism controls the poetry: the clarity, simplicity, and concreteness of word choice; the absence of excess words; the condensation evident in the use of one detail to suggest a world of daily routine and sudden emotion (the chattering child, playing with her mother's workbasket, stopped in midstream by her mother's glance); and most importantly, the presentation of an "intellectual and emotional complex" through the image. Helen's dissatisfaction as a wife and mother, her feelings in leaving, and her child's intuitive recognition of the truth are condensed, embodied, and frozen into tableau. The focal point of the picture is the intense glance shared by the mother and daughter, a hieroglyphic moment transcending time that contains the essence of Helen's life. H.D. uses repetition for emphasis: the child "stared / with wide eyes in a white face, / at a stranger—and stared at her mother, / a stranger—that was all." Helen, trapped in the satin cage of the supposedly ideal marriage, is a "stranger," unknown to her husband, her child, and most importantly to herself. She had repressed the flight with Paris to find herself because that rebellion violated the norms for devoted motherhood that she had internalized. It is perhaps the last memory to resurface because abandonment of a child for self-discovery is a taboo far more intense in our culture than rejection of a husband. Helen is able to recover and accept this memory only after she has explored new contexts and norms from which to understand her actions.

The release and interpretation of a single hieroglyphic tableau from the unconscious serves as the basic building block of H.D.'s epic much as Pound's ideogram does in *The Cantos*. To give her epic structural coherence and continuity, H.D. used a number of psychic hieroglyphs as motifs repeated throughout the epic. Some of these hieroglyphs are visual memories recovered from the unconscious, like the frozen glance between mother and child. Others are intense moments in which ordinary perceptions of space and time are suspended. Products of "supernormal," nonrational states of mind, they represent fundamental truths pictorially. They are essentially visual epiphanies rendered imagistically, hieroglyphs that must be returned to repeatedly for interpretation. Achilles, for example, recalls the powerful glance that caused his death and set in motion his ultimate reunion with Helen on Leuké:

> I can see you still, a mist
> or a fountain of water
>
> in that desert; we died of thirst;
>
> .   .   .   .
>
> I stooped to fasten a greave
> that was loose at the ankle,
>
> when she turned; I stood
> indifferent to the rasp of metal,
> and her eyes met mine;
>
> you say, I could not see her eyes
> across the field of battle,
> I could not see their light
>
> shimmering as light on the changeable sea?
> All things would change but never
> the glance she exchanged with me. (*H.E.*, pp. 48, 54).

Achilles, like Helen, is a questor in the epic, and the mystery of his full identity is contained in the hieroglyph of this moment. The parallel moment for Helen is her first meeting with Achilles on the desolate beach when his violent attack becomes a loving embrace. This tableau of hate-become-love is repeatedly imaged for Helen as "a flash in the heaven at noon / that blinds the sun" (*H.E.*, p. 100). It is a hieroglyphic moment outside of time whose hidden meanings clarify the essential patterns of life in time. Throughout the epic Helen returns to this hieroglyph to decode all its possible associations with both her past and future.

The repetition of hieroglyphic motif is an important structural device in *Helen in Egypt*, but of even greater significance is the effect that psychological tableau had on H.D.'s use of plot and structure. The transformation of the image from aesthetic object to psychological hieroglyph led naturally to a structure of quest modeled substantially on the experience of psychoanalysis. For H.D. in Freud's study, for Helen on the desolate beach in Egypt, the focus of spiritual quest is on the process of translation or interpretation. Helen's identity and the meaning of war are contained enigmatically in heightened moments or tableaux. The action of the epic is the "reading" of those moments, just as the "action" of psychoanalysis is the interpretation of the unconscious. The corresponding type of plot is meditative, not active; it moves through reflection and association, not through external circumstance or logic. The present tense of action is nearly nonexistent in *Helen in Egypt*—in fact, the "plot" summary presented by way of introduction to a difficult epic was gleaned almost entirely from Helen's reflective stream of consciousness. External action is fragmentary, emerging suddenly and briefly out of extended periods of reflection when Helen is alone with her thoughts. In "Pallinode," Helen and Achilles meet and converse while Thetis ends the "song against" by urging Helen to join Achilles on Leuké. In "Leuké," Helen calls Paris to her and together they re-create the Trojan past and argue about her future with Achilles; then Helen goes to Athens to see Theseus. In "Eidolon," Achilles draws Helen back to him in Egypt, but their direct conversation is brief and the final part of the epic centers on Helen alone in an undefined dimension of space. Ordinary conventions of epic narrative are consistently violated. H.D. deliberately obscures for most of the epic the cornerstones of external reality and conventional narrative: the factual location of characters in space and time. Helen, for example, has used her magic to bring the dead Achilles and the dead Paris to her. Is, then, the "setting" her mind? the afterworld? Since both dead men speak of a future with her, is she even alive? Paris insists that he saw her killed on the marble stair of Troy while Helen answers simply that Achilles' love "sustained" her (*H.E.*, pp. 141–44). Helen's physical whereabouts during the Trojan War are never clarified. In fact, her simultaneous presence in both Egypt and Troy defies ordinary spatial reality and sequential chronology.

H.D.'s dissolution of the external reality that conventionally forms the backdrop of epics helps to establish the locus of quest as the psyche and the process of search as associational reflection. In this sense, her meditative epic is phenomenological. The exploration of consciousness that distills essential reality, however, is patterned on the psychoanalysis of Freud, not the philosophy of Husserl. A carefully controlled level of material reality appears in the epic as the fragments of memory that must be translated to reveal the hidden mysteries of the psyche. H.D. never implied that the war was an illusion; death and its most violent manifestations in rape, murder, and war are facts whose impact and meaning must be interpreted. In the *tableau vivant* of extraordinary moments, the details of external reality are precisely rendered because these hieroglyphic moments bring the eternal into time and space. This form of imagistic incarnation reinforces the reflective dimension of the epic because much of the "action" revolves around translation of these ephemeral moments when "out-of-time" manifests in the "in-time" (*H.E.*, pp. 11, 20, 107, 201, 202, 204).

Even the most extended sequence of almost conventional narrative in the epic links H.D.'s epic form with psychoanalysis. Helen's conversations with Theseus in Athens cover many books in the epic, but Theseus is unmistakably Freud himself as he warms the tired Helen, "blown by the wind, the snow," with the embers of yet another important brazier and chooses some "fleece-lined shoes" for her from his "cedar-chest" (*H.E.*, pp. 147–52). His gentle questioning urges Helen to follow out the train of her associations, recover painful memories such as the moment she left Hermione, and reconcile the fragments of her identity represented by her various loves. Her discussions with Theseus are a microcosm of the reflective quest that structures the whole epic.

In H.D.'s psychoanalytic epic, action is process, not event. Like so many modernist texts in a variety of genres, H.D.'s emphasis is on the search itself, never on the answer or the end result. Freud once said that the analysis of any one dream is never complete until analysis itself is complete. With H.D., their interpretations were multiple and open ended, not definitive. Freud also told Bryher that if she were really interested in psychoanalysis, she "would want to go on with analysis to the end" of her days.[23] Similarly in H.D.'s epic, Helen's translations of her life's hieroglyphs never reach stasis, but remain in flux—even after she is reunited with Achilles on Leuké, even after their child is born. Both of these "actions" could have served as the epic's conventional climax, but instead we learn of them casually, as they appear in reflection. Like Helen's search, H.D.'s epic form does not have a definitive end. As Pearson wrote in comparing H.D. and Stevens, the quest for art and the realm of the imagination never led to "*the* permanent poem but rather [to] acts of the imagination, the process of imagination, the constancy of search" (*T.F.*, pp. xlii–xliii). The epic once completed became itself the hieroglyph for the poet's reflection. H.D. superimposed the prose voice that interprets each sequence of poetry *after* she finished writing the entire epic in verse.[24] The alternating voices in poetry and prose in the final text serve as a constant reminder of "the constancy of search" and the reflective process that "unravels the tangled skeins" of truth.

Freud's influence was certainly not the only factor in H.D.'s development of a reflective epic form. The novels she wrote during the twenties—*Paint It Today* (1921), *Asphodel* (1921), *Palimpsest* (1926), *Her* (1927), and *Hedylus* (1928)—exhibit considerable experimentation with plot centered on reflection instead of action and with narration that rendered stream of consciousness. H.D. read and greatly admired the work of Virginia Woolf and James Joyce.[25] She not only respected Dorothy Richardson's *Pilgrimage*, but she and Bryher were close friends and correspondents with the pioneer of interior monologue.[26] Before she worked with Freud, H.D. had read Eliot's, Pound's, and Williams' expansion of poetic structure into what L.S. Dembo has called the "neo-epic" form.[27] *The Cantos, Four Quartets*, and *Paterson* disregard the conventions of epic plot and chronology in their development of the modernist epic. But, more than any of these writers, H.D. directly applied the modern novel's experimentations with stream of consciousness to the creation of her own neo-epic style. Her experience with Freud was a key factor in this transference of interior monologue and reflective plot from her prose to her poetry.

H.D.'s adaptation of psychoanalytic process in the development of her epic form troubled Kenneth Fields, who wrote in his generally excellent and sympathetic introduction to *Tribute to Freud:*

> The problem in H.D.'s case, does not lie in her recourse to mythology, but rather in the momentary nature of her accesses to perfection. . . . One does not need to be a euhemerist to realize that the greatest mythological figures embodied the political, legal, and ethical realities of a living culture; and they are thus treated in some of the best modern mythological writing: Gide's *Thesée*, Winters' 'Theseus' and 'Heracles,' Michael Ayrton's *The Maze Maker*. Reading these works gives us a sense of the possibilities of action and error, whereas reading H.D. gives us a sense of how to perceive and meditate from moment to moment. (*T.F.*, p. xliii)

To use the presence of external action as criteria for great—or even good—art eliminates by definition a great deal of modern literature, from Proust and the late James to Woolf and much of Faulkner. Woolf's discussion of Edwardian literature in "Mr. Bennett and Mrs. Brown" provides a necessary corrective to the celebration of action in "the political, legal, and ethical realities of a living culture" and serves as a context within which H.D.'s achievement can be understood. Woolf believed that the reality of experience was indeed ephemeral, momentary, and ultimately subjective. To capture the essence of human experience, the novelist must not limit himself or herself to rendering human behavior from the outside. As in H.D.'s poetry, Woolf's theoretical and actual focus was on perception, not action; on the subjective, not the objective.[28] For Woolf, this preference for perception over action was linked to her feminism. In *A Room of One's Own*, she argued eloquently that women have historically been denied access to "the political, legal and ethical realities of a living culture," to use Fields's phrase. Therefore, women's lives and women's art have reflected or should reflect their different experience, one not centered on heroic action and achievement. Excluded from the arena of action, women's creativity and power have been interpersonal, subjective, and intangible. Women's literature, Woolf predicted, would demonstrate a style and structure suited to women's traditional sphere.[29] Woolf's own work, particularly *To the Lighthouse*, embodies her feminist aesthetic. She deemphasized external action by its ordinariness and fragmentary presentation—a walk in the garden, a storytime for little James, a dinner party. She centered the novel on the flow of consciousness that weaves past, present, future, and fantasy. The "moments of being," specifically linked in her novel to woman's creativity, could bear fruitful comparison with H.D.'s hieroglyphs of the psyche.

What Woolf did in the novel, H.D. did in the epic. But since the epic, more than any other genre, has typically centered on heroic action in a masculine world, H.D.'s meditative epic is a more radical departure from literary convention and perhaps consequently less understood or accepted. In making the hero of her epic a woman, she had to redefine epic form to render Helen's reflective quest for identity and meaning. Freud himself considered art a masculine province and culture a masculine achievement. But paradoxically, his nonsequential, nonlogical, free-associational techniques for psychoanalysis helped provide H.D. with a structural model of quest particularly suited to a woman hero and a new woman's epic.

3

Delphi of the Mind

THE UNCONSCIOUS AS MUSE AND PROPHET

FREUD'S HYPOTHESES about the nature of the unconscious went beyond an epistemology of the inner psyche into an ontology of religion and art. His theories about the origins of artistic and religious inspiration profoundly reshaped H.D.'s understanding of her identity and destiny as an artist. Their translations of her dreams and memories influenced the explosion of her poetic voice into the dimension of prophecy. His theory that individual development recapitulates the patterns of growth in human history provided her with a way to connect her personal myth to the records of early civilization in both religion and art. The universalism implicit in Freud's concept of the unconscious therefore redirected and systematized her extensive reading in comparative mythologies and contributed to the shift in her poetic use of myth. With Freud, H.D. developed her own theory that the unconscious is the Delphi of the mind, the wellspring of art and religion. Throughout the rest of her life, it served as her Muse, a source of inspiration to her art that linked "the individual dream and the myth as the dream of the tribe."[1] H.D. wrote in her tribute: "*Know thyself*, said the ironic Delphic oracle, and the sage or priest who framed the utterance knew that to know yourself in the full sense of the words was to know everybody. *Know thyself*, said the Professor, and plunging time and again, he amassed that store of intimate revelation contained in his impressive volumes" (*T.F.*, pp. 72–73).

Although art and religion are not interchangeable in Freud's theory, he essentially saw them both as hieroglyphic embodiments of unconscious thoughts, analogous in many ways to dreams, daydreams, and neurotic symptoms. Counteracting the harsh nature of external necessity, art and religion originate in the unconscious desire for pleasure. Like dreams, the religious and artistic impulse have their source in fantasies that serve the purpose of wish fulfillment.

To be more specific, Freud's somewhat scattered comments on art made during the middle years of his career clarify the analogies he drew between unconscious thought and artistic creation and the aesthetic theory implicit in these comparisons. In "The Relation of the Poet to Daydreaming" (1908), for example, he argued that the artist creates "a world of fantasy" that parallels the processes of daydreaming and the imaginative play of the child. Like the child at play, the artist "rearranges the things of his world and orders it in a new way that pleases him better."[2] Artistic expression is a substitution for actual gratification of unconscious impulses. Since art actualizes the fantasies of the artist's unconscious, it is analogous to neurotic symptom and may in fact indicate a neurotic tendency in the artist:

> The artist has also an introverted disposition and has not far to go to become neurotic. He is one who is urged on by instinctual needs which are too clamorous; he longs to attain to honour, power, riches, fame, and the love of women; but he lacks the means of achieving these gratifications. So, like any other with an unsatisfied longing, he turns away from reality and transfers all his interest, and all his libido too, on to the creation of his wishes in the life of phantasy, from which the way might readily lead to neurosis.[3]

Influenced by the dark pessimism of his later years, *Civilization and Its Discontents* stressed the overwhelming "pressure of reality" and described art as an enjoyable "illusion" that serves as a "source of pleasure and consolation in life." Expressing a withdrawal from the real world, art consoles by creating an alternate reality based on fantasy. The "mild narcosis" art induces, however, is largely "transient"; its ephemeral nature cannot block out the "pressure of vital needs" or the pain of "real misery."[4] The common thread running throughout these and other references to art is Freud's belief that art has its ultimate source in the unconscious. As Philip Rieff wrote, "Every work of art is to Freud a museum piece of the unconscious, an occasion to contemplate the unconscious frozen into one of its possible gestures."[5] Freud's own analyses of actual works of art follow naturally from his basic assumption. In da Vinci's paintings, for example, Freud uncovered disguised elements of the artist's early childhood. His "translation" of Jensen's *Gravida* paid tribute to the artist's intuitive apprehension and expression of unconscious thought processes.[6] For Freud, art is a valuable source of knowledge about the unconscious precisely because its motivating impulses originate in the unconscious. Buried within the highly controlled and consciously produced "manifest content" of the work of art is the "latent content," the unconscious desires that demand expression in disguised form.

Religion, like art, is the adult expression of unconscious desires that were particularly strong in childhood, Freud wrote. Religious experience and doctrine both recapitulate themes that were present in the child's early relationships with the parents, he argued in *The Future of an Illusion* and *Civilization and Its Discontents*. Mystical experience of the divine reproduces the primal bond of mother and child, the earliest form of infantile pleasure buried deep within the unconscious of the adult. In answer to his friend's "sensation of 'eternity' " as proof of divine existence, Freud wrote that Romain Rolland's "oceanic feeling" was a vestige of infancy when the ego was unable to distinguish any object as separate from itself, when the whole universe—internal and external—seemed to be one. The religious experience of Oneness emerges out of the unconscious, re-creating the baby's subjective fusion with the mother in the oral phase of psychosexual development.[7] God the Father, on the other hand, is a projection into doctrine of the child's dependence on the father for love and protection from the harsh reality of the outside world. "The terrifying impression of helplessness" that begins in infancy and lasts throughout a lifetime has "made it necessary to cling to the existence of a father, but this time a more powerful one. Thus the benevolent rule of a divine Providence allays our fear of the dangers of life."[8]

In his writings, Freud created a scientific language to systematize his ideas, a terminology which was largely absent from his actual sessions with H.D. (*T.F.*, p. 87) and certainly missing from the later poetry he so deeply influenced. But the absence of such terms as "wish-fulfillment," "oral phase," or "psychosexual development" from her work should not obscure the presence of his theories on religion and art in her self-definitions and her art. She consciously translated his language into the terminology of religious and artistic quest. The unconscious is a " 'well of living water' " or the " 'still waters' " of the inner soul, for example (*T.F.*, p. 82). It is "a source of inspiration" that creates a "dream-picture . . . like a work of art or [that] is a work of art" (*T.F.*, pp. 35, 82–83). It produces the analogues of religious "inspiration, madness, creative idea, or the dregs of the dreariest symptoms of mental unrest and disease" (*T.F.*, p. 71). As the source of religious feeling, the unconscious is an oracle whose obscure messages contain divine truth; as the source of artistic vision, the unconscious is a muse whose dream symbols inspire conscious expression in aesthetic form. For H.D., psychoanalysis unsealed the blocked entrance to the "well of living water" buried by repression and gave her conscious self a pipeline to the "original spring or well-head" of creative vision (*T.F.*, pp. 82–83).

Their collaborative translations of H.D.'s personal oracle helped her to establish an artistic identity that would fuse the functions of art and religion. In *Tribute to Freud*, she singled out one particularly vivid dream whose concealed meaning, once deciphered, strengthened the direction of her subsequent development. In the dream, a dark lady wrapped in a saffron robe descended marble stairs to the river and found a baby nestled in a basket. Re-creating the associations she shared with Freud, H.D. remembered how she played with her doll in the study of her "aloof, distant" father, how she pored over the Doré illustration of Moses in the bulrushes in the family Bible. They established together that the Egyptian "dolls" or figures on Freud's shelf represent ancient dreams and that the Lady is a Princess and a "mother-symbol" (*T.F.*, pp. 35–41). As her mind wandered through the fragments of memory and mythology, Freud suggested that the latent thought imaged in the dream was her desire to be the baby Moses, "to be the founder of a new religion" (*T.F.*, p. 37).

She was only half convinced that Freud was right, but their translation of the "writing-on-the-wall," hallucinations she had in her Corfu hotel in 1920, reinforced Freud's belief in her hidden desire for an important destiny. Flickering lights mysteriously projected onto her wall had drawn a series of pictures: the head of Mercury; the mystic chalice; the Delphic tripod of religious and artistic oracle; the Jacob's ladder of light; and the female image of Niké, wingless Victory, fused with the male sundisk (*T.F.*, pp. 41–56). This writing was the "hieroglyph of the unconscious . . . actually in operation before our very eyes" (*T.F.*, p. 47). Deciphering the script, H.D. wrote:

> We can read my writing, the fact that there was writing, in two ways or in more than two ways. We can read or translate it as a suppressed desire for forbidden 'signs and wonders,' breaking bounds, a suppressed desire to be a Prophetess, to be important anyway, megalomania they call it—a hidden desire to 'found a new religion' which the Professor ferreted out in the later Moses picture. Or this writing-on-the-wall is merely an extension of the artist's mind, a *picture* or an illustrated poem, taken out of the actual dream or daydream content and projected from within (though apparently from outside). . . . (*T.F.*, p. 51)

One of the images that flickered across her hotel wall looked like her small "spirit-lamp," an exact replica of the "tripod of classic Delphi." Sacred to Apollo, the tripod was the seat of the Priestess or Pythoness who pronounced the ambiguous messages of the Delphic oracle in ancient Greece. It was the "symbol of prophecy, prophetic utterance or occult or hidden knowledge." "Delphi," she continued, "was the shrine of the Prophet and Musician, the inspiration of artists and the patron of physicians. . . . Religion, art, and medicine, through the latter ages, became separated; they grow further apart from day to day. These three working together, to form a new vehicle of expression or a new form of thinking or of living, might be symbolized by the tripod" (*T.F.*, pp. 50–51). The appearance of the sacred tripod to H.D. was like a Tarot card whose symbols contain the wisdom of the past and the direction of her future. Freud's role was to read the card and "tell her fortune" though "he would not call it telling fortunes—heaven forbid!" (*T.F.*, p. 40). In other words, Freud's science would help her understand the relationship between those messages from the unconscious and her future destiny as an artist.

As H.D. translated the oracular voice of the unconscious, she was to become the Pythoness of Delphi in her poetry, to reintegrate the separated branches of religion, art, and healing into a poetic "tripod" of wisdom.[9] The hieroglyphs of the psyche, therefore, confirmed H. D.'s destiny as a prophet-poet for the "city of ruin," the war-ravaged century. Freud's belief that H.D. wanted to be important to her mother by being the baby boy Moses could be psychoanalytically interpreted as conventional female "penis envy." But as she reflected on her sessions with Freud in the midst of the war, she heard the voices of the unconscious urge her on to break the bounds of traditional female destiny, to fulfill her suppressed desires and express a new religious vision in "pictures" of poetic form. This desire serves as the poetic premise of the *Trilogy*, completed in December 1944, just two months after she drafted *Tribute to Freud*.

Ten to twenty years before, many of H.D.'s fellow artists had adopted differing voices of prophecy in the mythological and religious poetry that followed the imagist era. Pound's learned Odyssean personae echoed through *The Cantos*. T.S. Eliot's voice revived a weary Tiresias in *The Waste Land* and became the deeply religious, agonized Anglican in *Four Quartets*. The American bedlamite, Hart Crane, sought demonic and apocalyptic dimensions of the organic past and technological present in *The Bridge*. William Carlos Williams abandoned the sparse objectivist point of view for the persona of the poet and city Paterson seeking the fusion of order and chaos, ideas and things in his quest poetry. Much more self-mocking, but still heroic in tone, Wallace Stevens became the creator of complex supreme fictions. H.D.'s *Trilogy*, whose poetic persona represented a radical departure from her lyric voice of the twenties, belongs in this mainstream of twentieth-century epic poetry where the poet has become the seer. More than any of these poets, however, H.D.'s religious poetry of prophecy in the *Trilogy* has its roots in her translations of the hieroglyphs of the unconscious.

The poem begins with the poet walking through the bombed-out streets of her London neighborhood the day after an air raid. Regarding the surrounding destruction, she announces her task as poet-prophet.

> Let us, however, recover the Sceptre,
> the rod of power:
>
> it is crowned with the lily-head
> or the lily-bud:
>
> it is Caduceus; among the dying
> it bears healing:
>
> or evoking the dead,
> it brings life to the living. (*T.*, p. 7)

The image that dominates this statement and much of the *Trilogy* is the "rod of power," not the Delphic tripod, but the function of synthesis is the same. The "rod of power" is Aaron's rod, the magician's staff of religious transformation. It "bears healing" because it is linked through mythological association with Caduceus, the rod of Asklepios that is entwined with the dual snakes of wisdom and resurrection. Asklepios' relation to Apollo and Aaron's connection with Moses secure the rod as an image of interconnected religious and artistic function. Rooted firmly in the unconscious as they were for Freud, religion and art are the twin serpents wound round her Caduceus of poetry. Like the woman whose dream put a girl-child in Moses' baby basket, the poet assumes the authority of a religious and artistic voice that "breaks bounds" to found a new type of religion. As "Priestess or Pythoness of Delphi" and "poetess," H.D. found validation within the unconscious to don the predominantly male roles of prophet and poet in literary and religious tradition.

Throughout the *Trilogy*, the unconscious continues to serve as the direct source of the poet's inspiration. Dream and ecstatic vision are the foundation of religious experience in the poet's quest. Each volume of the *Trilogy* contains forty-three sections that revolve around an intense moment of "supernormal" consciousness when the rational mind of the poet is overwhelmed by the enigmatic voice of the unconscious. Like *Helen in Egypt*, the *Trilogy* gains structural coherence from the parallel presentations of hieroglyphic images which the poet must decipher. In *The Walls Do Not Fall*, the first poem of the *Trilogy*, the poet moves toward an experience of male divinity disentangled from its "art-craft junk-shop / paint-and-plaster medieval jumble of pain-worship and death-symbol" (*T.*, p. 27). The "Dream" mediates between ossified, sterile tradition and vision:

> Now it appears very clear
> that the Holy Ghost,
>
> childhood's mysterious enigma,
> is the Dream;
>
> that way of inspiration
> is always open,
>
> and open to everyone;
> it acts as go-between, interpreter,
>
> it explains symbols of the past
> in to-day's imagery,

it merges the distant future
with most distant antiquity,

states economically
in a simple dream-equation

the most profound philosophy,
discloses the alchemist's secret

and follows the Mage
in the desert. (*T.*, p. 29)

The Dream "deftly stage-managed" a "bare, clean / early colonial interior" and brought her "*Amen*, . . . our Christos," the male divinity
with burning amber eyes who dominates *The Walls Do Not Fall*.

In *Tribute to the Angels*, the Dream returns to bring the image
of the Lady, an avatar of the Great Goddess whom the dream-work
has lifted out of her traditional roles of harlot or mother of god and
restored to her power of regenerative Love. Echoing Freud's theory on
the external stimuli of dreams, the poet's Dream is tied to material
reality:

for it was ticking minute by minute
(the clock at my bed-head,

with its dim, luminous disc)
when the Lady knocked;

.   .   .   .

I realized I had been dreaming,

that I lay awake now on my bed,
that the luminous light

was the phosphorescent face
of my little clock

and the faint knocking
was the clock ticking. (*T.*, pp. 89–90)[10]

She stands unveiled in the luminous light of the poet's clock, "as if she
had miraculously related herself to time here." The Dream incarnates
the Lady, literally gives a spiritual entity a visual presence through the
agency of the unconscious. The poet's search to unravel the Dream's
meaning for the war-torn world structurally and thematically dominates the final sequences of *Tribute to the Angels*.

The Lady's religious message of resurrecting Love has an artistic dimension as well. She appears in the Dream carrying a blank book which the poet herself must complete with the "tale of a Fisherman, / a tale of a jar or jars" (*T.*, p. 105). The "tale of jars" is *The Flowering of the Rod*, the final poem of the *Trilogy*. A mystical vision rather than the Dream presents the central hieroglyph of the tale, but H.D. makes clear that its origins are the same "well-head" of inspiration that produced the Dreams. The poet's story is an imaginative recreation of how the biblical Mary of Bethany found the precious myrrh with which she bathed the feet of Jesus in Simon's house. H.D. changed the biblical identity of this Mary to fuse Martha's sister Mary, the woman who didn't "care for house-work," and Mary Magdalene, the prostitute who was the first to bear witness to the resurrection of Christ (*T.*, p. 129).[11] According to H.D.'s tale, Mary goes to see the Arab merchant Kaspar to strike a bargain for his alabaster jar of myrrh (*T.*, p. 130). He is annoyed by her request, irritated by her refusal to accept his signal of dismissal, and offended by the sight of her unveiled hair—in toto, "it was unseemly that a woman / appear at all" (*T.*, p. 137). Scarcely in a receptive mood, Kaspar nonetheless becomes transported when he sees a "fleck of light" on her hair. In that "grain" of light, in that "point or shadow," he suddenly saw "the whole secret of the mystery . . . the speck, fleck, grain or seed / opened like a flower." As the flower "opened petal by petal," he "saw the circles and circles of islands / about the lost centre-island, Atlantis"; he "in that half-second, saw / the whole scope and plan / of our and his civilization" (*T.*, p. 152–57). Like H.D. in her Corfu hotel, Kaspar did not know "whether it was a sort of spiritual optical-illusion, / or whether he looked down the deep deep-well / of the so-far unknown / depth of pre-history" (*T.*, p. 166). But Kaspar's vision, produced by a moment of supernormal consciousness, transformed the arrogant "merchant" into the Mage worthy to bring an alabaster jar of myrrh to the Christ child in the final sections of the poem (*T.*, pp. 171–72).

The Dream in the first volume of the *Trilogy* produced an image of an authentic God the Father. Another Dream in the second volume resurrected the Goddess. Kaspar's vision led him, along with the poet, to the Child. Father, Mother, and Child are the family constellation buried in the unconscious and retrieved for H.D. through psychoanalysis. The messages of divine presence that they bring to the poet serve as both object and resolution for her religious-artistic quest.

H.D. was certainly not the first twentieth-century poet to intermingle the functions and symbols of religious and artistic mythmaking. Yeats, for example, created a religion of art, while Eliot made an art of religion and Lawrence's fictions called for a religion founded on the life force centered in unconsciousness. More than any of these writers, H.D. developed psychoanalytic ideas to locate the common origin of religion and art in the unconscious. Translation of the unconscious was for H.D. not only the personal quest of Psyche for the meaning of her identity, but also Psyche's search for the source of religious and artistic inspiration.

Both in her life and in her art, H.D. did not separate the dual quests of Psyche for self-definition and transcendence of self into the eternal dimension of religious-aesthetic experience. In other words, H.D. incorporated both the poet of the *Trilogy*, who looked for the divine presence in the midst of war, and the poet of *Helen in Egypt*, who attempted to answer the question "Helena? Who is she?" Freud's theory of the unconscious and his techniques of analysis allowed H.D. to regard the mysteries of self, religion, and art as intertwined by their common origins in the unconscious. Consequently, decoding the hieroglyphic voices of the unconscious led her ultimately beyond the exclusive realm of the personal into a study of past expressions of religious and artistic inspiration.

This simultaneous and parallel search into time and self emerges out of Freud's hypothesis that the psychic development of the individual corresponds in a broad sense to the evolution of civilization. The passage from childhood to adulthood must recapitulate the stages in the history of humankind from its infancy to its modern phase. The unconscious, as the repository of "infantile mental life," is a vestige of the early experience of both the young child and infant humanity. Freud wrote: "The era to which the dream-work takes us back is 'primitive' in a two-fold sense: in the first place, it means the early days of the *individual*—his childhood—and, secondly, in so far as each individual repeats in some abbreviated fashion during childhood the whole course of the development of the human race, the reference is *phylogenetic*."[12] As archeologist, the analyst uses the shards of both personal and human history to piece together the disguised contents of the human psyche. H.D. accurately paraphrased the recapitulation theory upon which Freud's archeological metaphors are based: "he had brought the past into the present with his *the childhood of the individual is the childhood of the race*—or is it the other way round? —*the childhood of the race is the childhood of the individual*" (T.F., p. 12).[13]

This correspondence set up two related equations for H.D. which greatly directed her search. Freud's recapitulation theory implied first that the study of historical records led to an understanding of the self and secondly that the exploration of the individual psyche led to knowledge of human history. Psychological quest is historical quest; the personal past is the cultural past. H.D. found in these formulae a way to relate the individual to time, and particularly to myth, religion, and art as records of time. They gave direction and context for the extensive research she had always done in mythological tradition. And they led directly out of the purely subjective into the universal patterns of human experience.

Freud's first formula led him naturally toward a method of psychoanalytic research that H.D. imitated and in so doing subtly revised her earlier approach to mythology. For Freud, ancient myth, religion, and art constituted a kind of psychic history of humanity that provided clues to the unconscious desires buried in the unconscious of each adult. To recapture the past of the individual, the analyst could turn to these records of time in the traditions and mythologies throughout the world. Freud brought the "past back into the present" by insisting that mythology was useful to the modern seeker of self-knowledge.

Freud regularly used an analysis of mythology to aid in the translation of the hieroglyphic dream back into latent unconscious thought. Dreams are often filled with objects or events about which the analyst knows nothing and for which no associations seem possible. Freud believed that the analyst could decode those objects or "dream-symbols" by turning to the "various fields [in which] the same symbolism occurs." His sources were "from fairy tales and myths, jokes and witticisms, from folklore, i.e. from what we know of the manners and customs, sayings and songs, of different peoples, and from poetic and colloquial usage of language."[14]

From childhood, H.D. had been drawn to fairy tales, and her first published poetry abounded with mythological figures like the oread and testified to much careful reading in mythological source material. Freud's use of fairy tale, folklore, and mythology to explain the layered, buried past of the individual gave new purpose to H.D.'s fascination with myth. Her account in *Tribute to Freud* of decoding the thistle and serpent dream-symbol shows how closely she paralleled Freud's method of interpretation. At first, she was completely puzzled as to the meaning of the two vivid images, the thistle and the serpent set side by side, that suddenly appeared in her sleep sometime before she went to Europe. How was she to translate its meaning for her, especially when she *later* saw exactly the same thistle and snake set side by side on a Graeco-Roman or Hellenistic seal in the Louvre (*T.F.,* pp. 64–65)? The answer, she believed, lay buried in the mythologies of the past. Following Freud's example, she researched Greek and Ptolemaic designs, examined Etruscan pottery, read about early esoteric traditions about the healing tao-cross of the serpent in W.B. Crow's pamphlets, and then let her mind wander at will through all these mythological, religious, and artistic sources. To H.D., the various associations linked her vision with the role Freud was to play in her life as the blameless physician, the modern Asklepios (*T.F.,* pp. 100–101).

How such symbols from the past could emerge in modern dreams puzzled Freud at first. He tentatively posited and then later affirmed the "racial inheritance" and "hereditary transmission" of these symbols in the human brain. As H.D. paraphrased Freud's theory of inherited "psychical contents," Freud "had dared to say that the dream-symbol could be interpreted; its language, its imagery were common to the whole race, not only of the living but of those ten thousand years dead" (*T.F.,* p. 71).[15]

H.D.'s decodings of dream-symbols seldom use the frequently reductionistic, allegorical equations that often appear in Freud's writing as well as the general psychoanalytic literature. For example, Freud at one point took her into the shadowy anteroom off the fourth wall of his study to show her his favorite treasure, a bronze statue of Pallas Athena; " 'She is perfect,' he said, *'only she has lost her spear.'* I did not say anything" (*T.F.,* p. 69). But H.D. reflected, "She has lost her spear. He might have been talking Greek" (*T.F.,* p. 69). Norman Holland is probably correct in suggesting that Freud showed H.D. the spear-less Athena as an image to counter the hopeless wish buried in her unconscious that she wanted to be a boy.[16] But if in fact Freud's indirect demonstration rested on an equation of the spear with a penis, H.D. rejected this translation of his "gift." H.D. saw the statue of

Athena as the goddess in her form as Niké A-pteros or Wingless Victory. The Acropolis in Athens housed a statue of wingless Athena to secure the future safety of the city: "Niké A-pteros, she was called, the Wingless Victory, for Victory could never, would never fly away from Athens" (T.F., p. 69). H.D. explored the mythological associations of Niké A-pteros as a way of understanding her own future in the inevitable war to come. Linked as it was with Freud and the experience of analysis, the statue became an image of strength, not deficiency, to H.D. The nonpsychoanalytic cast to her interpretations of myth or mythic objects, however, should not obscure the similarity of her method with Freud's. For both of them myths were significant for what they could reveal about the individual psyche, for their links to the personal life of people in modern times.

This use of ancient mythology as personal oracle represents a subtle shift away from H.D.'s approach to myth in her imagist poetry. In poems like "Oread," H.D. used mythological figures as personae for her own contemporary experience. Freud's phylogenetic formula helped transform myth as personal metaphor into myth as the voice of the unconscious recorded through time. H.D.'s later notion of myth included the Freudian concept of myths as historical analogues to dreams, both carrying messages of great personal relevance for those who could interpret their enigmatic language. Myth no longer primarily provided a mask for contemporary experience; it more importantly contained another version of that experience, of the spiritual reality embodied in the hieroglyphic voices of the unconscious. Freud's insistence that ancient mythology shed light on the personal unconscious provided a psychological context for H.D.'s expanding research into a variety of mythological, religious, and artistic sources. Although H.D. surely read widely enough to be a classical pedant, she was not one. As her use of these materials in her late poetry shows, she read with a purpose and a coherence. She found her own inner life in the twentieth century reflected in all these ancient traditions. In a way that directed and focused her interests, Freud brought the past back into the present.

Conversely, Freud brought the present back into the past by the second equation of his recapitulation theory. If the analyst can interpret myth to understand contemporary expressions of unconscious, then it stands to reason that he or she can explore the inner self to learn about the early psychic history of humankind. This reasoning informs the methodology of such works as *Totem and Taboo* and clarifies the logic by which H.D. could transcend the isolation of the single self existing in an instant of historical time. As H.D. understood the implications of Freud's theory, exploration of her own psyche was not ultimately solipsistic or narcissistic. By recapturing her own childhood, she could recapture the past of the human race. "The dead were living in so far as they lived in memory or were recalled in dream," H.D. wrote (*T.F.*, p. 14). As Joseph Riddel so correctly wrote about H.D.'s reading of the Corfu visions: "Interpreting the writing, H.D. discovers that she bears within herself, in a sense, the 'whole race' and relives in her own consciousness the recurrent and hence real experience of all history."[17] Discovery of the patterns shaping the dynamics of the subjective self simultaneously included revelation of parallel patterns structuring human history.

The simultaneity of personal and historical quest is an assumption that characterizes all H.D.'s later long poems, but Freud's two formulae are particularly condensed and artistically embodied in *Helen in Egypt*. H.D.'s relationship to Helen is analogous to the self-portrait of an artist painting herself painting a self-portrait. Helen explores the myth of Isis and Osiris to understand her own family history, particularly the story of her sister Clytaemnestra. She also examines the hieroglyphs of her own present moment in order to translate the hidden dynamics of historic event (Trojan War) and mythic struggle recorded in the Amen-temple (Osiris-Set-Isis-Horus). But Helen herself is the perfect persona for H.D.; like Janus, she faces two ways. Within the story, she represents the subjective psyche seeking knowledge of self and time through an exploration of myth and the unconscious. But from H.D.'s perspective, Helen is also the myth through which the artist can examine her own personal identity and its parallels in myth. H.D.'s re-creation of Helen's myth represented her attempt to achieve union with her mother Helen Wolle (*T.F.*, pp. 17, 30, 33, 44, 49, 123, 184). She used the myth of Helen, who incarnates the spirit of the mother Goddess, to explore her personal identification with her mother. And in reverse, her feelings about her mother helped to shape her unique recreation of Helen's myth and the nature of the female divine spirit of Love. Demonstrating the interlocking formulae of Freud's recapitulation theory, H.D. explored both the psyche and the myth by reviving a mythic hero who is herself an image of personal quest through myth.

This portrait of overlapping personal and mythic quest in *Helen in Egypt* represents H.D.'s development of a universalistic tendency implicit in Freud's work. As Freud turned from the individual on his couch, to the ancient records of human dream and symbol, back to contemporary experience, he found correspondences in the unconscious life of human beings in all cultures, throughout all times. Neurotic symptoms may differ from society to society as the culture determines to some extent how an individual would handle his or her problems. But implicit in all of Freud's writings is the assumption that the unconscious impulses are universal. Freud himself does not explicitly discuss the universalist implications of his theories: nevertheless, his disciples as well as his critics seem to have understood. Jones wrote that Freud found that unconscious conflicts were not peculiar to his neurotic patients: "The conflicts themselves were common to all humanity."[18] Geza Roheim, the Freudian anthropologist, devoted almost two years of fieldwork with Australian aborigines to show that the Oedipus complex described the mental fantasies of little boys in the bush as well as in the drawing room.[19] The "diffusionist" anthropologists, who explain human behavior in terms of cultural context instead of universal characteristics, attacked Freud for applying what might be true of his predominantly wealthy Austrian, Victorian patients to people with totally different backgrounds. H.D. was aware of this charge because Jones discussed it in his pamphlet. He refuted their charge by asserting the universality of humankind in the deepest layers of the psyche.[20]

H.D., as Freud's poetic "disciple," understood the full universalist implications of his theories. She appreciated the assumption beneath Freud's description of the unconscious—that the unconscious transcends space and time. The primary expression of unconscious desires is the dream. Once translated, the dreams of all humans—not only those of sybils, mystics, and prophets—are found to be the "same . . . today as in Joseph's day" (*T.F.*, p. 71). The world of the dream not only dissolves differences of time; it also cuts across all cultures. The dream-symbols, the latent contents of the dream, and the picture-making processes of the dream-work are the same everywhere. H.D. restated Freud's universalist assumption in perhaps more definite and generalized form than Freud, but the unity of humanity she described is consistent with the implications of his theories: "He had dared to say that it ["the unexplored depth in man's consciousness"] was the same ocean of universal consciousness, and even if not stated in so many words, he had dared to imply that this consciousness proclaimed all men one; all nations and races met in the universal world of the dream. . . . The picture-writing, the hieroglyph of the dream was the common property of the whole race; in the dream, man, as at the beginning of time, spoke a universal language" (*T.F.*, p. 71).

The dream's transcendence of space and time gave direction and purpose to H.D.'s curiosity about her own dreams and about the dreams embodied in the mythologies and art of scattered cultures. The universality of humankind's deepest desires and fears allowed H.D. to link not only herself to others, but also each culture to all the others. Freud provided H.D. with the logic by which she could relate the Greeks to the Egyptians, the Egyptians to the Jews, the Jews to modern Christians, and all of these to herself. Norman Pearson explained succinctly how H.D. applied Freud's notion that the personal dream was universal:

> when H.D. began to understand man's dream and myths and saw how they took different metaphorical shapes from culture to culture, she could begin to reassemble her life. . . . Freud helped her understand that there are interchangeable parts in dreams, and that there is a relationship between the individual dream and the myth as the dream of the tribe. In this sense, whatever she was to say about the search for Helen, or by Helen, was related to the Count Zinzendorf myth or to Egyptian myth or to her own personal experience, and she put these all together as Pound has done so brilliantly in the *Cantos*.[21]

In the face of war, "with the black wing of man's growing power of destruction and threat of racial separateness," H.D. found the foundation of future peace in Freud's affirmation of common humanity. Fortified by Freud's theories and techniques for understanding this shared "ocean of universal consciousness," she believed that she could confront the war directly and find beneath its terrors the route to "the clearest fountain head of highest truth" (*T.F.*, pp. 82, 71, 92). Freud's equations of the present and the past, the personal and the universal, formed a bridge from her private experience to that of other people, from her present age to those recorded in the mythologies of the world. Freud's conceptions of religion and art helped to fulfill her original desire for their sessions: to "root out" her "personal weeds," to "strengthen" her purpose, to "reaffirm" her belief, and to "canalize" her energies (*T.F.*, p. 91). In so doing, however, Freud's influence paradoxically confirmed for her a set of premises about the nature of reality that were diametrically opposed to his own. The "transcendental argument" that resulted, the subject of the subsequent chapter, was as important to the formulation of H.D.'s poetic voice as the ideas she absorbed without debate.

4

"Transcendental Issues"

ARTIST AND SCIENTIST IN DEBATE

FREUD'S ENORMOUS influence as a catalyst to H.D.'s artistic self-definition was paradoxically dependent on her capacity to disagree with his most fundamental presuppositions about the nature of reality. H.D. referred to this "argument implicit in our very bones" as a disagreement about "the greater transcendental issues" (*T.F.*, p. 13). The immediate context of her reference is her concern over Freud's disbelief in immortality (*T.F.*, p. 43). But the quarrel that remained unspoken in their relationship was much broader than the issue of the soul's fate after death. Upon their specific disagreement over immortality hinged a whole way of seeing and ordering human experience.

The cornerstone of those "greater transcendental issues" was their opposing premises on the nature of reality itself. What constitutes absolute reality and the contingent mode of perception were questions about which H.D. and Freud were in fundamental disagreement. Freud ultimately assessed the reality of the unconscious realm he explored from the perspectives of materialism and rationalism. While H.D. accepted Freud's categories for the unconscious and his methods of translation, she valued this psychic reality and its expressions in dream, art, and religion from a nonmaterialist, nonrationalist perspective. Freud's influence on H.D. records a debate that personifies artistic and scientific conceptions of reality. Understanding the philosophical issues in that debate will not only clarify the dialectical nature of their collaboration, but also provide the context for a comprehension of H.D.'s modernist aesthetic, particularly as she first expressed it in the *Trilogy*. Freud's evaluative premises about the nature of reality and the value of dreams, art, and religion permeate his canon just as they do H.D.'s. No doubt violating the subtle give and take that characterized H.D.'s interchanges with Freud, this chapter will nonetheless draw the lines of opposition firmly between them. In the interests of clarity, what occurred between them as free associational conversation must be presented as if the two great debaters each had one chance to speak. The lines of argument delineated, the chapter will then conclude with a discussion of the principles and perspectives by which H.D. resolved the conflict between them.

In his writings, Freud confronted the ridicule and bitter attack that he faced over a lifetime with the image, language, and defenses of Science. His continual goal was to establish psychoanalysis as a science, to have his methods and discoveries accepted as analogous to the experiments and laws of the physicist or chemist. Freud saw his work as an extension of nineteenth-century materialist science and positivist philosophy to the realm of mental phenomena. What Darwin did with his explorations of human biology, Freud hoped to do with his observations and interpretations of human psychology.[1] As many have said of Freud, this modern explorer, whose ideas proved to be such a catalyst for H.D. and other artists, was a "rationalist" writing within an intellectual tradition that placed its faith in reason and science. Except for the most loyal of Freudians like Ernest Jones, few commentators on Freud today consider his methods of research to be genuinely empirical.[2] But Freud's self-conscious image as a scientist and his identification with the rationalist tradition had important consequences in his conception of reality, which in turn created the context for his valuation of the unconscious and its expressions.

Freud defined primary reality as the tangible and measurable— in short, the material. Knowledge of reality must be objective, based on external evidence, not on subjective experience. In denying the authority of religious experience, Freud asserted that "there is no appeal to a court above that of reason." In identifying the "general tendency of mankind to credulity," he defined belief as "a resistance . . . against the relentlessness and monotony of the laws of thought and against the demands of reality-testing." Freud quoted Goethe to affirm that "Reason and Science [are] the highest strength possessed by man." By reality-testing, Freud meant simply "the process of testing things to see if they are real."[3] He quoted a rhyme from his childhood as a prototype for "reality-testing" and thereby revealed his materialist presuppositions: "The Town of Constance lies on the Bodensee. 'If you don't believe it, go and see.' "[4] Truth is responsive to the logical eye and is therefore ultimately rational and reasonable. What cannot be measured, what opposes reason by a "logic" of its own is automatically consigned to the realm of wish fulfillment in Freud's empiricist view of the world. An immeasurably infinite divinity or an intuited truth are beyond the boundaries of reality which Freud repeatedly identified with the "external world." Reality is everything outside consciousness. It is that hard world of necessity and natural catastrophe against which the psyche must struggle in its search for pleasure.[5]

To establish what is real, what opinions "deserve belief," Freud believed we need only obey the "relentless laws of reason and concrete observation." As he wrote in his paper "Dreams and Occultism," occult phenomena pose "a question of fact: is what the occultists tell us true or not? It must, after all, be possible to decide this by observation."[6] This paradigm of Freudian "reality-testing" embodies his empirical demand for tangibility and his belief that only those who can measure reality can discover it. Scientists are the only people who work with facts, the world external to subjective experience, and therefore with objective truth. Freud wrote: "But scientific work is the only road which can lead us to a knowledge of reality outside ourselves. It is once again merely an illusion to expect anything from intuition and introspection; they give us nothing but particulars about our own mental life."[7]

These "particulars" of the "mental life," all the intuitions, dreams, daydreams, and fantasies of the inner psyche, do have a certain reality for Freud, a "psychical reality" that should in no way be confused with "material reality." In a lecture delivered during the middle years of his career, Freud clarified a distinction that was to remain the fundamental context for all his discussions of the unconscious, religion, and art: "In contrast to *material* reality these phantasies possess psychical reality, and we gradually come to understand that *in the world of neurosis* PSYCHICAL REALITY *is the determining factor.*"[8] While Freud insisted that the analyst must focus on the "psychical reality," the things the patient believed to be true, he never lost sight of the "material reality" beyond consciousness, the touchstone by which all symptoms of the unconscious must ultimately be judged. "According to our way of thinking," he continued, "heaven and earth are not farther apart than fiction [psychical reality] from reality, and we value the two quite differently."[9] The fictions of the psyche are useful for understanding neurosis and helping to eliminate it, but this significance does not make them true or objectively real.

The distinction Freud made between the reality of the external world and the reality "created by the patient" parallels the perpetual conflict he identified between the "reality-principle" and the "pleasure-principle." Reality continually denies the child, then the adult, the pleasures which the instincts never cease to demand. The development of the ego coincides with the ego's increasing ability to apprehend the necessities of external reality and control the urge to pleasure: "You know that the ego in man is gradually trained by the influence of external necessity to appreciate reality and to pursue the reality-principle and that in so doing it must renounce temporarily or permanently various of the objects and aims—not only sexual—of its desires for pleasure."[10] As compensation for the harsh demands of the reality principle, the psyche resorts to the freedom of fantasy, dream, and illusion:

> man . . . has evolved for himself a mental activity in which all these relinquished sources of pleasure and abandoned paths of gratification are permitted their existence, a form of existence in which they are free from the demands of reality and from what we call the exercise of 'testing reality.' . . . In phantasy, therefore, man can continue to enjoy a freedom from the grip of the external world, one which he has long relinquished in actuality.[11]

To escape material reality and serve the pleasure principle, the unconscious creates the psychical realities that are denied during the day. Thus Freud's theories on the unconscious, its expressions and its relation to consciousness are set in a bipolar context which contrasts the absolute material reality and the relative subjective reality serving escapist needs for pleasure.

Freud's materialist conception of reality is itself evidence that his science was not so objective and presuppositionless as he liked to believe. His opposition of material and psychical reality is in fact circular because it already contains a premise of primary reality. If what is true must be tangibly observable, then reality has already been limited by definition to what is essentially material. Even before a "reality-test" can be made, any spiritual phenomenon, any product of unconscious thought, has already been disqualified. Freud's deep trust in the externality of reality and scientific methods thus ironically led him away from the empirical objectivity he so prized. In spite of his self-image as a value-free empirical scientist, Freud's assumptions about reality and perception became a framework of categories that ultimately judged as they described the particulars of psychic reality. Measured against the light of the rational and the external, all aspects of the unconscious life—its mode of thinking, its desires, its creations —seemed darkly regressive and inferior to Freud.

The value judgments Freud made on the mode of perception characteristic of the unconscious are linguistically implicit in his descriptions of the dream-work. His theories of the picture-making perception and expression of the dream greatly attracted the artists of the time who valued imagery, the ambiguity of the visual symbol, and the hidden depths of a poem or novel. But Freud himself called the visual expression of the dream an "archaic" and "regressive" way to think and communicate, a mode humankind used in its infancy, before science developed and reason took precedence. In the following description of the dream-work, for example, Freud's nondescriptive terms violate his own empirical ideal: "We have said that it [the dream-work] goes back to phases in our intellectual development which we have long outgrown—to hieroglyphic writing, to symbolic connections, possibly to conditions which existed before the language of thought was evolved. On this account we called the form of expression employed by the dream-work *archaic* or *regressive*."[12]

Freud's bias against the dream-work's archaic and regressive hieroglyphics originated in his identification with the philosophical traditions of the Enlightenment. These traditions not only celebrated reason and science, but they also assumed that time moves humanity ever forward, that evolution inevitably brings progress, and that the ancient is inferior to the modern. This linear, evolutionary view of history formed an evaluative base for Freud's theory that the childhood of the individual must recapitulate the childhood of humanity. The world that takes hold of us at night is a "regression" to our "infantile," "archaic" past—the early days of the child and the race. This backward-sliding path we take every night is the reverse of a twofold evolution: ethical and epistemological. Primitive people lived out in reality what we just dream: "The evil impulses of our dreams are merely infantile, a reversion to the beginnings of our ethical development."[13] The dream world of modern people, in fact the unconscious of each adult, is a psychic vestige of ancient realities when people acted in response to the pleasure principle instead of the reality principle. Primitive people thought consciously in the picture-making mode which we use in the dream and which we see as reminders in the ancient hieroglyphic scripts. Abstract, conceptual thought has replaced the inferior perceptual thought of visual images. Within the context of his recapitulation theory, Freud's analogy between the dream-work and hieroglyphics is not a flattering one. He considered the "picture-writing" of Chinese and Egyptian characters to be "primitive systems . . . necessarily accompanied by ambiguity and indefiniteness." Poets may work hard to achieve ambiguity, but Freud said that "we would not tolerate" the ambiguity of "ancient systems of expression in our writings today."[14] By analogy, Freud would not seek a visual language or picture thinking as a useful path to reality.

The language of science is precise and logical, not vague and analogical, Freud argued. Its methods are governed by the reality principle, not the pleasure principle. Since science deals in a rational, measurable way with material reality, it is superior as a form of knowledge to any perceptions rooted in the psychical realities of the unconscious. Particularly in *The Future of an Illusion* and *Civilization and Its Discontents*, Freud set science—and its "god" Logos or reason —far above art and religion in a hierarchy of knowledge constituted by his materialist definition of reality. Freud paid tribute to the artistic explorations of psychical reality that preceded his science of psychoanalysis. But for Freud, art was fundamentally fantasy, serving the pleasure principle in the unconscious of both the artist and the audience. Art functions as escape from ultimate, external reality; it makes "oneself independent of the external world." In contrast to science, art creates a world of illusion that pleases precisely because it contradicts reality:

> In it [art], the connection with reality is further loosened; satisfaction is obtained from illusions, which are recognized as such without the discrepancy between them and reality being allowed to interfere with enjoyment. The region from which these illusions arise is the life of the imagination; at the time when the development of the sense of reality took place, this region was expressly exempted from the demands of

reality-testing and was set apart for the purpose of fulfilling wishes which were difficult to carry out. At the head of these satisfactions through phantasy stands the enjoyment of works of art. . . .[15]

As Rieff argued, "The usable truth Freud acknowledged in art was, of course, of a lower order than that in science."[16] Much as Freud surrounded himself with art, he never elevated art or the achievement of artists to the high level of science.

The fundamental dualism of material and psychic realities that separates science from art provides an evaluative framework that further condemns religion. While Freud expressed great respect for the consolation art offers, he had only scorn for the escape religion provides. *The Future of an Illusion* and *Civilization and Its Discontents* contain his major attacks against religion, attacks which grew in bitterness and intensity from the first work to the second. Originating in the attempt to escape harsh necessity ("Ananké"), religion is "incongruous with reality," Freud stated bluntly. Its epistemology is not empirical, and its doctrines are called "illusions" in his first book on religion and finally "mass-delusions" in the second.[17] The fact that religion has an "infantile" prototype in the child's early relations with the mother and father simply emphasized for Freud that religion embodies the unconscious drive for pleasure and rejects the voice of reason and the ties to reality. *The Future of an Illusion* concludes with a celebration of science and logos and the hope that the objective reality of science will one day eliminate the need to create such illusions as religion.[18] The evolutionary optimism of *The Future of an Illusion* was somewhat dampened by the time he wrote *Civilization and Its Discontents*. With the rise of Hitler, it no longer appeared so obvious that the passage of time would bring the ever-growing dominance of reason and the ever-diminishing presence of infantile desires and nonrational modes of thought. He described religions as "mass-delusions" based in destructive "delusional remoulding of reality." His condemnation was scathing and bitter: "The whole thing is so patently infantile, so foreign to reality, that to anyone with a friendly attitude to humanity it is painful to think that the great majority of mortals will never be able to rise above this view of life. It is still more humiliating to discover how large a number of people living to-day, who cannot but see that this religion is not tenable, nevertheless try to defend it piece by piece in a series of pitiable rear-guard actions."[19]

The evaluative context for Freud's theories about the unconscious has an ethical dimension as well as an epistemological one. Just as he denied objective reality to the expressions of the unconscious, so he largely condemned the thoughts and desires of the realm he explored. Freud's revelations about the unknown part of the psyche caused a furor in the intellectual world: men who refused to accept that they wanted to sleep with their mothers or kill their fathers attacked Freud bitterly as a sex maniac. What went unnoticed in the duststorm of battle was that Freud definitely did not condone the wishes he thought basic to the unconscious.[20] In the authorized English translations, Freud's discussions of unconscious desires are permeated with traditional ethical categories that inevitably judge as they describe. His most comprehensive volume produced during the middle years of his career, *A General Introduction to Psychoanalysis*, consistently assumes that unconscious desires are "abhorrent" or "evil." He wrote, for example, that the dream thoughts against which the censorship understandably operates "are invariably of an objectionable nature, offensive from the ethical, aesthetic or social point of view, things about which we do not dare to think at all, or think of only with abhorrence." Dreams, daydreams, fantasies, and neurotic symptoms are all "manifestations of a boundless and ruthless egoism" that serve the pleasure principle. Freud himself did not hide from these ethically abhorrent wishes, and he believed that psychoanalysis would help people to "dare" to bring the "ruthlessness" and "evil" of buried desires to the light of consciousness where the ego could be absolved of guilt. As soon as the analysand realizes that *"the Unconscious is the infantile mental life* . . . the objectionable impression that so much evil lurks in human nature grows somewhat less. For this terrible evil is simply what is original, primitive, and infantile in mental life, what we find in operation in the child. . . . If the evil impulses of our dreams are merely infantile, a reversion to the beginnings of our ethical development, the dream simply making us children again in thought and feeling, it is surely not reasonable to be ashamed of these evil dreams."[21]

In his later speculative books on religion and civilization, Freud extended his ethical categories from the individual psyche to the formation and continuance of culture itself. In *Civilization and Its Discontents*, Freud formulated a psychoanalytic variation on the social contract theories of the Enlightenment. Humanity in a state of nature represented the unconscious unleashed to wreak its havoc of offensive desires on all, thus making communal existence impossible. The evolution of civilization depended upon the repression of these abhorrent instincts. Freud understood the danger of too much repression, especially sexual repression. The energy of the id could no longer be successfully sublimated into the creations of civilization since the ego would succumb to neurosis. But while he argued against the Victorian disapproval of sex as a "source of pleasure in its own right," he never questioned the necessity for repression of unconscious desires.[22] Some of the criticism leveled at Freud, particularly from the neo-Freudians, and some of the praise he has received, relate specifically to his bleak judgment on the dark, ethically "primitive" nature of the unconscious. The profound pessimism which permeates his later essays on society and civilization is based fundamentally on his belief that there is a deep core to every human being which is impervious to environment and social conditioning.[23]

Freud found the conscious self—the ego, as he called it—to be everything the unconscious was not. In the first place, the ego is not cut off from reality like the unconscious. In fact, it develops out of the unconscious as the demands of the real, external world impinge upon the unconscious' desire for pleasure. Instinct may push for a person to make love with his mother, but the ego has learned that it is fathers, not children, that sleep with mothers. The ego is also aware that social custom frowns on such incestuous desires. Thus, responsive to the social world as it is and as it claims it should be, the ego tries to silence the pleasure-seeking, unrealistic desires of the unconscious. In preventing the "evil wishes" of the id from escaping into action, the ego is necessarily in Freud's scheme of things a force for "good" in society and in the individual. Perhaps because the ego is in touch with reality and the needs of the whole society, it is not restricted to the limited and ambiguous perception of the unconscious. The ego has intellect; it reasons instead of intuiting. It can resort to logic while the unconscious is pushed uncontrollably in the direction of its desires.[24]

The ego and the unconscious are thus far different both ethically and epistemologically. This difference is not, however, a static one in Freud's system of things. At best, in Freud's view, the elements in a person's psyche exist in a state of conflict, and at worst, he or she lives in the midst of a civil war. The unfortunate person whose ego suffered excessively in the early stages of its development cannot handle this constant tension. The ego is too weak; it begins to lose its ties to reality, the external world. At this point in neurosis, the analyst steps in to take the side of the ego; he or she strengthens the rational, relatively moral part of the patient: "Our plan of cure is based upon these views. The ego has been weakened by the internal conflict; we must come to its aid. The position is like a civil war which can only be decided by the help of an ally from without. The analytical physician and the weakened ego of the patient, basing themselves upon the real external world, are to combine against the enemies, the instinctual demands of the id, and the moral demands of the superego. We form a pact with each other."[25] The goal of the good physician, then, is to strengthen the ego—to help it create greater ties with the "real external world" and control the instincts of the unconscious with less conflict. The ego becomes rejuvenated as soon as it can bring to self-awareness what has been repressed or forgotten. Knowledge is power. When the secrets of the unconscious are put in the light of reason, much of their power to haunt and control the ego is lost. Because of its ties to external reality, Freud saw the ego as the seat of reason and intellect. And thus, as the analyst, he struggled to bring what he perceived as the irrational part of humanity into the domain of rational consciousness. Rieff wrote that Freud held out a "rationalist promise"—that conscious knowledge of unconscious contents will bring " 'mastery over the lost provinces of the mental life.' "[26] The fundamental purpose of this mastery is not the release, but the control of the unconscious. As Trilling argued, "Freud would never have accepted the role which Mann seems to give him as the legitimizer of the myth and the dark, irrational ways of the mind. If Freud discovered the darkness for science, he never endorsed it. On the contrary, his rationalism supports all the ideas of the Enlightenment that deny validity to myth or religion; he holds to a simple materialism, to a simple determinism, to a rather limited sort of epistemology."[27]

To summarize Freud's side of the debate, his theoretical perspective established a bipolar context that contrasted material reality with psychical reality, the reality principle with the pleasure principle, logical thought with hieroglyphic thought, the ego with the id, and finally science with art and religion. The paradox of his life work is that his alliance with the conscious mind ultimately devalued the unconscious realm which was the center of his scientific inquiry and fascination.

The nature of his influence on H.D. and other twentieth-century artists begins at this point of paradox.

In order for Freud's ideas to serve as catalyst, H.D. and her fellow artists in the modernist tradition had to leave him far behind in the dust of his imagined empiricism. His materialist conception of reality and the resulting negative valuation of psychical realities had to be rejected if his rich insights into nonrational thought processes were to have an impact on art. Since Freud's bias ultimately denies the power of art to deal with primary reality, rejection of his rationalist presuppositions is practically intrinsic to any artist—who, after all, would dedicate a life to artistic creativity all the while believing that art was by nature insignificant in the face of reason and science?

But modernists like H.D. had additional reasons to transcend Freud's rationalist boundaries in their own explorations of nonmaterial realities. H.D.'s disagreement with Freud reproduces the pivotal point of modernist art. The starting point of modernism is the crisis of belief that pervades twentieth-century western culture: loss of faith, experience of fragmentation and disintegration, and shattering of cultural symbols and norms. At the center of this crisis were the new technologies and methodologies of science, the epistemology of logical positivism, and the relativism of functionalist thought—in short, major aspects of the philosophical perspectives that Freud embodied. The rationalism of science and philosophy attacked the validity of traditional religious and artistic symbols while the growing technology of the industrialized world produced the catastrophes of war on the one hand and the atomization of human beings on the other. Art produced after the First World War recorded the emotional impact of this crisis; despair, hopelessness, paralysis angst, and a sense of meaninglessness dominated the scenarios of various waste lands in modernist literature. But these writers refused finally to be satisfied with the seeming meaninglessness, chaos, and fragmentation of material reality. In a variety of ways suited to their own religious, literary, mythological, occult, political, or existentialist perspectives, they emerged from the paralysis of absolute despair to an active search for meaning. The search for order and pattern began in its own negation, in the overwhelming sense of disorder and fragmentation caused by the modern materialist world. The artist as seer would attempt to create what the culture could no longer produce: symbol and meaning in the dimension of art, brought into being through the agency of language, the Word or Logos of the twentieth century. The emphasis in modernist literature is generally on the search itself rather than on any given answer. Between absolute disbelief and belief the artist moved in a dynamic process of often agonized quest. But the initial turning point of that search was a refusal to accept the materialist definitions of reality that establish so devastatingly the spiritual waste land of modern life.

H.D.'s "transcendental" argument with Freud over the nature of reality dramatizes—indeed almost personifies—the process of interaction between art and science in the first half of the twentieth century. She transformed many of his ideas about the unconscious into the hieroglyphic image and structure of the modernist quest for new meaning. His theories about psychical reality become in her poetry the artistic argument that counters a simple positivist view of perception or a materialist view of reality. H.D. paradoxically used his own science to create spiritual, symbolic alternatives to his world view. In the *Trilogy*, she calls this nonmaterial reality simply "spiritual realism" (*T.*, p. 48), a term that forcefully joins together the conceptual poles of Freud's thought.

The roots of H.D.'s "spiritual realism" and her transcendental argument with Freud go back to the premodernist, prewar days of imagism. Pound's concept of the image may have come directly from Freud through the psychologist Bernard Hart, but imagist aesthetics and poetry are an inversion of Freud's rationalist hierarchy of realities. Intrinsic to the notion of poetic image is the assumption that visual language and thought can capture a reality inexpressible in conceptual discourse. To think and communicate visually as the unconscious does is therefore superior to reason and logic. Precisely because it can instantaneously render complex subjective realities, poetic language can make concrete a whole nonmaterial, intangible realm of human experience that is not accessible to empirical reality-testing.

While "Oread" demonstrates the connections between H.D.'s poetics and Freud's theories, it also illustrates the gulf between their conceptions of reality. Freud would surely have been interested in "Oread" as a reflection of H.D.'s fantasies, but he would not have agreed that the poem expressed ultimate reality, the "reality outside ourselves." Precisely because the realities of "Oread" are experiential, not "outside ourselves," they could never pass Freud's reality test.

Waves are not made of pine trees; the land is not the sea—"if you don't believe it go and see." The fusion of land and sea, active and passive, masculine and feminine could never be "authenticated." In fact, the whole paradoxical direction of the poem—to unite opposites which are at the same time affirmed—is foreign to the "rigid laws of reason" which separate and emphasize differences. For Freud, then, the reality of "Oread" would have been hopelessly subjective. But for H.D., Freud's external reality would have been hopelessly incomplete. By using the visual modes of perception and expression which he viewed as regressive and inferior to reason, she fixed in a poem the otherwise indefinable reality of an experience. Robert Duncan referred to this visual *"condensare* of the dream or poem" as the creation in form of "What Is."[28] Freud would not have accepted his idea that the pictures of the unconscious or the nonrational images of the poem express "What Is" because their reality is part of consciousness, not external to it. But, as Cyrena Pondrom said about the imagist circle in general, this poem operates on "a belief in art, in poetry, as the expression of a higher realism."[29]

Freud devoted his whole life to the study of consciousness—in its conscious and unconscious forms. But ultimately, he turned his back on the reality of what he studied when he insisted that the truths of conscious experience had to be measured ultimately against external standards. Even in her imagist days, H.D. turned her gaze inward to what was not measurable, not concrete. There she found the center of what is humanly real.

The subjective nature of reality in "Oread" reveals a great deal about the perspective with which H.D. must have greeted Freud's materialist categories. *Tribute to Freud* indicates indirectly H.D.'s acute awareness of the philosophical chasm between herself and her guide. It also clearly indicates her rejection of his epistemological and ethical biases as she turned increasingly to the unconscious as an oracle of "spiritual realism." Her account, for example, of her first meeting with Freud is couched in terms of their different modes of perception and her belief in the superiority of her own. As she entered his study, Freud was worried that his dog Yofi would bite "the stranger." But H.D., making immediate friends with the little chow, believed that Freud's literal thought which designated her a "stranger" could not see into the other "region of cause and effect" where the dog could sense instantly that she was no "stranger" to Freud and all that he loved. In spite of his greatness, her insight was sometimes superior because it was not limited to rational modes of thought:

> my form of rightness, my intuition, sometimes functioned by the split-second (that makes all the difference in spiritual time-computations) the quicker. I was swifter in some intuitive instances, and sometimes a small tendril of a root from that great common Tree of Knowledge went deeper into the sub-soil. His were the great giant roots of that tree, but mine, with hair-like almost invisible feelers, sometimes quivered a warning or resolved a problem, as for instance at the impact of that word *stranger*. "We'll show him," retorts the invisible intuitive rootlet. . . . "Show him that you have ways of finding out things about people, other than looking at their mere outward ordinary appearance." My intuition challenges the Professor, though not in words. (*T.F.*, pp. 98–99)

H.D.'s philosophical challenge to the Professor was evident even in her first meeting with Freud because she brought to analysis a perspective that assumed subjective realities intuitively or imagistically perceived to be a higher form of reality than the material. Her immediate rejection of Freud's rationalism was the catalyst that transformed the personal subjective reality of her imagist poetry to the spiritual realism of her later modernist epics. Her knowing denial of Freud's materialist bias against the inner voice of the self, art, and religion helped the early poetic image become the later hieroglyph that contained in coded form the wisdom necessary to confront modern chaos. By ignoring his Enlightenment framework, H.D. could gain access to "the clearest fountain-head of highest truth," the source for her of artistic identity, aesthetic form, and religious vision (*T.F.*, p. 92).

H.D.'s rejection of Freud's materialism was thus the essential interaction liberating his rich influence on her work. H.D.'s own awareness of this paradox is sharply evident in *Tribute to Freud* as she discussed their opposing perspectives on her Corfu visions. Freud saw the light-pictures projected on her hotel wall as a "dangerous symptom" of "neurosis" (*T.F.*, pp. 41, 51). The fact that H.D.'s suppressed desires could break into daytime consciousness, even to appear external to consciousness, must have suggested to Freud that H.D.'s ego was dangerously weakened. He as analyst would have to help reestablish the healthy ego's strong ties to reality and thus its capacity to keep the unconscious in check. H.D.'s "megalomania" and its symptoms in waking life would then gradually disappear.

H.D. paired his word "symptom" with her own "inspiration" (*T.F.*, 41, 51), a word choice that vividly contrasts their different purposes in their collaboration to decode the unconscious. For H.D., her ego was not in danger from the riotous impulses of an id in revolt; it was instead in need of direction as it drifted down the river of a chaotic century (*T.F.*, p. 13). She was not eager to translate the writing-on-the-wall so as to readjust her ties to external reality. As "signs" rather than "symptoms," these visions brought messages that could reaffirm her belief in and her knowledge of "highest truth." As indicators of her ability to fuse art, religion, and healing, these visions did not point to a "ruthless egoism" or dangerous megalomania, but rather to a new destiny as a poet-prophet. The very qualities of the unconscious that condemned it in Freud's eyes were the source of its special value for H.D. For Psyche as artist, the voices of the unconscious could fertilize the conscious mind which remains sterile and mechanical without some source of imaginative inspiration. For Psyche as seeker of transcendent truth, the unconscious could open doors to religious experience and wisdom. The goal of analysis, then, was not to control the unconscious by destroying its illusions and delusions in the light of rational consciousness. It was to enrich the limited, inadequate knowledge of reason that H.D. set out to explore the unconscious.

Before H.D. embarked on the *Trilogy*, she read and reread a book she called her Bible, one that must have reinforced her lines of debate with Freud and confirmed her rejection of Freud's materialist evaluation of the unconscious. Denis de Rougemont's *Love in the Western World* clarifies further that H.D. was perfectly aware of the philosophical issues at stake in her "transcendental" argument with Freud. In his examination of variants of the Tristan-Iseult myth, de Rougemont sharply contrasted the prevailing epistemologies of the Middle Ages and twentieth-century Europe that revolve around the issues of material reality vs. spiritual reality, empiricism vs. symbolic or visual perception, and science vs. religion and art. The spirit of the modern age is "materialistic," he argued. The "contemporary mind" presumes that "the physical is *more true and more real* than the mental, and hence that the physical is at the foundation of all things and is the principle of all explanation." De Rougemont turned the tables on materialist detractors of subjective reality by calling their belief in the tangible the new superstition or obsession of the time in spite of their claim to scientific truth: "The superstition of our time expresses itself in a mania . . . [that] usurps the name of 'scientific integrity,' and is defended on the ground that it emancipates the mind from delusions of the spirit." While de Rougemont used a Freudian method of interpreting the Tristan myth, he placed Freud squarely in the center of the materialist tradition he found so mistaken, just as H.D. herself learned from Freud how to translate dreams at the same time that she denied his denunciation of dreams as illusions.[30]

In opposition to a materialist epistemology, religion depends on a symbolic mode of discourse analogous to art, de Rougemont continued. Mystical experience occurs without language or thought, and consequently the mystic must resort to symbolic expression to convey the vision to others. In short, the mystic must become a poet. The poet, in touch with the inner spirit, is like the mystic. Art and religion are potentially tied together by their symbolic mode of thought and their refusal to limit the real to the material. Rooted in the unconscious, originally fused in function, religion and art capture the transcendent truths invisible to empirical reality-testing. De Rougemont's discussion of reality, art, religion, and science recapitulates the themes of H.D.'s disagreement with Freud.

Rejection of materialism and the consequent search for spiritual realism is the central poetic act of the *Trilogy*, which therefore reproduces indirectly H.D.'s dialogue with Freud and demonstrates the essential pattern of much modernist art. In these poems about social destruction, H.D. attempts to bridge the chasm between the internal world of the dream and the external world of objective fact. Art is used to confront the reality of war, not to escape its horror through the creation of fantasies and illusions, as Freud might have argued.

The initial experience of the *Trilogy* is immersion in the harsh reality of the contemporary world. The conditions under which H.D. wrote underline the philosophical starting point of the poem and help dispel the frequent critical notion that H.D. was essentially escapist in her art and too fragile for the modern world.[31] Throughout the war, H.D. remained in London, the center of the air war in Britain. As an American, she could have easily returned to the States. Or she could have taken the urgent advice of her friends who implored her to leave the city for the relative safety of the countryside. Instead, she chose to remain. The fear, exhilaration, and final affirmation of spirit that she felt in London are evident in her explanation to Viola Jordan:

"It's been a continuous night-mare but when one has things so bad, one sort of turns a corner and is so thankful just for LIFE in large Caps. Don't want a sticky-end, myself, but it is a sort of triumph of the spirit to have been able to endure this. . . . I have friends . . . near the Sitwells' beautiful old estate, they urge me to move down there; I may go for a time in the spring and summer but I feel so lost in the country; I am so conditioned now to this life and really it is exciting and stimulating and people are so wonderful" (14 February 1944).[32]

Like the woman Hilda Doolittle, the poet of the *Trilogy* makes no attempt to escape the gaping walls and constant death that surround her. The poem begins with the poet walking through the ruined city just after a bombing raid. Staring in desolation at the destruction, she records her impressions in the first section:

. . . —we pass on

to another cellar, to another sliced wall

where poor utensils show
like rare objects in a museum;

Pompeii has nothing to teach us,
we know crack of volcanic fissure,
slow flow of terrible lava,

pressure on heart, lungs, the brain
about to burst its brittle case
(what the skull can endure!):

over us, Apocryphal fire,
under us, the earth sway, dip of a floor,
slope of a pavement   (*T.*, p. 4)

But even as she is immersed in the concrete, actual horror of the war, she refuses to limit her understanding of the destruction to the material rubble in front of her. The ruins remind her of Pompeii—another instance of sudden catastrophe in human experience. This is no escape back into time; rather, H.D.'s comparison foreshadows her insistence throughout the poem that the ultimate reality of any single moment in history is contained in a pattern of essential experience which informs all time. The fire in London, like the fire in Pompeii, is a special kind of flame—Apocryphal fire, destruction which brings rebirth. H.D. approaches external reality in the same way she learned to read the mysterious script of psychical reality from Freud. The rubble contains, she believes, a coded message whose interpretation can reveal an order underlying the surface reality of chaos.

The Walls Do Not Fall, the first poem in the Trilogy, records the poet's attempt to translate the hidden meaning of external reality. Like much modernist literature, however, this quest is permeated with despair engendered by the "real" world whose message is at best ambivalent. The Walls ends with a starkly rendered expression of the modernist nightmare world:

Still the walls do not fall,
I do not know why;

there is zrr-hiss,
lightning is a not-known,

unregistered dimension;
we are powerless,

dust and powder fill our lungs
our bodies blunder

through doors twisted on hinges,
and the lintels slant

cross-wise;
we walk continually

on thin air
that thickens to a blind fog,

then step swiftly aside,
for even the air

is independable,
thick where it should be fine

and tenuous
where wings separate and open,

and the ether
is heavier than the floor,

and the floor sags
like a ship floundering;

we know no rule
of procedure,

we are voyagers, discoverers
of the not-known,

the unrecorded;
we have no map;

possibly we will reach haven,
heaven. (T., pp. 58–59)

The techniques of imagism are used to describe concretely the physical reality to suggest the correlative and collective state of mind of the modern world. The dust, powder, and smoke from the bombs suffocate and blind the spirit of the ruined city; bodies lurch in the rubble without security and direction. Doorways lead to nowhere, and the city is a "floundering ship." Cultural symbols and traditions can offer no direction any more. Simple facts are clear, but their significance—if they have any—is hidden in the spiritual fog. The "zrr-hiss" and lightning flashes in the sky are certainly bombs, but they may contain a sign from some "unregistered dimension," some alternate reality. The "wings that separate and open" release destruction, but suggest also the protective wings of angels. "We are powerless" in the face of reality, but not ultimately paralyzed. With full knowledge of material reality, the poet will take an existential leap of faith to begin the search for transcendent reality—"we are voyagers, discoverers / of the not-known / the unrecorded." What gives this quest its particular modernist quality is the recognition of potential failure and the underlying uncertainty of goal. Who runs the castle in Kafka's *Castle*; is there even a castle that sends messages? Who is Godot in Beckett's *Waiting for Godot*; if he even exists, is he benevolent? Without any tangible evidence to validate the search, the poet must act as if there were an alternate life-giving reality to be discovered or created—"possibly we will reach haven, / heaven." We may or may not reach an end-point in this quest; the safe "haven" from death may or may not be "heaven." Living in a world that defines reality empirically, the poet must nonetheless continue the search for the "unregistered dimension" that can incorporate as it transcends that reality.

Contributing greatly to the difficulty of this task, the rationalist cultural norms mock the nonutilitarian efforts and intangible realities of the poet (T., pp. 14, 16, 17, 19, 22). Traditional religion, on the other hand, has been shattered into "art-craft junk-shop / paint-and-plaster medieval jumble," and has little to offer (*T.*, p. 27). Direction emerges instead out of the poet's defiance of simple materialism and trust in intangible religious experience revealed through the inner voices of the psyche. As she walks through the desolate streets, "inspiration stalks us . . . Spirit announces the Presence" (*T.*, pp. 3, 83–87). Dreams bring male and female images of divine spirit (*T.*, pp. 25–29, 89–105). The poet's persona, the "worm" who spins its shroud, is a dual image of both snake and caterpillar who shed past selves to be reborn anew (*T.*, pp. 11–12, 13, 20, 22, 23, 53, 103). These affirmations of divine presence and resurrection pattern are not testable in the empirical sense. Their authority is experiential, not scientific. Yet in defiance, the poet urges "let us . . . re-dedicate our gifts / to spiritual realism, / scrape a palette, / point pen or brush" (*T.*, p. 48). Art will define the "spiritual realism" inaccessible to science. To do so, it must abandon the limited vision of reason: "the elixir of life, the philosopher's stone / is yours if you surrender / sterile logic, trivial reason" (*T.*, p. 40). The danger of "mind dispersed" is great: "lost in sea-depth, / sub-conscious ocean where Fish / move two-ways, devour . . . illusion, reversion of old values, / oneness lost, madness" (*T.*, pp. 40–41). H.D. recognized that madness and illusions were possible results of loosening the ego's ties to external reality. But if the seeker had the courage to "dare, seek, seek further, dare more," the "secret doors" to "spiritual realism" would be unlocked (*T.*, p. 40).[33]

Interpretation of the psychical reality provided the key to those doors because spiritual reality is prior to physical reality. H.D. gives a psychoanalytic cast to John's Word and Plato's Idea:

> . . . remember, O Sword,
> you are the younger brother, the latter-born,
>
> your Triumph, however exultant,
> must one day be over,
>
> *in the beginning*
> *was the Word.*
>
> Without thought, invention,
> you would not have been, O Sword,
>
> without idea and the Word's mediation,
> you would have remained

unmanifest in the dim dimension
where thought dwells,

and beyond thought and idea,
their begetter,

Dream,
Vision.   (*T.*, pp. 17–18)

Condensation or metonymy accomplishes a complex philosophical argument. The "Sword" in the *Trilogy* represents the world at war, the forces of death and destruction, and the materialist world view that would deny the power or existence of spiritual reality. H.D. counters the Sword's claim to ultimate power with a Platonic world view that sees the mental as prior to the physical. Rational thought precedes the material, and Dream or Vision precede the intellect. H.D. has turned Freud's hierarchy of realities upside down and affirmed the primacy of the intangible spirit.

At the same time, however, H.D. attempts to achieve a synthesis of material and psychical reality in her concept of "spiritual realism." Even the choice of words forcibly yokes together the opposing poles of reality. The roots of this fusion may even go back to imagist days. Cyrena Pondrom argued that the "higher realism" of the imagists showed the "impact of mechanistic and scientific philosophies" in the post-symbolist world. The imagists abandoned the "mystical aesthetic of spiritual vision" that characterized the symbolists and adopted a concept of "higher realism" that was based in the "empirical consciousness of the artist."[34] The image of subjective reality was chosen on the basis of the artist's precise observation of concrete reality.

In the *Trilogy*, however, it is not careful observation but the concept of incarnation that synthesizes spiritual and physical realities. Dream and Vision are prior to the material world of war—the "Sword." But they are also manifest or incarnate in the physical dimension that mysteriously reveals as it conceals the "higher realism." The wings of war are simultaneously the wings of angels; the "whirr and roar" of the terrifying planes is also the "Voice louder, / though its speech was lower / than a whisper" (*T.*, p. 19). The fire of incendiary bombs is the purifying apocalyptic flame that allows a new civilization to rise like a phoenix from the ashes (*T.*, pp. 4, 35). The "lightning" that "shattered earth / and splintered sky" is the divine fire personified by Uriel, one of the seven angels around God's throne (*T.*, pp. 68, 69, 79). As the fires slowly die out, the charred but still blossoming apple tree is a "sign": "this is the flowering of the rood, / this is the flowering of the wood," an "incarnate symbol of the Holy Ghost" (*T.*, pp. 87, 101). And in the "tale of jars," the "unseemly" hair of Mary Magdalene reveals the "dynamic centre," the "lost centre-island, Atlantis" (*T.*, p. 153).

Material reality itself presents a hieroglyphic script that the poet must translate. The measurable, testable facts of the external world are for H.D. analogous to the manifest content of a dream. Facts are signs or symbols incarnating spiritual reality. These images allow the poet a glimpse of a reality more "real" than the material fact of destruction. Moreover, these signs reveal patterns of divine process that order the chaos and catastrophe of the present.

Reading these signs depends on the rejection of materialism and a faith in the various hieroglyphic voices of psychical realities. Denial of Freud's empirical world view is thus the initial poetic act which allows for the creation of meaning rooted in the revelations of the unconscious. From Freud's perspective as scientist, H.D.'s artistic formulation of spiritual realism is based in fantasy and the need for wish fulfillment. From her perspective as artist, Freud's empirical reality reduces spirit to the tangible fact of destruction and thus embodies a form of nihilism. H.D. turned her quest for the meaning amidst destruction to the realm of vision and imagination. While Freud saw this type of artistic search as escape, H.D. experienced her exploration of psychic realms as liberation from the confines of material reality.

H.D.'s concept of spiritual realism also freed her to expand the universalistic tendencies in Freud's work into her own theory of time and related valuation of myth. Freud's Enlightenment presuppositions about evolution caused him ultimately to emphasize the differences among cultures and historical periods even though his contribution to psychology was a theory of commonality. From her earliest to her latest work, however, H.D. never portrayed time as evolutionary. She returned many times to the image of palimpsest to embody her essentialist view of history. For H.D., the superposition of new writings upon the old in a "palimpsest" paralleled history as a "palimpsest" of repeated events whose essential meaning is embodied in the various forms of chronological time. Her attitude toward chronological time parallels her view of external reality. Since "the real" for H.D. is what transcends the ever-changing surface of the tangible, time does not bring "real" change.

In her poetry, H.D. often explored the paradox of an ever-changing, changeless procession of events in time. When the luminous Lady appears in the poet's dream in the *Trilogy*, for example, the poet recognizes her as "Our Lady" who has been portrayed by artists in all times and places. With precise imagist craft, the poet catalogues the different forms in which the Lady has appeared, but concludes that the Lady in her dream has "the same—different—the same attributes, / different yet the same as before" (*T.*, pp. 93–105). Time is a paradox: simultaneously unique and universal, the Lady is constantly changing as she appears in the religious and artistic dreams of differing cultures and epochs, but she is always the same. As the poet says of another Lady in *Vale Ave*, "nothing was changed where everything was different."[35] In the palimpsest of history the Lady's changeless essence shines through all the erasures of external change.

The resolution of the paradox rested for H.D. in her concept of time as incarnation. Spiritual reality manifests itself in the created forms of the actual world in chronological time. Each age or each individual provides the situations, the details, the particulars through which eternal reality gains form or flesh. Like the latent and manifest content of the dream, history is composed of an inner core of meaning and the enigmatic, visual form of external reality. It was a torrent of fire and ashes in Pompeii; it was the screeching bombs from German planes in London of the forties; "it had happened before / it would happen again," says the poet in the *Trilogy* (*T.*, p. 161). For Freud, history brought progress, and the planes do, after all, represent technological advances since the days of Pompeii. For H.D., history embodied the out-of-time realities in time. Like the dreamer interpreting the dream, the poet seeks to translate the enigma of time.

A central image for eternal reality in *Helen in Egypt* is based on the shape-shifter Proteus. In Greek myth, Menelaus learned that he could return home to Sparta, if he could catch Proteus and not let the god who could change his form slip through his fingers. Menelaus would never have managed to hold on to Proteus if he had ignored the different shapes Proteus so swiftly assumed. Similarly, time is protean for H.D. In contrast to Indian philosophy and the theosophists it influenced, H.D. never suggested that the surface manifestations of reality were "maya," illusion. Each new form is "real," and must be understood in all its particularity. Helen in the epic and the poet in the *Trilogy* must fully absorb the unique quality of their own personal experience. The poet says of the other artists, "But none of these, none of these suggest her as I saw her" (*T.*, p. 96). To understand the Lady's special message to her at that particular moment of incarnation, the poet must explore the significance of the Lady's new form. The particularity of the actual in a moment of time is a hieroglyph of the universal, timeless dimension of spiritual realism.

The essence in H.D.'s timeless dimension is most often a structure for a pattern of relations rather than a static type of Platonic idea. Her translation of a fragmentary memory in *Tribute to Freud* clarifies the structuralist quality of H.D.'s concept of time and reality. She visualized the time she and her brother sat on the curb and refused to follow their laughing mother home: "But there we sit . . . making a little group, design, an image at the crossroads. It appears variously in Greek tragedies with Greek names and it can be found in your original Grimm's tales or in your nursery translation, called Little-Brother, Little-Sister." All the variants "make a group, a constellation, they make a groove or a pattern into which or upon which other patterns fit, or are placed unfitted and are cut by circumstance to fit" (*T.F.*, pp. 28–29). Riddel referred to this "pattern" in H.D.'s work as the "*Ur*-myth," "*Ur*-form," or "*Ur*-pattern" which he described as "unity-alienation-struggle-return, the 'resurrection myth' and the 'resurrection reality.'" He continued: "The personal event realized in the individual poem is simply one more variation on the *Ur*-myth, of which all recorded myths, all writing-on-the-wall, all history, is simply a recurring instant." H.D.'s view of the poet's task, Riddel argued, is "to disentangle the pattern of reality from the chaos of its present manifestation—to discover [for example] . . . that the Christos image is . . . itself only another, single variation on the *Ur*-myth."[36] Riddel's designation of an "*Ur*-myth" is perhaps reductionistic. Although H.D. sought the pattern amidst multiplicity, she never claimed that there is only one pattern or monomyth for all experience. But Riddel was certainly correct in his description of the quest for essential patterns as the cornerstone of her concept of history and approach to myth.

The essentialist concept of time in H.D.'s work is perhaps best understood when placed within the context of structuralism, an intellectual system that she anticipated in her use of Freud's ideas to search for universal formulae. Edmund Leach wrote of Claude Lévi-Strauss, for example, that he was not primarily interested in the endless detail of myth collected by such comparativists as James Frazer or functionalists like Bronislaw Malinowski. Instead, he argued that "universals of human culture exist only at the level of structure never at the level of manifest fact." Leach's comparison of Lévi-Strauss with Freud clarifies H.D.'s place in a structuralist context: "Lévi-Strauss postulates that behind the manifest sense of the stories there must be another nonsense, a message wrapped up in code. In other words, he assumes with Freud that a myth is a kind of collective dream and that it should be capable of interpretation so as to reveal the hidden meaning." Both H.D. and Lévi-Strauss could use Freud's theory of the dream if they rejected Freud's concept of evolution. History "bodies forth in time—rather in the manner of a *tableau vivant* certain fundamental properties of the physical and psychical universe."[37] These "fundamental properties" imaged in the *tableau vivant* of the unconscious structure the lives of all people, at all periods of history, H.D. believed.

H.D.'s notion of time as protean incarnation and her search for the fundamental patterns embodied in myth are welded most completely in one of the last, long poems she wrote, *Vale Ave*. The poem begins with myth, which as Mircea Eliade wrote, is a "sacred history" that "takes place in primordial time, the fabled time of the 'beginnings.'"[38] Lucifer and Lilith are the primordial man and woman and the prototypical lovers in H.D.'s poem. Their nature, their relationship, and especially the effect of death upon them is explored in the poem through their incarnations or avatars in several varying epochs of history and culture. In a brief prose introduction to the poetic text, H.D. defined the subject of her epic as the mythic "formula" which is recreated through time: "The Lucifer-Lilith, Adam-Eve formula may be applied to all men and women, though here we follow the processus, through the characters of Elizabeth and Sir Walter, meeting and parting, *Vale Ave*, through time—specifically Late Rome, dynastic Egypt, legendary Provence, early seventeenth-century England and contemporary London" (*V.A.*, p. 2). To make her point that the Lucifer-Lilith formula is universal, H.D. relied not only on the structural parallels in the experience of the lovers, but also on a mixing of the motifs from one time period with those of another. The eagles of war, a recurring image in the story of Rome, appear in modern London:

> his eyes stared as his eyes had stared before,
> nothing was changed, where everything was different,
>
> the eagles and the legions, death and war,
> the bronze-edged sandal of a charioteer,
>
> London as always, it was just the same,
> the coast-guards and the signals and the fire (V.A., p. 2)

Further, the various women "remember" the lives of the other women and echo the poetic motifs associated with each time period. Lizeth the Elizabethan remembers the purple tent of Julia in Rome. Lizeth is not a reincarnation of the Roman Julia, however. Julia "remembers" the penance of the nun in Provence and the tower of Lizeth in London (V.A., pp. 15, 33).

H.D. referred to these memories that transcend chronological time as the "alchemy of memory," and she used the technique of poetic motif to create the fourth dimension of time, the "processus" of Lilith and Lucifer. Because this concept of time as "processus" and incarnation denies Freud's notion of progress, H.D.'s valuation and ultimate use of the past is quite different than Freud's. Since the essential pattern of the past is the same as the present, she did not denigrate the records of the past as superstitious, vague, or inadequate. Instead the visions of ancient peoples, the desires of the child, and the inspirations of the modern adult are woven together into a poetic tapestry of spiritual reality.

Although H.D. rejected Freud's bias against the traditions of the past, she did not see the past as a kind of Golden Age from which everything has degenerated, never to return to its formerly pure state. Critics who have seen H.D. as the poet seeking escape into the imagined purity of classical Greece implicitly assumed that H.D. conceived of time as a downward path of degeneration. But more accurately, H. D. looked to the past to see what will happen in the future. History is not a progression; it is a "processus" of re-created essences. Freud has a reputation among scholars for his "pessimism." But H.D.'s belief in the continuity of pattern ordering the multiplicity of historical event is actually a darker view than Freud's in some ways. Freud held on tentatively to his faith that the rational would control the irrational while H.D. saw no evolutionary change for the future. The logic of death and rebirth discovered in the *Trilogy* structured the past, orders the present, and will continue to shape human destiny in the future. An apocalyptic vision of history does not negate cataclysm; it merely incorporates it into a larger pattern that also includes regeneration.

H.D.'s use of the Atlantis myth as a thematic center in *The Flowering of the Rod* appears to posit an ideal time, a fantasy of perfection that once existed in a past that was superior to the present. But H.D. developed this variant myth of a Golden Age into a set of cycle images that not only affirms the unchanging "formulae" of time, but also reproduces her dialogue with Freud. The poet identifies her search with the flight of the wild geese, whose circling is likened to a "bee-line" toward resurrection (*T.*, p. 123). "Resurrection is a sense of direction," a spiral quest, not a static ideal. These "snow-geese of the Arctic circle" come to "hover / over the lost island, Atlantis," the "Golden Age," the "Paradise," the "islands of the Blest." They "find no rest / till they drop from the highest point of the spiral." But they continue the search because "they remember, they remember, as they sway and hover, / what once was . . . they have known bliss, / the fruit that satisfies" of the "golden-apple trees" (*T.*, pp. 119–20).

Their "circling" in "certain ecstasy" parallels the poet's quest for resurrection within the material hieroglyphics of war and death. This circling contrasts with the "foolish circling" of the materialists who deny the Paradise of the Hesperides because they cannot authenticate Atlantis through empirical "reality-testing":

> I would rather beat in the wind, crying to these others:
>
> yours is the more foolish circling,
> yours is the senseless wheeling
>
> round and round—yours has no reason—
> I am seeking heaven;
>
> yours has no vision,
> I see what is beneath me, what is above me,
>
> what men say is-not—I remember,
> I remember, I remember—you have forgot:
>
> you think, even before it is half-over,
> that your cycle is at an end,

> but you repeat your foolish circling—again, again, again;
> again, the steel sharpened on the stone;
>
> again, the pyramid of skulls;
>
> .   .   .   .
>
> only love is holy and love's ecstasy
>
> that turns and turns and turns about one centre,
> reckless, regardless, blind to reality,
>
> that knows the Islands of the Blest are there,
> for *many waters can not quench love's fire.* (T., pp. 121–22)

The others, the "you" in this passage, are the rationalist voices that are blinded to the higher realism of art, religion, dream, and vision throughout the *Trilogy*. They represent the "other" side in the debate between art and science that took place in the poet's mind throughout the *Trilogy*, that underlay H.D.'s interactions with Freud, and that motivated much modernist art. The poet "defeats" the voices of reason in part through ironic reversal of the words "senseless" and "reason." Throughout the *Trilogy*, the poet has confronted the accusations of the utilitarian materialists who believe that poetry in wartime is doubly without reason—being visionary, poetry is nonrational; being mere words, poetry provides no material goods for the war effort. The poet in turn accuses her materialist critics: "yours" is the "foolish," "senseless wheeling" without "reason," without purpose. To her critics, the "cycle" ends with the "skulls" of death because their literal eyes cannot perceive the resurrection half of the cycle. Seeing beyond material reality, however, the poet can move beyond the vortex to the "Islands of the Blest":

> I am the first or the last to renounce
> iron, steel, metal;
>
> I have gone forward,
> I have gone backward,
>
> I have gone onward from bronze and iron,
> into the Golden Age.   (T., p. 124)

By imagist metonymy, steel and iron are the Sword—the material fact of destruction which was earlier contrasted to the Dream, Vision, its "elder" in the sequence of creation. By association, the Sword is linked with the earlier "stages" of civilization which are identified by their predominant metal. The poet says that her "hovering" above the image of Atlantis can potentially usher in a Golden Age that leaves behind the imperfect, destructive metals of the Sword. Atlantis is not a literal Golden Age in the ancient past or the imagined future. Based like the unconscious on spatial and temporal metaphor, Atlantis is instead an image of the timeless, changeless, perfect realm of spiritual reality that manifests itself in time, in concrete existence. This transcendent realm is accessible to the poet because she does not close her eyes to "what men say is-not." The Golden Age is not a time period; it is a dimension of the mind. Exploring vision, dream, art, and myth, she "remembers" what the modern materialist world has "forgot."

Freud and H.D. vividly personify the opposing *Weltanschauungen* of Science and Art in the modern world. Yet Freud's perspective on the dimension of the mind that contained Atlantis was one of the most significant and clearly defined instances of the "other" voice in H.D.'s life. Paradoxically, the materialist who called religion a pitiable delusion succeeded in reaffirming H.D.'s beliefs; the scientist who saw art as pleasurable wish fulfillment stimulated the poetry of spiritual realism; the rationalist who denigrated the "primitive" past helped H.D. "remember" the ancient wisdom recorded in time.

But, given their fundamental differences, it nonetheless seems remarkable that in *Tribute to Freud* H.D. praised and mythologized someone with whom she so basically disagreed. Her admiration for his explorations into the hinterlands of the psyche would appear to be misplaced, or at least to be based on a profound misunderstanding of his work. How did she resolve the contradictions of their collaboration?

Undoubtedly, the many hours spent in quiet intimacy with the famous old man engendered strong feelings of loyalty. Certainly she was emotionally and intellectually dependent on him for the psychoanalytic process she imaged as the rebirth of Psyche. A psychoanalyst might further add that H.D. had never broken the stronghold of the "transference" after her analysis was interrupted. A misogynist like John Cournos, who scorned H.D. as an overemotional, silly woman, might say that she was above her head in the deep waters of abstract thought.[39]

But loyalty to Freud does not satisfactorily explain why, ten years later, she would write a book that is more an exploration of her experience of analysis than a defense of the great man himself. Read carefully, *Tribute to Freud* is neither nostalgic memoir nor "enchanting ornament," as Ernest Jones termed it (*T.F.*, p. viii). Transference also has limited relevance, for it can only explain why H.D. transformed Freud into a mythic figure; it leaves unanswered the question of why H.D. mythologized her experience in psychoanalysis as spiritual quest. As for the argument that H.D. must have misunderstood or misread Freud, it disappears in the light of evidence from de Rougement's *Love in the Western World* and her repeated testimony in *Tribute to Freud* that she was precisely aware of the philosophical bases of her argument with Freud.

In *Tribute to Freud*, H.D. indirectly posed a transcendence of their debate at the same time that she explored the polarity of their perspectives. Her portrait of Freud transforms his own self-image as a scientist and suggests that he often thought, acted, and judged in ways that were antithetical to the materialist philosophy he espoused. She examined his own modes of thought, his joy in the discoveries of his science, and his veneration for the past, and thereby concluded that he deserved a different place in the history of ideas than he gave himself.

Tribute to Freud, for example, uses Freud's own *Autobiographical Study* to dissolve his bias against intuitive, artistic modes of thought. After contrasting the great root of reason with the superior rootlets of intuitive thought, H.D. insisted that Freud's work was really the result of both modes of thought. She knew that Freud believed that he always worked by hypothesis and observation. But she used her own "intuitive imagination" to pose an alternative history of "when and how the Professor happened on the idea that led to his linking up neurotic states of megalomania with, in certain instances, fantasies of youth and childhood" (*T.F.*, pp. 76–77). When she asked her question of another analyst, he answered her "correctly and conventionally; he said that Freud did not happen upon ideas." He "repeated what already, of course, I was supposed to know": Freud's "whole established body of work was founded on accurate and accumulated data of scientific observation" (*T.F.*, p. 77). H.D. was aware of the components of empirical method and did not deny Freud that period of empirical testing in the development of his final theories. But she was sure that the initial thrust for experimentation came to

Freud from "a flash of inspiration" and "intuitive reasoning." She imagined for us "at what exact moment, and in what manner, there came that flash of inspiration, that thing that clicked, that sounded, that shouted in the inner Freud mind, heart or soul, *this is it*" (T.F., p. 77). Freud may have insisted in his writings that his theories emerged inductively from his data; but H.D. maintained that when his mind suddenly began to see a pattern, an order in a "disconnected sequence of apparently unrelated actions," he was thinking as the artist does when he or she bursts upon the *"theme"*: "Yes, musical terms do seem relevant to the curious and original process of the Professor's intuitive reasoning that led up to, developed, amplified, simplified the first astonishing findings of the young Viennese doctor" (T. F., pp. 78, 82).

In the context of her "imaginative intuitions" about how Freud's mind really worked, her various associations of him with the great artists of western tradition take on added significance. H.D. bridged the chasm between herself and Freud by portraying him as an artist whose medium was science.[40] Perhaps for symbolic emphasis, the first event in her relationship with Freud becomes the last event to be described in her tribute. It encapsulates her transformation of the man of science into the artist of vision. When she first entered his office, she turned silently to look at all his ancient art treasures. He said to her "a little sadly": " 'You are the only person who has ever come into this room and looked at the things in the room before looking at me' " (T.F., p. 98). Freud did not understand that H.D. was becoming directly acquainted with him by approaching him through his treasures. "He is at home here. He is part and parcel of these treasures" (T.F., p. 97). Before this reality, his materialist bias, ultimately negating the realm of the unconscious and vision it inspires, fades away.

H.D.'s revision of Freud's relationship to religion lies in her analysis of Freud's language. She understood that Freud would have to speak the language of science. The medium in which he worked was the matter-of-fact contemporary world which scoffed at religion and faith. Therefore, his discoveries about the depths of the human psyche would naturally "manifest" in a scientific "script" or "hieroglyphic": "The Professor spoke of this source of inspiration in terms of oil. It focused the abstraction, made it concrete, a modern business symbol. Although it was obvious that he was speaking of a vague, vast abstraction, he used a common, almost a commonplace, symbol for it. He used the idiom or slang of the counting-house, of Wall Street, a business man's concrete definite image for a successful run of luck or hope of success in the if-we-should-strike-oil or old-so-and-so-has-struck-oil-again manner" (*T.F.*, p. 83). What he called an oil well, those back "in the old days" would have said was "a well of living water" or " 'still waters' " (*T.F.*, p. 83). For all the apparent differences in the meaning of these terms, H.D. suggested that the essence of their message about the unconscious remains the same. H.D. translated Freud's thought into her own religious language just to demonstrate the simultaneous difference of form and similarity of content:

> It is difficult to imagine the Professor saying solemnly, "I drew by right of inheritance from the great source of inspiration of Israel and the Psalmist—Jeremiah, some might call me. I stumbled on a well of living water, the river of life. It ran muddy or bright. It was blocked by fallen logs, some petrified—and an accumulation of decaying leaves and branches. I saw the course of the river and how it ran, and I, personally, cleared away a bit of rubbish, so that at least a small section of the river should run clear. . . ." But no, that was not the Professor's way of talking. "I struck oil" suggests business enterprise. We visualize stark uprights and skeleton-like steel cages, like unfinished Eiffel Towers. (*T.F.*, p. 83)

H.D. was saying that she didn't expect the man who embodied the modern scientific age to come out talking like a Prophet of Israel, but nonetheless he is a prophet for his own times. Behind H.D.'s association of Freud with the Prophets of Israel lies neither transference nor miscomprehension, but instead her own protean view of history. Prophets of all times have been in touch with the well spring of inspiration, but the shape and message of each prophet has taken forms as various as the changing surface of history itself. Even while their language illustrates the particularity of their age, their capacity to express spiritual reality has remained constant. H.D.'s continual identification of Freud with the great thinkers and artists of all times represents her insistence that he be lifted out of the limitations of a single time and be placed in the context of all history. In that broad perspective, Freud does for modern times what the prophets did for Israel, Shakespeare for the Elizabethans, and Sophocles for the Greeks.

Just as H.D. used her belief in the superiority of intuitive vision to transform Freud into an artist, so she applied her concept of history to resolve their conflict. Although many of her ideas about time and reality continued to develop in dialectical opposition to Freud, she ultimately insisted on placing his discoveries within her own framework of assumptions and not those of a materialist psychology. As she transformed the scientist into the artist and prophet, she was reassessing the value of his work and suggesting that she understood its implications better than he himself did. In so doing, H.D. accomplished what some later admirers and interpreters of Freud have also done. Writers like Herbert Marcuse, Norman O. Brown, and Geza Roheim, as well as H.D., have ignored Freud's value judgments reflecting his Victorian context, have developed the implications of Freud's explorations further than he could go, and thereby have given him a different place in the history of ideas than he would have given himself.

H.D.'s intuitive reasoning and impressionistic style is a different "language" from the conceptual argument of Marcuse, Brown, and Roheim. But poet, philosopher, anthropologist, and critic alike took a similar direction in their reading of Freud: all ignored Freud's negative judgment against the unconscious, his sympathy with the ego and the status quo (external reality), and his glorification of scientific achievements in the west. They all suggested instead that Freud's work had more radical implications. Marcuse and Brown argued that by releasing the energy of the unconscious with his discoveries, Freud had pointed the way to the liberation of the individual from the confines of an oppressive civilization which had developed in the first place out of the repression of the id.[41] While H.D. never dealt with the overtly political dimension of Freud's work, she too saw the liberating and inspirational potential of a recovered unconscious. Roheim, while loyal to Freud, developed the universalist implications of Freud's work as he studied "primitive" peoples and found their lives and culture in no way inferior to western, white civilization. Similarly, H.D. expanded Freud's theory of the universality of the unconscious into her own belief that all people are one and that therefore the teachings of ancient peoples are as wise today as they were before.

Tribute to Freud presents a reassessment of Freud the man, as well as the implications of his theories. When she suggested that his genius operated first through intuition or that his treasured art collection revealed more of his nature than his aesthetic theories, she implied the existence of contradictions beneath the surface of his avowed identity as empirical scientist. In his "Introduction" to Freud's *Beyond the Pleasure Principle*, Gregory Zilboorg argued that many have been deceived by the "aggressive, trenchant, emphatic tone of his writings, which seem to be full of conviction and devoid of doubt." In reality, Zilboorg believed, Freud was drawn back and forth in a struggle of "heroic proportions" between his deep attractions for science and mysticism, material fact and artistic vision:

> As one studies Freud, one can develop the strong suspicion that he was more attracted by many mystics than by physico-chemical hypotheses [in spite of his "faith" the "whole complexity of human reactions . . . could be reduced to some . . . physico-chemical reactions"], and that he struggled with all the might of his great mind against openly giving in to the attraction of the mystical aspects of human life. In other words, the man . . . seems throughout this span of time [between his article on Michelangelo's *Moses* and *Moses and Monotheism*] to have been preoccupied with the greatness of human intuitions and the universality of human strivings not only to solve but to participate in the mysteries of life.[42]

In other words, Freud was neither materialist nor mystic, neither scientist nor artist in some continuous, static way. Instead, his own psyche was engaged in a dynamic dialogue or interplay of opposing voices. H.D.'s portrait of the prophet-scientist is consistent with Zilboorg's analysis. A man of paradoxes, Freud carried on internally the debate between art and science that H.D. characterized as the "argument implicit in our very bones." And as H.D. explored the world of her own family with Freud, she discovered the same debate in her own psyche, a dialogue she literally lived through as a child growing up with a mother who represented art and a father who embodied science. H.D.'s transcendental argument with Freud led her ultimately back down to the concrete, personal world of the family and her own struggles to establish her destiny as a woman artist.

5

"The Professor Was Not Always Right"

WOMAN AND MAN IN CONFLICT

"I WAS RATHER annoyed with the Professor in one of his volumes. He said (as I remember) that women did not creatively amount to anything or amount to much, unless they had a male counterpart or a male companion from whom they drew their inspiration. Perhaps he is right and my dream of 'salting' my typewriter with the tell-tale transference symbol is further proof of his infallibility," says H.D.'s journal entry for March 10, 1933, during the period when she was seeing Freud daily (T.F., p. 149).

This brief statement constitutes H.D.'s only direct and explicit comment on Freud's theories about women among her published writings. *Tribute to Freud* openly addresses H.D.'s confrontation with Freud about immortality, but on the subject of the "woman question" her memoir is largely silent. This silence is even more strikingly significant in the light of her letters to Bryher from this period and the poem about Freud that she never published. Their discussions frequently revolved around her identity as a woman, and her poem "The Master" expresses bluntly not only her adulation of Freud as the wise oracle, but also the anger absent from her published texts: "I was angry with the old man / with his talk of the man-strength, / I was angry with his mystery, his mysteries, / I argued till day-break."[1]

This poem, as well as H.D.'s comment on Freud's ideas about female creativity, expresses a disagreement with "the old man" that had an immediate and concrete relevance to her identity as a woman artist. It also poses a dilemma concerning her relationship with him that is

even more puzzling than their confrontations over such "transcendental issues" as the nature of reality, perception, and time. Freud's theories of psychosexual development are explicitly based on the premise
that male physiology and psychology constitute the human norm,
while female physiology and psychology embody the deviant and
deficient. He believed that sex roles reflect the biologically determined
differences between men and women and that civilization has largely
been the accomplishment of men. Their fundamental disagreement
about standard philosophical issues can be viewed as a dialogue between colleagues, a modern form of a very old debate where both
"sides" rest on centuries of tradition. But Freud's theories about wom-
en implicitly challenged the very legitimacy of H.D.'s claim to be an
artist. How then could a woman find new strength and direction for
her identity as artist from a guide who asserted with all the weight
of science and objectivity that female anatomy requires a specifically
feminine destiny?

The paradox is by no means easy to resolve. Complicated by the
infrequency with which H.D.'s journals and memoirs directly address
the issue, the complex process by which she reshaped Freud's ideas on
women to create an authentic female voice in her poetry is largely
hidden. Ultimately her poetry itself is the richest source for understanding the metamorphosis she wrought. But discussion of the female
voice in her poetry will be more soundly based if we examine the psychological workshop in which H.D. began to construct the fusion
of selves evident in her epic poems. *Tribute to Freud*, in particular the
less censored "Advent," provides many clues to the nature of their
discussions about women's identity and destiny. They included not
only his diagnosis of her "symptoms," but also his theories about
femininity, bisexuality, and lesbianism. The mother-daughter relationship constituted the central theme of their discussions, particularly as
H.D.'s feelings about her mother deeply influenced her sexuality, her
adult relationships, her visionary experiences, and her artistic destiny.
This chapter will clarify the theoretical roots of their discussions, il-
lustrate the impact of these ideas on her poetry, and then demonstrate the principles by which H.D. bridged their differences.

Freud did not write extensively about the psychology of women,
and what he did write frequently contained qualifications referring to
the "incomplete and fragmentary nature" of psychoanalytic knowledge on the subject of women.[2] Nonetheless, his theory of the psycho-

sexual development of women was well formulated by the late twenties and early thirties when his influence on H.D. was so enormous. Freud believed that the passage of boys and girls through the oral, anal, and phallic stages of "normal" psychosexual development is essentially similar. All infants begin life without sexual differentiation, equally motivated in their search for pleasure. Using the male as the model for the human, Freud wrote that the little girl is in all respects "a little man," just as intelligent, active, aggressive, and self-sufficient as a little boy.[3] During the phallic phase, when sexual pleasure is localized in the genitals, both the girl and the boy regard their mother with love and sexual desire; they achieve sexual gratification mainly through masturbation—the boy with his penis and the girl with her "penis substitute," the clitoris.

This intense love for the mother is interrupted, Freud believed, by the traumatic discovery of anatomical sex differences. Both boys and girls experience a "castration complex," but the nature of their psychological development is no longer the same. For boys, the sight of women's genitals introduces the notion that they too could be "castrated." Their fear of castration leads them to repress their love for the mother and thereby ends the Oedipus complex. For girls, Freud argued, the sight of male genitals inflicts a severe blow to their self-image. Girls "feel seriously wronged, often declare that they want to 'have something like it too,' and fall victim to 'envy for the penis.'" The girl's castration complex is not fear of what *might* happen to her, but a discovery of what *has* happened, in Freud's view, and her response to it determines the course of her subsequent development: "The discovery that she is castrated is a turning-point in a girl's growth. Three possible lines of development start from it: one leads to sexual inhibition or to neurosis, the second to change of character in the sense of a masculinity complex, the third, finally to normal femininity."[4] The neurotic woman is so traumatized by her discovery as a child that severe repression leads to sexual inhibition in adulthood. The girl enroute to "normal femininity" holds her mother responsible for the lack of a penis and angrily abandons her as a love object: "The turning away from the mother is accompanied by hostility; the attachment to the mother ends in hate." Her castration complex does not destroy the Oedipus complex; it creates it. Rejection of her mother allows her to transfer her attachment to her father, a love that serves as a prototype for her future relationships with men. Seeking ways to "compensate herself for the [anatomical] defect," the girl who will exhibit "a normal feminine attitude" begins to adopt a passive attitude in relation to men and sublimates her desire for a penis into the "most powerful feminine wish," the longing for a baby, "quite especially so if the baby is a little boy who brings the longed for penis with him." The active, even aggressive behavior of her "masculine phase" disappears as "passivity takes the upper hand." After puberty, the "normal" woman's erotic center is transferred from the clitoris to the "truly feminine vagina."[5]

The third response to castration trauma outlined by Freud is the development of the "masculine" woman whose "powerful masculinity-complex" does not allow her to abandon her envy of the penis, to accept a passive role in relation to men, or in "extreme" cases to regard men as love objects. The drive of the "masculine" woman to compete with men in the public sphere originates in her unconscious wish for a penis and her refusal to accept her biologically determined destiny.

"Masculine" and "feminine" women are alike in their self-mortification, alike even in their hostility to their non-phallic mothers, but they are profoundly antithetical in subsequent psychological development. The "feminine" girl, according to Freud, passes safely into the "haven" of the Oedipus complex to sublimate her desire for a penis into the "feminine" wish for a child. But the "masculine" woman sublimates her envy into her desire for achievement in a "masculine vocation." Her inability to accept a passive mode of being greatly inhibits her capacity for heterosexual fulfillment, and instead of directing her love first toward her father and later toward other men, she frequently regresses to her pre-Oedipal, erotic attachment to her mother.

Lesbianism represents an "extreme" development of this "regression" since the erotic love for women reproduces the early mother-daughter relationship. Freud believed that women who "fell victim to homosexuality" had not successfully transferred their affection from their mother to their father during their passage through the Oedipus complex or the frequent revival of Oedipal feelings during puberty. Instead of rejecting their mothers, lesbians experience "mother-fixation," choosing women as "love objects" who could substitute for the mother they still desire at an unconscious level. As Freud described the "mother-fixation" in his "The Psychogenesis of a Case of Homosexuality in a Woman," the lesbian's search for mother-figures includes a component of penis envy and the strong, unconscious desire to be a boy. Buried in the unconscious, a strong "masculinity-complex" and "mother-fixation" go hand in hand to create the adult lesbian. Freud may even have believed these related complexes to be the psychosexual origin of feminism; for he wrote about the young lesbian in his study:

> A spirited girl, always ready to fight, she was not at all prepared to be second to her slightly older brother; after inspecting his genital organs she had developed a pronounced envy of the penis, and the thoughts derived from this envy still continued to fill her mind. She was in fact a feminist; she felt it to be unjust that girls should not enjoy the same freedom as boys, and rebelled against the lot of women in general. . . . the girl's behavior, as described above [homosexual pursuit of women], was exactly what would follow from the combined effect in a person with a strong mother-fixation of the two influences of her mother's indifference [toward her after birth of a son] and of her comparison of her genital organs with her brothers.[6]

As distinct as the "masculine" and "feminine" women are in Freud's schema, their development of selfhood depends equally, though differently, on a negation of femaleness and an implicit acceptance of women's inherent inferiority to man. Self-hatred and misogyny are inescapably central to the female psyche as Freud described it. Whether they develop into "masculine" or "feminine" women, young girls feel betrayed by their "castrated" mothers and come to hate them—first because their mothers were unveiled as inadequate and secondly because their mothers had not given their daughters the "far superior equipment" of male anatomy. Rejection of their mothers as women extends outward to a rejection of all women and inward to a hatred of their own femaleness. The "feminine" woman differs from the "masculine" woman primarily in her resignation to her own inferiority and her consequent search to attach herself to a man who has the "superior equipment" that she lacks. The "masculine" woman accepts the inferiority of castration, but at an unconscious level refuses to believe that she does not have or cannot acquire a penis. The very envy of men that motivates her aggressive competition with them begins in a rejection of her own womanhood. If she becomes a lesbian, even her love for women is based on a denial of her self as woman; for the lesbian's "object choice" represents her regression to the pre-Oedipal, masculine phase when she loved her "phallic" mother—that is, the mother as she appeared to the daughter before the "fact" of castration had been discovered.

In the context of his own historical era, Freud's theory of psychosexual development for women and men must surely be credited with a pioneering brilliance that contained liberating implications, particularly in the area of sexuality. Emerging as he did out of a nineteenth-century cultural tradition whose medical and moral "experts" described sexual response in adult women as abnormal, Freud's discussions of female sexuality opened the door for explorations that ultimately led far beyond his initial contribution. In addition, Freud's theory accomplished a fundamentally important "naming" of such frequently overlooked psychic phenomena as female envy and anger with men, hostility between mother and daughter, and women's passive identification with the active achievements of husbands and sons. Among those writing about Freud's contributions to an understanding of women, there has always been considerable disagreement on a final evaluation. However, attack has characteristically fueled the fires of support, even among feminist writers.[7]

The central controversy revolves around an issue crucial to *all* H.D.'s interactions with Freud: the attempt to determine what evaluative framework, if any, lies encoded in Freud's theories. When Freud used words such as "normal," "abnormal," "inversion," "deviation," or "regression," was he prescribing a norm of healthy adult behavior, a psychological goal toward which all right-minded people should direct themselves? If so, on what grounds did he justify his norms— ethical, political, psychological, biological? As demonstrated in chapter 4, Freud's materialist epistemology clearly determined a set of values that allowed him to judge such creations of the unconscious as religion or art as inferior forms of knowledge. Because of Freud's epistemological presuppositions, the process of influence necessarily involved the abandonment of his negative evaluative framework so that his discoveries about the unconscious could nourish a new integration of the unconscious and conscious minds. Were parallel values operating in his hypotheses about psychosexual development? And did the process of influence in H.D.'s case require a negation of those values in order for his ideas to permeate her identity as artist and woman?

Juliet Mitchell has argued, unpersuasively, I think, that Freud's theories were scientific descriptions of psychological development within a patriarchal society. According to Mitchell, Freud's discussions of the "normal" and "abnormal" are simply the descriptions of an objective observer of society as it exists, not the normative prescriptions of a value-laden perspective.[8] In contrast, I would argue that Mitchell's approach, first developed in any case by Karen Horney, *may* point the way to a useful adaptation of Freud's theories, but as a reading of Freud himself, it represents a serious distortion of his work. Understanding the process of influence—in particular, Freud's influence on a creative woman in search of authentic identity—requires not only a careful reading of Freud, but also an unflinching confrontation with the prejudice of the brilliant and kind-hearted pioneer of modern psychology.

The prescriptive norms encoded in Freud's theories are founded on the way he related nature and culture to the psychological development of women and men. His "description" of psychological sex differences should be recognized as a theory of innate female inferiority based ultimately on biology. Mitchell is quite correct in pointing out Freud's occasional references to the power of cultural conditioning in the creation of sex differences.[9] But such statements only acted as qualifications of his theory of psychosexual development; the theory itself did not take cultural conditioning into account. In his expositions of his theory, Freud returned repeatedly to the theme of an ultimate biological, *not* cultural, determinism. Culture helps to accomplish what biology determines, but psychological sex differences originate in the material "facts" of physiology. "After all," he wrote, "the anatomical distinction (between the sexes) must express itself in psychical consequences."[10] Anatomy controls the antithetical nature of the castration complex for boys and girls, and this complex in turn is the single most "specific factor" in the different psychology of men and women.

Freud basically regarded culture as an extension of nature in the psychosexual development of women and men. Anatomy is the "bedrock" of the psyche and determines a range of psychological differences that invalidate the claims of feminists: "The feminist demand for equal rights between the sexes does not carry far here; the morphological difference must express itself in differences in the development of the mind. 'Anatomy is Destiny,' to vary a saying of Napoleon's."[11] Socialization accomplishes what has been biologically prescribed, a process evident in Freud's description of passivity in the girl who achieves the "normal feminine attitude": "The suppression of women's aggressiveness which is *prescribed for them con-stitutionally* and *imposed on them socially* favours the development of powerful masochistic impulses."[12] According to his own evaluation, the central question his theory posed about women is this: "how does a girl pass from her mother to an attachment to her father? or in other words, how does she pass from her masculine phase to the feminine one to which she is biologically destined?"[13]

Freud warned that "we must beware in this of underestimating the influence of social customs, which similarly force women into passive situations," but he never seriously examined the "influence of social customs" as a controlling force in the genesis of "normal" gender identities and roles. His prescriptive concept of normality does not reflect ethical or social norms, but rather emerges from an evaluative schema based upon a biological norm. Or, to be precise, Freud's biological norm rests upon his *perception* of anatomy. From his androcentric perspective, male anatomy embodies the human norm, and according to its standard, the female body is inherently deficient. The clitoris is not a sexual organ in its own right; it is a "penis equivalent" whose small size makes it a "stunted penis" in Freud's view. Astoundingly enough for a man who considered himself to be an empirical scientist basing his theories on "nothing but observed facts," Freud wrote about female castration as a *fact* of external reality.[14] Freud's materialist epistemology reinforced his belief that the superiority he perceived in male physiology was a "fact" of nature, not a product of culture.

The biological base Freud gave to his concept of normality established the evaluative context for his related theories of psychological bisexuality and homosexuality. Throughout his long career, Freud repeatedly warned against the simplistic equation of masculinity with men and femininity with women. He premised his theory of psychosexual development on a belief in the psychologically bisexual or androgynous nature of each individual psyche. As he wrote in the twenties, "all human individuals, as a result of their bisexual disposition and of cross-inheritance, combine in themselves both masculine and feminine characteristics, so that pure masculinity and femininity remain theoretical constructions of uncertain content."[15] But Freud's description of psychological bisexuality did not validate nourishment of relatively equal amounts of masculinity and femininity in the individual human psyche—a state of mind that many feminists today call "androgynous" and associate with mental health, flexibility, and creativity.[16] In fact, his theories invalidate such psychic bisexuality in adults by relating its existence to unresolved castration complexes, neurosis, and/or homosexuality—all signs to Freud of *abnormal* psychosexual development. While he did not equate masculinity with men or femininity with women, he *did* associate masculinity and its opposite, femininity, with men and women who experience "normal" development. Psychological bisexuality never completely disappears, but in the "normal" adult, either masculine or feminine behavior predominates. Biological destiny is most completely fulfilled when the androgynous child becomes the masculine man or the feminine woman. For women, this destiny involves the repression of aggressive behavior in relation to men and acceptance of passive "aims"; for men, it involves the repression of passive behavior in relation to men and the pursuit of active "aims." Failure of such repression to operate results in the psychologically bisexual adult. The presence of strong masculine and feminine components in an individual indicated to Freud the likelihood of neurotic symptoms and/or homosexuality. Freud's insistence on the bisexual nature of all psyches proved liberating to people like H.D. who could not limit themselves to the half life of either masculinity or femininity. But Freud's value-laden perspective did not legitimate such transcendence of traditional gender identities and sex roles.

Nor did his discussions of homosexuality affirm the normality or desirability of homosexuality. Unlike so much of the psychiatric establishment that followed him, Freud did not describe all homosexuality as mental illness; nor did he believe that psychoanalysis could or should regularly reverse a homosexual "object choice" to a heterosexual one. Furthermore, Freud did not accept the "trapped-soul" theories of homosexuality prevalent among such writers as Havelock Ellis and illustrated by such books as Bryher's *Two Selves* and Radclyffe Hall's *The Well of Loneliness*. Nor did he agree with the theory that homosexuality was causally connected with either physical or psychical hermaphroditism—the so-called "third sex" theory of homosexuality. Freud's radical contribution to psychology was in fact the assertion that homosexuality is a psychic component of *all* human beings; he argued that the libido of everyone "normally oscillates between male and female objects."[17] However, Freud's relatively nonjudgmental attitude toward homosexuality and his theory of its universality should not be confused with a value-free perspective. Again, his concept of a biologically based norm is central. He believed that in "normal" adults, homosexual "object choice" exists primarily at an unconscious level. Developing the word "inversion" commonly used for homosexuality in his day, Freud saw homosexuality as a literal "inversion" of heterosexual object choice: homosexuals repressed their heterosexual desires and acted out on a conscious level the "inverted" desires that remain buried in the unconscious of heterosexuals. The cause of such "inversion," he believed, was a "disturbance" in "normal development" occurring during one or more of the stages of psychosexual development. Words such as "disturbance," "aberration," "deviance," and "inversion" frequently appear in Freud's description of homosexuality and do not describe sexual preference from an objective point of view. Instead, such words emerge from a perspective that assumes heterosexuality to be the human norm while all other forms of sexual expression are different, deviant, and implicitly inferior. Unlike most homophobic attacks on homosexuality, Freud's normative presuppositions are not ethical, religious, or even medical in nature. Rather, he viewed homosexuality as aberrant because it does not allow for the fulfillment of what he assumed to be a given of external reality: the biological destiny prescribed by the "anatomical distinction between the sexes."

Freud's materialist epistemology and consequent belief in his own objectivity blinded him to the related androcentric and heterocentric biases of his work. He believed that he was merely describing what nature had prescribed rather than what culture has wrought. His nascent sociobiology served—and still serves—to rationalize the ideology and institutions of patriarchy in both public and private spheres. Freud was well aware of feminist critiques of his work, but he maintained till the end that "we must not allow ourselves to be deflected from such conclusions [the ethical and intellectual inferiority of women] by the denial of feminists, who are anxious to force us to regard the two sexes as completely equal in position and worth."[18]

Combined with these biases, Freud's belief in his own objectivity and in the self-evident validity of the "facts" he observed made him dangerous to any woman, particularly any lesbian woman, who came to him for guidance in her quest for authentic womanhood. If H.D. had not prided herself on her "difference," if she had not so clearly enjoyed sparring with the famous old man, she might have been highly vulnerable to internalizing Freud's negative image of woman's nature and potential. Although Freud apparently sidestepped much of the technical jargon of psychoanalysis in his sessions with H.D., her account of analysis reveals the omnipresence of his theory of psychosexual development in their discussions. H.D. wrote that she especially desired Freud's help in deciphering the occult, visionary experiences she had had in the years immediately following her breakdown in 1919—the writing on the wall in Corfu; the hallucinations of Mr. Van Eck on the boat to Greece; and the feeling of being suspended in a "bell-jar" (*T.F.*, pp. 39–56, 153–62, 168, 176). Freud considered these experiences to be "dangerous symptoms" of neurosis reflecting problems H.D. had during childhood in completing the difficult route to "normal" femininity. Freud's comments on these symptoms and her dreams as they are reported by H.D. center on her repressed feelings about her mother, her father, and her resistance to acceptance of a feminine destiny.

As H.D. repeatedly wrote, Freud translated her occult experiences as an unresolved attachment to her mother, Helen Wolle Doolittle (*T. F.*, pp. 17, 30, 33, 37, 41, 49, 123, 136, 176, 184). Paralleling what he had written about religious experience in general, Freud concluded that H.D. longed to fuse with her mother, to recreate the early period in infancy when the ego is as yet undifferentiated and cannot distinguish itself from the mother. As H.D. herself wrote in remembering her mother, "But one can never get near enough, or if one gets near, it is because one has measles or scarlet fever. *If* one could stay near her always, there would be no break in consciousness" (*T.F.*, p. 33). The experience of "no break in consciousness" between subject and object is a regression to infantile desire for union with her mother, in Freud's view. Her Scilly Isles experience—"the transcendental feeling of the two globes or the two half-globes enclosing me"—was a form of "prenatal fantasy" (*T.F.*, p. 168). Her trip to Greece (Hellas) in 1920 with Bryher was a projection of her wish to find her mother (Helen) (*T.F.*, p. 44). The oracle of Delphi which figures so centrally in the writing on the wall was the "main objective" of her journey in Greece because it is the shrine of Helios, again associated with Hellas and Helen (*T.F.*, p. 49). The writing on the wall was, or so "the Professor said, . . . really a sort of display or entertainment for my *mother*" (*T.F.*, p. 176). H.D. wrote Bryher that Freud believed such displays, as well as her interest in acting, provided "a clue to a lot of my inhibitions about my writing" (26 March 1933). Part of the "cure" for her writer's block in the thirties was to bring to consciousness her "mother-fix," as H.D. casually referred to it in her letters to Bryher (23 March 1933; 25 March 1933). Full of the excitement of discovery, H.D. told Bryher about Freud's diagnosis of her "special kind of fixation": "F. says mine is absolutely FIRST layer, I got stuck at the earliest pre-OE stage, and 'back to the womb' seems to be my only solution. Hence islands, sea, Greek primitives and so on. It's all too, too wonder-making" (23 March 1933).

Both Freud and H.D. linked Bryher with Helen Wolle, thereby suggesting that H.D.'s longing for her mother was projected onto her relationship with Bryher. Bryher was not only present during H.D.'s psychic experiences at Corfu and the Scilly Isles, but she was also necessary to the completion of the writing on the wall. H.D. wrote that Bryher's friendship in Greece so soon after her illness and breakdown "seemed to have adjusted me to normal conditions of life. Freud qualified, 'Not normal, so much as ideal' " (T.F., p. 168). He implied, I believe, that H.D.'s happiness with Bryher was based on a re-creation of a mother-child relationship. H.D.'s own record of dreams she discussed with Freud reinforces the connection they made between Bryher and Helen Wolle. In one dream, for example, H.D. defended a beautiful box with great "vehemence" and "passion" because it was a present from her mother. Actually, H.D. recalled with Freud, Bryher had given her that jewel box in Florence (T.F., p. 165).[19]

Since Vienna was the city where Helen Wolle spent her honeymoon, Freud believed that H.D. came to see him in Vienna to find her mother (T.F., p. 17). From Freud's point of view, he was the mother in transference with H.D. (T.F., pp. 146–47). As he told H.D., he was somewhat uncomfortable in this role: "I do not like to be the mother in transference—it always surprises and shocks me a little. I feel so very masculine" (T.F., pp. 146–47). H.D., on the other hand, associated him more frequently with her father, grandfather, and D.H. Lawrence (T.F., pp. 116, 124–25, 127–28, 140–44). In her letters to Bryher, her code name for Freud became "Papa" very shortly after analysis began. Even if H.D. and Freud differed in their analysis of transference, H.D.'s account strongly suggests that Freud made her relationship with her mother the central theme of analysis. Freud explicitly related these discussions of her desire for her mother to his theory of the young girl's psychosexual development. H.D. recalled:

"The Professor speaks of the mother-layer of fixation being the same in girls and boys, but the girl usually transfers her affection or (if it happens) her fixation to her father. Not always. . . . The Professor went on about the growth of psychoanalysis and how mistakes were made in the beginning, as it was not sufficiently understood that the girl did not invariably transfer her emotions to her father" (*T.F.*, p. 175).

Interwoven with H.D.'s unconscious search for her mother were, in Freud's view, a strong desire to be a boy and an emotional detachment from her father. H.D. recalled: "The Professor said I had not made the conventional transference from mother to father, as is usual with a girl at adolescence. He said he thought my father was a cold man" (*T.F.*, p. 136). Freud apparently indicated to H.D. that she had not as a child abandoned her erotic love for her mother and attached herself to her father as "normal" progress through the Oedipus complex prescribes. As the last piece of the psychological puzzle, Freud found evidence of H.D.'s desire to be a boy in the dreams she reported to him. In the luminous Princess dream Freud saw a "mother-symbol" and H.D.'s megalomaniac desire to be a boy—that is, to be important in her mother's eyes: "But the Professor insisted I myself wanted to be Moses; not only did I want to be a boy but I wanted to be a hero" (*T.F.*, p. 120).

To use the language of Freud's own essays on female psychology, Freud probably regarded H.D.'s "symptoms" and dreams as signs of regression to the pre-Oedipal, "masculine" phase of a girl's psychosexual development. Within the context of Freud's theories, H.D.'s unconscious desire to be a boy and her strong attachment to her mother reflected her failure to resolve her castration complex by falling in love with her father and sublimating her desire for a penis into the wish of having his baby. The combination of "mother-complex" and "masculinity complex" in Freud's comments on H.D. makes his diagnosis of her symptoms strikingly similar to what he wrote about the young lesbian in "The Psychogenesis of a Case of Homosexuality in a Woman." But precisely what discussions of H.D.'s sexuality took place in Freud's office is not clear from *Tribute to Freud*. As an illustration of his belief that all neurosis contains unconscious homosexual desires, Freud may have been telling H.D. that her "symptoms" indicated *latent* lesbian attachments that inhibited her conscious heterosexual experiences. Or paralleling his analysis of the young lesbian in his essay, Freud may have told H.D. that Gregg and Bryher were her "mother substitutes" and that her relationships with women reflected her "deviance" from "normal" development and repression of heterosexual object choice. In either case, however, Freud did not see H.D. as a woman who had achieved the "normal feminine attitude" in relation to men. What direction Freud sought for H.D. in analysis is not fully clear from *Tribute to Freud*. Did he hope to bring her unconscious desires to consciousness so that she could transfer affection from women to men? Did he attempt to nourish the development of femininity so that she could fulfill the destiny to which he believed women are biologically determined? What value judgments did he make or avoid making about a woman who had strong lesbian feelings, who dedicated her life to a form of creation that Freud considered a masculine province?

"Advent" itself provides some evidence that Freud's biological determinism hurt H.D. in at least one instance. His insistence that she could never have been "biologically happy" with Gregg probably sounded like a rejection to H.D. (*T.F.*, p. 152). Although Freud generally held out little hope for changing homosexuality through psychoanalysis, he did think there was some chance of "success" for patients whose sexual orientation had been bisexual.[20] H.D.'s bisexual behavior certainly placed her in this category, and Freud may have hoped to encourage H.D. to abandon her attachment to women who functioned as her mother substitutes. But there is no evidence to suggest that Freud tried to separate H.D. from Bryher. In looking at a photograph of Bryher, he did say that "she is *only* a boy" and that she looked so " 'decisive' and 'unyielding,' " but he found her letters " 'very kind, very pliable,' " (*T.F.*, p. 170). At one point, he urged H.D. to "use her influence" on Bryher "to better advantage" to make Bryher, who wanted to fight Hitler, "less warlike."[21] When Freud expressed his delight at the prospect of seeing Bryher, H.D. felt "very happy" (*T.F.*, p. 170). Freud's friendship with both women, and with Perdita as well, perhaps signalled a kind of acceptance that erased the rejection implicit in his comment about Gregg.

Although Freud's androcentric and heterocentric perspective must have been evident in his sessions with H.D., I suspect that H.D.'s "abnormal" womanhood would not in itself have concerned him. Freud did not, it should be remembered, consider all "masculine" women and lesbians to be neurotic. What appeared dangerous to him were H.D.'s "symptoms," the daytime hallucinations that revealed the power he believed H.D.'s unconscious, unresolved complexes had to impinge on her consciousness and weaken her ego's ties to external reality. From his perspective, H.D.'s infantile attachment to her mother not only interfered with her achievement of "normal" womanhood, but, more importantly, it was threatening her ego's ability to distinguish between hallucination and reality. Freud's general purpose in therapy, he had written elsewhere, was to strengthen the ego by weakening the hold of unconscious desires on the rational self. In the context of H.D.'s analysis, he would help her recover and interpret the fragments of her dreams and visions so that the neurotic symptoms rooted in desire for union with her mother would disappear.

H.D., however, wanted access to the unconscious not to control it, but to benefit from its inspiration and revelation. The process of influence that characterized H.D.'s interactions with Freud in the formulation of her religious aesthetic continued to operate in her search for authentic womanhood through psychoanalysis. The key to Freud's influence on H.D.'s identity as woman-artist was her fundamental disagreement with his evaluative framework. Perhaps her arguments with Freud over "transcendental issues" helped to establish the pattern of disagreement upon which her survival, as a woman in analysis with a man who believed in female inferiority, ultimately depended. Whatever the cause, H.D. was able to disregard the prescriptions for "normal" femininity implicit in Freud's general theory of female development. Self-hatred is a crippling starting point for any artist. To avoid it, H.D. had to counter Freud's belief that women were a deficient form of human being who could achieve biological fulfillment only by recognizing the inferiority of their anatomy, experiencing a "healthy" hostility toward their mothers, and attaching themselves to a man who embodies the superiority they envy. Rejection of his norms, rooted in his biased perception of physiology, freed H.D. to bypass the hatred of female anatomy and consequent hostility to women which Freud regarded as the motivating factor in the psyches of all women. Denial of these norms allowed her to dismiss the negative value judgments encoded in his discussion of psychic bisexuality or homosexuality in adults as a "regression" to pre-Oedipal stages of individual and historical development. For a woman whose art simultaneously developed positive female symbols and placed her as poet in the heroic mold traditionally reserved for male questors, such denials were essential.

H.D.'s philosophic idealism proved invaluable as a reinforcement in the development of her capacity to disagree with Freud's value-laden perspective on women. Her general insistence on the priority of psychic reality over material reality made it easier for her to deny Freud's belief that the superiority of men resided ultimately in nature, in the material facts of physiology. Freud's materialist epistemology led him to equate his androcentric perspective with objective truth because he believed that the inferiority he perceived exists as fact in the external reality beyond consciousness. H.D.'s idealist epistemology, on the other hand, allowed her to counter such perceptions with her own alternative perspective precisely because she believed that truth exists in the subjective realm of a spiritual reality created through consciousness.

The role H.D.'s epistemology played in freeing her from Freud's androcentrism and misogyny is not idiosyncratic, but rather a characteristic tendency of all groups of people who differ from the dominant culture because of their sex, race, ethnic heritage, age, religion, sexual preference, class, disability—and all the additional forms of "otherness" that have yet to be named. People who live on the fringes of society experience an epistemological imperative to philosophic idealism. Many, of course, internalize the values of the powerful mainstream, and learn to perceive their own difference through the negative perspectives of the dominant ethos. But those rebellious ones in search of authenticity have a stake in denying the ultimate reality of the status quo. Their survival depends on a belief that the oppressive world of external reality has been created by culture, not determined by the objective forces of nature. A belief in the power of the human mind to define the ultimate realities liberates the imagination of oppressed peoples to pose alternatives to the structures of the status quo. The starting point of freedom is the mind's capacity to dream.[22]

Within Freud's epistemological system, the healthy ego equates the existing world with the external reality to which it must adjust according to the demands of the reality principle. Unconscious desires that pose alternatives to external reality are potentially a threat to the ego when they begin to control conscious behavior through "symptoms." Within H.D.'s epistemological system, the woman's ego is confined by external reality and must seek the world of the dream in its search for authenticity. For H.D., the unconscious is the wellspring of truth. What this meant for her as a woman was that she could turn to the unconscious in her search for alternatives to the misogynist ideologies of the dominant culture. Within this context, Freud's specific diagnosis of her "mother-fixation" stimulated her to explore her feelings about her mother, to forge a strong bond of identification with her mother, and to connect her personal experience with the universal mother-symbols of myth. Out of the fragments of memory and dream, Freud helped H.D. to bring her mother back to life. As she wrote to Viola Jordan, "I think people do actually come to us in dreams. I dream of my mother, simply confused dreams, mixed-up, that don't count—then one so clear and exact, with such perfect detail, that I KNOW that this time, I have actually been with her" (30 July 1941). This recovery of her mother was a crucial step in her search for full womanhood, but not because she could then transfer her affection to a father-symbol and men in general. Instead, this identification and bond with her mother freed her to explore the meaning of woman's experience in a male-dominated world. The impact of psychoanalysis on H.D. as a woman follows the same dialectical process of influence that has been evident in her use of Freud to formulate her religious aesthetic and her concept of history as protean palimpsest of an essential spiritual reality. To reiterate the pattern of influence, H.D. took Freud's theories, dismissed their evaluative framework, and developed his ideas in a direction ultimately antithetical to his own perspective.

The spiritual reunion with her mother that she experienced in the realm of dream and vision helped to confirm art as a possible female destiny in a world that designated aesthetic genius and creation as the province of men. Helen Wolle was an accomplished musician and painter who taught music at her father's Moravian seminary in Bethlehem, Pennsylvania, before the family moved to the outskirts of Philadelphia when Hilda was eight years old. It was her mother who first taught music to her Uncle Fred Wolle, the organist who founded the Bach Festivals in Bethlehem (*T.F.*, p. x). As H.D. wrote, "Obviously, this is my inheritance. I derive my imaginative faculties through my musician-artist mother" (*T.F.*, p. 121). To H.D., her parents embodied a choice she had to make between art and science. As a student at Bryn Mawr in particular, H.D. felt caught between the two: "I must choose, because my life depends upon it, between the artist and the scientist. . . . I felt there [at Bryn Mawr] I had fallen between two stools, what with my mother's musical connection and my father's and half-brother's stars!" (*T.F.*, pp. xii–xiii).[23] Failing in science and math, H.D. chose to follow in her mother's footsteps. Analysis with Freud six years after her mother's death helped to restore to consciousness the vivid figure of her mother as a creative woman full of warm life and laughter. "I wanted to paint like my mother, though she laughed at her pictures we admired so," H.D. recalled in the notes she took of her sessions with Freud (*T.F.*, p. 117).

The Gift, completed just before she began writing the *Trilogy*, centers on her matrilineal inheritance—the "gift"—passed down to her through her mother and her mother's mother. Without being fully aware of her own significance to her daughter's nascent "gift," Helen Wolle not only demonstrated the reality of the woman artist to her daughter, but she also countered her child's fear that the relative invisibility of women artists meant that women were incapable of creative achievement. H.D. remembered this conversation with her mother when she asked about artists in the family:

> "Well, I don't know—well—to be *artistic*—I suppose you might say your Aunt Belle was *artistic*—"
> "Then can ladies be just the same as men?"
> "Just the same what?"
> "I mean what you said—about writing a book?"
> "Why yes, ladies write books of course, lots of ladies write very good books."
> "Like Louisa M. Alcott?"
> "Yes, like Louisa Alcott and like Harriet Beecher Stowe."[24]

Her mother took the children to see a performance of *Uncle Tom's Cabin*, and H.D. returned to the magic of that drama as the beginning point of her aesthetic awakening as a child.

Recalling her mother's example and encouragement helped H.D. transcend the double bind of the woman artist who is taught to feel that womanhood and artistic creativity are mutually exclusive. Certainly such books as *Palimpsest* and *Her* demonstrate that H.D. fell victim to this trap, especially in her relationships with men. But Freud returned her again and again to her yearning for her mother. This analysis of her dreams and visions helped to restore the strong emotional bond with her mother that had been loosened somewhat in her years of rebellion against her family's demands for respectability. Helen Wolle appeared in *Asphodel* and *Her* drawn in the mocking tone of the daughter who sees her mother as the embodiment of Victorian social convention. She is, at best, a negative model for her daughter and evokes more bitterness than positive identification.[25] But in such later prose accounts as "Advent," *The Gift*, and *Tribute to Freud*, H.D.'s recollections of her mother have lost their ironic cast and taken on a tone of compassion, even reverence, as they move back in time to her early childhood and to the years before she was born.

For example, on March 20, 1933, H.D. recorded one dream in which she was struggling to return to her London flat when a man and a boy, associated in her mind with the "news of fresh Nazi atrocities," threatened her and barred her way. Terrified, she stood out in the street and called "Mother." Looking up at her window, she saw the reassuring figure of her mother: "A figure is standing there, holding a lighted candle. It is my mother. I was overpowered with happiness and all trace of terror vanished" (*T.F.*, pp. 174–75). In this instance, as in all of her fears connected with the Nazis, H.D. could not tell Freud about her association of the man and boy with the Nazi reign of terror that she knew would come (*T.F.*, p. 94). But she did discuss this dream with Freud. With his general theory and his specific analysis of H.D. as context, we can speculate on his perspective. H.D.'s dream returned her to the pre-Oedipal stage of development, to her love for the "phallic mother." Her terror of the man and boy would signify her flight from femininity, her failure to transfer attachment from women to men. But analysis of this dream functioned very differently for H.D. It brought back into the troubled consciousness of an adult woman the primal bond of protective love between mother and daughter. In dream, Helen Wolle could "return" to her daughter as a Demeter-figure whose loyal strength would guard her beloved Persephone trapped in the man-created Hades of a world approaching the second holocaust of the century.[26]

Established through dream and recovered through analysis, this union with her mother could serve as a source of support in H.D.'s search for identity and the means to survive in a hostile world. Because her mother was so closely associated in her mind with art, this restored bond with her mother helped H.D. to define her creative center as female. As she turned backward in time and inward in consciousness for artistic inspiration, she rediscovered the primal mother who then served as her muse. As she wrote, in reference to *Helen in Egypt*, "the mother is the Muse, the Creator, and in my case especially, as my mother's name was Helen."[27]

For Helen Wolle to serve as her daughter's inspirational muse and model, however, she had to undergo considerable transformation. While she consistently signified in H.D.'s writings women's artistic potential, she also represented the woman whose talent had been thwarted and mind diverted by her identification with her husband, sons, and masculine culture in general. H.D.'s identification with her artist-mother could not in itself free the daughter from the confines of a feminine destiny. Herself a victim of masculine culture, Helen Wolle had been insecure and self-denigrating about her own considerable "gifts." H.D. remembered telling Freud, for example, that "painting reminded me of my mother. I told him how as children we had admired her painting and boasted to visitors, 'My mother *painted* that.' My mother was morbidly self-effacing" (*T.F.*, p. 164). When Freud asked if her mother ever sang to her, H.D. replied that "she had a resonant beautiful voice but that she had some sort of block or repression about singing" (*T.F.*, p. 176). Another memory revealed Helen Wolle to be a young victim of the male mockery and criticism that has silenced or crippled so many women artists. Her mother had explained her block to Hilda by recalling "how when she was little and singing, her father said who is making all that noise. She was so hurt she never sang again."[28] Like many mothers, Helen Wolle was prevented by her own victimization from being a model of autonomy for her daughter. H.D.'s identification with her mother carried with it the destructive potential of becoming "morbidly self-effacing" and dependent on men for validation.

William Carlos Williams' brief portrait of Helen Wolle suggests that her self-effacement as an artist was well matched by an erosion of individual identity accomplished through her duties as the wife of a famous astronomer and the mother of many children. H.D.'s father was the center of the household around whose needs everyone else revolved. "On January nights towards dawn," Williams recalled for an example, "the doctor's wife . . . would go out with a kettle of boiling water to thaw the hairs of his whiskers that during the night-long vigil had become frozen to the eyepiece of the machine."[29] H.D. captured the contradictions of her mother's life by comparing her to the powerful Demeter who is yet powerless to restore her stolen daughter to life: "Eugenia moving through [her husband's work world] powerless, all powerful ... one should sing a hymn of worship to her, powerless, all-powerful ... and what am I between them?" (*Her*, p. 111). Like Virginia Woolf, H.D. grew up in a home with parents who fulfilled the mutually exclusive norms of masculinity and femininity. Her attempt to develop fully as both woman and artist was hurt by the image of her gifted mother who sacrificed her autonomy and capacity for enduring achievement to the demands of "normal" feminine destiny. Just as Woolf's growth as an artist depended upon a partial rejection of her mother as a model, H.D.'s artistic development involved a denial of the femininity her mother embodied.

The powerlessness of Demeter to save her daughter from the traps of a male-dominated world, however, took on the overtones of betrayal for H.D. as she recalled Helen Wolle's attitude toward her children. Although her mother encouraged her daughter's writing, H.D. believed that her mother did not recognize her daughter's artistic and psychic "gifts." In *The Gift*, H.D. remembered her mother's description of the fortune teller who predicted that she would have a gifted child. *The Gift* recounts how hurt the young Hilda felt to hear her mother lament the failure of the fortune teller's prophecy to be realized. As a compassionate adult, however, H.D. recognized what she didn't understand as a child—that her mother's denial of her daughter's gift was a projection of her own self-hate: "How could I know that this apparent disappointment that her children were not 'gifted,' was itself her own sense of inadequacy and frustration, carried a step further."[30]

Her mother's "sense of inadequacy and frustration" deepened to a rejection of her only daughter, according to H.D., who believed that her mother had openly favored her son Gilbert (*T.F.*, pp. 29, 33). As fantasies that countered rejection, some of H.D.'s dreams recorded in the thirties re-create the child Hilda attempting to prove to her mother that she is special, more gifted or important than her brother (*T.F.*, pp. 36–39, 119–23, 170–71). They are painful dreams which express the explosive ambivalence of mother-daughter relationships evident in such divergent works as George Eliot's *Mill on the Floss* and Rita Mae Brown's *Rubyfruit Jungle*.

Freud explained H.D.'s longing for closeness with her mother as her desire to be a boy, her need to be important to her mother (*T.F.*,

p. 120). Although H.D. made no reference to it, Freud's theory of female psychosexual development suggests that he would have explained her sense of rejection as the healthy hostility that a young girl feels toward her mother after the "fact of her castration" has been discovered. Her mother's preference for her son simply reflects the unconscious residue of her own penis envy: "The difference in a mother's reaction to the birth of a son or a daughter shows that the old factor of lack of a penis has even now not lost its strength. A mother is only brought unlimited satisfaction by her relation to a son; this is altogether the most perfect, the most free from ambivalence of all human relationships."[31] The ambivalence evident in the relationship between H.D. and her mother would have been for Freud part of a psychological chain reaction set in motion by the anatomical distinction between the sexes and the inherent superiority of male physiology. Never the materialist, H.D. rejected Freud's ultimately biological explanation of ambivalence in her relationship with her mother. Instead, she implicitly understood that in a patriarchal society, the mother has often helped to perpetuate the dominant norms in her relationship with her daughter. Whether engaging in the practice of footbinding or the more subtle process of "mindbinding," the mother has sometimes acted on behalf of men to injure her daughter physically or psychically. The potentially creative bond of love and identification between mother and daughter has been distorted by patriarchal culture. To restore this bond as center of her artistic identity, H.D. used Freud's diagnosis of her desire for union with her mother to transform her mother from the wounded woman of the patriarchal world to an ideal mother-symbol who is free to nourish her daughter. Her mother's existence as her daughter's muse represents H.D.'s liberation of her mother from imprisonment in her Victorian context. In the realm of the imagination fed by the inspirational river of the unconscious, H.D. could re-create the image of the whole mother, the all-powerful Demeter who is prevented in the material world of the patriarchy from loving and protecting her daughter.

However, the affirmation of womanhood represented by H.D.'s re-creation of an authentic mother-symbol did not ultimately lead H.D. in a separatist direction, the form of woman-identification that creates exclusive "woman-space" and abandons strong emotional ties to men—fathers, brothers, friends, and especially lovers.[32] If anything, psychoanalysis convinced her of the need to explore the significance of her interactions with men as well as women. The prose and poetry written after the resurgence of creativity during World War II reveal an artist who believed that her search to unite the fragments of female identity was inextricably interwoven with her desire to understand the patterns of male-female relationship. Freud's theory that the child's early erotic desires in the intense world of the nuclear family determine the nature of adult relationships had a profound impact on H.D. Parallel to her attachment to her mother, her relationship with her father served as a paradigm for later involvements with men. Adapting Freud's ideas to her own life, H.D. regarded her father, mother, brothers, and even the sister who died as personal prototypes for the men and women for whom she cared most deeply during her adult life. She fused Freud's theory of the family with her own notion of palimpsest, the "superposition" of the present on the past. She accepted, without any moral hesitation, the incestuous base of erotic passion implicit in Freud's theory of adult sexual love. In *Helen in Egypt*, the myth of Isis and Osiris most particularly embodies the erotic interconnections between generations of family members: as archetypes of love, they are simultaneously husband and wife, father and mother, brother and sister.[33] As a consequence of this personal palimpsest, H.D. believed that she could discover the patterns of love and betrayal in her relationships with such men as Pound and Aldington through psychoanalysis of her early feelings about her father and her more recent dreams centering on father-symbols.

Her search for the personal father in her adult life led her to reverse Freud's analysis of the transference in their sessions together. She wrote in *Compassionate Friendship* that Freud was the "perfect father image," and her dream records and associations continuously link Professor Freud with Professor Doolittle, not with Helen Wolle.[34] As an extension of this personal search, poems like the *Trilogy*, *Helen in Egypt*, *Vale Ave*, and *Sagesse* develop the poet's quest in two opposing directions variously portrayed as father and mother, father-symbol and mother-symbol, God and Goddess. Thus, "The Dream / deftly stage-managed" a stark male image of the "world-father" whose "amber shining" eyes pierced the dark in the *Trilogy* (*T.*, pp. 25–34). The *Trilogy*'s "All-Father" reappears as "Amen, All-father" in *Helen in Egypt*, the creator whose presence and will dominate Book One of the "Pallinode" (*H.E.*, pp. 1–17). And in *Vale Ave*, light-bearing and falsely defiled Lucifer pairs with Lilith as the archetypal father and mother whose relationship is incarnated in each historical era.

Like the disparity between H.D.'s ideal mother symbol and her actual mother, her quest for the protective care of the ideal father figure was often clouded by her memories of her somewhat "chilly" father. If the mother-archetype in a patriarchy always contains the potential of victimization, the father-archetype correspondingly incorporates the possibility of oppressive power, even violence. H.D.'s dream of her mother being raped by a father-figure and her nightmare of being strangled as a child by her brother are both psychological archetypes inevitable in a patriarchy (Hirslanden I, pp. 1–4). While H.D. attempted in her poetry to free her father-symbols from the oppressive trap of their own dehumanization, she was on the whole less successful with them than she was with transforming the powerless Demeter. Her poetry as well as her diaries and unpublished memoirs repeatedly portray man's betrayal of woman, man's near-destruction of Psyche. The pattern of victimization, imprinted on the mind of the child in the nuclear family, follows a rhythm of the woman's all-embracing fascination for her male lover and his subsequent rejection of her. As Helen feels at one point in *Winter Love*, a sequel to *Helen in Egypt*, "the Gods decree / that Helen is deserted utterly." Rachel Blau DuPlessis has characterized this pattern as "romantic thralldom" and argued persuasively that H.D.'s art attempted to pose solutions to the victimization she experienced in her own life as a result of patriarchal sexual politics.[35]

While H.D.'s search for the ideal father-symbol parallels the creation of her powerful mother-symbol, these personal and poetic quests are not evenly balanced because their purpose and context were different. H.D.'s identity as a woman in a male-dominated society made her transformation of the mother-figure an act of survival and a source of her own strength. In addition, Freud's ideas and diagnosis led her to reverse his portrait of women as the second sex in a gynocentric direction so that women became the first sex and men a sex toward which women express considerable ambivalence. Supported by Freud's theory of the family in both personal and cultural development, H.D. believed that the mother holds a prior, even primal position in the unconscious of the individual and the collective unconscious of the race. Beneath many layers of memory stands the mother, the first life-giver and nourisher. To recover the mother, H.D. felt, is to reach the foundation of the psyche. The father too must be recaptured from the buried fragments of the unconscious, for he greatly influenced the woman's adult relationships with men. But the return to the mother is a journey to beginnings which makes the rebirth of Psyche possible. Because the childhood of the individual recapitulates the childhood of the race, resurrection of the ancient mother-symbols who predated the "All-Fathers" of patriarchy represents a return to the most "primitive" stages of the human race according to Freud's adaption of J.J. Bachofen. H.D.'s disagreement with Freud's Enlightenment view of progress served her well as a woman in search of her roots. As she celebrated the "primitivism" of hieroglyphic thought, so she rejoiced at the creative potential of her return to historical and personal origins in her visionary reunions with her mother. Freud's own emphasis in their sessions on H.D.'s desire for her mother intensified her quest to restore the primal bond between mother and daughter. *The Gift* represents the fulfillment of that quest and paved the way for the poetry that followed about her reconstituted mother and matrilineage: "Mary, Maia, Miriam, Mut, Madre, Mere, Mother, pray for us. . . . This is Gaia, this is the beginning. This is the end. Under every shrine to Zeus, to Jupiter, to Zeus-pater of Theus-pater or God-the-father . . . there is an earlier altar. There is, beneath the carved superstructure of every temple to God-the-father, the dark cave or grotto or inner hall or cellar to Mary, Mere, Mut, mutter, pray for us."[36]

Without exception, such mother-symbols appear in H.D.'s epics to inspire the daughter's search for autonomous identity and the principle of love in a hate-filled world dominated by the forces of death. Usually embodied in one of the many protean forms of Near Eastern goddess figures, H.D.'s ideal mother-symbol serves as a model of whole womanhood, lifts the veil to reveal the secret mysteries of spiritual reality, and inspires the poet to write. Protean forms of the male archetype also figure significantly in these poems. But the structure of search follows the pattern of childhood as H.D. frequently begins with the father-symbols and moves backward in time to recover the primal mother, the source of birth and rebirth. Although this pattern, so antithetical to Freud's belief in female inferiority, repeats itself in all of H.D.'s long poems, it is especially evident in the last poem she wrote—*Hermetic Definition*. In this poem H.D. focused on an exploration of her identity as woman artist after years of relative silence on the topic. While the mother-symbol's service as muse operates implicitly in poems like the *Trilogy, Helen in Egypt,* or *Sagesse, Hermetic Definition* explicitly links the mother's function as muse to the capacity of the woman to write autonomously, without fear of male mockery or excessive male influence. Although these earlier poems incorporate the search for father-symbols, her final poem expresses more directly her ambivalence toward the explosive power of man to overwhelm woman in matters of heart and mind, passion and art.

The three-part poem records H.D.'s obsessions with two men— one as lover, one as poet—and her struggle to find her own "way." As the acronym of the poem (*H.D.*) suggests, the poetic product of her quest as she stands on the threshold of death is also a self-definition: the poet H.D. is united with her poem, *Hermetic Definition.* The overall structure of the poem frames the dialectical process of her mediative quest: the eighteen sections of Part One, "Red Rose and a Beggar," balance the eighteen sections of Part Two, "Grove of Academe," and the poem concludes with the eight sections of Part Three, "Star of Day," in which the poet transcends the opposing obsessions of the first two parts.

In "Red Rose and a Beggar," the bedridden poet falls in love with the young reporter who comes to interview her for a magazine article in April. She sees him again briefly in May when she goes to the United States to receive her gold medal for poetry awarded by the American Academy of Arts and Letters. After a short exchange of letters, she is crushed when he stops writing (*H.D.*, pp. 47, 54). Equally devastating is the dismissal of her art in his review of her book— " 'fascinating . . . / if you can stand its preciousness,' " he wrote. Like much of H.D.'s poetry, this section is rooted in key events in her life. Lionel Durand, a Haitian who was the chief of the Paris Bureau of *Newsweek*, visited H.D. in April and met her briefly in New York the following month. His review of *Bid Me to Live* was condescending at best, and H.D.'s diary notebooks record her passion for him, her pain at his double rejection, and the power his image retained in her dreams. He had a serious heart condition and was not allowed cigarettes, alcohol, or salt, restrictions to which H.D. referred repeatedly in the poem (*H.D.*, pp. 10, 11, 12, 13). News of his sudden death in January 1961 stimulated H.D. to write the final section of the poem, "Star of Day."[37]

Since the personal dream is the universal myth in H.D.'s world view, her love for Durand and his rejection of it incarnated an archetypal meaning that she attempted to translate in her poetry. She is old, he is young, and her passion is "unseemly, impossible, / even slightly scandalous": "Why did you come / to trouble my decline," she asks (*H.D.*, p. 3). But the "reddest rose" of her love transcends age and continues to unfold. He embodies a palimpsest of personal and mythic male lovers with the amber-eyed Paris, Bar-Isis (son of Isis) as the prototype.[38] As Paris, he is the archetypally masculine "Lover," whom H.D. associates with the games at Olympia, and the newest avatar of what she described as *"the tall god standing / where the race is run"* in *Red Roses for Bronze* (*H.D.*, pp. 14–15). The "torch" of "ecstasy" and "fever" he has lighted in her love parallels that of the Olympic Decathlon star of 1960:

> There is living bronze there,
> the vibration of sun, desperate endeavour,
> ambition, achievement, simplicity,
>
> sheer strength reaching sublimity (*H.D.*, p. 15)

She is, however, "prisoner" to his strength because his power "smudges" out her separate identity much as Ezra Pound's kisses did in *Her*. She compares him to "some thundering pack / of steers, bulls" whose impact is her own "total abasement" (*H.D.*, p. 10). In the "fervour" of her love, she seeks to be absorbed into his being, a loss of personal identity that was celebrated in both Victorian and Freudian ideologies of femininity:

> Take me anywhere, anywhere;
> I walk into you,
> Doge—Venice—
>
> you are my whole estate;
> I would hide in your mind
> as a child hides in an attic (*H.D.*, p. 4)

This loss of Self that results from "romantic thralldom" repeats the pattern of what she has experienced before with previous incarnations of the male lover. In personal palimpsest of love and victimization, Durand has taken the place of Pound and Aldington: "as you are new to me, different, / but of an old, old sphere. . . . the torch was lit from another before you, / and another and another before that.

. . ." (*H.D.*, pp. 11, 14). As a subtle key to the association between old lovers and new, H.D. echoes Pound's Canto 106 in her image of "the reddest rose" and connects Durand with Venice, the city she visited with Aldington. Pound's and Aldington's rejection of H.D. set the pattern for Durand's dismissal.

The intensity of Durand's rejection of her as woman is compounded by his mocking "praise" of her art. "I am judged—prisoner? / the reddest rose unfolds, / can I endure this?" the poet asks. The hermetic frame of the poem is the esoteric mysteries embedded in the symbols of Notre Dame, especially its three major doorways. Durand is associated with the "middle door . . . Judgement," the only doorway representing masculine iconography.[39] Durand's "judgement" of her art and the love that holds her prisoner nearly paralyzes her capacity to write. At this critical moment, a paradigm for the woman artist trapped in a male tradition, H.D.'s mother-symbol appears to restore her daughter's identity and compel her to write. The first and third doors of Notre Dame are female and matrilineal, like H.D.'s artistic inheritance described in *The Gift*. Saint Anne, the third door, is the Christian version of "Cybele . . . the grand-mother," while the Virgin Mother is in reality the Egyptian goddess Isis (*H.D.*, pp. 5, 9). Isis, the mother of Paris in the poem, tells her daughter to free herself from the son. Instead of preferring the son (as H.D.'s mother did), instead of nourishing the son (as Isis and Mary do in western art), H.D.'s mother-symbol inspires her daughter to write and thereby regain her lost Self.

> why must I write?
> you would not care for this,
> but She draws the veil aside,
>
> unbinds my eyes,
> commands,
> write, write or die.   (*H.D.*, p. 7)

In Part One, the reddest rose of passion reduces the poet to "beggar," and she gratefully leaves the intoxication of ecstasy and the "abasement" of femininity behind in the relative calm of the "grove of academe." St.-John Perse's steadying gesture when she nearly falls on her way to the podium at the Academy's award ceremony represents his acceptance of her as his colleague in poetry. She leaves behind the paralyzing sexual politics of Part One for the validation of artistic identity she feel emanating from his action: "our curious pre-occupation with stylus and pencil, / was re-born at your touch" (*H.D.*, pp. 24, 26). Perse, whose "cool laurel" is the antithesis of the "reddest rose," introduces her to a new absorption: an intellectual passion with the *"île de promesse"* of his vast poetic system (*H.D.*, pp. 37, 41). His "guardian" is Athené, particularly in her form as Hygeia, the goddess whose serpent feeds from her cup (*H.D.*, pp. 33, 35). His mythic prototype is "Perseus, man and hero" (*H.D.*, p. 37).

While there is a new "ecstasy and healing / in her acceptance" of his poetic "fantasy," there is also danger in the woman poet's total absorption as she is "swept away / in the orgy of your poetry" (*H.D.*, pp. 33–34). Not at all the Lover, Perse is nonetheless a form of arche-typal male, this time the poet whose very grandeur diminishes the woman poet's self-esteem. She makes the inevitable comparisons, and the more she becomes involved in his poetry, the more his influence begins to paralyze her capacity to write autonomously. She thinks: "your mind's thought and range / exceeds mine / out of all propor-tion" (*H.D.*, p. 25). The "storm" of his "poem's dimension" moves gradually from reducing her own dimension to absorbing her com-pletely into his "vast concept." She is no longer his companion, but rather an object in his poem. She compares herself to "Cassiopea on her star-chair, / moving round the pole, / moving with the whole, / part of your giant-concept" (*H.D.*, p. 32). Following the *"lois de trans-humance"* she finds in his *Exil*, she leaves behind "all fretful traces of humanity" to become the "small snake" of his patron, Athené Hygeia (*H.D.*, pp. 36–39). No longer poet herself, she is the male magician-poet's "intimate" and "familiar" (*H.D.*, p. 35). H.D. returns to her imagist craft to render her loss of Self and merger with the wildlife, rock, woods, and waters of his poetry (*H.D.*, pp. 36–39). The intel-lectual origins of her own objectification are different from the roman-tic thralldom of "Red Rose and a Beggar," but the end result is similar: loss of autonomy.

The point of total absorption is also the moment the pendulum begins to move back. Memory of Isis, Paris Bar-Isis, and the *"Notre Dame* revelation" return the poet to herself so that she can abandon the influence that overwhelmed her individual, "human" identity. *"Seigneur,"* she says to Perse, "it is no good, / your perfection carried me along, / but it's gone; / . . . / I want my old habit, / . . . / *Seig-neur,* you must forgive my deflection" (*H.D.*, p. 44). H.D. realizes that another poet's "invocations" and "magnificent rhythms" cannot free her from the prison of her love for Durand. Nor could his intellectual law of "transhumance" explain the "human equation" of "ordinary time-sequence, / neither insect, reptile / nor illimitable sun-ray" (*H. D.*, p. 44). To find the "answer," H.D. had to restore the autonomous Self of the woman poet: the object of Part Three, "Star of Day."

H.D.'s exploration of the difficulties of artistic influence parallels Harold Bloom's approach to the problem in *The Anxiety of Influence*. But while he described the male artist as the son who needed to declare his independence from the father, H.D. writes of the woman whose artistic autonomy depends on her ability to throw off the overwhelming male presence in literary tradition. To succeed, she must affirm her creative center as female.[40] Once again, H.D. turns to her mother-symbol for inspiration and a model for female creativity: the all-powerful Isis, "générateur, générant, / never to be gainsaid, / who ordered, ordained or controlled this, / and compelled my stylus, pen or pencil / as I wrote" (*H.D.*, pp. 49–50). To free herself, the daughter becomes the mother in the realm of poetry. In creative identification with her mother-symbol, she will "give birth" to Durand just as Isis bore Paris. Woman's physiological capacity to conceive and give birth becomes her paradigm for the processes of artistic creation.

The metaphor of birth is complex in its multiple dimensions and dependent for its meaning on biographical coincidence.[41] News of Durand's death just nine months after their meeting leads H.D. to regard that period as a "pregnancy" that will result in the "birth" of her completed poem and Durand's "rebirth" as a resurrected being (*H.D.*, p. 48). "Star of Day," the final section, written after Durand's death, accomplishes this double birth, the resolution of her "curious 'condition' " (*H.D.*, p. 49). Her meetings with Durand and the writing of Parts One and Two are now viewed as stages in the pregnancy when he was "five months" and "six months 'on the way' " (*H.D.*, pp. 48–49, 52). She had imagined that she had "walked into you," but now she realizes "that it was you who walked into me" as the unborn fetus growing in the fertile mind of the poet. During the summer when she felt "cast out" and "thrown away," she wrote "Red Rose and a Beggar" to "recover identity." Now she realizes that "the writing was the un-born, / the conception" which would lead to the multiple births in "Star of Day" (*H.D.*, p. 54). As she reflected later in her

Durand diary, "I take on myself the role of mother" in the last sequence, and his "death was his birth" (21 May 1961).

Giving birth to her poem frees her from Durand's possession of her being. As she wrote in the diary, "His death relieved me of personal, emotional tangles."[42] And in the poem, she asks: "Now you are born / and it's all over, / will you leave me alone?" (*H.D.*, p. 55). Although her question hints at the possibility of recurring possession, Durand's "birth" into immortality across the threshold of death in the completion of the poem restores her autonomy. And because her poem incorporates the "human" passion of the "reddest rose" as well as Perse's abstract *"unalterable law,"* it also establishes her independence from the dominance of masculine "intellect and achievement" (*H.D.*, pp. 51, 55). Indeed, her final act of poetic motherhood allows her to transcend in her "own way" the many dialectical polarities established in the poem's imagery and structure: Durand and Perse; Paris and Perseus; Egypt and Greece; emotion and intellect; heart and mind; *"right, left"*; *"win, lose"*; human, *transhumance*; the "reddest rose" and "silver-green" laurel; Night and Day; and most fundamentally, life and death. Her labor is troubled, but she achieves a final synthesis by returning to her female capacity to create new life. Many male writers have made the analogy between their own creativity and woman's ability to give birth. But in *Hermetic Definition*, this conventional metaphor takes on a new dimension of meaning. To create poems of hermetic vision that fuse the traditionally male functions of religion and art, she does not have to abandon her womanhood, as Freud's theory would imply. Instead, her creativity is rooted in her Self as woman.[43] When the dominance or scorn of the male world threatens that creativity, the mother-symbol reveals herself in epiphany and dream to strengthen the woman poet and redirect her quest. Isis and the female processes of pregnancy and childbirth serve as the poet's prototype of artistic creation and liberation. H.D.'s poetic motherhood gives birth to the poem and frees her from the romantic thralldom and intellectual domination that victimize so many women in a patriarchal culture.

H.D.'s poetry, then, creates its own "vast concept" of womanhood that is utterly antithetical to Freud's portrait of women as castrated men, inferior physiologically, intellectually, and morally. Yet in the paradox most crucial to her identity as woman artist, H.D. used Freud's ideas about women and particularly his analysis of her "mother-fixation" to express a vision of whole womanhood. H.D.'s transformation of Freud's work is even more extraordinary when we recall that it was not the result of an intellectual exercise by two brilliant minds exchanging ideas in a vacuum of abstractions. H.D. was Freud's analysand in the highly charged emotional atmosphere of a partially therapeutic situation—precisely the conditions in which so many women have been psychologically crippled by sexist therapists. How did H.D. survive to develop a woman-identified poetry? I believe the answer lies in the dialectical dynamics of her interactions with Freud and the brilliance of her final reevaluation of his life and work. Her delight in disagreement, a crucial factor in his ultimate influence on her work, allowed her to abandon the evaluative presuppositions of his perspective and develop his ideas in a direction that could nourish and unite artist and woman. It allowed her as well to present the world with a portrait of Freud, a reinterpretation of his significance that differed diametrically from his own self-image of the "so very masculine," empirical scientist.

The pattern of H.D.'s own life and work is profoundly dialectical. She repeatedly established clearly defined, imagistically rendered polar oppositions so that she could ultimately move toward a transcendent synthesis, a new whole that would incorporate the thesis and antithesis of argument. To H.D., Freud's association with science was extremely important—she played the artist and mystic in opposition to his science of the psyche. But she resolved the consequent epistemological disagreement between them by ultimately perceiving the intuitive artist permeate the rational scientist in a transcendent whole. Similarly, she developed the polarity between his Enlightenment celebration of reason and her return to "infantile," "primitive" religious faith. But, she posed a synthesis of this opposition in her final portrait of the modern-day "oil driller" as the newest avatar of the prophets of Israel recalling their lost flock to the residue of divinity buried in the unconscious. And finally, she recognized somewhat humorously the war of the sexes embodied in her interactions with Freud. But she dissolved the potentially destructive, misogynist bite of his theories about women by seeing him as an androgynous synthesis of masculine-feminine, reason and emotion, science and art, father and mother.

To Freud, he was the mother in transference during his sessions with H.D. But to her, he was the "perfect father-symbol." Consequently, in an ultimate sense, he became both mother and father to her as he fused her mother's art and her father's science in the mysteries of psychoanalysis. She wrote in her journal on March 8, 1933: "I am on the fringes or in the penumbra of the light of my father's science and my mother's art—the psychology or philosophy of Sigmund Freud" (*T.F.*, p. 145). H.D. experienced a "schism in consciousness" with all the "two's and two's and two's in my life"—the primary dualism of mother and father reproduced itself in such "two's" as Bethlehem and Philadelphia, England and America, Puritan background and Moravian inheritance (*T.F.*, pp. 31–33; *T.*, p. 49). "What is this mother-father / to tear at our entrails? / what is this unsatisfied duality?" she wrote in the *Trilogy* (*T.*, p. 72). Always she sought a way to "bridge over" and "heal old breaks in consciousness" (*T.F.*, p. 32; *T.*, pp. 49, 54). In *The Gift*, she wrote, "Science and art must beget a new creative medium."[44] The mother and the father unite to beget the child, and the "child" incorporates both of them to produce the poem: "I know the father, the mother, the third of the trio or trilogy, the poem, the creation, the thing they begat or conceived between them" (Hirslanden III, p. 27).

H.D. responded not to the condescending gallantry of the misogynist persona of his writings, but rather to the human being she visited every day for months. According to H.D.'s account, Freud in person did not act the role of the arrogant patriarch of psychoanalysis who silenced rebellious dissenters and trivialized the arguments of such female disciples as Karen Horney. Nor did his great love of art and his nonjudgmental explorations of the unconscious seem consistent with the harsh rationalist narrator of *The Future of an Illusion*. In H.D.'s tribute, he was both analytical in his "detached" questions and passionate in his reactions to her—as when he said, "*you do not think it worth your while to love me*" (*T.F.*, pp. 14, 16, 18). He was, it is true, the austere, famous old man, but he was also considerate, gracious, and nurturant in his concern for H.D. and her family. H.D. felt the great weight of his intellect, but she also responded to his sensitivity in his personal relationship with her. The correspondence between them that is reprinted in *Tribute to Freud* attests to his capacity to understand the subtlest nuance of suggestion in a warm friendship.

Psychologically bisexual in H.D.'s view, Freud was a man whose own psyche had not followed the pattern of "normal" development prescribed by his theories. "Normal" masculinity required the suppression of the feminine attitude, but H.D. found Freud to be a person like herself who combined in relatively equal amounts the qualities traditionally designated masculine and feminine. Theseus in *Helen in Egypt* is H.D.'s poetic tribute to Freud, and the fusion of tenderness and strength in his treatment of Helen reproduces Freud's healing interactions with H.D. Helen, buffeted by the "heart-storms" of her experiences with Paris and Achilles, arrives at the shelter of Theseus, the *"legendary hero-king of Athens."* Much as Freud listened to H.D., Theseus helps Helen translate the hieroglyphs of self and experience. Images of nurturance serve as objective correlatives for the old "Hermit" who served as a model of androgynous transcendence for H.D.:

> why do you weep, Helen?
>
> what cruel path have you trod?
> these heavy thongs,
> let me unclasp them;
>
> .   .   .   .
>
> your feet are wounded
>
> with this huntsman's gear;
> who wore these clumsy boots?
> there—there—let the fire cheer you;
>
> will you choose from the cedar-chest there,
> your own fleece-lined shoes?
> or shall I choose for you?   (*H.E.*, pp. 151–52)

Part II

H.D. and Religious Tradition

6

Initiations

BIOGRAPHICAL ROOTS OF OCCULT INFLUENCE

"I MUST DROWN completely and come out on the other side, or rise to the surface after the third time down, not dead to this life but with a new set of values, my treasure dredged from the depth. I must be born again or break utterly," H.D. wrote about her "psychic or occult experiences" at Corfu (*T.F.*, pp. 39, 54). A female Christ figure, Psyche's confrontation with death and emergence into new life was a process H.D. repeated many times in the rituals of mysticism and psychoanalysis in "the city of ruin," the twentieth century that seemed "almost past redemption" (*T.F.*, p. 84). H.D. found visions of spiritual realism that held out the promise of redemption through her extensive immersion in a variety of mystical and occult traditions, an involvement that was as necessary to the rebirth of Psyche as psychoanalysis.

To the rationalist, the expansion of H.D.'s esoteric explorations would represent a retreat from reality, an escape into the realm of consoling illusion. As a rationalist, Freud was himself fascinated with occult phenomena, but he classified them with other "symptoms" of "psychical reality" that served the needs of the pleasure principle.[1] Paradoxically and defiantly, H.D. remembered Freud as "the *alchemist si remarkable*" who "guards my room, almost my sanctuary." In the alchemy of her memory she returned to "my session or my séance" with Freud in which he had conjured up from the unconscious the dead voices of her mother and father as well as the mother-father symbols they embodied. She believed that her initiation into mystical traditions depended fundamentally upon his psychoanalytic séance. As she wrote in *Compassionate Friendship*: "I had my questions and my answers in that period of War II London, but without my preliminary work with the Professor, I could never have faced this final stage of the initiation."[2] As H.D. defined Freud's role, he was important to her initiation not because he helped restore the ties between the ego and external reality, but because he released her from the prison of the material. Under his guidance as she defined it herself, her retreat from material reality led to a direct confrontation with its limitations and an affirmation of spiritual reality. Like a religious "retreat," like Thoreau's "retreat," H.D.'s plunge into the esoteric only seemed to be a withdrawal. From her perspective, hermetic tradition offered a pattern of meaning in coded form to the initiate. For the transcendentalists of the nineteenth century, nature was a symbol for spirit. For the poet of the modernist era, the harsh world of necessity that Freud described is itself the "rune" that must be deciphered. The "true-rune and right spell" of esoteric tradition contained the code for H.D. in her search to translate the inner meaning of material reality.

H.D.'s nonrationalist perspective requires a phenomenological methodology for the assessment of occult influence. The temptation to evaluate her mysticism from a rationalist or psychoanalytic perspective may be great. But to understand how a modernist poet interacted with esoteric tradition and transformed it into art, an examination of how *she* experienced this mythmaking process is more fruitful. How, for example, did she resolve for herself the paradox of Freud as the rationalist initiator and psychoanalysis as the scientific *sagesse*? How, in fact, could opposite systems of explanation coexist as parallel forms of creative quest? How did *she* explain her involvement in the occult? What did she learn from esoteric tradition about the direction, nature, and function of her artistic destiny? What were her own criteria for psychic phenomena and religious faith? What mythologies did she adapt? Which ones did she transform? What, in short, is the religious vision that she brought to the modern world in her art?

No one figure like Freud stood as the guardian of H.D.'s esoteric beginnings, and *Tribute to Freud* has no companion piece in which she assessed the process and significance of a wide-ranging hermetic tradition on her development as an artist. However, the story of that diffuse influence emerges from her correspondence, journals, unpublished novels, and the books she kept in her library. These various sources provide extensive material that documents the nature of her involvement and illustrates her purpose in esoteric study. Like her collaboration with Freud, her capacity to transform the tradition she found enriching permeates her absorption of occult influence. This chapter will outline the factual aspects of her involvement and then discuss how she perceived the qualitative nature of her esoteric quest.

While H.D.'s serious study of esoterica did not begin until the late twenties, her fascination with visionary experience probably started in the same place as her early introduction to psychoanalysis: her relationship with Frances Gregg. As portrayed in *Her*, Gregg's intensity frequently bordered on psychic trance, and the novel depicts two central scenes in which Gregg prophecies H.D.'s destiny as an occultist who expresses her visions in art (*Her*, pp. 181–96). H.D. found confirmation of Gregg's prophecy in the series of occult experiences she had on the boat to Greece in 1920 and in the hotel room at Corfu. Indeed, one of her many reasons for seeing Freud was to get his help in translating the "things [that] had happened in my life, pictures, 'real dreams,' actual psychic or occult experiences that were superficially at least, outside the province of established psychoanalysis" (*T.F.*, p. 39). One of the "cards" she wanted to lay on the table so that Freud could "tell my fortune" was an example of "occult phenomena" in which time stopped, the material world became an ideal world, and the figure of Peter Van Eck seemed to join her on board the "Argo." H.D.'s code name for Van Eck, Peter Rodeck, was an architect who had helped Sir Arthur Evans restore Cretan vases at the palace of Knossos. H.D. had with him what she refers to as a rather "conventional meeting or voyage-out romance" (*T.F.*, p. 164). One night, however, a "violet light" covered the suddenly calm sea as she stood on deck to enjoy the air. Peter Van Eck appeared beside her and together they watched the dolphins "leaping in rhythmic order like crescent moons. . . . on a sea that is level yet broken in a thousand perfectly peaked wavelets like the waves in the background of a Botticelli" (*T.F.*, pp. 158, 160). It was a "supremely natural moment," but "an exact moment, [when] the boat slipped into enchantment" (*T.F.*, pp. 160, 161). Later, she discovered that there had been no dolphins in the sea that night, that Peter Van Eck had no memory of this moment of beauty and communion. To hold on to the enchantment of the "Man on the boat," H.D. dismissed Van Eck's advances and let the living man go (*T.F.*, p. 162).[3] While Gregg's visions became associated in H.D.'s mind with the ideal of a sister (or mother)-lover, her own vision of Van Eck created the idea of a brother (or father)-lover. H.D. experienced both visions as an initiation into a realm that transcended the ordinary and conventional.

This experience, along with the puzzling projections of light on the Corfu hotel wall, probably provided H.D. with the greatest impetus to begin serious study of esoteric traditions in the twenties. W.B. Yeats, with his poetic blend of theosophy and myth may have had some influence on H.D.[4] But Madame Blavatsky and the Theosophical Society, major influences on Yeats's occult interests, held little or no attraction for H.D. as she first delved into the occult. Probably more significant than Yeats's example was the general interest in occult phenomena among literary people in London during the twenties. While Bryher stimulated H.D.'s interest in psychoanalysis, Kenneth Macpherson most likely served as the immediate catalyst for greater involvement in esoteric study. In her "Autobiographical Notes," H.D. commented that Gregg sent Macpherson to her in 1926 and that by 1927 "K. does my numerology." In "Narthex," an autobiographical sketch she wrote in 1927 about the complicated triangle of herself, Bryher, and Macpherson, she described him variously as the "crystal ball," the "slim rod. . . . the neophyte's wand," the "neophyte narthex" and the "Elusinian wandbearer." The "narthex" is a "wand carried by initiates ... original plant-stalk by means of which Prometheus brought fire from heaven." In the story, the "metallic" intellect of Gareth (Bryher) and these "swallow-spirals" of Daniel's (Kenneth's) thought are symbolically contrasted to suggest the inner conflict in H.D. between rational and occult knowledge.[5]

Whoever or whatever served as the initiator into the more popularized forms of the occult, it is clear that H.D. began experimenting with Tarot, astrology, and numerology in the late twenties. In 1929 her rather mundane correspondence with Viola Jordan burst into another dimension of communication. H.D. found in Jordan a friend who was sympathetic to her esoteric interests, who wanted to share her own experiences with occult phenomena, and who exchanged information on useful books and pamphlets of the occult underground. Jordan served as H.D.'s occult correspondent from the late twenties till the end of World War II, with particularly substantial letters on esoterica coming in the years 1929, 1930, 1933, 1934, 1941–42, 1944–45.[6] These letters establish that H.D. read extensively, first in numerology, then Tarot and astrology—especially the more complex and arcane rather than the popularized versions of occult tradition. Upon occasion, she consulted a woman who had worked out "a sort of chart of 'inner numbers' ": "Her 'fortunes' are so terribly clear and right that she has to take the greatest care herself, not to abuse her power. Twice she has told me things of the utmost value, but I always keep these matters for moments of the greatest perplexity. In fact, I have only twice in a long period of friendship actually 'consulted' her" (24 May 1930). H.D. not only worked out number charts for herself, family, and friends, but she also learned to "read" the symbols of the Tarot cards, a power of her own that she used in special circumstances. In 1930, for example, she did a reading for Jordan, who had written to her about a psychic experience (see Figure 1). H.D. explained her reading by saying "I don't do these cards often. . . . and only when I really am anxious and want to 'help' . . . . Do be sure that all I say is in a most sincere and really 'simple' manner. I do know and I do believe. . . . I can tell when the cards seem to indicate something direct and real. These fell into order as if by pre-arrangement" (12 February 1930). Both numerology and Tarot served as a sort of Delphic oracle whose cryptic visual messages contained the secrets of personal destiny.[7]

The books H.D. read on numerology and Tarot linked these forms of the occult with astrology. H.D. felt a personal imperative for astrology because of her father's astronomy. She associated the mystique of his work with the "hieroglyphs" from the Zodiac that he sketched at the top of his columns (*T.F.*, p. 25). She had caused him great disappointment by failing at math, but she could follow in his footsteps by researching the esoteric dimension of astronomy. H.D.'s immersion in classical mythology also served as an important foundation of associations for her involvement in astrology because the Mars, Venus, and Mercury of a horoscope are planetary versions of the Greek and Egyptian pantheons. The connections H.D. made between mythology and astrology are demonstrated in her copies of Lewis Richard Farnell's *Cults of the Greek States*—in all five volumes, she placed the astrological symbols for the planets in the margins next to the relevant god or goddess mentioned in the text.

H.D. was hindered in her construction of her own horoscope be-

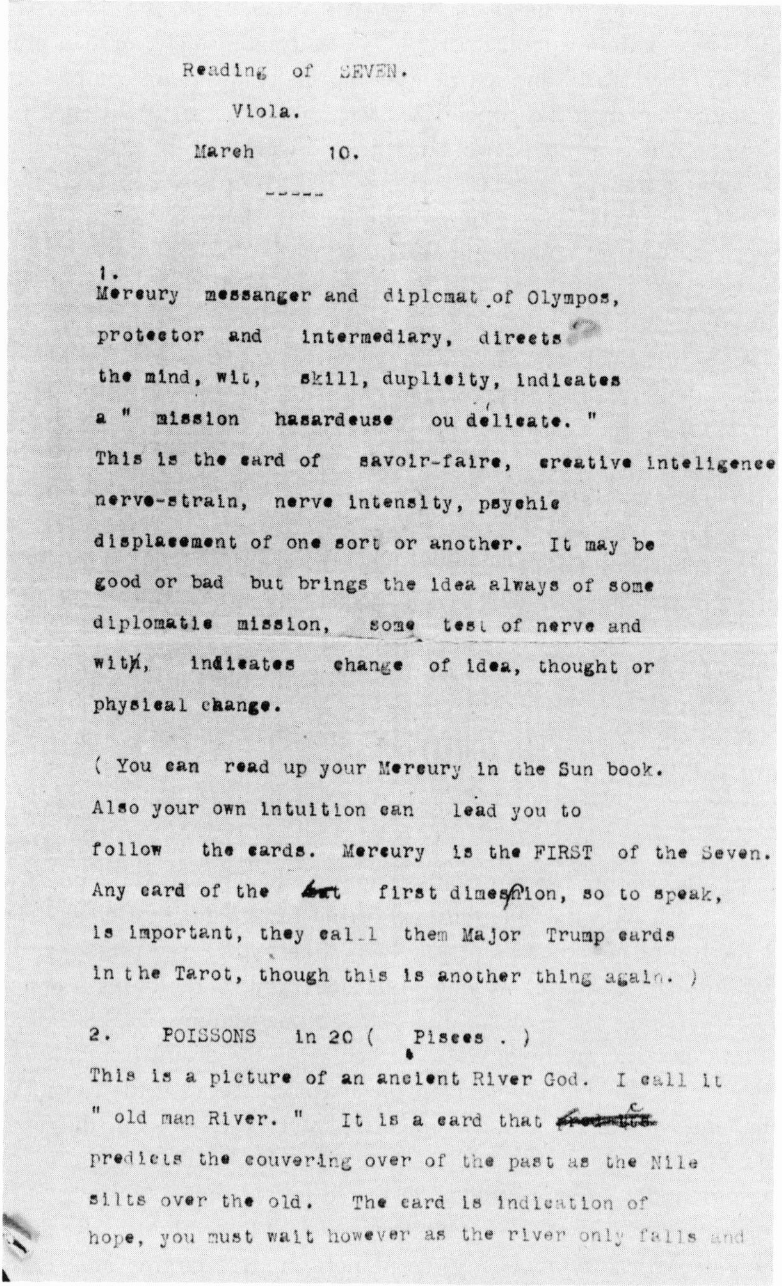

Reading of SEVEN.

Viola.

March   10.

- - - - - -

1.
Mercury messanger and diplcmat of Olympos,
protector and   intermediary, directs
the mind, wit,   skill, duplicity, indicates
a " mission   hasardeuse   ou delicate. "
This is the card of   savoir-faire, creative inteligence
nerve-strain, nerve intensity, psychic
displacement of one sort or another. It may be
good or bad but brings the idea always of some
diplomatic mission,   some test of nerve and
with,   indicates change of idea, thought or
physical change.

(You can read up your Mercury in the Sun book.
Also your own intuition can   lead you to
follow   the cards. Mercury is the FIRST of the Seven.
Any card of the first first dimension, so to speak,
is important, they call them Major Trump cards
in the Tarot, though this is another thing again.)

2.   POISSONS in 20 (Pisces .)
This is a picture of an ancient River God. I call it
" old man River. "   It is a card that predicts
predicts the couvering over of the past as the Nile
silts over the old. The card is indication of
hope, you must wait however as the river only falls and

Figure 1. H.D.'s second Tarot reading for Viola Jordan
(10 March 1933 letter from H.D. to Viola Jordan)

2.

rises at stated interval.   It is a card of
cosmic force and grandeur.   It is the end of
something, the last card in the set, the last of
the old year.   This card indicates " qu'il
ne faut pas desespérer, il n'y a   aucune raison
pour que la vie ne se poursuivre pas,   que
le consultant laisse agir le temps, il sera le
meilleur de ses   appuis. "

3.   Gemeaux (Gemini   )   This represents
good taste, the arts, love of music etc.
You can judge for yourself and supply for yourself ho'
and in what instance the card of the two boy-twins
helps.

4.   Lion.   This as you know is a Sun symbol,
meaning again great power backing you, the Sun
and what pertains. This rather works in with the
other reading where the Sun constanty
turned up, in rather super-abundance. I suppose
you are at some turn of your psyche life and
are being constantly guarded.

C'est   une carte cruelle, puissante ,
menacante , ambitieuse et orgueilleuse, qui
donne   le pouvoir   et les richesses mais par
les moyens violents. //
You can apply the text ... I quote without
refurbishing. If I knew more I could apply
this better.

Figure 1. (continued)

3.

(This ~~Lion~~ Leo is the centre card of the seven,
showing that it is the key-stone, the
column so to speak to the edifice.)

5.   Cancer in 19, shows some
inimical force at work. This force though
entirely present and so to speak , embodied is
however modified by the great intensity of
th SUN card, the LEO that is the centre of the
design.   The Cancer card shows a young man
standing on a jet of rock in full bright
day-light. He is smitten as from a flash from " the
blue. "   This shows danger of course but as I
say, the other cards about it, ~~alleviate~~
alleviate the power of this one.   The next card
shows danger too, but a danger from within -

6.   'Lion 20.   This is the Leo in the
descendant . It is the Hydra headed monster, later slain
by Hercules. Saturn is in the sky. It
indicates a monster that grown with the slaying.
It is Psychic terror and pessimism and
presentement.   " Il faut   se débarraser
de la torpeur ... "   This however leads
on to another card, perfectly in unison, one of
the most beautiful -

7 .   Belier (Ram)   in 10.

Figure 1. (continued)

4.

This card represents Andromache on the rock.

It is chaste, severe Beauty, chained to circumstance.

This figure is being threatened by a sea-monster.

(This monster can be interpreted by the succeeding card

the hydra-headed snake-monster, psychic terror again .)

Out of the sky appears the majic figure on the

winged horse, Perseus.   ... # "c'est la

Volonte intelligent   et hardie   qui   anime la

bonte agissante   et courageuse,   apportant

la delivirance   at le triumph   compensateur   de

l'Hymen heureux. "

The dignificance is triumph after sacrifice,

it   predicts honors   and wealth   after a

thousand   disappointments.

The Sun is in " exaltation " here supported by

Juppiter and Mars.

It is difficult to predict exactly what this means

but it is an infallable indication of

Beauty threatened and at length miraculously

set free.   Perseus is of course one of the

younger Sun   symbols, a sort of prince, slayer

of that monster of inanition and hate, jealousy,

guilt-complex etc. etc, the Gorgan.

As I said of the other set, I would not send this

but at the moment it seems indicated.

You will judge and
modify for yourself.

Figure 1. (continued)

cause she did not know her exact time of birth, the fact upon which the whole natal chart rests. H.D. wrote several times to Jordan that she did not really know her time of birth, but that she and her astrologer had "reconstructed" one that allowed them to proceed with a birth chart (see Figure 2). In 1936 or 1937, her friend Silvia Dobson, who did a number of complex astrological calculations, and Silvia's sister, Molly, designed for H.D. a handmade book entitled "Horoscopes H.D." The cover of the book is delicately scrolled with penned Zodiac designs that are drawn in the style of the Cretan vases H.D. referred to in connection with Peter Van Eck. It contains some forty hand-drawn and decorated horoscopes for herself and her friends, including Bryher, Perdita, Freud, Lawrence, and Pound.[8] For herself, the book contains her birth chart (based on time of birth), her conception chart (based on time of conception), and three progressed charts for the years 1935, 1936, and 1938 (based on placement of planets in a given year).

H.D.'s manuscript materials do not reveal what year she first had her natal chart cast. But her letters to Bryher in the spring of 1933 indicate that her sessions with Freud coincided significantly with extensive research in astrology as well as the general reawakening of interest in her occult experiences in the Scilly Isles and Corfu. On April 25, for example, she wrote Bryher, "I have been simply wallowing in the star-book. It is very helpful and may eventually lead to something possibly creative" (25 April 1933). Although she was clearly cautious about showing Freud how deeply she cared about astrology, her interest in the stars came up in their discussions of her father. Both Freud and H.D. regarded her fascination for esoteric astronomy as her unconscious attempt to approach her distant, cold, scientific father. They interpreted one particularly important dream with the help of astrological symbolism. At one point in the lengthy exegesis, H.D. wrote Bryher:

> The clue is the fear and dread of the Scorpio, my father, a cold, distant, upright, devoted father and husband but for whose profession I had only terror, a blind fear of space and the distances of the planets and the fixed stars. But no Scorpio grew wings in my dream. I ran forward across a floor to open a door so that this deadly insect might run out. But as soon as I open the door, he spreads bright translucent needle-like wings and with a sword like directness, flies into the branches of a small tree, in the dark hall-way. We have not inter-

preted this finally, but it is obvious that the fear is removed, the mystery, the glamour remains, and is now recognizable in my reading and romantic interpretation of star-values which my father measured with cruel (to me) and exquisite accuracy, with a cold hermit logic and detachment. (27 April 1933)

If astrology's connections to astronomy helped bring H.D. closer to her father, the esoteric side of her father's science also became the symbolic point of her disagreement with Freud, her "Papa" in the séance of analysis. H.D.'s letter to Bryher about her conflict with Freud specifies the "transcendental issues" over which they disagreed so profoundly:

> . . . as S.F. once or twice has given such a snort when I have gone into star-states, it sort of cripples me. But I think that is it. I am not, as you know a sloppy theosophist or horoscope-ist, but as you know, I do believe in these things and think there is a whole other-science of them. And that is where, in a way, S.F. and I part company. I suppose that too, is symbolical of my leaving my own home and its surroundings and the strictly, so-called "scientific." But I think you will agree that star-fish stuff [astrology and psychic phenomena] is my real world, and that getting that, I am, in a way, being "in love" also with my father . . . I write this, as it all helps to tell you, and also S.F. may nip it in the bud to-morrow. But I don't think he will. I think I must simply have it straight out with him. He is good, you know, too good and he has to stick to his scientific guns, but I have to stick to mine too. These Jews, I think, hold that any dealings with "lore" and that sort of craft is wrong. I think so too, when it is WRONG!!!!! But it isn't always. And I want to write my vol. to prove it. (28 May 1933)

Although the year 1933 was perhaps a high point of her interest in astrology, H.D.'s letters to Jordan stress its continuing importance to her and refer repeatedly to a community of friends who shared her interest. In particular, she thanked Jordan many times for her gifts of *Astrology: Your Place in the Sun* and *Astrology: Your Place among the Stars*, by the well-known American astrologer Evangeline Adams.[9] In 1933, for example, H.D. wrote: "You did me a great, great service when you sent me that first book. I have bought three sets of the books for different people and they have all been psychically helped immensely, so you see it was your doing to begin with. I was born with the Sagittarius rising,—so that counteracts a lot of the Virgo primness, as you must see. Also, it means I WANT to help, and do when I can, also do not forget others who have given me a

Summary

Sun Sign: Virgo   *Ascendant:*   Sagittarius

Placement of Planets in Signs: Moon in Aquarius, Neptune in Taurus, Pluto in Gemini, Saturn in Cancer, Venus in Leo, Mercury in Virgo, Uranus and Jupiter in Libra, Mars in Scorpio

Placement of Planets in Houses: Moon in 2nd House (money and possessions); Neptune and Pluto in 6th House (work, health); Saturn in 8th House (death); Venus, Mercury, and Sun in 9th House (religious and philosophical views, dreams); Uranus and Jupiter in 10th House (career); Mars in 11th House (friends)

Aspects:

Sextiles (easy): Sun and Saturn, Sun and Mars,
    Saturn and Neptune, Mercury and Mars

Squares (hard): Mars and Neptune, Jupiter and Saturn,
    Venus and Neptune, Mercury and Neptune, Moon and Mars,
    Pluto and Venus, Pluto and Mercury

Trines (easy): Moon and Uranus, Moon and Jupiter, Pluto
    and Uranus, Pluto and Jupiter, Uranus and Neptune

Conjunction (intensification): Jupiter and Uranus, Mercury and
    Venus, Neptune and Pluto

Opposition (hard): Moon and Venus

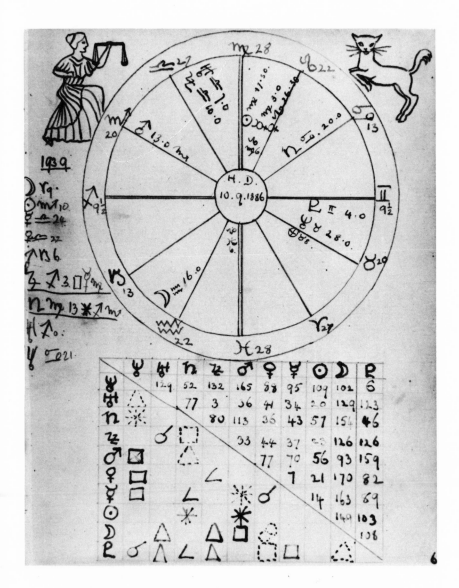

Figure 2. H.D.'s Natal Horoscope (reproduced from the ink drawing in her horoscope journal, "Horoscopes H.D."). Among her intimate friends, one of her code names was CAT, hence the feline sketched in one corner.

hunch of the right thing" (1 June 1933). In the same year, when H.D.
was so troubled by the rise of Hitler to power, she found evidence of
her war phobia in the poor placement of Mars in her chart: "The star-
epigrams are all excellent. I think that *Mars* touch is explainable, as
I had, as you know, been up against all sorts of troubles, in the *War*.
And I still 'see red' when people get foolishly patriotic, in the wrong
way. I mean, all sorts of peoples, English and French and German and
American equally. The thing is to keep out of *War*, but I have been
flung into constant cycles of war-scares and war-talk and I hate it
all" (9 January 1933). When the dreaded war finally arrived, H.D.
returned with renewed intensity to astrology and the Adams books:
"I want you to know that those Astrology books you sent me have
simply been more-than-heaven and balm to me. I have a friend, a
lady doctor, who is quite a good astrologer and has been re-working
various aspects for us. I lent her Place in the Sun, but can't let Among
the Stars for, as suddenly it is life for me to pick out various star-
aspects—my own and friends" (15 February 1945).[10]

World War II most likely renewed H.D.'s interest in the occult,
raised it to a level of great intensity, and expanded it into a study of
many different mystical traditions. Though she did not attend church
or join organizations, the occult helped H.D. endure the omnipresence
of sudden, random death. On one level, H.D. wrote, "the supernatural,
within reason, is anodyne" that softens the pain of both fear and the
dreariness of rationed life in wartime where getting food for supper
could occupy a whole day (5 October 1941). In another sense, H.D.
found predictions or guidance to the "day's possibilities" in the Tarot
cards and the Zodiac (1 May 1941). But on the deepest level, the destruction of war made acute her need to find meaning embedded in
the harsh realities of a nightmarish existence.

During the war, this imperative to understand destruction went
deeply in two directions, both of which ultimately fed into her art:
extensive reading about past esoteric traditions and actual experience
in current forms of occult practice. While H.D.'s involvement during
the twenties and thirties gave her some mastery over the details of difficult occult disciplines, she learned from her reading in the forties
how they were all linked together into a single, syncretist tradition.
Denis de Rougemont's *Love in the Western World*, which H.D. read
in the first French edition in 1939, was probably the initial stimulant
for research. He argued that western mystical sects were interconnect-

ed currents of an evolving Manichaean tradition that originated in the mystery religions of the middle east. Its fundamental dogma was the dualism of Light and Dark, the imprisonment of the divine soul in the matter of creation, and the fatal search of the soul for total reabsorption into the Divine. Love was synonymous with Divine Spirit, and through Love, the initiate could attempt transcendence of matter and the force of evil.[11]

De Rougemont asserted that this tradition has occasionally been the official one, but has more often been the religious sect driven underground by the Establishment of the times, persecuted as a group, and forced to meet in secret and to pass its wisdom down from person to person, sometimes even orally. Nonetheless, it continued to evolve as the mystical undercurrents in Judaism, expressed especially in the Kabbalah, and in Christianity, expressed particularly in the descendants of Gnosticism within the church. The most brilliant "flare-up" of this tradition was the Cathar heresy during the twelfth and thirteenth centuries in Europe. De Rougemont's controversial argument further claims that the tradition of Courtly Love was Cathar in origin and that the troubadours expounded a mysticism of Divine Love coded in the language of human passion. For initiates, the poetry and celebration of joy had an inner mystery. Art, through these roving musicians and poets, kept alive the Church of Love. Art became the central expression and record of religious vision and commitment.[12]

De Rougemont's important fusion of art and religion in the esoteric Church of Love may be controversial to medievalists, but his theory of a single current of mysticism permeated H.D.'s additional esoteric reading. W.B. Crow, the writer H.D. mentioned in *Tribute to Freud*, argued for example that "there exists one single Pandean or Catholic religion of which all cults are more or less modified variations." Each religion is "one form of the esoteric and divine secret knowledge" which Crow, as astrologer, believed was always in part astrological.[13] With his occult base in the Tarot, Jean Chaboseau insisted that traditions like the Tarot and alchemy are only parts of a single "Tradition" that he called "Hermeticism." Hermeticism is more a way of thinking than a set of doctrines, he argued. It "is the more subtle side of Philosophy, the more mysterious if you wish. It incorporates the totality of 'secret' spoken knowledge—Kabbalah or the science of letters and numbers, astrology, alchemy. Each has different aspects, but they are held together in a whole." Hermeticism is a "remembrance of a survival of forgotten or dispersed races." But it has been recorded in the temples, works of art, and books of certain artists throughout the ages who have been sensitive to "these manifestations of Spirit." "The principal end of Hermeticism," Chaboseau continued, "is Reintegration—the conquest of divine Knowledge."[14]

The syncretist Robert Ambelain provided H.D. with her most comprehensive discussion of mystical sects. He described the "fermentation" of mysticism as an evolving process of loosely connected esoteric sects who affirmed a secret wisdom often disguised in the official texts of established religions. In *Dans l'ombre des cathédrales*, for example, Ambelain decoded the hermetic symbols that he claimed had been secretly encased by artisans who built the cathedral of Notre Dame. The Christian saints Anne and Mary that stand above the various portals were earlier "pagan" goddesses Cybele and Isis, clothed in the acceptable garments of Christianity.[15] Their presence recalled the mystery, magic, and wisdom associated with the ancient esoteric cults that were celebrated in goddess religions of the Near East. Similarly, all the established religions of the ancient Near East contained a component of followers who extended the symbols of the religion into a concealed dimension of mysticism. The religious scholar or mystic who can break the code can experience and contribute to the tradition of "la Sagesse." This religion centers on a transcendent deity bearing little resemblance to the jealous Jehovah of Genesis who tried to keep Adam and Eve in ignorance and punished their search for "la Sagesse" so severely. Ambelain argued that the secret codes and mythologies of this religion have been handed down through the generations, often orally, but sometimes in esoteric texts, visual forms, and art.[16]

H.D.'s careful reading of these modern scholars of mysticism provided a philosophical context for her long-established interest in the popularized forms of the occult. She considered, for example, the contemporary cult of St. Theresa as a modern version of the protean tradition, one in which she could participate.[17] But Spiritualism was the branch of the occult that offered her the most extended personal experience of that tradition during the war. Spiritualism affirmed the continuing existence of the soul after death and the possibility of communication with the dead through some form of medium. The transmission of messages from the dead to the living is said to come in the form of table-rapping or knocking, the "possession" of a psychic individual, or some such phenomenon that denies rational conceptions of space and time. H.D.'s introduction to Spiritualism began when she joined the Society for Psychical Research in London so that she could use their library and attend lectures.[18] Founded in 1882, this Society did not advocate Spiritualism or any other form of the occult. It was established to scientifically investigate the claims of psychic phenomena, and over the years it recorded an enormous number of such claims. At the Society, she heard the psychic medium Arthur Bhaduri lecture. She wrote to Jordan that she considered him to be "very gifted, in fact, he is a 'seer,' " and that he had asked her help in finding him some lecture engagements in the United States (28 July 1942).

Bhaduri's "gift" became evident to H.D. when he described the events surrounding Peter Van Eck and spoke with startling clarity about her mother. She sent Bryher to Bhaduri for advice about some "dangerous war work" she wanted to undertake. Bryher in turn was so impressed that she invited Bhaduri and his mother to the flat in Lowndes Square. In 1943, the two of them joined Bryher and H.D. once a week for a séance on the small, oak tripod table built and originally owned by William Morris.[19] In the Hirslanden Notebooks, H.D. recalled her joy in their sessions, which she called a "kindergarten" where Bhaduri taught them the "alphabet (1 tap for yes, 2 for no)" for spirit talk (III, p. 6). Most of the séances, however, were trivial, H.D. recounted in the matter-of-fact style and often ironic tone of the first section of *The Sword Went Out to Sea*: "One felt sometimes that Manisi [Bhaduri] was simply reading one's thoughts, not that that made what he said any the less effective, from the psychic or psychological angle, but why sit in the dark and be told things accurately and in nice detail, that one already knows?" (*Sword*, pp. 18–19). Finally, H.D. and Bhaduri had a few sessions alone that produced visions of vivid clarity, hieroglyphs that helped shape H.D.'s growing involvement with Spiritualism and provided important symbols for her later novels and poems.

H.D. regarded her work with Bhaduri as preparation for the more important séances she held alone after she heard Lord Hugh Dowding lecture on his communications with his dead pilots. Dowding had been relieved of his post as Chief Air Marshal of the Royal Air Force shortly after his victory in the Battle of Britain. He continued to be a prominent public figure through his lectures all over Britain as an advocate of Spiritualism. H.D. read his books on Spiritualism and sent his *Many Mansions* to Jordan.[20] H.D. heard him lecture twice and began a correspondence with him, she wrote in the Hirslanden Notebooks (III, p. 7).[21] In 1945 she met with him seven times, a number whose mystical significance in numerology seemed to be a sign to H.D. of the nature of their relationship. One of his letters to her asked her to join his "home-circle," but when she "consulted" her own "circle," the table rapped "no" (*Sword*, pp. 25–30). When Bhaduri's marriage alienated H.D. from him, she began to hold séances on the William Morris table by herself (*Sword*, pp. 30, 37, 51–66). During one of these sessions on September 3, 1945, H.D. believed that she received the first of a series of messages from five of Dowding's dead RAF pilots. She expressed considerable uncertainty on how to explain these events:

> When I was alone, the table came to life immediately. It's true we started with a lot of questions on my part, and with yes or no from the table. I didn't know who was answering but that didn't make any difference. I kept, more or less, to the surface of things. . . . I may have jogged the yes and the no from the table each time, by contracting or expanding those arm and wrist muscles, at the prompting of the unconscious mind—or I may not have. . . . Nor can I say positively, that Lad and Larry, Ralph, John and the rest were disembodied spirits, or whether I made them up. (*Sword*, pp. 53, 94)

But in spite of this uncertainty, she never doubted her own integrity or their spiritual truth, whatever their empirical reality may have been: "If this was a fairy-tale, it was very real to me. It was true. I never for a moment, doubted the integrity of Lad and Larry, of Ralph, of John, of Howell, of myself. That is, I never doubted his sincerity nor my own" (*Sword*, p. 63).

The messages themselves were not nearly so puzzling as the messengers who brought them. The pilots urgently demanded that H.D. carry their concerns to Dowding because his own "home-circle" would not receive them. As H.D. "read" the letters rapped out on the table, the pilots wanted to warn the world of the terrible dangers and natural disasters that would ensue from the release of atomic energy (*Sword*, pp. 189–90). H.D. recorded their messages and invited Dowding to tea. She saw Dowding three times alone, and each time he refused to talk with her about the pilots' warning. At first, he was very upset and insisted that the pilots must be a "lower order" of disembodied spirits—certainly not on the level of his sources—and finally he kept changing the subject back to himself and his work. On February 14, 1946, H.D. received a letter from him in which he wrote: "No. I can not be expected to receive messages of this sort. They are both frivolous and uninspiring. Of course, it is none of my business but it would be better if you gave up this work" (*Sword*, p. 74). For H.D., his letter was an ultimate "repudiation," a rejection of her that was superimposed on a series of betrayals by ideal male figures, many of whom were connected in some way with war. Dowding's letter was the immediate catalyst for her period of severe illness in 1946.[22]

After her recovery, H.D. never returned to conducting or participating in Spiritualist séances. During the fifties, she continued to explore the significance of astrology, as her chart for Erich Heydt and her letters from her astrologer demonstrate. But the central direction of her esoteric involvement was the syncretist Kabbalah of Robert Ambelain and the hermeticism of Jean Chaboseau. She had absorbed the occult mysticism of these and other writers during the forties, but during her years at Küsnacht Klinik, the eloquent theology of Ambelain's *La Kabbale practique* became the focus of her occult activities. Her quest for an alternative to modernist nihilism found haven in the Kabbalistic doctrine of the En-Soph—the Divine One that manifests itself in a multiplicity of emanations encompassing all creation in meaningful pattern. Although H.D. ignored Ambelain's minute prescriptions for elaborate rituals of invocation, she did experiment in her own way with his "practical Kabbalah"—the invocation of the seventy-two angels who embody different attributes of the En-Soph and rule all the hours of the day. Gustav Davidson, author of *Dictionary of Angels*, acknowledged H.D.'s help in the completion of his reference book and thereby revealed how extensive her interest in the Kabbalah had become in the fifties: "I would be remiss if I did not speak here of the help accorded me by the late H.D. (Hilda Doolittle), noted American poet long resident abroad. She was an avid reader in esoterica; also a devout believer in angels, whom she invoked by name and apostrophized in song. From Zurich, where she made her home for many years until her recent death, she sent me rare books in practical cabala 'for our mutual benefit.' Our friendship, though brief and late in coming, I count among my most cherished memories."[23] *Sagesse* was the song in which H.D. invoked the guardian spirits of the En-Soph, and its imagery is thoroughly based on "Le Grande Arbre Kabbalistique of Oedipus Aegyptiacus" reproduced in *La Kabbale practique* (see Figure 3).

The underlying motivations for the expansion of H.D.'s esoteric search from the Tarot of the twenties to the invocations of the fifties were the same cluster of reasons that brought her to Freud: the search for direction in a "drifting" century; the need to fortify herself for the impending war; the quest to avoid the destruction wrought by "racial separateness" by linking the personal dream with the myths of everyone, everywhere; the desire to explore and confirm beliefs; and the hope that such knowledge would "canalize" her energies into the visionary expressions of her art (*T.F.*, pp. 13, 93–94). In short, the foundation of H.D.'s esoteric involvement was the dual dimension of modernism: the awareness of fragmentation and the consequent search to create new meanings.

H.D.'s modernist impulse toward the inner explorations of esoteric tradition and psychoanalysis was not a rejection of the external world as irrelevant, but an attempt to find a vision that would explain it. It is important to remember that H.D. was neither apolitical nor oblivious to the rise of social movements that tore apart the fabric of the twentieth century. *Tribute to Freud* attests to her astute awareness of the significance of Hitler's rise to power in the early thirties, as well as her commitment to the symbolic-political act of defiance. Once, for example, H.D. braved the empty streets of Vienna, deliberately following the swastikas chalked on the sidewalk leading up to Freud's door, to attend her usual session. "Why did you come," Freud wanted to know. "*I am here because no one else has come*. As if again, symbolically, I must be different" (*T.F.*, p. 61). During the early thirties H.D. was involved with Bryher in "refugee work" with Jews escaping the growing tide of anti-Semitism. Pound's politics, especially his anti-Semitism, appalled H.D. and caused the estrangement in their friendship that was not healed until his commitment to St. Elizabeth's.[24] During the forties, H.D. explained her decision to remain in London as her refusal to be safe while the people of her adopted country were in danger.[25] Even the messages she interpreted from the RAF pilots and her subsequent descent into madness attest to her concern with the political world which she correctly perceived as dangerously headed in the direction of atomic war.

Although H.D.'s esoteric and psychoanalytic explorations did not

Figure 3. Le Grand Arbre Kabbalistique, d'après Kircher (Œdipus Ægyptiacus), from Robert Ambelain, *La Kabbale practique*

result from a desire to escape external reality, their emphasis on the priority of psychical reality did result partially from a self-conscious alienation from political involvement as an effective way to usher in a new age. Before World War II, H.D. had been impatient with the "brilliant" political talk of her friends whom she compared to those who knew the "flood" was coming, but only "counted the nails and measured the planks with endless exact mathematical formulas, but didn't seem to have the very least idea of how to put the Ark together" (T.F., p. 57). After the war, she believed that external organizations merely reproduced inner chaos on a grand scale and that change must begin within the individual to be realized on a societal level. Esoteric study as well as psychoanalysis was the starting point of such change. She wrote in *The Sword Went Out to Sea*:

> . . . if you are consoled or integrated, you help console and integrate the scattered remnant. I don't think society can be reconstructed from outside. I have said if there is comfort, it is solitary. When the ego or centre of our amorphous, scattered personality crystallizes out, then and then only, are we of use to ourselves and other people. I have said it is *sauve qui peut*, even for the best of us. In saving myself, one creates a shell, not the isolated, highly individual spiral-shell I spoke of, but a minute coral-shell, one of a million, or a single wax-cell of the honeycomb.
>
> If we think of policies or politics, we are forced to think in vague generalities. As the outer world has expanded, so has the inner. Probably it was the struggle to comprehend the incomprehensible actions that were taking place outside, that forced me by a law of compensation, to try to grapple with the forces inside myself, or outside the material world. (*Sword*, p. 41)[26]

The psychic experiences H.D. had over the forty-year period of her involvement in esoteric tradition convinced her that she had a special "gift" that destined her to make important contributions to the "coral-shell" communities of the world through her art. The appeal of orthodoxy, so compelling for fellow modernist T.S. Eliot, fell on deaf ears in H.D.'s case. She deliberately and consistently avoided centering her search for meaning in mainstream religious traditions. As she wanted to tell Freud, she was "different" and that "difference" was a source of direction as well as pain (T.F., pp. 26, 32, 61–63, 74, 98, 106–107). H.D.'s "difference" included not only the unorthodox forms of her womanhood, but also her attraction to the esoteric traditions often persecuted for their difference from the establishment forms of Christianity or Judaism. As a woman, H.D. was particularly sensitive to the concept of divinity in esoteric tradition which differed sharply from the masculine monotheism of the mainstream. H.D.'s journals and unpublished novels establish that she perceived the difference between orthodox and heterodox traditions in terms of their contrasting treatment of woman as both symbol and believer.

The orthodox traditions created a masculine imagery of God and used this ideology to justify taboos against women in the priesthood and to rationalize cultural beliefs in male superiority.[27] The heterodox mystical traditions, on the other hand, legitimized the place of woman as symbol in the divine pantheon. Although the names differed, they all posited the primal existence of a divine One, a latent androgynous Whole that incorporates equally both masculine and feminine potential. The gods and goddesses of various mythic traditions were said to incarnate those dual principles of the androgynous One. As dualistic theologies, these loosely connected traditions taught that the dualism of masculine and feminine structures all manifest creation and governs all other dualisms such as light-dark, good-evil, positive-negative, spirit-flesh, active-passive, life-death, reason-intuition, rational-emotional, and sun-moon.[28]

Such traditions restored a Feminine Principle to the concept of divinity. At times, this aspect of their mythologies influenced established religious traditions. According to de Rougemont, for example, the Virgin Mary achieved her stronghold in the Catholic Church as a result of the Cathar heresy and the Albigensian Crusade. While the Inquisition succeeded in driving underground the Church of Love, in which Mary played a central symbolic role, the Catholic Church instituted a major cult of the Virgin mother to hold the loyalty of its wavering followers.[29] The current of mysticism in Judaism developed extensive mythologies of the Shekinah, the female form of the divine spirit. Under this influence, the mainstream traditions of Judaism, which emphasized the Law given to Moses, made room for the Shekinah who is welcomed into the home in the Sabbath ceremonies performed by women every Friday night.[30] Nonetheless, woman as symbol remained at the periphery of orthodox Christianity and Judaism. In contrast, esoteric sects brought female symbols into the center of their mythological systems.

In both *Her* and *Asphodel*, H.D. wrote about the different roles allowed to woman as both believer and symbol in mystical and mainstream traditions. Saint Joan in both novels appears as a mystic whose capacity to see visions interconnects with her rebellion against traditional norms of femininity. Her defiance wins her persecution by the Church, on the one hand, but also worship of sorts by her modern "sisters." Hermione (H.D.) and Fayne (Gregg) identify with Joan as they fuse their early rejection of heterosexual conventions, their love for each other, and their psychic potential for visionary experience. As they look at a statue of Joan in Rouen, Joan functions simultaneously as a hero who validates their own life choices and as a warning of the costs of being "different": "They [the Church] had trapped her, a girl who was a boy and they would always do that. They would always trap them . . . break them, for seeing things, having 'visions' seeing things like she did and like Fayne Rabb. This was a warning. Joan of Arc."[31]

Completed shortly after *Her*, H.D.'s unpublished historical novel *Pilate's Wife* similarly combines the discovery of mysticism with the affirmation of woman as symbol in the pantheon of divine spirit. The novel records the religious conversion of Veronica, Pilate's wife, to the new religion of Jesus, the Jew. But this religion bears little relationship to the later Christianity of the Church Fathers. Influenced by Arthur Weigall's *The Paganism in Our Christianity*, H.D. believed that Christianity arose out of a convergence of mystery cults, especially those associated with Mithraism and the worship of Isis. A decade before she read Ambelain, H.D. already accepted the theory of some religious scholars that the cult of Jesus was linked with a number of other esoteric sects active in the middle east. Veronica's conversion, perhaps a version of H.D.'s own attraction to mysticism, depends finally upon Isis and the role of women in the new religion. At the beginning of the novel Veronica is indeed "Pilate's wife," a woman with only a hazy sense of any identity outside of her role as wife. As the novel opens, she is trying to say her name: "she spelled her own [name] arduously, sensing in its hard and pebble-like lustre, some unknown lustre. . . . 'I am Veronica.' She could say that and sense it, bite it and feel it. . . . 'I am Veronica' sounded stranger to her, more irreconcilable than the domina and augusta, the my-lady and your-highness, that echoed about her. . . . She walked listlessly, at times, in mock solemnity, always a little out of step with the procession she was, of necessity, part of."[32] The novel ends with her ability to name herself without ambivalence: " 'I am Veronica,' said Veronica, realizing at last, that she was a person" (*P.W.*, p. 167).

Veronica's transformation from "wife" to "person" results from her involvement with the mystical cults introduced to her by two lovers: Mnevis, a priestess of Isis from Crete, and Fabius, a man entranced with the "ideal brother-love" he found in the Roman soldier's cult of Mithra. Fabius acquaints Veronica with Mithraism and broadly hints to her that Jesus is at the center of the cult. Although Veronica is fascinated with tales of the young Jew, she feels left out of Fabius' description of "ideal brother-love" and annoyed with his dismissal of her need to find "an ideal sister." She concludes that the cult of Mithra "leaves . . . out women" (*P.W.*, p. 62).

Veronica finds her "ideal sister" and the image of "perfect Woman" in her lover Mnevis and the Goddess whom Mnevis embodies. Isis has a "wholeness" that Veronica emulates and then finds in her love for Mnevis: "Isis was a magician and goddess of wisdom. The Greeks, for all their immense pragmatism and logical philosophy, had had to split the perfect image of the perfect Woman, say here is Love, faithless [Aphrodite] and here is Wisdom, loveless [Athene]. Yet even Aphrodite and Athene, re-modelled, flung into some blasting furnace, to return, one perfectly welded figure, would yet lack something—something of the magic that Isis held in Egypt" (*P.W.*, p. 25). Isis fuses Love and Wisdom in her magic, and the passion Veronica feels for Mnevis brings the spirit of Isis into her search for identity. She thinks: "It occurred to Veronica suddenly that her visits to Mnevis *were* by way of searching a feminine counter-part of deity" (*P.W.*, p. 110). Rediscovery of female divinity is tied to her love for Mnevis. And that love becomes a form of self-love, a kind of self-acceptance that makes Veronica's transformation possible: "Sister to sister, lover to lover, Veronica had loved Mnevis, as one grown satiated with too much admiration, turns to view a familiar face, washed clear as in spring water, and realizes with no vanity that that face is one's own" (*P.W.*, p. 88).

After the flowering of her love for the spiritual and human symbols of Woman, Veronica is ripe for conversion to the cult of Jesus. Mnevis reveals that she is a disciple of Jesus, and explains to Veronica that his cult is especially open to women. In Veronica's meditations of Jesus she often wonders whether or not he "leaves out women":

"Anyhow, what use had Jews for women? But that was the whole point. From the first Mnevis had insisted that this [Jesus] was some sort of paragon who loved women, yet was no lover. Yet who was a lover" (*P.W.*, p. 71). And later, she thinks: "This Jesus had given new shape to the vine, the vine in blossom. . . . He had spoken of love and the outcast woman" (*P.W.*, p. 167). At one point she summarized the "intrinsic wisdom" of Jesus' message: "that all men are gods. What he was and could do, he constantly asserted, all men could do and would do. All men and (this was the oddest thing about it) all women. What Eastern prophet had ever given women a place in the spiritual hierarchy?" (*P.W.*, p. 130). Veronica decides that Jesus gives women an equal place in the spiritual hierarchy because he is androgynous: numerology shows her that the number of his name (6) is the same as the number for Aphrodite (6). She doesn't use the word "androgyny," but she finds in his creed of Love and his symbols (lilies, doves, trees, and fruit) evidence that he incorporates the occult mysteries of Isis. Her discovery that Mnevis and the worshippers of Mithra have managed to steal the body of Jesus from his tomb completes her conversion. Fabius was mistaken in his belief that Jesus represented only ideal brother-love. Veronica approaches the new mystery religion through Isis and an ideal sister-love. She accepts Jesus because his religion makes room for women in its spiritual hierarchy. With her discovery of wholeness in mythic symbols, she emerges out of her role as wife into acceptance of her self as woman, as person.

Veronica's healing conversion embodies the special appeal esoteric tradition had for H.D. as a woman. But the incorporation of female symbols in the divine does not fully explain H.D.'s sense of her own individual "gift." She was convinced that the occult phenomena she had directly experienced were "signs" indicating an important destiny she would fulfill in her art. As she wrote to Jordan about Tarot, "I don't advise people 'playing' with these things, forces, etc. Only you see I have had some sort of 'initiation.' I am sure you know I am not boasting. I mean ... what I do, sometimes, I believe is 'directed' " (10 March 1930). In the thirties Freud decoded her dreams and "symptoms" as her wish to be a Pythoness and the founder of a new religion. Throughout her life, H.D. found confirmation for his "readings" in the Delphic utterances of the occult. These directives had a profound influence on the transformation of her art from the imagist "gem" to the cosmic poetry of her later years.

H.D. believed that her psychic powers were her inheritance from her mother, especially from her mother's Moravian heritage. H.D.'s explosion into poetry of prophecy in the *Trilogy* resulted in part from the sense of personal initiation she felt as she read extensively in Moravian Church history in the early forties. Much to her surprise, she found that the "staid," "respectable" Moravian Church of her childhood was the descendent of a mystical sect often known as the Unitas Fratrum that was established in the fifteenth century in Moravia, persecuted in the sixteenth and seventeenth centuries, and revived by Count Zinzendorf in 1722. *The Mystery*, an unpublished novel H.D. wrote in 1951, centers on her reconstruction of overlapping family and church history.[33] But *The Gift*, her "childhood autobiography," is even more important as evidence for H.D.'s sense of personal initiation. The central action of *The Gift* is a revelation of forgotten Moravian mystery when Hilda's grandmother tells the story of her husband's discovery of secret church documents. The contemporary church regarded Moravian rituals such as the "love feast" and the "kiss of peace" as "scandal" best to be forgotten. But Mammalie's history of the "Hidden Church" reveals the mystical significance of these rituals that existed "underground" from the time of the Templars. Many Moravians were burned for witchcraft, but they continued to worship secretly with a cup decorated with an "S." This "S" did not represent the serpent of the Devil, but an earlier serpent symbol that signified the "Sanctus Spiritus, the Holy Spirit." Mammalie explained the symbols to her grandchild because she believed Hilda had "the gift," that is the capacity to comprehend and experience the mystery. Her "gift" to her grandchild was to initiate Hilda by recalling her own mystical experience for the child. As she listened to music one day, she recalled, she felt suddenly possessed by the joy of Love: "I could not tell you of that laughter, it was the laughter of the water; indeed it was the outpouring of the Mystic Chalice that Paxnous' priest too had a name for; it poured from the sky or from the inner realm of the Spirit, this laughter that ran over us."[34] In the alchemy of memory, H.D. felt marked or chosen by this religion of Love; and to counter imminent death from the Nazi forces of hate, H.D. "pieced

together" the significance of her childhood initiation. The Nazi nightmare became in part a modern instance of a centuries-old persecution.

The sense of initiation to which H.D. believed her Moravian
heritage destined her permeated her experiences in Corfu and her
readings of Tarot cards and numbers. But even more importantly, her
natal horoscope predicted a destiny based on the powers of psychic
intuition and expressed in the prophecies of her art. Chart reading is
an admittedly subjective art, even for the most experienced astrologer. There is no single, definitive reading of a horoscope any more than
there can be an objective analysis of a dream. Unfortunately, H.D.
left only fragmentary indications in her letters to Jordan about what
significance she found in her horoscope. Nonetheless, speculation on
how H.D. read her chart is possible and valuable because her chart
contains elements that are strikingly similar to the messages she found
in her dreams with Freud's help. Read as a complex whole, her chart
affirmed her special destiny as an artist and designated the cosmic
dimensions of esoteric philosophy and religion as her special gift.[35]

At first glance, H.D.'s horoscope seems to pose nothing but contradictions and raise the immediate question of how she found any
validation for herself as creative artist in her chart. Her Sun sign, determined by the placement of the Sun in relationship to the Zodiac
at the time of birth, was Virgo, a sign that Adams described in unrelievedly negative terms. She wrote that the Virgo native is practical
and interested in the details of material advantage: "His outlook is
apt to be petty and his reason itself hampered by the perpetual in-
trusion of the pragmatical viewpoint. He is, therefore, practically incapable of producing anything with the fire of true genius."[36] When
H.D. wrote that "my [Virgo] keeps me stacking papers and paying
bills," she echoed Adams: "the native of Virgo is extraordinarily well
adapted to routine business. . . . Virgo makes an excellent bank clerk
or cashier." H.D. seems to have missed her calling. If she believed that
these Virgo qualities expressed her basic potentialities, why did she
attempt to create, to strike sparks of genius, to pursue a religious
vision? Or, since she did attempt these things, why didn't she reject
astrology and turn elsewhere for guidance? That H.D. did not abandon astrology completely after reading Adams demonstrates much
about her method of astrological quest. She was not tied to a literal
reading of a chart as a static map of the psyche; her vision expanded
to a comprehension of her chart, and therefore her psyche, as a dynamic interaction of conflicting potentialities. Read as a whole, her

chart contains a cluster of factors that "counteracts a lot of the Virgo primness," as H.D. wrote to Jordan, and indicates creativity, exceptional mental powers, and strong interest in religion and philosophy. First, Mercury was the ruler of H.D.'s Sun sign. Since Adams described Mercury extensively in terms of his roots with the Greek Hermes and the Egyptian Thoth, H.D. most likely looked beyond his attribute as the god of commerce to an inner reading she based on his symbolical associations with the Greek Hermes, the Egyptian Thoth, Hermes Psychopompous, Hermes Trismegistus, and the Christian "Word."[37] As Thoth, he invented writing; as Psychopompous, his magic wand Caduceus led the dead souls to a new life in the underworld; as Trismegistus, he was the patron of alchemy and hermetic wisdom; as the Greek Hermes, he was the patron of both science and art; as the Christian "Word," he was the agent of creation and salvation. Hermes is the dominant force in H.D.'s chart, and he appears as her personal patron in the *Trilogy* with all these symbolic associations (*T.*, pp. 7, 14–17, 63, 71–77). The central role Hermes plays in the *Trilogy* emerges partially, I would argue, from the sense of personal initiation H.D. found in her horoscope.

The second factor in H.D.'s horoscope that pointed to a special religious destiny is her Ascendant, the sign on the horizon at the moment of birth. The qualities of Sagittarius, she wrote to Jordan, "make all the difference" and no doubt appeared to H.D. to draw out the symbolic associations of Hermes. As a force in her psyche, Sagittarius confirmed the messages Freud read in her Princess dream —that she wanted to be a Moses, a founder of a new religion. The symbol of Sagittarius is an arrow shooting off into the heavens. Its sigil is the rainbow, that vision of hope and promise which God showed to Noah as his covenant to humanity and that prism of colors and "rainbow feathers" which serve as central image of divinity in the *Trilogy* (pp. 109–10). Ambelain wrote in *Adam, dieu rouge* that Lucifer, the lightbearer, was associated with Sagittarius and linked the sign with spiritual journey, religion, wisdom, and initiation.[38] Adams clearly identified the sign with the gift of prophecy, for "it is swift and accurate in thought" and its "objective and subjective mind work harmoniously together."[39] Like H.D. in *Tribute to Freud*, Adams echoed the prophet Joel to describe the Sagittarian potential: "The Sagittarian is a born idealist; he is the young man who sees visions and the old man who dreams dreams" (*T.F.*, p. 36).

The placement of two important planets in H.D.'s horoscope is the third aspect of her chart that must have reinforced her reading of Sagittarius. Jupiter and Uranus both appear in the sign Libra, significantly in the House of Profession (Tenth House) where their influence would center on H.D.'s chosen profession as an artist. Adams' interpretations of Jupiter and Uranus in Libra must have strengthened H.D.'s belief that she had been chosen to express a new religious vision through her art. Uranus in Libra is a particularly strong placement that allows Uranus' potential for explosive and occult genius to be materialized. "This planet," Adams wrote, "is the planet of genius, the planet of the secret magical power in man."[40] An unconventional genius, it "desires the infinite"; it is "the essence of volcanic fire. There is no planet so strange, so revolutionary, so occult and mysterious. . . . Uranus gives tremendous occult forces; which, fused constructively, can make Uranian natives powers in their own sphere and enable them to be the vehicles through which comes a message to mankind. That message may be uttered in terms of art, science or philosophy." The planet Jupiter, also well placed in Libra, strengthened the tendencies of Uranus and made it more likely that those psychic gifts could be channeled into achievement. The message of both Uranus and Jupiter in the House of Profession paralleled the latent content H.D. found in her Corfu visions. Both her horoscope and her "symptoms" suggested an artistic destiny in which she would unite prophecy, art, and healing into a message of resurrection for the modern "city of ruin."

H.D. regarded the psychic phenomena she experienced through Spiritualism as her culminating "initiation" whose full meaning on both a personal and universal level would gradually unfold as she continued her research into esoteric tradition. Bhaduri started the process for H.D. in October 1943, when he saw a "Viking Ship" come across the sea bearing messages for her. Seeing a pattern in which the personal and the mythic were superimposed, H.D. "read" the leader as one of the "heros fatal" or the "Prince Lointain" of fairy tale who had always haunted her life.[41] This faraway Prince originated in her father and the father-symbols buried in her unconscious. In Bhaduri's vision, she watched the questing male figure of heroic proportions enter her life, engage her love, and then reject or betray that relationship. In *The Sword Went Out to Sea*, she attempted to decipher the meaning of the Viking Ship for her personal life:

For in my search for the impossible, Le Prince Lointain, shall we say, the old fairy-tale ideal, I somehow never turned back. I went round the labyrinth, but each turn of the spiral brought me a new personi-fication of the lost companion, the twin. There was Geoffrey [Alding-ton], of course. Then Peter Van Eck, dynamic and somewhat older. I suppose Frederick von Alten [Walter von Schmideberg] is really out of this, on the other hand, perhaps the attractive young officer looking down from the wall reminded me of Geoffrey, and von Alten himself was the beneficent father. It was my own father who had inflicted the first blow, given what I believe is known as the "psychic wound" [opposition to her marriage to Pound].

I do not blame him for that. Actually, this "psychic wound" saved me from I do not know what vicissitudes. . . . I had superimposed on Geoffrey—a hero in a small way—on Allen Flint [Pound], a traitor. (*Sword*, pp. 119, 125)

The idealized male hero on the Viking Ship took many forms in her art, but one of them was William Morris, the builder of the séance table and the man H.D. considered her spiritual father (*Sword*, p. 256). H.D. wrote *White Rose and the Red* about William Morris and his "circle" of Pre-Raphaelites as another form of the Viking Ship message.[42] But in her eyes, the most important manifestation of the "Prince Lointain" was Lord Dowding. She believed that Bhaduri's vision of the Viking Ship presaged her meetings with Dowding, their Spiritualist work with the dead pilots, and his betrayal of their rela-tionship. The RAF pilots had selected her to be their Cassandra of atomic doom, but neither Dowding nor the materialist world was will-ing to hear her message of future wars. This microcosmic event of her initiation, victimization, and subsequent attempt to understand the pattern motivated a great deal of her writing in the late forties and fifties. In *Helen in Egypt*, the meditative action of the epic originates in Helen's first meeting with Achilles after the caravel of Osiris leaves the *"legendary* heros fatal" on the beach (*H.E.*, p. 26). Although Achilles exists in multiple dimensions in the imaginative world of the poem, he corresponds to Dowding in H.D.'s own life, as H.D. noted in the Hirslanden Notebooks (I, pp. 24–25; III, p. 27). H.D.'s attempt to translate the hieroglyph of her "initiation" with Dowding and his repudiation of her is the model for Helen's quest to understand the significance of her meeting with Achilles. Dowding was the idealized "heros fatal" not only in *Helen in Egypt*, but also in *White Rose and the Red*, *The Mystery*, and *Vale Ave*. The Hirslanden Notebooks,

Magic Mirror, Compassionate Friendship, and "Thorn Thicket" repeatedly reflect on Dowding's significance in her life and the universal
patterns she felt her experience embodied.

H.D.'s designation of Freud as the "alchemist" who made initiation possible was a specific reference to psychoanalytic séance as preparation for esoteric séance with Dowding. Freud himself would surely
have been uncomfortable with his role as psychic initiator if he had
known that his "séance" would lead to messages from dead RAF pilots. But for H.D., the polarities of science and religion could be integrated. Her portraits of the man of science as the seer of hermetic
vision have their roots in her esoteric studies. Hermeticism provided
H.D. with the philosophical lens through which she perceived Freud's
materialist framework and re-created him as a symbol of the integration she sought. Released from the confines of empirical conceptions
of space and time, H.D. was free to experience seemingly antithetical
forms of knowledge as essentially parallel quests that enriched each
other and revealed the same truths in different language. Her experiences with psychoanalysis gave a psychological cast to her study of
myth, and her immersion in mysticism provided a religious dimension
to her study of the psyche.

A dream she discussed with Erich Heydt in 1957 provides the key
for understanding how H.D. transformed science and religion, inveterate enemies in the twentieth century, into mutually supportive companions in the same quest. In her dream, she led her distinguished
father up the steps of the cathedral to meet the Queen. She felt that
this union of mother and father related to the reconciliation of her
father's science and her mother's art, a synthesis that integrated
science and religion, intellect and vision. H.D. concluded: "They and
the dream reconcile my father's purely formal, rational, scientific
mathematics + astronomy with the inner mystery of the letters and
numbers + the astrology + star lore + 'myth' of the *Kabballe.* . . .
Mathematical Astronomy + 'mystical' religious or esoteric Astrology
are reconciled. Or reality + fantasy ... or intellect + imagination ...
or science + art ... + so on" (Hirslanden IV, p. 22).

H.D.'s reading of this dream presents schematically her belief
that knowledge and knowing are dual in nature. The stars, for example, can be seen from the perspectives of mathematical astronomy
or esoteric astrology, and each form of perception captures an aspect
of essence. Like Janus, reality itself is double-faced, incorporating the

esoteric and the exoteric, the inner and the outer, the spiritual and the empirical. Consequently, the quest for knowledge is also dual, encompassing both science and religion, or science and art. For knowledge to bring "integration" and healing "consolation," it must be a synthesis of dialectical opposites. Compelled by a longing for wholeness, H.D. attempted to join science and religion in a single process of quest.

This philosophical perspective freed H.D. to develop some of the striking similarities between Freud's psychoanalysis and esoteric traditions. A fundamental assumption common to both psychoanalysis and the occult is that all fragments of the psyche are significant, though often obscure, aspects of a coherent whole. In *The Interpretation of Dreams*, for example, Freud established his new science on the astounding presupposition that "every dream . . . has a meaning," a notion that few scientists or psychologists of his day would have accepted. He went on to argue in *The Psychopathology of Everyday Life* and *Jokes and Their Relation to the Unconscious* that jokes, slips of the tongue, accidents, and other such seemingly chance occurrences are in reality important signifiers of the forces at work in human psychology (*T.F.*, p. 104). Similarly, in various forms of occult tradition nothing is without some transcendent significance—no number or letter, no image or event, no fragment of text is random or unconnected to a larger pattern of meaning. Psychoanalysis found the locus o meaning in the individual unconscious, while the occult located th center of significance in a universal spirit. But both joined in th search for the connecting links in an overdetermined world.

Significant fragments of the psyche often manifest in visual form according to both Freud and esoteric tradition. Tarot cards in particu lar are an external projection of internal dream symbols onto th esoteric records of time. The products of an ancient time when, a Freud would say, humanity was in its infancy, the Tarot cards spea in code, in visual language, just as the unconscious does. The *tablea vivant* of the luminous dream is materialized, schematized into symbolic system, and handed down through the generations of Tar readers. One of H.D.'s books on the Tarot, for example, claimed th the Tarot is a universal book, but a "mute" one because it is a co lection of images. These images cannot be translated by reading book filled with verbal formulas, for words lie, never being an a curate intermediary for spirit. The truth is hidden in the person depths: "We can only discover it in ourselves, in the obscure depth of our personality." In a passage that H.D. underlined heavily, Wirth continued that the good reader has learned the art of active meditation: "he meditates, reflects intensely, searches, reasons, compares until an Apollonian light rises in his spirit."[43] Given her interest in psychoanalysis at a time when she was using the Tarot regularly, H.D. would probably have seen an analogy between meditation on the Tarot and free association on her dreams in the semi-darkness of Freud's office: no matter how different their language, both psychoanalysis and the Tarot made possible some contact with a strange and mysterious realm.

David Bakan, in *Sigmund Freud and the Jewish Mystical Tradition*, argued that the similarity between psychoanalysis and esoteric tradition is not accidental. It emerged, he wrote, out of Freud's Jewish roots and generalized awareness of the basic tenets of Jewish mysticism, particularly the Kabbalah.[44] Whether or not Freud was directly influenced by esoteric Judaism, his fundamental assumption that expressions of the unconscious always appear in disguised form parallels a similar premise in esoteric tradition. The Kabbalah and most other forms of esoterica presume that wisdom is a "Mystery"—hidden, obscure, and known only to those who have the key. H.D.'s extensive esoteric reading provided her with the codes with which to pierce the symbolic disguises. The seemingly random numbers associated with a person's name and birthday, for example, expressed the secrets of destiny, according to numerologists who knew how to decode their meaning. The ancient symbols of the Rose and the Cross, deciphered in their full mystical context, embodied the esoteric wisdom of the centuries-old Rosicrucian sect. Christian cathedral sculpture disguised a hidden celebration of mystery cults as the Christian saints of a monotheistic, masculine religion were clothed with the attributes and symbols of ancient female deities. Jewish mysticism in the Kabbalah held that the Mystery, the Absolute, the Eternal was revealed in the Bible and other sacred texts, but that this truth was hidden in a secret language handed down by tradition. Only the initiated have the key to the translation of the secret doctrines buried in the Bible. Genesis is like the manifest content of a dream. After Kabbalistic analysis, which relies on translation of puns, anagrams, and the hidden meanings of letters, numbers, and symbols, the seeker arrives at the "latent" or underlying true material.[45]

The dimensions of the occult traditions and psychology are certainly different. One deals with the vast eternal; the other deals with the individual psyche in time. But the logic of search is similar. The unconscious is buried, unknown to the conscious mind; the Absolute is hidden, invisible to the ordinary eye. The unconscious is expressed in the difficult code of dreams and neurotic symptoms, undecipherable to most people; the Eternal is revealed in visions and ancient texts for which few people have the key. The unconscious can be partially retrieved with the guidance of the analyst, who has learned to translate the code; the "Mystery" can be understood in some degree by those initiated into the esoteric traditions.

De Rougemont understood these parallels between Freud's concept of disguise and the various myths associated with the submerged mystical tradition. In *Love in the Western World,* he placed both the phenomenon of myth in general and the forms of the Tristan-Iseult myth in particular in the context of these parallels. Given H.D.'s simultaneous exploration of psychoanalysis and mysticism, de Rougemont's discussion of disguise must have underlined for her the synthesis she sought. He wrote that a myth is always "obscure"; its contents "disguised"; its meaning "veiled and hidden." But for those who know the code, the language of myth "betrays" the deeper, real content because it reveals at the same time it conceals, he argued. In writing about the Tristan myth, de Rougemont echoed Freud's metaphor of the dream as "hieroglyph": "A forbidden passion or a shameful love finds expression in the symbols of a hieroglyphic language which consciousness leaves undeciphered."[46] Just as Freud saw the dream as a compromise between the unconscious wish's desire for expression and the ego's need to censor, so de Rougemont understood a myth to satisfy two opposite needs: first, the need to have various submerged thoughts expressed—such as the death wish in the Tristan myth; and second, the need to veil those thoughts and wishes so that the conscious mind cannot understand what has been expressed. De Rougemont referred equally to individual dreams and myth when he wrote: "It is now known that a repressed wish is bound to be manifested, though in such a way as to disguise the nature of this wish."[47]

Freud's theory of disguise was curiously enough C.G. Jung's point of departure from Freud, as he himself described the origins of his school of Analytical Psychology.[48] Since Jung avowed a form of psychological mysticism, it seems ironic that Freud, not Jung, developed ideas that were fundamental to many mystical traditions. But this difference between them is a partial explanation for H.D.'s refusal to meet Jung or consider herself a Jungian. As she wrote in defense of the *"alchemist si remarkable,"* "there is no conflict in my mind between him and the redoubtable Carl Jung, whose house lies several gardens beyond, outside my window, by the lake. I have read very little of Jung and not everything of Freud. But Jung left as they say, medicine for mysticism and as I have said, I studied my mysticism or magic from the French writers Ambelain and Chaboseau."[49]

H.D. found mysticism *in* Freud's medicine, not separate from it, because his theories of the psyche posed principles of esoteric "psychology" in the language of science. The parallels were not limited to the theory of disguise, not even to the similarity of messages that H.D. "read" concerning her artistic identity and destiny. Astrology is a traditional form of psychology, a collection of ancient symbols believed by some to be a complete typology of human behavior. The astrologer's goal, like that of the psychoanalyst, is to teach a person what forces are at work in his or her psyche and environment so that the person can achieve some kind of fulfillment. Adams, for example, stated her psychological purpose in astrology: "Astrology has no more useful function than this, to discover the inmost nature of a man, and to bring it out into his consciousness, that he may fulfill it according to the law of light."[50]

Astrology's claims as a psychology parallel the psychoanalytic hypothesis of the psyche as a dynamic battleground of conflicting impulses. The destiny that an astrologer reads in any one horoscope is no more deterministic than an analyst's diagnosis of neurosis is final; it is a prediction of the potential dynamics or the unique interplay of universal forces active in that person's life. As H.D. wrote to Jordan, the placement of planets in the signs show, not actual deeds, but "tendencies" which may either be developed or ignored depending on other factors in the chart (1 January 1929). If Freud was a "healer" who made neuroses disappear by teaching his patients to understand themselves, so was Adams; she wrote: "The horoscope shows the good points and the bad. The Astrologer must show how to strengthen the one and atrophy the other. . . . it shows tendencies rather than deeds. Tendencies may be unavoidable; deeds are what the individual makes them according to his success in overcoming bad tendencies

and strengthening good ones. Man *can* be the master of his Fate."[51]
Seeming contradictions in a chart point, not to the inaccuracy of astrology, but rather to an area of perpetual conflict which the person
must try to resolve, for example, in H.D.'s horoscope where Venus
appears in the sign Leo, indicating great warmth and love in her
relations with people, and Mercury in the sign Virgo, suggesting
coldness and lack of feeling. Similarly, Freud argued that opposing
forces are always at war within each person, a battle which can lead
to neurosis if some kind of uneasy truce is not established. H.D.'s
two guides, Freud and Adams, believed that increased self-knowledge
of the forces at work beneath the surface creates a far greater chance
of happiness or fulfillment. Both urged H.D. to follow the commands
of the Delphic oracle: "Know Thyself."[52]

From Freud's materialist perspective, astrology and psychoanalysis are inveterate enemies and opposing systems for explaining the
psyche: astrology assumes that human destiny is determined by the
movement of the stars; psychoanalysis assumes that the adult is a
product of childhood and the unceasing conflict between the demands
of the pleasure principle and the reality principle. But from H.D.'s
occultist perspective, the correspondence of inner and outer realities
bridges the chasm between the opposing conceptions of causation in
astrology and psychoanalysis.

H.D. found the logic of reconciliation in the doctrine of Correspondence that permeates esoteric tradition. Occultists consistently
presume a "Correspondence" between the individual and the cosmos,
the personal and the universal, the inner and the outer. What is above
is like that which is below, as Hermes Trismegistus wrote on the
Emerald Tablet. Honoré de Balzac's *Seraphita*, a book H.D. read with
Pound and reflected on repeatedly in *End to Torment*, demonstrates
the principle by which she identified psychoanalysis and mysticism as
dual forms of the same quest.[53] *Seraphita* expounds the mysticism of
Swedenborg by presenting the transcendent figure of the androgynous
Seraphita-Seraphitus. At one point a Norwegian minister explains the
"law of CORRESPONDENCES" by which Seraphita-Seraphitus
achieves her-his integration with Logos:

> To know the Correspondences of the World with Heaven; to know the
> Correspondences which exist between the things visible and ponderable
> in the terrestrial world and the things invisible and imponderable in the

spiritual world, is to hold heaven within our comprehension. All the objects of the manifold creations having emanated from God necessarily enfold a hidden meaning.[54]

By using the law of Correspondence itself, H.D. saw Freud as an androgynous Seraphitus-Seraphita who mediated between the perception of external truths and internal realities. The law of Correspondence also explains her attitude toward the "real" source of her Corfu visions. While Freud would have insisted that to understand her experience, the writing-on-the-wall had to be recognized as hallucination of external truths and internal realities. The law of Correspon-"Whether that hand or person is myself, projecting the images as a sign, a warning or a guiding sign-post from my own subconscious mind, or whether they are projected from outside—they are at least clear enough . . ." (T.F., p. 46).

For Freud, psychological "projection" of images from the unconscious guaranteed their unreality. But for H.D., inner and outer forms of "projection" were interchangeable hieroglyphs of ultimate reality, the "spiritual realism" that underlies the material. This logic governs H.D.'s attitude toward spiritualist phenomena. Rather than claim that the spirit messages were "real" in the empirical sense, she used the correspondence of inner and outer to affirm the bond between the individual psyche investigated by psychoanalysis and the larger realm of spirit that has been explored in esoteric tradition. In *The Sword Went Out to Sea*, she wrote:

> Biologically, I can accept the fact of some inter-relation between dead and living. But I think the whole content of psychic communication can be related, as I said before, to the dream-life of the individual.
>
> We know very little about that dream-life. But we do know that it is only possible to approach the dream-world subjectively. The same might be said of the world of psychic phenomena. . . . It is the legitimate reward of my devotion to the "work," the intense, broken sessions when I concentrated so feverishly on the messages from the RAF, or when if you will, I drew on the submerged content of my own subconscious mind and created a group of lovers or of brothers, to compensate for my own loss and disappointment. However it came about, I found the thread and followed it through the labyrinth. (*Sword*, pp. 143, 233–34)

The possibility that the RAF messages might have originated in her unconscious desires did not challenge their significance to her lifelong search for the patterns that make sense of life's labyrinth. In H.D.'s mind, recognition of the nonempirical foundation of occult phenomena coexisted with certainty of their spiritual reality.

H.D.'s synthesis of inner and outer in the protean forms of psychoanalysis and the occult was based ultimately on the distinction she made between ordinary and "supernormal" states of mind. When the images formed on her hotel wall at Corfu, she referred to this moment as "an unusual dimension, an unusual way to *think*" (*T.F.*, p. 47). Rational notions of space and time are altered as this "unusual way to think" transcends the empirically possible and collapses past, present, and future into the eternal moment. In *Tribute to Freud*, H.D. explained the common origins of dream and occult phenomena in an altered consciousness:

> The series of shadow- or of light-pictures I saw projected on the wall . . . belong in the sense of quality and intensity, of clarity and authenticity, to the same psychic category as the dream of the Princess. . . . For myself I consider this sort of dream or projected picture or vision as a sort of halfway state between ordinary dream and the vision of those who, for lack of a more definite term, we must call psychics or clairvoyants. Memories too, like the two I have recorded of my father in the garden and my mother on Church Street, are in a sense super-memories; they are ordinary, "normal" memories but retained with so vivid a detail that they become almost events out of time, like the Princess dream and the writing-on-the-wall. They are steps in the so-far superficially catalogued or built-up mechanism of supernormal, abnormal (or subnormal) states of mind. (*T.F.*, pp. 41–42)

To describe this state of mind, H.D. twice used an analogy to drugs.[55] The chemical processes set in motion by drugs like LSD and peyote alter conventional notions of space and time and allow images unattached to "objective" reality to predominate. But as Anaïs Nin wrote in her diaries, there are also nonchemical pathways to the altered states of mind, as many artists and mystics have known for centuries.[56] Many of the esoteric writers H.D. was reading warned that the realm of spiritual reality had to be experienced directly and not approached through research alone. In psychoanalysis the buried layers of childhood cannot be recaptured solely by reading textbooks. Each seeker must leave behind for a time the rational thought processes of the conscious mind to let the spontaneous play of free association restore fragments of the unconscious. Similarly, H.D.'s occult reading required direct revelation through altered consciousness. The experience of a transcendent realm may be deciphered through esoteric study just as the psychoanalyst helps to translate the hieroglyphs of the unconscious. But direct experience is essential, as Ambelain admonished in *La Kabbale practique*. Ambelain argued that the seeker must at first be familiar with the doctrines of tradition. But the goal is mystical enlightenment which can only be achieved if the ordinary, rational ways of seeing are left behind and a level of superordinary consciousness achieved. The mysteries, Ambelain continued, will always be inaccessible to scientists because the critical intellect measuring for truth cannot perceive the intangible realities of "la Sagesse" —"all dissection, all explication, can reach nothing of their reality." Historians and critics—the doubters—believe they have explored and described the sanctuary of wisdom, but because genuine experience or revelation is closed off from them by their materialist conception of reality, they can only scratch the surface of the "Temple" whose magical perfume and profound secrets are reserved for "the Children of Love."[57]

What H.D. did with the occultists' validation of nonordinary consciousness, intuition, and meditation was to fuse them with what she had learned about the unconscious from Freud. Her celebration of "supernormal states of mind" bears a resemblance to the transrational modes of perception sought by other modern poets like Williams and Pound. But her version of the transrational is firmly rooted in her experience with mysticism and psychoanalysis. She approached the revelation of divinity necessary to the mystic, the nonrational apprehension of the hidden reality, through the unconscious. The unconscious became her " 'well of living water,' " her "spring" through which she escaped ordinary perception and loosened her ties to the material world. The dreams, daydreams, and hallucinations emerging from her own unconscious provided the medium for her direct, mystical experience of the hidden reality. Freud was important to her precisely because he could help her decipher those direct manifestations of mystery that paralleled what she found in the sacred texts of tradition.

Art increasingly became for H.D. the projection of these supernormal states of mind into the codes of aesthetic form. Art was the materialization or incarnation of the vision that originated in the unconscious. Locating creative inspiration in the psyche's capacity to enter the "4th dimension" of space and time, H.D. considered the occult, like the dream, a "fountain-head" of art (*T.F.*, pp. 23, 92). In describing why the Tarot readings meant "a great deal" to her, for example, H.D. told Jordan that this occult study "feeds some creative imaginative centre" (12 February 1930). In the next letter to Jordan, her account of a London friend who constructed a chart of the "real 'inner' numbers" doubles as a brief self-portrait because the combination of psychoanalysis and psychic phenomenon results in artistic creation: "This woman in London I speak of had a most elaborate [psychic] experience but of course [a] nerve specialist [analyst] understood her. She is now glad of that, as she got at bed-rock finally and is now doing a creative novel, very good, dealing with some such 'trial' and interpreting the whole thing in terms of two symbols as you say you have been doing" (10 March 1930).

The process outlined as her friend's experience became the pattern of the forties for H.D.: intense psychic experience and research combined with psychoanalysis in the cauldron of war produced an outpouring of poetry and prose. Looking back at that process in the Hirslanden Notebooks, H.D. clarified the role the esoteric played in artistic inspiration. Neither rejection by Dowding nor the collapse that followed could break the link between the occult and her art:

> That marriage [to Aldington] had gone on the rocks of course, like my engagement to Ezra Pound. I had not thought of any actual reward of marriage or engagement. But I am "engaged" to the A.M. [Air Marshal] in this mystery of the table and the Viking Ship. . . . We had come together through + for the messages. There was a feeling of exaltation in my later discovery, it was not I personally, who was repudiated. An "engagement" was broken, but broken on a new level, a "marriage" went on the rocks, but it was not the Viking Ship . . . that was wrecked. The Ship was sacred. The messages were sacred, the experience was recorded. My life was enriched, my creative energy was almost abnormal, after I got over the first shock of leaving London. I wrote *Avon*, I wrote three "works" (unpublished) on my unparalleled experiences. I wrote the long *Helen* Sequence, did the recordings for the *Helen*. I wrote on another level, *Magic Mirror*, an account of some of the enigmatic, fascinating people that I met at Küsnacht. (III, p. 24)

The importance of psychic phenomena and the occult to her art in no sense identifies H.D. with those who equated the outpourings of a medium with art. Yeats's recordings of his wife's trancelike utterances in *A Vision* or the aesthetics of automatic writing bear little similarity

to what H.D. meant by saying that the occult fed her "creative imaginative centre" and stimulated artistic expression. Like dreams, psychic
phenomena and esoteric visions had to be translated after an extensive
period of meditation similar to the free association of psychoanalysis.
Like the latent content of dreams encoded in the disguise of the
manifest content, the inner mysteries of transcendent vision were encased in visual forms that concealed meanings as they revealed them.
In projecting these visions into the material forms of art, H.D. never
reproduced them literally or photographically. They first had to be deciphered and then recast in the consciously controlled codes of art. The
careful craft of the imagist poet, parallel to the dream-work in some
of its techniques, had to distill the vision and give it finite form. Occult
experience, then, functioned as a sort of religious muse that inspired
her art.

Distillation of vision in preparation for its projection into artistic
form included an element of judgment. Unlike many occultists, H.D.
did not accept the authenticity or significance of all psychic phenomena produced by supernormal states of mind. Her attitude toward
authority, whether mystic or scientific, was never passive or receptive.
She did not use empirical criteria for "reality-testing" because such
criteria presuppose rational definitions of space and time, the very
perspectives altered by heightened consciousness. But H.D. did not
abandon discrimination, evaluation, and the process of weeding out
the insignificant. Unlike Freud, who valued all fragments of the unconscious equally for what they could reveal of the hidden self, H.D.
insisted upon "differentiation with the utmost felicity and fidelity"
between the "luminous *real* dream" and "the most trivial and tiresome
dreams, the newspaper class" (*T.F.*, p. 92). Because she saw the dream
linked to the occult and the mystical by the role of altered states of
mind, she used the same standards for evaluating all psychic phenomena. "Intensity," "clarity," and "authenticity" are the words she used
to describe the products of "supernormal" consciousness (*T.F.*, p. 41).
They constitute criteria for visions that bear general resemblance to
the twentieth-century concept of epiphany. Less aesthetic that Joyce's,
more religious than Woolf's, less sexual than Lawrence's, and more
psychological than any of them, H.D.'s epiphanies are moments of
great intensity when the unconscious projects "illuminated" hieroglyphs of spiritual realism onto the conscious mind—often in open
defiance of reason and "objective" reality. "Control" of consciousness

by a force beyond consciousness partially accounts for the psychic phenomena that are "authentic." H.D. wrote to Jordan, for example, "I can tell when the cards seem to indicate something direct and real. These fell into order as if by pre-arrangement" (10 March 1930). This "control" is not so much a reference to the supernatural as it is a testament to the power of supernormal states of mind in which "sterile logic, trivial reason" are overwhelmed in epiphany. Religious experience, memory, a reading of the Tarot, dream, invocation of protective angel spirits, communications with the dead—all were potential sources of epiphany for H.D. Their forms were assuredly different, but all were avatars of the unconscious and therefore expressions of "the clearest fountain-head of highest truth" (*T.F.*, p. 92).

The authenticity, clarity, and intensity she looked for in all visionary experience led her to regard with scepticism and some detachment many forms of the occult. Just as she looked at the institution of the Church with suspicion, she felt considerable alienation from popularized versions of the occult. She was quick to assure Jordan on several occasions that she had little to do with the "superficial sensation hunter who uses these things for 'parlor games'" (24 May 1929), and she sharply separated the charlatans from those she considered to be psychically gifted and dedicated to a lifelong search into the complex mysteries of esoteric wisdom. In the months shortly after her most severe breakdown, Spiritualism was the form of the occult that received both her highest praise as the "crowning" initiation of her life and her greatest scepticism. Most spiritualist messages, she wrote in *The Sword Went Out to Sea*, lack the clarity of authenticity:

> For my own part, I have found the boundaries so far explored by psychic-research workers, cloudy and amorphous. My chief objection to the recorded findings of the spiritualists is that their messages and voices seem to come from a vague and commonplace no-man's-land. . . . when the literary resources of the "disembodied" are over-taxed, they seem to have a neat trick of saying, "All this defies description, words can not possibly convey any idea of what is going on over here." This being the case, why does not some robust Robert Browning or some sensitive but competent John Keats step forward and fill in the gap? Recent communications, purporting to come from the poet Shelley, are illiterate to a degree, and the stanzas palmed off as his "disembodied" utterances, are a desecration to his memory. . . . We hear of so-and-so having an Egyptian, a Chinese or a Hindu "guide," or more usually, a Red Feather or a Prairie Flower. But all the recorded

messages I have read from these sources, are indistinguishable from one another. It is almost as if their wordy and amorphous manner of expression were a badge of authenticity. (*Sword*, pp. 265–67).

The "authenticity" of the exotic had no appeal to H.D. whatsoever, and it is no accident that the only organization connected with the occult that she ever joined was the Society for Psychical Research, an avowedly "objective" organization dedicated to an investigation, not a propagandization, of psychic phenomena. Many of the esoteric books H.D. used as resources in her search for "la Sagesse" were connected with secret societies: the Curtisses were leaders in the "Order of the 15," a mystic Christian sect; Ambelain wrote about the contemporary Martinists, Rosicrucians, and French Masons; Mabel Collins was an important writer and leader in the Theosophical Society.[58] But unlike Yeats, H.D. never joined any such organizations. In part, her syncretist approach prevented her from converting to any one pathway to spiritual realism. But also, her self-image suggests an element of detached evaluation. As she wrote in the Hirslanden Notebooks: "the Professor of Astronomy and Mathematics . . . wanted eventually (he even said so) to make a higher mathematician of me or research worker or scientist like (he even said) Madame Curie. He did make a research worker of me but in another dimension" (III, p. 4). When Jordan apparently expressed concern over H.D.'s involvement in Spiritualism and the Catholic cult of St. Theresa, H.D. defended herself by describing the intellectual component in her version of spiritual quest: "I am interested but because I follow a movement it does not mean I am either a 'spiritualist' or a 'catholic.' I am a student of various religious trends" (13 March 1944). Just as she was both patient and student in analysis with Freud, her attitude toward the occult was a blend of both faith and skepticism. As she wrote in reference to Spiritualism, "The inventors of the engines of destruction have no inhibitions about using their minds," and those who would counter the forces of war with a vision of spirit must not abandon the intellect completely (*Sword*, p. 268).

H.D.'s need for critical intelligence to complement the states of supernormal consciousness included a desire for what she called "sanity" and reliability. Her letters to Jordan about her occult friends consistently demonstrate her insistence that clairvoyance and inner vision be accompanied by a healthy grounding in the reality of the external world. Dowding, for example, was in part appealing to H.D.

because he was a military man, she reassured Jordan, a "level-headed bloke" who "made a good plea for the 'straight deal'" (13 March 1944). And the woman who did Tarot readings convinced H.D. of her authenticity: "But this one woman is 'reliable' and SANE. That is why I trust her and believe her ... of course 'insanity' would be the cry of the outside" (10 March 1930).

H.D. associated "sanity" with reliable seers, with those whose epiphanies had "authenticity," "clarity," and "intensity." But she recognized that all such vision appeared "insane" from the perspectives of social convention and the rationalist definitions of reality that have predominated in western culture. As Lowdnes (Pound) said to Hermione in *Her*, she and her psychic friend Fayne would have been burned as witches a few centuries earlier. H.D.'s letters to Jordan never lost sight of how these occult pursuits appeared in the eyes of many, and she often repeated an appeal for discretion and secrecy. Her revelations about the mystery of "'inner numbers'" were accompanied by the warning: "This is of course for YOU as I do not like my great 'discovery' abused by the wrong people. You know how it is . . . I am sure you feel the same" (24 May 1929). In encouraging Jordan to write her about her psychic experience, she wrote: "I shall be so glad to hear from you. Just write everything ... you can depend on my discretion. . . . I should go on just as per usual and not tell people too much. Anything like that makes people say 'mad'" (10 March 1930). Later in the same letter, she ended her Tarot reading with a plea for secrecy: "As I said before, this is between ourselves. I mean, you KNOW what people are like." William Carlos Williams was apparently one of those whose mocking voice H.D. most feared, for she wrote to Jordan, "Now please do NOT tell Bill Williams or anyone like that, that I 'dabble' in this sort of thing. Because it means a great deal to me and from time to time, in a small way, I have been able to help people a little" (12 February 1930). Another voice of skepticism was apparently even closer to home than Williams, however, for in asking for confidentiality about St. Theresa, H.D. revealed some hostility on the part of Bryher, who sometimes represented to H.D. the epitome of intellect: "My friend Bryher is like a bull with a red rage when I mention any thing supernatural, though she is interested, too. That little suggestion about T. was *BETWEEN OURSELVES*" (30 July 1941).[59] Shortly thereafter, Bryher's distress about H.D.'s fascination with the supernatural also turned to pleas for secrecy when she and

H.D. began holding séances in their flat. "Gareth [Bryher] had insisted—and she was right there—that we keep the fact of our 'circle'
strictly to ourselves. That had meant intrigue and awkwardness from
the beginning," H.D. wrote (*Sword*, p. 42).

Familiar with the forms of persecution experienced for centuries
by initiates of esoteric tradition, H.D. feared the mocking voice of the
modern inquisitors—the rationalists for whom the occult was a heresy
against science. Her correspondence with Jordan is a useful indicator
of how she handled that fear. In revealing any new aspect of her
fascination, she was cautious and somewhat defensive with such
qualifiers as "It [numerology] sounds silly but isn't really" (1 January
1929) or "do not think I have reached second childhood or anything"
(28 April 1942). In renewing her discussions about astrology and
Tarot with Jordan after six years of silence, H.D. again wore a casual
mask that hid her own intensity until her testing query got a sympathetic response: "It's nice to hear you speak of stars, Uranus or any
other—I have a pack of Tarot cards—do you know them? They link
up with the astrological signs and are fun to do, as a sort of guide to
the day's possibilities. It's something to go on—but I don't take them
too seriously. I wonder if you get them in USA? I got one pack in
Vienna and have an English one with rather silly pictures—I would
send you, but fear I can't. It's the link up with star-symbolism that I
find so fascinating" (1 May 1941). It is of course possible that H.D.
did not take the cards seriously and that the occult was an enjoyable
diversion from the war. But it is more likely that such flip references
to the occult must be placed in the context of her need to test out her
friend's sympathy and her fear of being thought "crazy." Her memoirs and novels of the war years attest beyond a doubt to the seriousness of her "psychic research." And her response to Jordan's lack of
sympathy about Spiritualism shows clearly the operation of a defensive mask that protected her from rejection. Like the mollusk that
serves as metaphor for self in the *Trilogy*, her shell slammed shut in
this sharp note to Jordan in regard to her request for information
about theosophical churches in America: "I am sorry you misunderstood me, re 'occult' matters, I thought I made clear I was asking you
because I myself was so entirely ignorant about anything of the sort
and hated to seem indifferent to the question as to what sort of
'churches' there were. And I thought I could ask you, where I could
not ask other people, without being misunderstood" (4 July 1942).

The guise of the research scholar—the "student of various religious trends"—was partially the rational front that H.D. adopted to deflect the disapproval of her friends. But it also represented an internal voice of her own that warned her of the danger of excessive involvement in the occult. The intensity, exhilaration, and power of supernormal states of mind produced the psychic phenomena that led H.D. to the spiritual realism she sought. But their very power also brought the real threat of madness, a complete loss of touch with ordinary states of mind. "I think any sort of medium stuff (in excess) does drain one's vitality and is dangerous," she wrote Jordan (28 July 1942). And in *Tribute to Freud*, she described the intoxication of her Corfu visions as a kind of "drowning": "In a sense, it seems I am drowning; already half-drowned to the ordinary dimensions of space and time" (*T.F.*, p. 56). In her search for the heavens, H.D. felt a strong need to keep some contact with the earth, some hold on "the ordinary dimensions of space and time." The luminous sight of the dream, the vision, or occult experience had, for H.D., to be balanced by the rational perception of the conscious mind. As she wrote in *The Gift*, "science and art must beget a new creative medium. Medium? Yet we must not step right over into the transcendental, we must crouch near the grass and near to the earth that made us. And the people who created us. For the mechanism, the very complicated coils and wheels and springs that are brain-matter or the nerves and living tissues or the brain itself, can be unhinged by dissociation, can be broken; shock can scatter the contents of this strange *camera obscura*."[60]

When apocalyptic vision, freed from the confines of a materialist reality, loses all contact with the external world it transcends, divine madness can give way to insanity. In the *Trilogy*, H.D. foreshadowed her own coming illness in the poet's meditation on the Zodiac. Previously the beneficent wheel of life, it becomes a frightening march through the signs toward complete submersion or drowning in the unconscious, imaged by the sea sign Pisces:

> I heard Scorpion [Scorpio] whet his knife,
> I feared Archer [Sagittarius] (taut his bow),
>
> Goat's [Capricorn] horns were threat,
> would climb high? then fall low;
>
> across the abyss
> the Waterman [Aquarius] waited,

> this is the age of the new dimension,
> dare, seek, seek further, dare more,
>
> here is the alchemist's key,
> it unlocks secret doors,
>
> the present goes a step further
> toward fine distillation of emotion,
>
> the elixir of life, the philosopher's stone
> is yours if you surrender
>
> sterile logic, trivial reason;
> so mind dispersed, dared occult lore,
>
> found secret doors unlocked,
> floundered, was lost in sea-depth,
>
> sub-conscious ocean where Fish [Pisces]
> move two-ways, devour;
>
> when identity in the depth,
> would merge with the best,
>
> octopus or shark rise
> from the sea-floor:
>
> illusion, reversion of old values,
> oneness lost, madness. (T., pp. 40–41)

Reason or logic by themselves are sterile, but occult lore by itself potentially drowns the questor in the sea of the unconscious. In seeking "oneness," "integration," and "consolation," H.D. strove for the synthesis of intellect and vision, science and religion. The enigmatic "S's" that appear and reappear throughout *Tribute to Freud* symbolize both the dualism she perceived and the transcendence she sought in the mediums of psychoanalysis and religion. The "S" form appeared as one of her Corfu visions: it faced the angel and looked like a question mark: "But now I think this inverted S-pattern may have represented a series of question marks, the questions that have been asked through all the ages, that the ages will go on asking" (T.F., p. 55). The "S" form reappeared as the hidden symbol in her puzzling vision of the thistle and the serpent. The "S" is not a sign of skepticism, but is rather the sigil of resurrection, the mystery of Caduceus: "Another question, another question mark, a half-S, the other way round, S for seal, symbol, serpent certainly, signet, Sigmund" (T.F.,

p. 88). The "S" is also the "Sophia" or "Sanctus Spiritus" of Moravian mysticism, the "S" engraved on the sacred chalice. From one angle of vision, the "S" is skepticism, science; from another, it is sophia. What H.D. hoped to do was to apprehend the whole, transcend the dualism. From the perspective of "integration," there is the mysticism of "Sophia" in Freud and his science. And there is the perpetual question mark of science in the mystery of the "Sanctus Spiritus."

Ultimately, H.D. related this bridge in the schisms of consciousness or the dual forms of knowledge to the symbolic figures of her mother and father who represent the two aspects of her own self. In *The Sword Went Out to Sea*, she wrote of her exploration in Spiritualism as an attempt at this kind of synthesis:

> I had thought myself above the usual type of sensational or hysterical seeker. I still think so. But my valiant—if I may say so—effort to make a bridge between the conscious or scientific mind and the unconscious or dream-mind, met with scant recognition. Thrown back on myself, myself becomes the arbiter. . . . I have just said that biologically, I feel we may continue our relationship with certain people after death. We are and we remain physically, part of our mother and our father. My own mother did seem a living presence, on the occasion of my first talk alone with Ben Manisi. . . . You may say that the mother represents the emotional, creative or dream-self, while the father represents the intellectual, critical or constructive self." (*Sword*, pp. 143–44)

H.D.'s distant, scientific father and warm, artistic mother happened to coincide with conventional norms of masculinity, femininity, and sex roles. Her parents easily came to represent for her the duality of knowledge and perception. As their child, she identified with neither one exclusively, but rather attempted to fuse the poles they represented into an androgynous whole. This synthesis of the dream self and the critical self, vision and reason, male and female, psychoanalysis and *sagesse*, was partially what H.D. meant by her desire for "integration" and "consolation." Although she did not use the term "androgyny," her concept of synthesis belongs in the context of Woolf's discussion of androgyny in *A Room of One's Own*, a book H.D. read, as the source of creativity. "A great mind is androgynous. It is when this fusion takes place that the mind is fully fertilised and uses all its faculties," Woolf paraphrased Samuel Coleridge's statement about creative genius.[61]

Like the dream in which she brought her father up the steps of the cathedral to meet the Queen, the reconciliation of duality signified the wholeness she sought and fed the streams of creativity in her art. In this search for integration, she looked for the mystic in Freud and the science in the esoteric. Her transformation of tradition was rooted in her need to bring the perspective of psychoanalysis to her study of mysticism and the visions of the esoteric to her experience with science. The result of her search for synthesis was the ritual of poetry where she recorded the "true-rune" of spiritual realism.

7

"Companions of the Flame"

SYNCRETIST MYTHMAKING IN THE CRUCIBLE OF WAR

PERSONAL INITIATION became poetry of prophecy as H.D. transformed her psychic experiences and esoteric researches into art. The flaming ruins of war served as the catalyst, Hermes was her patron, and alchemy was her metaphor for artistic creation. The city aflame functioned hermetically as the crucible in which she could transmute into art many years of psychoanalytic probing, several sequences of psychic experience, multiple sources of esoteric lore, and the questions raised by the harsh realities of the modern world. Out of the person Hilda Doolittle, who explored hermetic tradition, ultimately grew the artist H.D., who drew on those resources to incarnate her own visions into the symbolic forms of art. In acquiring the forms of H.D.'s art, these religious traditions were altered profoundly. Reservoir of symbol and epiphany, they served as a source of her poetry, never as the poem itself. Mediating between source and poem was always the artist whose interaction with tradition ultimately transformed it.

While the "Mystery" was central to H.D.'s religious vision, there is nothing mysterious about the process in which H.D. was engaged. Mythmaking as the central artistic act is a familiar phenomenon in the modernist and postmodernist era. The collapse of the old European order made complete by World War I left a dearth of viable symbols that could inspire belief and render the chaos of human events meaningful. A number of artists, many of whom H.D. read and knew personally, attempted to fill the gaps left by established church and state by defying the normal processes of cultural evolution and creating new symbols and myths to replace the old. Artists, increasingly devalued by the materialist temper of the times, had a special role as mythmakers, if only they could make themselves heard above the voices of science and utilitarianism. Descendants of Shelley's poet-prophet and Whitman's democratic bard, they projected images of the heroic poet whose prophetic voice first described the shattered value systems of the twentieth century and then increasingly sought to transcend the fragments of self and society by developing new living mythologies. Because of the individual nature of each poet's vision, however, poetic mythmaking resulted in the proliferation of individual mythologies rather than a single mythic system that could permeate and explain the whole culture. For example, Ezra Pound's fascistic heroes, absolute leaders of their society, and William Carlos Williams' poet Paterson, the man who *is* the city, not its ruler, have little in common, althoug! the mythmaking process by which they were created is similar. Poets as mythmakers were caught in a contradiction: as poet-prophets for their societies, they were attempting to do by means of the individual act of artistic creation what is usually the result of general cultural evolution.

As unique as each mythmaker was, not one created symbolic systems *ex nihilo*. In the act of making a new tradition, all engaged in a search through existing traditions for the symbols and patterns that could bring meaning to the realities of the present. W.B. Yeats, for example, began early in his poetic career to bypass Christian mythologies and attempt the restoration of an Irish linguistic, literary, and mythological tradition. Ultimately he combined nationalist forms of tradition with theosophy and various other branches of the occult to develop his systems of cycle, gyres, and masks. As a young man, Pound delved into the artistic and historical traditions of Greece, Provence, Japan, China, and Anglo-Saxon Britain until, as a mature poet, he fused translations, allusions, paraphrasings, and his own visions into the ideograms of *The Cantos*. With the work of comparativists like James Frazer, Jessie Weston, and Jane Harrison as background, T.S. Eliot used mystery cults of the ancient and medieval world to explore the roots of spiritual despair and the potential directions for spiritual rebirth. For Eliot, this abandonment of a bankrupt Christianity ultimately became the first step in a circuitous route through the non-Christian myths of seasonal death and rebirth back to the cycle of wound and healing, despair and salvation in Catholic-

ism. Interested like Eliot in non-Christian deities, especially the Goddess, Williams merged American history and culture with mythologies
of nature in his epic of Paterson, the modern poet and city.[1]

Eliot supplemented his search in various religious traditions with
an insistence on the signficance of past literary traditions for the
writer's "individual talent." In 1919, he published his widely known
essay "Tradition and the Individual Talent" that served as a theoretical justification for the turn to tradition in his poetry and in that of
many of his literary companions of that period. He argued that a poet
should write "not merely with his own generation in his bones," but
with the whole of European literary tradition simultaneously coexisting in his mind with the works of his own era.[2] In his book *T.S. Eliot*,
Bernard Bergonzi speculated that the narrow idea of tradition as literary in Eliot's 1919 essay expanded to "acquire a wider reference and
to embrace religious and political meanings."[3] Read in the light of
this extended tradition, Eliot's critical theory as well as his poetic
practice (with the possible exception of the *Four Quartets*) expressed
the contradictory core of modern poetic mythmaking. To create new
myths, poets must be imbued with the old mythologies—not any *one*
tradition as sufficient in itself, but a whole range of parallel traditions,
each one of which has lost its claim to individual authenticity. Then,
according to the parameters of personal vision and experience, the
poet adapts, modifies, and molds these traditions to establish a new
synthesis in the world of the poem. Poetic mythmaking therefore
combines individual and traditional elements in a creative fusion of
old mythologies into new symbolic systems relevant to the modern
world. Consequently, a central question for the critic is the exploration
of how the poet interacts with tradition in all its various forms. Although identification of influential sources is part of that process, the
focus must ultimately be turned toward an examination of poetic
transformation.

H.D. belongs squarely in the center of this modernist mythmaking tradition, even though her first substantial poem in this mode came
some twenty-odd years after the earliest examples of it. The *Trilogy's*
portrait of the modernist nightmare and the poet's search to recover
old truths and synthesize new ones establish this poem as a kind of
primer of poetic mythmaking—all the more so because of the self-
conscious dimension of the poem. H.D. made the poet's creative interaction with seemingly dead mythological traditions the framework

of the poem and her existence within those traditions the core of her self-definition as an artist. The mythic system that emerges from the *Trilogy* and later poems is more religious than Williams or Pound, more esoteric than Eliot, and more syncretist than Yeats.

However, H.D. differed from these poets not only as an individual artist, but also as a woman. Like any art, the works of Yeats, Pound, Eliot, Williams, and H.D. did not come out of a vacuum, but emerged out of the personal experiences and perspectives of their creators. These perspectives in turn reflected in varying degrees elements of their differing ethnic, religious, class, race and sex backgrounds. Stephen Dedalus, if not Joyce, would surely disagree with my critical presupposition that the artist's personal and societal environment are germane to the work of art he or she creates, for he espoused a theory of the art object as a luminous entity separated utterly from its creator, audience, and general historical context.[4] But, Dedalus and the critical perspective he articulated aside, the new myths of these poets reflected not only fragments of old mythologies, but also familiar aspects of the ongoing societal norms. Pound, for example, did not invent anti-Semitism; rather, he gave new expression to a centuries-old tradition of hatred in his demonology of the modern world. Yeats's early poetic celebration of Irish culture and his later alienation from the bourgeois Irish who refused his appeal to restore Gaelic life reflected both nationalist and elitist currents common in the ethos of his times. As different as Yeats, Pound, Williams, and Eliot were in their backgrounds and vision, however, they all shared the experience of being male artists in a predominantly masculine culture. Their myth-making emerged from male perspectives validated and reinforced by the dominant norms and institutions of society. Although authors like Henrik Ibsen demonstrate male potential for transcendence of such perspectives, the new mythologies of these poets, not surprisingly, show the impact of biographical and cultural context by the pervasive androcentrism of the texts.

Androcentrism has a number of dimensions, but in its most direct form it includes the use of male experience as the human norm and the assumption that what is male is superior to what is female. Yeats's poem "Leda and the Swan," for example, uses rape as a metaphor for the divine implantation of potent knowledge and mystery into the receptive vessel of the human flesh. The familiar cast of mythological characters may obscure the androcentrism of Yeats's vision, but his association in this poem of divinity with masculine imagery and physical rape with the implantation of knowledge encapsulates in poetic myth a pattern of sexual mythology that has dominated Judeo-Christian culture.[5] Similarly, in his great epic *Paterson*, Williams anthropomorphized the fertility of mind-less nature in the passive figure of the Goddess, reclining in the form of the city's beautiful but often desecrated park. Out of the dualism of nature and culture arises the active figure of Paterson: the man Paterson whose mind is a chaos of ideas, the poet-questor Paterson who seeks order through union with nature, and the city in modern America which represents the city of man in the broadest dimension of meaning. Paterson divorced from the Goddess is surely inadequate, even sterile, in the symbolic system of the epic, and his quest for the Goddess represents the attempt to unite "thing" (matter) with "idea" (thought). This union established in the world of the poem through the agency of language operates fundamentally on an androcentric dualism that denigrates woman as symbol under the guise of reverence. Paterson may be impotent without the Goddess, but she as passive female embodies matter without mind while he as active male represents the human as distinct from nature. Like Yeats, Williams did not invent this dualism, but gave expression to a modern, secular version of an ideology that flourished in Christianity, particularly the patristic tradition, but predated the church fathers by many centuries.[6]

H.D. felt "different" as the only girl in a family of brothers, and she *was* "different" as the only poet in this circle of mythmakers to write from a woman's perspective—not *the* woman's perspective since there is no monolith of female experience any more than there is a single male perspective. Nonetheless, her new mythologies emerged like the butterfly of the *Trilogy*—"out of the cocoon" spun in part out of her life as a woman in a male-dominated society (*T.*, p. 103). The old mythologies that she worked with were all patriarchal in a variety of ways—many of them the same as the ones Yeats and Williams re-created in "Leda and the Swan" and *Paterson*. Consequently, as woman mythmaker, H.D. was faced with raw materials of poetic vision that did not validate her experience or perspective as authentic, but rather projected a feminine image of woman's "otherness" or deviation from the masculine human norm. To construct a new symbolic system that did not objectify her self as woman, her mythmaking necessarily included a subversive aspect that set her distinctly apart from her fellow poets. Like them, her transformation of old myth-ologies was a new synthesis of symbol. But unlike them, her syn-thesis included a revision of patriarchal foundations. For H.D., myth-making from a woman's perspective began in a negation of male perspectives. But since she used the traditional sources in which she was immersed, this negation ultimately involved a dialectical process that developed aspects of the old into antithetical myths which vali-dated female experience, female quest, and female vision.

H.D.'s mythmaking metamorphoses are consequently a complex intersection of individual vision and female re-vision. Examination of her interaction with tradition in the creation of modern myths must include two dimensions of analysis: first, the development of the in-dividual poet-prophet whose vision attempts to restore meaning to modernist nihilism, the subject of this chapter; and, second, the crea-tion of the female questor whose birth brings authenticity to women as a group, the focus of the following chapter.

Perhaps the added complexity of the mythmaking process for the woman who refuses to project androcentric feminine images in her poetry led H.D. to a heightened self-awareness about her relationship to tradition. Or perhaps Freud's equation of cultural myths with per-sonal dream involved her in a self-conscious attempt to define the links between tradition and individual vision. Possibly, the emphasis on tra-dition in the underground esoteric sects she studied necessitated her exploration of the presence of the old in the creation of new mytholo-ogies. The word "Kabbalah" itself means "received tradition," and as a poet who sought to bring Kabbalah into her prophecies for the mod-ern world, she would quite naturally examine the concept of "tradi-tion" as well as its substance.[7] Whatever the actual convergence of influences on H.D., "tradition" is subject as well as content in her artistic explosion of works in the early forties. The *Trilogy* in particu-lar focuses simultaneously on the relationship of tradition to artistic identity, the processes of transforming tradition in poetic mythmak-ing, and the revelation of a newly synthesized mythic tradition.

The *Trilogy* develops the theme of initiation woven throughout H.D.'s life and establishes the core of the poet's identity as her mem-bership in a band of initiates tied to ancient esoteric traditions. The prophetic voice of the poet does not emerge newly created *ex nihilo*. The religious experience that inspires the poet to decode the runes of destruction and reveal the patterns of spiritual realism depends upon

the poet's strong identification with an ongoing mystical tradition.
The repeated opposition of pronouns—"we" and "you"—in *The
Walls Do Not Fall* establishes this identification and gradually builds
an image of a community ("we") dedicated to preserving the ancient
traditions that the cultural mainstream ("you") continually mocks.
Early in the poem, the prophet Samuel is a prototype for the modern
poet as his sudden possession by the Divine Spirit simultaneously
helps her name her own experience after a bombing raid and links
her contemporary vision to a longstanding tradition of mysticism:

> . . . through our desolation,
> thoughts stir, inspiration stalks us
> through gloom:
>
> unaware, Spirit announces the Presence;
> shivering overtakes us,
> as of old, Samuel: (*T.*, p. 3)

Later in the poem, the poet's identification with Samuel expands
to an affirmation of collective experience preserved in the mystical
tradition. She is not alone as she walks through the "city of ruin."
She is instead "surrounded by companions / in this mystery," her
fellow "initiates" who share with her an identification with esoteric
tradition:

> The Presence was spectrum-blue,
> ultimate blue ray,
>
> rare as radium, as healing;
> my old self, wrapped round me,
>
> was shroud (I speak of myself individually
> but I was surrounded by companions
>
> in this mystery);
> do you wonder we are proud,
>
> aloof,
> indifferent to your good and evil?
>
> peril, strangely encountered, strangely endured,
> marks us;
>
> we know each other
> by secret symbols,
>
> though, remote, speechless,
> we pass each other on the pavement,

at the turn of the stair;
though no word pass between us,

there is subtle appraisement;
even if we snarl a brief greeting

or do not speak at all,
we know our Name,

we nameless initiates,
born of one mother,

companions
of the flame.   (*T.*, pp. 20–21)

H.D.'s esoteric research into the syncretist traditions of "la Sagesse" becomes the foundation of poetic identity in the world of the poem. Robert Ambelain, Jean Chaboseau, Denis de Rougemont, and W.B. Crow had all described for H.D. a protean tradition of mysticism and hermetic wisdom "born of one mother"—that is, originating in a common source. In the *Trilogy*, the poet announces her initiation into that religious tradition and explores her artistic contribution to the secret "mystery," whose forms are ever changing, whose essence is ever the same. As mythmaker, H.D. did not see herself as an isolated creator of new mythologies. She instead experienced a spiritual bond with a community of initiates who are "companions in this mystery," "companions of the flame." Echoing H.D.'s own alienation from any religious organizations, orthodox or heterodox, the poet's snarled greetings and speechless communication with her companions suggest that H.D. was not referring to formal initiation into a group like the Theosophical Society or the Order of 15. Rather, initiation develops out of the poet's knowledge of "secret symbols" and her sense of belonging to an ongoing, hidden tradition kept alive by others like her.

H.D.'s announcement of identification with esoteric tradition in section thirteen is itself a text whose images simultaneously reveal and conceal hermetic dimensions of meaning. Decoded with the help of other sections in the poem and H.D.'s esoteric sources, this section strongly links the *Trilogy* to the syncretist tradition described by Ambelain and others. H.D. used the concepts of the Gnostics and the Ophites, for example, to build her metaphors of Psyche's search for rebirth in a death-centered world at war. The Gnostics in particular developed the doctrine of the soul's preexistence in the realm of the spirit. At the birth of a child, an unwilling soul is assigned to the imperfect world of manifest form to live out its life cycle, trapped in the human body. For the soul forever yearning to return "home," death is a liberation from the bonds of the flesh, an experience that purifies the soul from the taint of material existence. Material death is simultaneously spiritual birth, or more accurately rebirth. Within this context, the Gnostics regarded Jehovah, the god of Genesis and the creator of material forms, as a temperamental lesser deity who jealously guarded the Tree of Knowledge so that the souls attached to Adam and Eve could not rejoin the spiritual realm of pure wisdom.[8]

The Ophites, a mystical sect that flourished in the century before Jesus' birth, developed related doctrines of resurrection as they decoded the esoteric meanings in Genesis. The Ophites worshipped the serpent of Genesis as a symbol of rebirth and condemned Jehovah for cursing the serpent in the Garden of Eden and consigning the human race to ignorance and death. The serpent, long associated with resurrection in many Near Eastern religions, offered Eve knowledge of the Divine One and the eternal life of the spirit. Like Prometheus and Asklepios in the Greek tradition, the serpent was punished for its attempted gift to the human race. The Ophite attempt to transcend the spiritual limitations imposed by Jehovah revolved around worship of the serpent and all others who had rebelled against tyranny, including such conventionally maligned figures as Lucifer and Lilith. H.D. read about Ophite doctrine in Ambelain's *Adam, dieu rouge*: "In the beginning of Genesis or *Sepher Bereschit*, the serpent, we know, symbolizes the Supreme Being, Elohim, the adversary of the Creator of the Material World. The serpent awakened the intelligence of Man and Woman by making them eat the fruit of the Tree of Knowledge. This is why the serpent became the symbol of Medicine and the symbol of the Saviour."[9]

H.D.'s image of the "old self" as "shroud" enclosing the newly emerging self identified with other companions in mystery develops Gnostic and Ophite doctrines to portray the central action and symbolism of *The Walls Do Not Fall*. Adapting the syncretist process of esoteric tradition, H.D. fused the Ophite serpent and Gnostic soul to create the poem's recurring image of the human spirit struggling to survive and transcend the Nazi engines of death. The "shroud" is a reference to the poet's frequent portrayal of herself as a "worm" elsewhere in the poem:

In me (the worm) clearly
is no righteousness, but this—

persistence; I escaped spider-snare,
bird-claw, scavenger bird-beak,

clung to grass-blade,
the back of a leaf

when storm-wind
tore it from its stem;

I escaped, I explored
rose-thorn forest,

was rain-swept
down the valley of a leaf;

.   .   .   .

. . . I profit
by every calamity;

I eat my way out of it;
gorged on vine-leaf and mulberry,

parasite, I find nourishment:
when you cry in disgust,

a worm on the leaf,
a worm in the dust,

a worm on the ear-of-wheat,
I am yet unrepentant,

for I know how the Lord God
is about to manifest, when I,

the industrious worm,
spin my own shroud.   (T., pp. 11–12)

The diminution of the human is faintly mock-heroic, the craft is
strikingly imagist, but the symbolic associations of the poet's self-
portrait are distinctly esoteric. The "industrious worm" who spins her
own shroud is H.D.'s version of the Gnostic soul whose human "garment" is a shroud of material existence and morality. The defiant persistence of the "worm's" journey through a storm-tossed, mocking
world is analogous to the Gnostic's belief that the soul is out of place
in its material form and yearns to complete its life cycle to be free.
The poet echoes Gnostic language in her reference to her companions

who have "done their worm-cycle" and to the "latter-day twice-born . . . dragging the forlorn husk of self" (*T.*, pp. 15, 22). The soul's second birth leaves behind the "old self" and initiates the new self into the service of "this mystery," the Sophia of Gnostic tradition.

While developing Gnostic notions of rebirth, H.D. nonetheless shifted the grounds of spiritual alienation considerably. The Gnostic soul's disgust for the flesh in general and sexuality in particular has little relevance to the *Trilogy*. The world of material existence that the soul yearns to transcend becomes in H.D.'s poem the modern world at war and the materialist perspective that would deny spiritual realism. Initiation or rebirth in H.D.'s symbolic system is not the Gnostic escape from the world of forms, but the soul's discovery of the esoteric wisdom underlying the hieroglyphs of war. The persistent "worm" spins its cocoon and becomes a butterfly, one of the "companions of the flame":

> we pull at this dead shell,
> struggle but we must wait
>
> till the new Sun dries off
> the old-body humours;   (*T.*, p. 22)[10]

In the "*condensare*" of syncretism, however, the "worm" as caterpillar is simultaneously the Ophite serpent. "*Be ye wise /* as asps, scorpions, as *serpents*," the poet warns, and her "worm" persona links her with esoteric symbols of resurrection and wisdom. The "you" of orthodox traditions have made the "worm" a symbol of death, by metonymy the agent of corporeal disintegration. A "worm on a leaf / a worm in the dust" inspires disgust and represents the mortal, not divine, aspect of human nature. But the "we" of esoteric traditions recognize the lowly worm as the serpent cursed by Jehovah. This serpent, the poet learns in the process of spiritual transformation, is the same as the healing serpents entwined on the winged Caduceus of Hermes Psychopompous; the uraeus worn by Egyptian deities and pharaohs; the horned headdress of Hathor, associated by H.D. with insect antennae; and the serpent rod of the biblical magician Aaron. The shortest section in *The Walls Do Not Fall* condenses serpent and insect into the single image of the worm, and it synthesizes Greek, Egyptian, and Hebrew traditions into a single current of esoteric wisdom:

Gods, goddesses
wear the winged head-dress

of horns, as the butterfly
antennae,

or the erect king-cobra crest
to show how the worm turns. (*T.*, p. 13)

Conventional associations triggered by "the worm turns" suggest the inevitable processes of decay after burial in the earth as the worm "turns" in the dead flesh it consumes. But esoteric translation of this death symbol transforms the movement of "turning" into the processes of metamorphosis. The lowly "worm in the dust" industriously spins the cocoon of its own rebirth. Similarly, the poet-initiate "turns" the evil serpent of Genesis into the redemptive symbol of wisdom through her association with esoteric tradition. Along with her "companions in this mystery," she can use the "secret symbols" she has learned to discover hidden dimensions of meaning in conventional religions.

Even more importantly, however, her association with mystical traditions allows her to decode the runes of material reality, the rubble of war. She and her fellow initiates are "companions of the flame" as well as "companions in this mystery." To interpret the "flame" of war, she and her companions abandon the conventional ethics of the Judeo-Christian tradition. She calls herself a worm without "righteousness"; she is "indifferent to your good and evil." Like the Gnostics, Ophites, and Luciferians before her, the poet discards the orthodox definitions of evil and proceeds to find the symbols of Sagesse in the heart of death itself. The "flames" of death become the purifying fire of rebirth. By extension the fiery destruction of London becomes the apocalypse that will usher in the new age of Aquarius, a "woman's age" as H.D. wrote to Viola Jordan (2 July 1941). The meaning of the word "apocalypse" itself fuses the hermetic significance of fire and the process of revelation. As William Loftus Hare wrote in a book H.D. read carefully, an "apocalypse" is not only a redemptive cataclysm, but also "the *revelation* or *uncovering* of something by the expedient of obtaining a point of view from which it can be seen in its true significance (*apo*—removal from a place; *kalupto*—to envelop, to conceal, to darken)."[11] The task of the poet-prophet is the "uncovering" of spiritual realism enveloped in the dark flame of war.

Tribute to the Angels, the second poem of the *Trilogy*, explores the esoteric dimension of the fires of war. The hidden significance of the poet's persona as worm in *The Walls Do Not Fall* implied the possibility of metamorphosis. Translating the hieroglyph of fire in the second poem spells out the conditions of transformation. Ambelain concluded *Adam, dieu rouge* with an admonition for Rosicrucians: " 'Listen to your teachers, Sons of Fire' " and an explanation of their doctrines: "it is by Fire that Nature renews itself."[12] H.D. identified with these "companions of the flame" and embodied their belief in regenerating fire in the image patterns of her tribute to the angels. Ambelain argued that the Rosicrucians were direct descendants of numerous ancient mystical sects that identified divinity with fire. An undercurrent of mysticism was strong in Judaism itself. In the Bible, God appears to Moses in the form of a burning bush (Exodus 3:4), to Ezekiel in his vision of the wheels of fire (Ezekiel 10:1–22), and to Daniel in his dream of God seated on a throne of "fiery flame" (Daniel 7:9). Neighbors of the Jewish prophets, the Zoroastrians worshipped fire as the physical representation of spiritual divinity, a symbolic association that H.D. made central in her novel about the origins of Christianity, *Pilate's Wife*.[13] Ambelain argued that the Zoroastrians were only one among many sects who associated salvation with fire. In the first century B.C., he claimed, there were a number of esoteric sects, including Jewish ones, that worshipped a savior called in Hebrew "Ieshu," the "son of fire." The Hebrew word for fire is "iesh," he wrote, and the name "Jesus" is etymologically related to "iesh." Ambelain based his defense of syncretism largely upon this "single," yet protean tradition of fire worshippers that preceded the birth of Jesus, greatly influenced Christianity, and continued to thrive through centuries of persecution by the established church.[14]

Fire is the central agent of transformation in *Tribute to the Angels*, a text that represents H.D.'s contribution to hermetic tradition and a text that is itself hermetic. The poet's task is to find the resurrection pattern embedded in images and material realities of the London Blitz. The poet appropriately begins by invoking the guardian spirit of hermeticism, Hermes in his guise as Hermes Trismegistus, "patron of alchemists" (*T.*, p. 63). His "clients" are "orators, thieves and poets," and she asks his help in gathering together the "shards" of seemingly dead traditions. Like all modern mythmakers, she must "plunder" the past:

> steal then, O orator,
> plunder, O poet,
>
> take what the old-church
> found in Mithra's tomb,
>
> candle and script and bell,
> take what the new-church spat upon
>
> and broke and shattered;
> collect the fragments of the splintered glass
>
> and of your fire and breath,
> melt down and integrate,
>
> re-invoke, re-create
> opal, onyx, obsidian
>
> now scattered in the shards
> men tread upon.   (*T.*, p. 63)

The alchemists' purifying fire, fed by the desecrated sacred fires of Persian fire worshippers, is the "breath" that allows the mythmaking process to "melt down and integrate" the ancient fragments into a new whole. The poet's gem of distilled vision is the result of a metamorphosis wrought by fire. London under attack is a crucible in the alchemy of war. Decoded as living symbols of *sagesse*, the bombs that light up the dark sky are the material forms of Divine Fire. Adapted to the scientific medium of the modern age, Divine Fire takes on technological forms. Reflecting the language of physics and chemistry, the "Presence" itself manifests as a healing flash of light in the darkened city at war: "spectrum-blue, / ultimate blue ray, / rare as radium, as healing." The modern technology of destruction in World War II is the same purifying fire the alchemists used in their "Grand Work," the same "lake of fire" that ushered in the new Jerusalem in John's Revelation (20:14).

The poet's identification with Hermes Trismegistus and the alchemists allows her to decipher the redemptive pattern structuring the lightning flash of bombs and the inevitable aftermath of burning buildings and charred trees. But an equally important "companion" of the "flame" is the mystic John. The analogues between his visions and her own experience affirm the apocalyptic nature of the fiery war. John's Revelation begins with his vision of seven golden candle-sticks that later reemerge as the "seven lamps of fire burning before the throne, which are the seven Spirits of God" (Revelation 1:12–13; 20; 4:5). The middle "candlestick" holds "seven stars" in "his" hand and explains to John "the mystery of the seven stars . . . and the seven golden candlesticks." H.D.'s revelation similarly begins with her ability to see the flames of war as the "seven fires," the angels that guard the throne of God, "the seven Spirits, / set before God / as lamps on a high-altar" (*T.*, p. 80). Naming these angels, each of whom represents one aspect of divinity, structures the poet's simul-taneous record of destruction and prayer of thanks in this section of the *Trilogy*. The discrete units of the long poem loosely join together as "the sequence of candle and fire / and the law of the seven" (*T.*, p. 92). Reinforcing her bond with John, she sees these fiery "compan-ions" as "candles," "lamps," and "stars" (*T.*, pp. 65, 67–70, 79, 80, 92, 99, 108–09). The "lightning shattered earth / and splintered sky" of modern warfare are hermetic hieroglyphs of apocalypse. Decoded in the context of esoteric revelation, the "fire-to-endure" comes ulti-mately from God and transforms destruction into resurrection. The precondition of rebirth is death: to live through her "worm-cycle," the poet must be immersed in the "lake of fire," the "red-death" of war (*T.*, pp. 68, 70, 79).[15]

H.D.'s hermetic translations of modern realities depends ulti-mately on her identification with her "companions in this mystery," on her sense of community with the nameless initiates tied to an evolving esoteric tradition. Her emphasis on spiritual community strikingly contrasts to John's expression of individual vision and his curse leveled at any who dared change a single word of his revela-tion. H.D.'s repeated affirmation of "we" signals membership in a centuries-old, collaborative tradition. Her expression of a secret desti-ny shared with numerous other "receivers" of tradition directly echoes her primary teachers—Ambelain, de Rougemont, and Chaboseau. In a religious dimension, H.D. paralleled Eliot's dictum to write with tra-dition "simultaneously coexisting" in her mind along with "individ-ual talent" or vision.

But if H.D. gave Eliot's theory a religious cast, she conversely provided esoteric tradition with her own artistic emphasis. As poet drawn to all forms of art, H.D. must have been greatly attracted to the role Ambelain and de Rougemont assigned to artists in their descriptions of hermetic tradition. Both pointed out that artists, whose modes of expression are more consistently symbolic than the often rational discourse of theologians, have frequently given enduring forms to the doctrines of esoteric mysticism. The lyrics of the troubadours bore a coded message of the heretical Church of Love. The paintings of mother and child contained cult objects of an outlawed syncretist tradition. And the cathedrals themselves were architectural symbols of forbidden Manichaean doctrine. In the *Trilogy*, H.D. gave the artists of esoteric tradition an even more central role than did her guides. Developing Freud's theory of the common origins of art and religion into the cornerstone of her religious aesthetic, H.D. broke down the distinctions between artists and mystics. In the *Trilogy*, her religious community of initiates, the "we" with whom she identifies, are all poets. The traditional persecution of these companions by the established church has an added dimension in the modern world: the materialist condemnation of poetry as nonutilitarian or escapist parallels the orthodox condemnation of heterodox tradition as heresy. H.D.'s defense of religious poetry flung in the face of her scornful critics clarifies her fusion of religious and artistic function and symbol:

> So we reveal our status
> with twin-horns, disk, erect serpent,
>
> though these or the double-plume or lotus
> are, you now tell us, trivial
>
> intellectual adornment;
> poets are useless,
>
> more than that,
> we, authentic relic,
>
> bearers of the secret wisdom,
> living remnant
>
> of the inner band
> of the sanctuaries' initiate,
>
> are not only 'non-utilitarian',
> we are 'pathetic':
>
> this is the new heresy;   (*T.*, p. 14)

For the first time in the *Trilogy*, explicit use of the word "poets" to describe the initiates of the "secret wisdom" unites art and religion. In the face of her attackers, who, it should be remembered, had so often termed her "escapist," H.D. announces that her allusions to the lotus, the twin-horns of Hathor, and the erect serpent on Pharaoh's brow are not decorative or even purely aesthetic.[16] These references bear religious significance; they appear in her poem as sacred symbols, as messengers of the secret wisdom to which she has been introduced. And as poet, she sees her task as a "bearer" of that wisdom.

To the rationalists and doubters, the words of the poet-initiate are "nonutilitarian" and "pathetic." But to H.D., her words embody "Logos" and provide access to spiritual realism. Invented by Thoth, words are "magic, indelibly stamped / on the atmosphere somewhere / forever" (*T.*, p. 17). Invented by Hermes, the lyre of art fuses with the script of Thoth, the Egyptian Hermes. "I am branded with a word," the poet says (*T.*, p. 124). As Joseph Blau wrote in an article in *Hemispheres* that H.D. read, the power of magic resides in the "wonder-working words" whose power is so great that their meaning has had to be concealed. All magicians face the same task: "to unravel the threads of concealment, to discover the compulsive names hidden by the deities." In the same issue, Johannes Urzidil explicitly connected the common power of the magician and the poet in the Word: "all artists are magicians, and the magic of all poetry resides in the Word."[17]

L. S. Dembo has argued persuasively that many modernist poets "regarded language as a mode of revelation, a logos that. . . . is the sole means by which man can transcend a world governed by Chance (*le Hasard*) and penetrate to an ultimate realm (*l'Absolu*), which, correspondingly, is expressed only through logos (*le Verbe*)."[18] Each poet, Dembo argued, developed a distinct version of Logos—from Eliot's Christian Logos to Pound's "*cheng ming.*" H.D.'s concept of Logos belongs in this modernist context. Her "Word," however, is her own synthesis of esoteric tradition and psychoanalysis. To the scoffers, she throws back her challenge: "but if you do not even understand what words say, / how can you expect to pass judgement / on what words conceal?" Words are like dreams, simultaneously revealing and concealing the "mystery": the "secret is stored / in man's very speech, / in the trivial or / the real dream" (*T.*, pp. 14–15). Words are like the myths de Rougemont described; like the dreams,

puns, and slips of the tongue Freud translated; and like the sacred
texts the Kabbalists deciphered. Words, the poet's medium, conceal
the inner mystery, but at the same time give expression to those
secrets. The poet seeks the coded wisdom within by learning the
traditional Kabbalistic techniques for "translation":

> . . . I know, I feel
> the meaning that words hide;
>
> they are anagrams, cryptograms,
> little boxes, conditioned
>
> to hatch butterflies ... (T., p. 53)

The anagrams and cryptograms that accomplish the rebirth of
Psyche parallel "temurah" and "notarikon," the Kabbalistic techniques of revelation based on manipulation of letters through anagrams
and substitutions.[19] The next section of the *Trilogy* demonstrates the
operation of H.D.'s Logos:

> For example:
> Osiris equates O-sir-is or O-Sire-is;
>
> Osiris,
> the star Sirius,
>
> relates resurrection myth
> and resurrection reality
>
> .   .   .   .
>
> . . . my thought
> would cover deplorable gaps
>
> in time, reveal the regrettable chasm,
> bridge that before-and-after schism,
>
> .   .   .   .
>
> recover the secret of Isis,
> which is: there was One
>
> in the beginning, Creator,
> Fosterer, Begetter, the Same-forever
>
> in the papyrus-swamp
> in the Judean meadow   (T., pp. 54–55)

As a Kabbalist poet, H.D. finds the hidden meaning of a resurrection deity by creating new words from the letters of the god's name. "Osiris" can be broken down into "Sirius" or "O-sir-is" or "O-Sire-is." To find "Sirius" hidden in the name of the god is to reveal not only his connection with yearly regeneration or resurrection, but also with the mother goddess Isis, his opposite; for the dog-star Sirius, Frazer wrote, was "a sign from heaven" announcing the rising waters of the Nile which brought new life and crops. Sirius, or Sothis as the Egyptians called this fixed star, appeared just before sunrise at the time of the summer solstice when the Nile began to flood. This symbol of returning life was also known as the star of Isis.[20] Buried in the name of the god is Binah, the female principle of regeneration; and by another anagram, H.D. finds Chokmah, the male or father: "Osiris" becomes "O-Sire-is," an affirmation of the existence of god as father or sire. Together Isis and Osiris unite to encompass the androgynous unity of the One, the "Creator, Fosterer, Begetter."

H.D.'s linguistic magic returns the "scribe" to her common origins in religion and art. Art has become the medium for the exploration and preservation of religious wisdom. The artist is a kind of Vestal Virgin, keeping the flame of divinity alive for humankind:

> we are the keepers of the secret,
> the carriers, the spinners
>
> of the rare intangible thread
> that binds all humanity
>
> to ancient wisdom,
> to antiquity;
>
> our joy is unique, to us,
> grape, knife, cup, wheat
>
> are symbols in eternity,
> and every concrete object
>
> has abstract value, is timeless
> in the dream parallel
>
> whose relative sigil has not changed
> since Nineveh and Babel. (*T.*, p. 24)

In her art, the poet spins the cocoon of words that will "hatch butterflies" (*T.*, p. 53). The "rare intangible thread" she spins emerges from her ability to translate "ancient cult symbols" of mystery re-

ligions ("grape, knife, cup, wheat") and the hieroglyphs of the
"dream parallel." H.D.'s years of quest with Freud and her occult
teachers come together into a single "intangible thread" of affirmation
in the *Trilogy*. This poem expresses the exhilaration of her discovery
of esoteric tradition and her place within it as an artist. It announces
boldly that she has found her sense of direction, that the "drifting"
which sent her to Freud in the first place has become meaningful
quest, and that even though she has not reached "haven / heaven,"
she now knows where to search for "treasure" in hermetic tradition
and its parallel in dream.

As modernist mythmaker, H.D. was deeply rooted in tradition
and committed to its preservation. But as one of the "keepers of the
secret, / the carriers, the spinners," she did not conceive of the poet
as a passive receptacle for the images and symbols of tradition as
Eliot had suggested in his "Tradition and the Individual Talent." Instead, the poet engages in an active, dialectical process of weaving
traditional and personal revelations into new patterns of vision. H.D.
condensed this complex revision of tradition into her image of the
poet as "carrier" and "spinner." The poet is simultaneously "carrier"
of the old and "spinner" of the new. Gershom G. Scholem, the leading authority on Jewish mysticism, has pointed out a basic contradiction in mysticism that aptly describes H.D.'s transformations of tradition. "All mysticism," he wrote, "has contradictory or complementary
aspects: the one conservative, the other revolutionary." Mystics, permeated with their own given religious tradition, have a unique personal experience of formless divinity which they then communicate
with the symbolic language of their own tradition. Scholem described
the contradictory components of mystical experience as a "dialectic"
that puts "new wine into old bottles."[21] This dialectical interaction
with tradition is not only the logic that governs H.D.'s modernist
mythmaking in the *Trilogy*, but it is also itself the subject. Throughout the poem, the poet builds a defense of her poetry against the attacks of the collective "you," the skeptical voices who mock the
relevance of art and religion to a world at war. The final attack
queries the uniqueness and therefore the significance of her vision:

> This search for historical parallels,
> research into psychic affinities,

has been done to death before,
will be done again;

. . . .

what new light can you possibly
throw upon them ["spiritual realities"]? (*T.*, p. 51)

The poet's answer presents in imagist terms an argument for the protean forms of spiritual reality that simultaneously allow for the uniqueness of personal vision and the common essence of tradition:

my mind (yours),
your way of thought (mine),

each has its peculiar intricate map,
threads weave over and under

the jungle-growth
of biological aptitudes,

inherited tendencies,
the intellectual effort

of the whole race,
its tide and ebb;

but my mind (yours)
has its peculiar ego-centric

personal approach
to the eternal realities,

and differs from every other
in minute particulars,

as the vein-paths on any leaf
differ from those of every other leaf

in the forest, as every snow-flake
has its particular star, coral or prism shape. (*T.*, pp. 51–52)

H.D.'s imagist craft carries the same message expounded by Scholem. The "revolutionary" aspect of her vision is the unique form of her apprehension of spiritual reality; like the snowflake, the design of her poem reproduces no other. The "conservative" element of her vision is her common bond with tradition; like the snowflake, her difference exists within the context of identity. Her aesthetic of mythmaking involves the creation of a tapestry of words that "weaves" a new pattern with the "threads" of tradition. In a modern world with "no maps," the poem combines the old and the new to draw its own "peculiar intricate map." The poem itself is the "map" that guides the modernist "voyagers, discoverers / of the not-known, / the unrecorded" (*T.*, p. 59).

Although H.D.'s poetic mysticism operates on the dialectic described by Scholem, the "revolutionary" aspect of her individual vision has a dimension that Scholem never intended. Because she was a woman working within a masculine tradition, she had to revise the patriarchal bias of that tradition so that she could speak with an authentic female voice as both the poet and hero of her own quest poetry. Like Eliot, Scholem established a contrast between individual vision and the collective tradition. But since women have been reviled as a caste in that tradition, H.D. understood that the emerging self of any woman cannot be created in a purely individual dimension. The rebirth of the poet as Psyche depends not only upon her unique weaving of resurrection mythologies, but also upon her creation of an authentic self and symbol for women as a group. Self-transformation for H.D. was tied to her capacity to "spin" a new group identity, a new mythology of womanhood. Psyche's search and rebirth took H.D. back to beginnings in which she discovered that the "companions of the flame" were not only born of one mother-tradition, but were also "born of one mother"—the primal Goddess from which all subsequent religions evolved. As the poet learns in *Sagesse*, she must journey to the origins of all life and myth in the echoing sea-shell chambers of the "Grand Mer." She prays for the Goddess to come, "to spread the picture-book upon my bed, / to show me who you are," to bring "the one special shell you chose for me," and to "hold it to my ear." Listening to the mother of life, Psyche hears the words that shape her quest:

> "listen, my child, fear not the ancient lore,
>
> (*Gymnosophes, Philosophes*), this echo is for you,
> listen, my child, it is enough,
>
> the echo of the sea, our secret
> and our simple mystery, *Grande Mer* ..." (*S.*, p. 75)

8

"Born of One Mother"

RE-VISION OF PATRIARCHAL TRADITION

> she carries a book but it is not
> the tome of the ancient wisdom,
>
> the pages, I imagine, are the blank pages
> of the unwritten volume of the new;
>
> all you say, is implicit,
> all that and much more;
>
> but she is not shut up in a cave
> like a Sibyl; she is not
>
> imprisoned in leaden bars
> in a coloured window;
>
> she is Psyche, the butterfly,
> out of the cocoon. (T., p. 103)

H.D.'s VISION of the Lady in the central dream of *Tribute to the An-gels* releases the Goddess from the leaden bars of patriarchal tradition and simultaneously accomplishes the rebirth of Psyche. The Goddess comes to the poet bearing "none of her usual attributes; / the Child was not with her" (T., p. 97). Instead, she carries the "Book of Life," whose pages are not weighted down by patriarchal wisdom, but blank for the poet to write the "unwritten volume of the new." In the *Trilogy*, the Lady is "Love, the Creator," who oversees the resurrection pattern evident in the flowering of her charred may-apple tree. In *Helen in Egypt*, she is Thetis-Isis, the "Empress and lure of the sea" and "Regent of heaven and the star-zone" who ultimately frees Helen from shame (*H.E.*, p. 253). In *Sagesse*, she is the "Grand Mer" who whispers the "simple mystery" of Love to her daughter, the poet, through the echo of a seashell. In *Vale Ave*, she is the unjustly desecrated Lilith, the prototype of woman-spirit incarnated throughout the "processus" of history. In *Hermetic Definition*, she is Isis, the embodiment of hermetic wisdom, who commands the aging poet to "write, write or die." Her name changes throughout the poems as H.D. fuses the protean forms of the ancient goddesses, but her core meaning remains essentially the same. She is the female divine spirit embodying the power of regenerative Love in the midst of a fragmented, death-centered modern world. Her manifestations in myth, dream, and religious experience transform the misogyny of patriarchal tradition and validate H.D. as woman, as poet. Her message of Love brings redemption to the "city of ruin" through her embodiment of "resurrection myth, resurrection reality."

Love is the primal force in H.D.'s syncretist mysticism, as it has been for many of the mystical sects she studied, including her own Moravian church. As Count Zinzendorf said, "Love institutes the very life and soul of belief, Love is the spiritus universalis of a true religion."[1] But these esoteric traditions to which she was tied as one of the "initiates born of one mother" had to undergo the process of revision in order to serve the personal and mythic needs of a woman poet. In her essay "When We Dead Awaken: Writing as Re-Vision," Adrienne Rich has defined that process of cultural transformation as the "looking back" (re-vision) that revises the images of woman projected for centuries:

> Re-vision—the act of looking back, of seeing with fresh eyes, of entering an old text from a new critical direction—is for us more than a chapter in cultural history: it is an act of survival. Until we can understand the assumptions in which we are drenched we cannot know ourselves. And this drive to self-knowledge, for woman, is more than a search for identity: it is part of her refusal of the self-destructiveness of male-dominated society. . . . We need to know the writing of the past, and know it differently than we have ever known it; not to pass on a tradition but to break its hold over us. . . . woman is becoming her own midwife, creating herself anew.[2]

H.D.'s poetic "re-visions" did not abandon traditional mythologies to create a new mythos of Love. Instead, H.D. approached religious tradition as she did psychoanalysis: she developed implicit aspects of hermetic tradition until she had created a woman's mythology antithetical to her source of inspiration.

Syncretist religions had a special appeal for H.D. because they incorporated female symbols in their divine pantheons and resurrected the ancient Goddess as living symbol. Freud's hypothesis that the childhood of the individual recapitulates the infancy of the human race presented her with a formula that allowed her to link the personal with the mythic. In the world of her daughter's dream and vision, Helen Wolle was a personal mother-symbol who incarnated the Goddess, the mother-symbol of myth. Because of this equation, H.D. experienced her research into the myths of the Goddess as an exploration of her own self as woman. Like Veronica in *Pilate's Wife*, H.D.'s liberation from unrelievedly masculine mythologies by esoteric tradition freed her to discover an authentic self.

But for the Goddess to inspire the process of self-transformation, H.D. had to revise syncretist tradition just as she did the psychoanalytical one. While this tradition did indeed grant recognition to a Female Principle largely denied in orthodox traditions, it was itself permeated with patriarchal assumptions about the nature of women. Veronica accepts the new religion of Jesus, but even she wonders if his emphasis on the Father betrays the Mother: "He had wanted final consummation, union with the ultimate, with the parent, father, his father. Why not his mother? . . . Perhaps he had made it impossible any more, for any one to visualize the mother—Demeter" (*P.W.*, p. 155). H.D.'s re-vision of esoteric Christianity gave the female divine symbol a more central role than she had in tradition. Christ, the beloved Son of God, incarnates the power of Logos and the force of Love in heterodox as well as orthodox traditions. Moravian mysticism in particular focuses its doctrines of Love and Redemption in the wounds of Christ, endlessly imaged in the hymns H.D. sang as a child. Similarly, the Manichaean dualisms of Gnosticism and the Kabbalah had to undergo transformation in order to serve their purpose in H.D.'s mythos of womanhood. The dualistic mythologies described by Robert Ambelain tend to equate the Female Principle with darkness, passivity, matter, evil, flesh, and death. In Gnosticism, for example, creation is a Fall from perfection where the Male Principle, the spark of the divine, is shrouded in the flesh of the female. Ambelain's summary of the dualisms inherent in syncretist traditions clarify the essentially negative valuation of woman as symbol: "the traditional symbol of Light is the Sun—the male principle, which is positive and the image of Day, of the Father, of Man. The symbol of Darkness is the Moon—the female principle, which is negative and the image of Night, of the Mother, of Woman. Here are the two origins of patriarchy and matriarchy, of the phallic and yonic cults, of Osiris and Isis (the 'dark virgin')."[3]

To use these traditions as the raw materials of woman's quest, H.D. had to revise them. She redefined the Goddess, reversed the traditional dualisms, and revalued the Female Principle. Once having discovered the Goddess in mystical tradition, H.D. abandoned the androcentric lens of that tradition to develop her personal and mythic mother-symbol into the cornerstone of her vision of salvation. On the level of personal dream, the mother-symbol in her Princess dream descends the stairs to find a beloved girl-child in the basket of baby Moses; in the "dream parallel" of her *Tribute to the Angels*, the Lady has replaced the Son as the symbol of Love and resurrection. The Goddess appears repeatedly in H.D.'s poetry to embody and inspire this dialectical process of re-vision, of revisionist mythmaking. She symbolizes both what has happened to women in patriarchal tradition and the potential of women to transcend the paralyzing definitions of "otherness." She is not so much a supernatural force outside women as a symbolic incarnation of the divine spark in women. The desecration of the Goddess in orthodox religions and the distortion of her primal power in esoteric traditions represents on a mythic scale the defilement of women in the historical dimension. The resurrection of the Goddess in H.D.'s poetry accomplishes the transformation of women as a group and the rebirth of Psyche.[4]

H.D.'s "revolutionary" re-vision of tradition did not spring into being full-grown with the publication of the *Trilogy*. Instead, it was rooted firmly in her imagist poetry and grew slowly as her early fascination with mythology deepened into the religious researches of her later years. Representing different decades of her poetic career, four poems centering on goddess figures can serve as a paradigm of the growing dialectic in H.D.'s use of traditional materials: "Helen" (1923), "Callypso Speaks" (1938), *Trilogy*, and *Helen in Egypt*. They clarify not only the process of transformation, but also the progression of a gradually developing imperative to create a new mythology for women as a group.

"Helen" takes as its subject the woman who has been the literary and mythic symbol of sexual beauty and illicit love in western culture. Much has been written about her, but H.D.'s poem does something new: it implicitly attacks the traditional imagery of Helen and implies that such perspectives have silenced Helen's own voice.

> All Greece hates
> the still eyes in the white face,
> the lustre as of olives
> where she stands,
> and the white hands.
>
> all Greece reviles
> the wan face when she smiles,
> hating it deeper still
> when it grows wan and white,
> remembering past enchantments
> and past ills.
>
> Greece sees, unmoved,
> God's daughter, born of love,
> the beauty of cool feet
> and slenderest knees,
> could love indeed the maid,
> only if she were laid,
> white ash amid funereal cypresses.   (*S.P.*, p. 48)

Like Edgar Allan Poe's poem about Helen, this poem draws a portrait with careful references to Helen's eyes, face, hands, feet, and knees.[5] But in contrast to Poe's poem, H.D.'s Helen does not stand alone, unveiled before the adoring eyes of the male poet. Instead, she is accompanied by a hate-filled gaze that never leaves the beauty of her body. H.D.'s poem operates on an opposition established between Helen and "all Greece," and the speaker stands outside this opposition to record the interaction between the two. Time, space, and situation are left uncertain with a sparse setting that presents an image rather than a realistic event. The action verbs outline the image: Helen "stands," "smiles" faintly, and grows more "wan and white" while "all Greece" regards first her face and then "sees . . . the beauty of cool feet / and slenderest knees."

The process the speaker watches is the growing hatred of Helen and the overwhelming effect it has upon her. The emotion directed in judgment against Helen is intense—we are aware of this not only because the verbs "hates" and "reviles" stand out so starkly, but also because the impersonality of "all Greece" generalizes the condemnation. In Poe's poem, he alone worships Helen. In W.B. Yeats's "No Second Troy," the poet's feelings for Helen are more ambivalent, but Yeats still records a private experience between himself and his mythic mask for Maude Gonne. In her poem, however, H.D. generalizes those who regard Helen until they take on the dimensions of a collective culture. "Greece" is a country, not a person, not even a people. H.D.'s choice of "Greece" in place of the more logical "Greeks" suggests that the entire weight of a cultural tradition "reviles" Helen. The structural repetition of "all" at the beginning of the first two stanzas reinforces the image of a whole culture set in powerful opposition to one woman. And the lack of a realistic setting in this portrait of "all Greece" regarding Helen underlines the real subject of the poem: woman's place in male-dominated tradition.

Helen's response to the hate-filled gaze of "all Greece" is not a static one. In fact, the stanzas of the poem subtly suggest the transformation of a living woman into a marble statue, a progression from life to death controlled by the force of hate. In the first stanza, Helen seems immobilized—her eyes are "still" and she simply "stands." The emphasis on the whiteness of her face and hands adds to this image of impassivity. But, read in the light of the last two stanzas, Helen in the first stanza still has the glow of life. The poet sees the rich "lustre as of olives / where she stands." This lustre begins to disappear in the second stanza. White hands and white face are conventional attributes of female beauty. But in the second stanza, white skin "grows wan and white" in the face of increasing hatred—that is, pale, bloodless, and seemingly lifeless. As if to appease "all Greece," her "wan face . . . smiles." According to some scholars, women have traditionally relied on a perpetual smile to render themselves more acceptable in an androcentric culture.[6] Helen too smiles in a desperate attempt to counteract the condemnation that is growing "deeper still" for her part in the Trojan War.

In the third stanza, "white" signals the final result of Greece's unmoving hatred, becoming the color of death: "white ash amid funereal cypresses." The word "unmoved" to describe a lack of compassion is something of a pun (un-moving) that echoes in reverse the increasing immobility of Helen. Her smiles win her no mercy, and the only way she can become loved is through her death. The opening image of Helen surrounded by the "lustre" of life yields to the con-

ditional fantasy of her death, a progression underlined by the change
in trees from olive to "funereal cypresses." Her feet are "cool," not
warm with life. The death imagery, however, has another dimension
of meaning in Helen's relationship to tradition. As the poem records
the change in Helen's reactions, it presents a dynamic image of Helen's
metamorphosis into a white marble statue adored for the beauty of
her "cool feet / and slenderest knees." Poe's poem ends with his
vision of Helen "in yon brilliant window-niche / How statue-like I
see thee stand." H.D. doesn't use the word "statue," but the central
image of Helen standing before the gaze of "all Greece" suggests it.
The poet watches the process of Helen's canonization as "God's
daughter, born of love." The growing whiteness of her skin signals
her death as a living woman and her birth as a statue, a symbol of
beauty in the eyes of "all Greece."

In Poe's poem, Helen's appearance as a statue is an affirmation.
But in H.D.'s poem, the speaker understands the connection between
the traditional worship of woman as symbol and the death of the
living woman. H.D.'s poem about Helen is a re-vision of the Medusa
myth and an implicit attack on the processes of masculine mythmaking with female symbols. According to Greek myth, a man's direct
sight of the fearful Medusa with her hair of snakes would turn him
to stone. In his famous interpretation of this myth, Freud argued
that Medusa's head represented the castrated state of female genitals,
and the myth embodied castration anxiety.[7] But in H.D.'s reversal of
psychoanalysis and myth, the hatred of a collective male tradition
turns woman to stone, literally a statue. An added complexity, however, is that hatred becomes love once Helen's paralysis is complete.
Like Joan of Arc, Helen, immobilized and silenced, is an object of
worship. Alive, she was an object of hatred, a threat to the dominant
culture ruled by men. As statue or symbol, she is safely controlled by
the tradition that defines her through its art. What seems to be an
adoration of woman, H.D. says, is rooted in reality in a hatred for
the living woman who has the capacity to speak for herself.

In "Helen," the poet cannot free Helen from the patriarchal cage
of traditional hate and adoration. She stands outside the process, helpless to prevent Helen's growing silence and paralysis. She can and does
attack tradition, but she cannot give the mute statue a voice. Because
of her mother's name, Helen was always a personal and mythic mother-symbol for H.D. But at this point in her life, her mother-symbol

was too overwhelmed by tradition to help her daughter the poet. To serve as "the Muse, the Creator" as the Goddess does in H.D.'s later poems, the daughter had to give birth to her own mother.

In "Callypso Speaks," H.D. blows life and speech back into the mute statue of the Goddess. She transforms over two thousand years of mythological and literary history by a slight shift in perspective and voice. The strange title signals the subject of the poem, with the verb "speaks" standing out starkly without its usual adverb or prepositional phrase to define the conditions or purpose of Callypso's speech. We have all heard Odysseus "speak"—from Homer to Joyce, he has held center stage and we have seen his adventures unfold in countless ways, but all variations of the myth have focused on how his trials related to his needs and desires. Even Penelope's suffering as she fends off her rude suitors is usually set in the context of their violation of Odysseus' honour.[8] Callypso appears in these myths as the goddess who saved Odysseus from shipwreck, offered her love in her island paradise beyond death, and sadly helped Odysseus provide for the continuation of his journey back to Ithaca when he grew restless with her love. Now, most probably for the first time in cultural history, "Callypso Speaks" her own story. As if to emphasize how many years an androcentric tradition has repressed Callypso's speech, the first section of the poem erupts in a violent volcano of anger:

Callypso

> O you clouds,
> here is my song;
> man is clumsy and evil
> a devil.
>
> O you sand,
> this is my command,
> drown all men in slow breathless suffocation—
> then they may understand.
>
> O you winds,
> beat his sails flat,
> shift a wave sideways
> that he suffocate.
>
> O you waves
> run counter to his oars,

waft him to blistering shores,
where he may die of thirst.

O you skies,
send rain
to wash salt from my eyes,

and witness, all earth and heaven,
it was of my heart-blood
his sails were woven;

witness, river and sea and land;
you, you must hear me—
man is a devil,
man will not understand. (*S.P.*, pp. 59–60)[9]

The anger of Callypso's first speech is raw and stark—not mask-ed by appeasing smiles, not even coded in natural image as H.D.'s poems about emotion so often are. She has "suffocated" in silence for centuries, and her "first song" in the open air is terrifyingly direct in its demand for vengeance. The first four stanzas of the poem are in fact a curse hurled with enormous power at the departing figure of Odysseus. Revised in H.D.'s rendering of mythic tradition, Callyp-so does not represent the "feminine" principle of submissiveness or passivity. Like the earliest goddess figures of ancient history, she is the Queen of heaven and earth, who commands the seas, the land, the rivers, and the sky. Her "song" begins as a "command" to the forces of nature to destroy Odysseus. The Callypso of tradition who sadly weeps at Odysseus' inevitable departure is unveiled in H.D.'s poem as a masculine fantasy of an androcentric culture. When a woman poet gives Callypso speech, the goddess reveals her own power and her real feelings at Odysseus' betrayal of her love. Rich's description of the new female anger in women's poetry illuminates the underlying significance of H.D.'s handling of traditional materials: "Convention and propriety are perhaps not the right words, but until recently this female anger and this furious awareness of the Man's power over her [elsewhere, Rich describes this as the power to domi-nate, tyrannize, choose, or reject the woman] were not available materials to the female poet, who tended to write of Love as the source of her suffering, and to view that victimization by Love as an almost inevitable fate."[10]

H.D. brings all her imagist craft in prosody to her desire to emphasize Callypso's explosion into speech. Like one who has been silenced for many years, Callypso's rhythms are not graceful, musical, and fluent. H.D. uses syntactical repetition at the beginning of each stanza, an unusually high number of spondees, and a preponderance of one-syllable words to underline the heaviness of her anger. The irregular rhyming patterns, not used in the rest of the poem, weave the threads of the curse even more tightly together and by their inconsistency suggest the passion of its source. A moral, even religious weight appears in the final stanzas of Callypso's speech as Callypso justifies her curse and asks "all earth and heaven" to bear "witness" to Odysseus' crime. In her court of law, "evil" is redefined. It does not involve the sin of female beauty and illicit sexuality as it does in the Greek tradition of Pandora and Helen. For Callypso, "evil" means insensitivity, egotism, and the betrayal of love, as we learn from the remainder of the poem.

As if to emphasize that insensitivity, Callypso repeats herself, with blunt rhythms and harsh words. She concludes by addressing a "you" that could be Odysseus or the male sex he represents: "you, you must hear me— / man is a devil, / man will not understand." For H.D., who always loved indirection and masks in her poetry, this is an extraordinarily direct statement of anger. It had to be. Extensive encoding of Callypso's speech would have ensured that her lone voice could never be heard amidst the overwhelming cumulation of masculine voices in the dominant literary and mythic tradition. Deconstructing Callypso's painfully blunt words does not involve complex explication of the poem nearly so much as it necessitates decoding the androcentric cultural context that has denied a voice to Callypso's perspective in the first place. To hear and understand Callypso's speech, the literary critic must discard the imprint of centuries, stop "listening" to the myriad voices of Odysseus, and hear anew the direct message in all its authenticity.

Callypso's fear that she will not be heard or understood by "man" is fulfilled in the next section of the poem, in which the poet shifts the perspective and the voice to unveil Odysseus' inner thoughts and reveal the accuracy of Callypso's charge. Odysseus, now far away at sea and ignorant of Callypso's curse, innocently sings a litany of praises to her generosity:

Odysseus (on the sea)

> She gave me fresh water in an earth-jar,
> strange fruits

to quench thirst,
a golden zither
to work magic on the water;

she gave me wine in a cup
and white wine in a crystal shell;
she gave me water and salt,
wrapped in a palm-leaf,
and palm-dates:

she gave me wool and a pelt of fur,
she gave me a pelt of silver-fox,
and a brown soft skin of a bear,

she gave me an ivory comb for my hair,
she washed brine and mud from my body,
and cool hands
held balm
for a rust-wound;

she gave me water
and fruit in a basket,
and shallow
baskets of pulse and grain, and a ball
of hemp
for mending the sail;

she gave me a willow-basket
for letting into the shallows
for eels;

she gave me peace in her cave. (*S.P.*, pp. 60–61)

Odysseus' speech proves Callypso right—"man" does not "understand." With his desire turned entirely toward his own needs, Odysseus celebrates her power and gifts with complete insensitivity to her needs. Unaware of his own self-centeredness, he reveals the underlying pattern of their relationship: she gave and gave and gave; he took and took and left. The syntactical repetition of "she gave" continues almost to the point of exaggerated caricature as if to underline the hidden structure of man's treatment of woman as H.D. sees it in this poem. Callypso's gifts are themselves a re-vision of tradition, however. They confirm the suggestion in Callypso's "command" that she embodies not the negative principles of passivity and darkness, nor the lesser female deities of the Olympian pantheon, but rather the pre-Olympian Goddess of heaven and earth. Through her magic, she heals and nurtures him with the fruits of land and sea, music, clothes, baskets, and most important "peace in her cave." She is the great Goddess whose powers regenerate and restore life. She embodies the Greek Pandora (pan=all; dora=giving) whose "gifts" were distorted in Hesiod's misogynist tales of creation.

Without the context of Callypso's angry speech, Odysseus' grateful hymn of praise would seem to share little with Hesiod's condemnation of woman's corrupting evil nature so deviously hidden beneath a surface of natural beauty. Like many artistic forms of male adoration, Odysseus appears to be worshipping the beautiful goddess who lovingly healed his wounds and repaired his boat for his homeward journey. The images function as a caress, and the heavy spondees are replaced by soft, lilting rhythms. But, read in the context of Callypso's anger, Odysseus' adoration takes on an ironic dimension. It parallels "Helen," where the Greeks can love Helen only when she becomes a dead statue fashioned by men as a symbol of beauty they desire. Through irony, H.D. establishes that the male celebration of woman as a positive symbol exists at the expense of living women. Tradition, she argues, must not only celebrate women; it must let woman speak for herself. The ironic juxtaposition of Odysseus' litany and Callypso's curse demonstrates that when man speaks for woman, he does not understand. H.D.'s manipulation of shifting perspectives helps to establish the thematic center of her poem: revisionist mythmaking, woman's re-vision of masculine tradition.

The tempo of alternating perspectives quickens in the final section of the poem as if to emphasize the issue of perspective as the thematic core of the poem.

Callypso (from land)
> He has gone,
> he has forgotten;
> he took my lute and my shell of crystal—
> he never looked back—

Odysseus (on the sea)
> She gave me a wooden flute
> and a mantle,
> she wove this wool—

Callypso (from land)
> For man is a brute and a fool. (*S.P.*, p. 61)

Callypso's curse reveals its origin in the pain of rejection. While Odysseus' first speech illustrates his own insensitivity, it also provides an important context for Callypso's explosion of hatred that gives no hint of prior love. The extent of her love was so great that she continued to give all she could even when she knew that her gifts would help Odysseus leave. Her final words from land as she watches Odysseus at sea incorporate a mixture of love and anger. "He has gone, / he has forgotten / . . . / he never looked back—" is a lament born of rejection. Callypso is of course wrong in one sense. We hear both sides of a dramatic dialogue while Callypso and Odysseus speak only to themselves. Odysseus does remember Callypso's gifts; he does nothing but "look back" toward her for his eight stanzas of the poem. But on another level, she is quite right. In always taking and never giving, he has betrayed her lute and shell of crystal, her wooden flute and woolen mantle. His memory merely charades as love because it reveals the egotism at the center of his feelings. As in Robert Browning's "My Last Duchess," dramatic irony intensifies Callypso's condemnation of Odysseus. The more he "remembers" Callypso's gifts, the more his adoration is unveiled as his capacity to exploit her selfless love without any understanding of her feelings or his own insensitivity. His own words of praise ironically demonstrate the accuracy of Callypso's final judgment: "For man is a brute and a fool." Odysseus, representative of men in general, has not understood that "it was of my heart-blood / his sails were woven."

The juxtaposition of voices in the poem helps to establish the poet's own perspective. At first glance, H.D.'s adaptation of a dramatic script to poetry seems to suggest a conventional lover's quarrel. First we hear "her side," then "his side" with the poet as arbiter, dispassionately revealing the breakdown in communication. But this poet is no more dispassionate or "objective" than the one who watched the growing paralysis of Helen in the earlier poem. In "Callypso Speaks," the poet only seems invisible because of the play's dramatic form, because in this poem, the poet no longer has to speak for the suffocated woman. Each speaker's monologue provides the context that reveals the poet's underlying sympathies. Odysseus' song of thanks clarifies the love that preceded Callypso's anger. Her curse establishes an ironic context for Odysseus' chronicle of her gifts. As the extent of Odysseus' insensitivity unfolds before our eyes, Callypso's anger and pain become the poet's as well. Callypso, a projection of fury softened only by her mythic nature, speaks the poet's own rage.

If H.D. had adopted the confessional mode of Sylvia Plath or Anne Sexton, her readers might have understood the raw fury in the poem for what it is. The use of mythic masks encodes the rebellion into "safer" forms so that her readers can avoid confronting the blunt message of the poem: "man is a brute and a fool." Readers immersed in the androcentric cultural tradition can dismiss the contemporary anger of this poem by seeing it only as a poem about Odysseus and Callypso, two mythic characters utterly removed from the present day. To do so would merely repeat what patriarchal perspectives have done for centuries: ignore, trivialize, or distort the very real presence of anger in the female literary tradition. Because of the absence of mythic masks in a poem like "Daddy," such dismissal has been more difficult in readings of Sylvia Plath's *Ariel*. One might justifiably say that H.D.'s insistence on using traditional materials distanced the perspectives she expressed and contributed to the misunderstanding of her poetry. I would argue, on the other hand, that "Callypso Speaks" belongs within the context of what Rich has written about anger in contemporary women's poetry. Revision of patriarchal tradition is the first step toward the liberation of woman's speech. That speech, however, must release an explosion of anger before the process of rebirth can be fulfilled: "Much of woman's poetry has been of the nature of the blues song: a cry of pain, of victimization, or a lyric of seduction. And today, much poetry by women—and prose for that matter—is charged with anger. . . . Both the victimization and the anger experienced by women are real, and have real sources, everywhere in the environment, built into society. They must go on being tapped and explored by poets, among others. We can neither deny them, nor can we rest there. They are our birth-pains, and we are bearing ourselves."[11]

"Callypso Speaks" taps the vein of hidden anger Rich believes essential to the birth of woman out of the ashes of patriarchal culture. But in this poem, Callypso herself is not reborn. While this poem gives expression to rage, it also portrays anger as inadequate as an end in itself. Callypso is certainly closer to self-definition than is H.D.'s earlier portrait of Helen. She is not paralyzed; she has finally spoken. But there is an overtone of futility in the poet's vision of the man and the woman set perpetually in opposition. Callypso's anger explodes only when Odysseus is too far away to hear her. In Odysseus' presence, she silenced her rage so effectively that he never guessed at the depths of her rebellion. Although her articulation of a woman's perspective is a gigantic step in mythological tradition, Callypso remains the victim in the world of the poem. Her situation is basically unchanged—like so many women, she remains behind while Odysseus uses her gifts to fulfill his destiny as hero. While Callypso's anger is the poet's as well, H.D. and the abandoned goddess are separate in another dimension of the poem's meaning. Callypso is fully immersed in her feelings, but H.D. stands outside Callypso's catharsis to ask implicitly where such anger will lead. There is no suggestion in the poem that Callypso will be able to break the pattern of victimization in the future. She suffers intensely from the selflessness of woman's love for man, but no quest for self-discovery emerges from her pain. The poet's anger in identification with Callypso is set within the larger context of despair. Anger as an end in itself is a dead-end. It may be necessary for woman's self-definition, but it cannot by itself accomplish transcendence.

"Callypso Speaks" is the only poem H.D. ever published that expresses the violent anger of women against men that Rich has described. Perhaps the atmosphere of futility that surrounds Callypso's nonetheless crucial speech characterized H.D.'s own attitude toward the function of hate in the transitional years between *Red Roses for Bronze* and the *Trilogy*. Or perhaps the poem had distant biographical roots in H.D.'s anger toward Aldington, emotions dredged to the surface with the lengthy divorce proceedings of the late thirties. Whatever its origins, "Callypso Speaks" is a pivotal poem standing between the mute Helen of "Helen" and the rebirth of the goddess figure as a potent, living symbol in the *Trilogy* and as paradigmatic questor in *Helen in Egypt*. The *Trilogy* carries woman's anger one step forward into the processes of transformation. Recognition of traditional forms of misogyny leads not to despair, but to an affirmation of the poet's power to purify patriarchal images of woman and to resurrect the Goddess as the spirit of regenerative Love in the modernist nightmare.

In his *Cantos*, Pound grounded his mythmaking in the "rectification" of language. In her *Trilogy*, H.D. centered her mythmaking

in the "rectification" of tradition itself. The dialectic that put new
wine in old bottles was for H.D. a process of purification, a restoration of spiritual realism in poetic form. In the contemporary world
at war, the familiar male images of deity were "beautiful yet static,
empty / old thought, old convention" (*T*, p. 26). To discover the
"new Sun / of regeneration," the poet has to rely on the "Dream"
to "deftly stage-manage" a stark vision of the "world-father" and the
"son" of salvation (*T.*, pp. 25–29). The first poem of the *Trilogy*
centers on the poet's recovery through dream of an authentic male
image of divine spirit. But the "amber eyes" of Christos are not
enough by themselves to uncover the pattern of rebirth structuring
the apocalyptic destruction of war. The poet recalls God's commandment: *"Thou shalt have none other gods but me,"* but she ends
by denying the monotheism of orthodox tradition (*T.*, pp. 50–51).
Not only will she defy the commandment to discover the "historical
parallels" and "psychic affinities" among male deities of various
cultures, but she must also resurrect the female deities expressly
forbidden by the masculine mythology of Judeo-Christianity. In the
Bible, the prophets of Israel denounced the goddesses of the mystery
religions while John designated Ishtar as the Whore of Babylon in
his Revelation. In revising tradition to bring a new mythos to the
modern world, H.D. saw her task as the restoration of the Goddess
to her original purity. The androcentric definition of woman that
paralyzed Helen and silenced Callypso must be dissolved in the "corrosive sublimate" of the poet's pen. H.D.'s initial call to "recover old
values" incorporates the poet's recognition of patriarchal desecration
and her rectification of tradition:

> but gods always face two-ways,
> so let us search the old highways
>
> for the true-rune, the right-spell,
> recover old values;
>
> nor listen if they shout out,
> your beauty, Isis, Aset or Astarte,
>
> is a harlot; you are retrogressive,
> zealot, hankering after old flesh-pots;
>
> your heart, moreover,
> is a dead canker,

they continue, and
your rhythm is the devil's hymn,

your stylus is dipped in corrosive sublimate,
how can you scratch out

indelible ink of the palimpsest
of past misadventure? (*T.*, pp 5–6)

The "palimpsest of past misadventure" is H.D.'s metaphor for centuries of misogynist tradition by which the goddesses and woman-symbols were reduced to evil, corrupting sexuality, material existence, and death. Woman's "rhythms" or cycles connect her with the devil. Woman's "flesh" is "retrogressive," man's beginning point ever after left behind by the individual and historical search for progress. Woman's "heart," woman's love, is a spreading canker of corruption and death designed to deceive and entrap men. H.D. found her own images to express the hatred and fear of woman that manifested most particularly in the patristic tradition. "You are the devil's gateway," Tertullian had warned the "daughters of Eve" in the second century: "You shattered that image of God: man!" Clement of Alexandria wrote: "Nothing disgraceful is proper for man, who is endowed with reason; much less for woman, to whom it brings shame even to reflect of what nature she is. . . . By no manner of means are women to be allowed to uncover and exhibit any part of their person, lest both fall—the men by being excited to look, they by drawing on themselves the eyes of men." And St. John Chrysostom summed up a whole tradition in the fourth century in his condemnation of Eve and by extension all women: "The woman taught once, and ruined all."[12] Given the weight of such negative judgment how can you "scratch out indelible ink" of tradition, the poet asks. Her image of "corrosive sublimate" foreshadows the chemical and alchemical processes of purification developed in full in *Tribute to the Angels*. Corrosive sublimate is a crystalline compound, mercury chloride, used to disinfect and purify. H.D.'s pen, her poetry, will "sublime" tradition —as a verb to define a chemical process, "to sublime" means to refine or purify, to convert something from an inferior state to a "sublime" one. H.D. began to "sublime" tradition in "Helen" and "Callypso Speaks." But in the *Trilogy*, particularly *Tribute to the Angels*, she makes the process of "subliming" the subject of a poetic quest that ultimately moves beyond paralysis and anger into transformation.

The chemistry of *The Walls Do Not Fall* becomes the esoteric alchemy interwoven with the symbols of John's Revelation in *Tribute to the Angels* as H.D. explores more fully the nature of cultural metamorphosis. She identifies with the apocalyptic mysticism of John, but the very parallels she draws between them lead her into the process of re-vision as Rich has defined it. *"I John saw. I testify* / to rainbow feathers, to the span of heaven and walls of colour, / the colonnades of jasper," the poet announces (*T.*, p. 109). But "when the jewel / melts in the crucible" of her poetry, John's vision has been radically transformed (*T.*, p 109).

In John's version, the Lamb's victory over the Whore of Babylon is the necessary precursor to the defeat of Satan that immediately follows. John's description of this woman, however, reveals her to be one of the protean forms of the Near Eastern Great Goddess whose religions so threatened the angry Jewish prophets. Often, she appeared as the queen of heaven and earth, the lady of beasts, and the embodiment of wisdom.[13] Like Hesiod's Pandora and the Eve of Genesis, John's portrait presents familiar attributes of the Goddess in a negative light: "I saw a woman sit upon a scarlet coloured beast, full of names of blasphemy, having seven heads and ten horns. And the woman was arrayed in purple and scarlet colour, and decked with gold and precious stones and pearls, having a golden cup in her hand full of abominations and filthiness of her fornication: And upon her forehead was a name written, MYSTERY, BABYLON THE GREAT, THE MOTHER OF HARLOTS AND ABOMINATIONS OF THE EARTH" (17:3–5). Anticipating the virulent misogyny of the patristic tradition, John's vision condemned the Goddess in favor of the masculine monotheism of patriarchal religion. Woman's beauty (the gems), menstrual fluid ("scarlet colour"), sexuality ("fornication"), and womb ("golden cup") represent to John the essence of abomination and the source of defilement for men (14:4). The defeat of the Whore makes possible the celebration of the Virgin in the following chapter. She appears to John as the mother of God—the "woman clothed with the sun, and the moon under her feet, and upon her head a crown of twelve stars" (12:1). Zodiacal imagery similarly connects her with the Great Goddess, but the source of her virtue is the redemption she gains through giving birth to the Son (12:3–5). Dethroned herself, the goddess figure gives birth to the masculine pantheon that supersedes her.[14]

Poetic alchemy, inspired by Hermes Trismegistus, becomes the poet's means of revising the misogyny of John and resurrecting the Goddess as a regenerative force in a death-centered world at war. To undo the "palimpsest of past misadventure," the poet's "corrosive sublimate" (mercury chloride) fuses Hermes (mercury) and "marah" (chloride, a salt) in a process of distillation that "sublimes" "marah" into "Star of the Sea, / Mother":

> Now polish the crucible
> and in the bowl distill
>
> a word most bitter, *marah*,
> a word bitterer still, *mar*,
>
> sea, brine, breaker, seducer,
> giver of life, giver of tears;
>
> Now polish the crucible
> and set the jet of flame
>
> under, till *marah-mar*
> are melted, fuse and join
>
> and change and alter,
> mer, mere, mère, mater, Maia, Mary,
>
> Star of the Sea,
> Mother. (*T.*, p. 71)

"Mara" or "Marah" is the Hebrew word for bitter. Moses named the first encampment in the desert "Mara" because the waters were too bitter or salty to drink (Exodus 15:23). And Naomi changed her name which means "beautiful" to Mara or "bitter" after the death of her family (Ruth 1:20). In the crucible of poetry, heated by the fire of war, H.D. distilled the words associated with sea water and bitterness to restore the origins of life, the Mother, to her pre–Judeo-Christian essence. John's words about the Babylonian Goddess were bitter indeed, but H.D.'s etymological alchemy purifies the negative imagery by transforming "mara" to "mère," "Star of the Sea, / Mother."[15] As Freud taught H.D., the childhood of the individual recapitulates the infancy of humankind. The "jewel" in the crucible is both the poet's mother and the Sea as "mother" of all life. Amniotic fluid cradles the beginnings of individual birth, and seawater, too bitter to drink, created the biochemistry favorable to organic evolution.

The poet does not immediately understand the meaning of the "bitter, bitter jewel / in the heart of the bowl" produced by her alchemy. "What is your colour? / what do you offer / to us who rebel," she asks the jewel (*T.*, p. 72). To answer her question, she must allow the alchemical process to unfold. As she relights the flame, she understands more precisely that she must "purify" the protean forms of the Goddess as they have been distorted by masculine monotheism:

> O swiftly, re-light the flame
> before the substance cool,
>
> for suddenly we saw your name
> desecrated; knaves and fools
>
> have done you impious wrong,
> Venus, for venery stands for impurity
>
> and Venus as desire
> is venereous, lascivious,
>
> while the very root of the word shrieks
> like a mandrake when foul witches pull
>
> its stem at midnight,
>
> .   .   .   .
>
> Swiftly re-light the flame,
> Aphrodite, holy name,
>
> Astarte, hull and spar
> of wrecked ships lost your star,
>
> forgot the light at dusk,
> forgot the prayer at dawn;
>
> return, O holiest one,
> Venus whose name is kin
>
> to venerate,
> venerator. (*T.*, pp. 74–75)

H.D.'s etymological alchemy distills the cultural accumulations of negative meaning into the word's "root," or pure essence. As Pound did in *The Cantos*, she engages in what he called *cheng ming* or rectification of the language.[16] Her patron, Hermes Trismegistus, is connected with Hermes and Thoth, Greek and Egyptian inventors of written language. Alchemy restores Logos, the Word, to a world that has distorted "Venus" into "venereous," a world that has lost its vision of "spiritual realism," a world dominated by "the Sword." The poet's alchemy counters the Sword's modern reality with an affirmation of her patron: "Mercury, Hermes, Thoth / invented the script, letters, palette. . . . remember, O Sword, / you are the younger brother, the latter-born, / . . . / *in the beginning / was the Word*" (*T.*, p. 17).

Alchemy serves as metaphor for cultural purification as well as for linguistic restoration. The "substance" heated by the poet's flame is the desecrated Goddess. The alchemy of a mythmaking poetic purifies tradition of its misogyny and releases the regenerative powers inherent in "Star of the Sea, / Mother." In condemning the protective forces originally represented by Venus, Aphrodite, and Astarte, the modern world is shipwrecked, lost, and blind to the guiding star, "star of the east, / star of the west, / Phosphorus at sun-rise, / Hesperus at sun-set" (*T*, p. 73). Precursor to Jesus as the "bright and morning star" in Revelation (22:16), this "star" is the planet Venus, the one that guided sailors lost in stormy seas safely back to land. It is also the star Sirius referred to in *The Walls Do Not Fall:* the star of Isis whose appearance in the spring heralded the return of life. As H.D. wrote to Viola Jordan in 1945, the Lady in *Tribute to the Angels* is "planetary." She is "VENUS! That great and good lady is shining now, full and splendid, out of my bedroom window—or into it. As we still have black-out, this is good for seeing stars. I never seem to have seen her anywhere so clear and bright, and last night, there was a tiny crescent moon with her . . . petals up, as if to receive Venus in a cup or flower-cup" (15 February and 25 March 1945). Poetic alchemy restores the brilliant star to its original purity as the Goddess of life and love and thereby "relates resurrection myth and resurrection reality" (*T.*, p. 54). Re-vision of tradition in the *Trilogy* consequently goes further than breaking the silences imposed on women by either a misogynist or a seemingly reverential masculine tradition. The "jewel" created by the poet's profoundly revisionist mythmaking is the "Star" that signifies the return of life in the spring, the "Star" that can restore protection and direction to the weary, shipwrecked questors. The rest of *Tribute to the Angels* centers on the poet's attempt to decipher the meaning of the "jewel."

The alchemical imagery of mythmaking process is ultimately inseparable from the alchemical myth which is the end result of that poetic process. The living jewel distilled in the crucible of words is not gold, not a traditional version of the long-sought philosopher's stone. The "bitter jewel" is organic, not metallic, and its fragrant heartbeat leads the poet to her final vision of the "resurrection myth and resurrection reality."[17] Its color is ever-changing, like the span of "rainbow feathers" and the "all-colour" white of the spectrum (*T.*, p. 109):

> "What is the jewel colour?"
> green-white, opalescent,
>
> with under-layer of changing blue,
> with rose-vein; a white agate
>
> with a pulse uncooled that beats yet,
> faint blue-violet;
>
> it lives, it breathes,
> it gives off—fragrance?
>
> I do not know what it gives,
> a vibration that we can not name
>
> for there is no name for it;
> my patron said, "name it";
>
> I said, I can not name it,
> there is no name;
>
> he said,
> "invent it." (*T.*, p. 76)

The poet disobeys Hermes Trismegistus and refuses to name the living jewel:

> I do not want to name it,
> I want to watch its faint
>
> heart-beat, pulse-beat
> as it quivers, I do not want
>
> to talk about it,
> I want to minimize thought,
>
> concentrate on it
> till I shrink,
>
> dematerialize
> and am drawn into it. (*T.*, p. 77)

To name the jewel would be to separate herself from it by a rational act. Instead, she wants to fuse with her creation, to break down all divisions between alchemist and stone, poet and poem, mystic and divine—and, we might add, woman and Goddess. For the jewel is the resurrected Goddess, the female manifestation of the divine, andro-gynous One. Merged with the jewel, the daughter is reunited with the Mother, and by extension the modern world returns to the womb to be reborn.

Once "drawn into" the gem she created, the poet can experience the "resurrection myth" and "resurrection reality" that underlie the apocalypse of modern war: first in her mystical experience of the Goddess and then in her vivid dream of the Lady. Learning to trans-late the hieroglyphs of "Vision" and "Dream," she uncovers the power of mystical Love that restores life to a world immersed in death. The living jewel first reemerges in the form of the flowering may-apple tree, "so delicate, green-white, opalescent / like our jewel in the crucible" (*T.*, p. 80). The poet comes suddenly upon the bloom-ing tree as she pokes through the "charred portico" and old "garden-square" of what was once a house:

> We see her visible and actual,
> beauty incarnate,
>
> .   .   .   .
>
> we asked for no sign
> but she gave a sign unto us;
>
> sealed with the seal of death,
> we thought not to entreat her
>
> but prepared us for burial;
> then she set a charred tree before us,
>
> burnt and stricken to the heart;
> was it may-tree or apple? (*T.*, p. 82)

The sight of the "half-burnt-out apple-tree blossoming" is a vision of "Love's sacred groves," the mystical Love of hermetic tradition and the "Holy Wisdom, / *Santa Sophia*, the SS of the *Sanctus Spiritus*" (*T.*, p. 101). It "strikes paralysing, / strikes dumb, / strikes the senses numb, / sets the nerves quivering" (*T.*, p. 85). The tree, attribute of the Goddess, does not symbolize the fall of man through woman's sin, as in Genesis. Instead, it incarnates the power of the

Goddess to re-create life out of the ashes of death. Salvation comes not through the Cross of the Son of God, but from the "wood" of the Goddess. The poet "reads" this religious experience as a sign of resurrection myth, resurrection reality. Subsituting female imagery for the masculine imagery of Christianity, she calls her may-apple tree "the flowering of the rood, . . . the flowering of the wood / where Annael, we pause to give / thanks that we rise again from death and live" (*T.*, p. 87).

Dream complements Vision, and the jewel's next emergence starts with the "luminous light" on the "phosphorescent face" of her clock (*T.*, p. 90). The clock's ticking becomes the Lady's knocking, and suddenly the Goddess appears in the poet's dream. The element of surprise repeats the unpredictable onset of epiphany in the courtyard and implies the process of cultural revision that the appearance of the Goddess represents. In her guise as a modern John, the poet had fallen asleep while meditating on the seven masculine angels that surround God's throne in Revelation (1:12–13; 4:5; 8–11, 15–17).[18] But the Lady interrupts this immersion in masculine imagery as if to empha-size her absence from tradition and the urgency of her restoration:

> I had been thinking of Gabriel,
> of the moon-cycle, of the moon-shell,
>
> of the moon-crescent
> and the moon at full:
>
> I had been thinking of Gabriel,
> the moon-regent, the Angel,
>
> and I had intended to recall him
> in the sequence of candle and fire
>
> and the law of the seven;
>
> .   .   .   .
>
> how could I imagine
> the Lady herself would come instead?   (*T.*, p. 92)

In mystical tradition, Gabriel had frequently supplanted the God-dess as the ruler of the Moon. Although deemphasized and often dis-torted, the existence of the Goddess was not wholly forgotten. The poet recognizes the Lady of her dream as Mary: "We have seen her / the world over . . . in cathedral, museum, cloister" (*T.*, pp. 93–94). Artists have "done very well by her," but the poet recognizes that there is a profound difference between the Lady who interrupts her meditations on Gabriel and the catalogue of images she can recall: "But none of these, none of these / suggest her as I saw her" (*T.*, p. 96). Released from traditional imagery as the Virgin Mother of God, the Lady is as different as the pulsating, opalescent jewel is from the cold gold of alchemical tradition. Echoing yet transforming John's descriptions of Jesus, the poet sees the Lady *"clothed with a garment / down to the foot,"* with veils *"white as snow"* (Revelation 1:13–14). But unlike Christ, she is *"not girt about with a golden girdle, /* there was no gold" (*T.*, p. 97; Revelation 1:13). She differs sharply from traditional representations of Mary: "she bore / none of her usual attributes; / the Child was not with her" and she carried the "Book of Life" with "the blank pages / of the unwritten volume of the new" (*T.*, pp. 97, 101, 103, 107). She is not the mother of God, nor is she the bride of Christ: "the Lamb was not with her, / either as Bridegroom or Child" (*T.*, p. 104). Instead, she *is* the divine spirit in its female manifestation as the force of Love and the power of rebirth. And "we are her bridegroom and lamb" (*T.*, p. 104). Her presence to the poet, initiated by the poet's own alchemy, ushers in the new Jerusalem where there is *"no need of the moon to shine ..."* (*T.*, p. 107; Revelation 21:23).

Revisionist alchemy is necessary, indeed so central, to the poet's quest because centuries of religious tradition have so systematically repressed or denigrated the female form in which the "One" has manifested. In purifying tradition of its misogyny, the poet's alchemy restores the Goddess, and the regenerating force of Love that she represents, to a world overwhelmed by the destructive force of hate. Alchemy serves as the metaphor of cultural metamorphosis, and the poet's "jewel" embodies the apocalyptic vision of life-in-death that directs the modernist search for transcendence.[19]

The Goddess, however, is a "revolutionary" vision not only as a female savior, but also as a symbolic representation of the metamorphosis open to women. The alchemy of poetic vision that resurrects the Goddess can also restore the individual woman to authenticity. In her next major poem, *Helen in Egypt*, H.D. returned to the personal dimension of woman's quest for identity, returned to the story of "hated Helen." The striking contrast between the woman paralyzed by hatred and adoration in "Helen" and the woman transcending male definition of woman in *Helen in Egypt* demonstrates forcefully the liberating power of the cultural transformation accomplished in the *Trilogy*. While the poet restores female imagery to the concept of the divine in the *Trilogy*, she examines the implications of that restoration for individual quest in *Helen in Egypt*. In the epic, Helen is no longer mute, dependent upon the poet to point out the processes of injustice. The poet enters fully into the perspective of Helen, who can now construct her own "defense" or "pallinode"—literally, in Greek, a "song against." H.D.'s "pallinode" is a "song against" misogynist tradition, a song that transforms the mythological materials it works with by a radical shift in perspective.

The stages of Helen's quest for identity correspond to the three structural unit of the epic: "Pallinode"; "Leuké"; and "Eidolon." "Pallinode" centers on Helen's development of an "apologia" or "defense" to counter the voices of tradition. It opens with Helen in a psychological frame of mind that echoes the poem H.D. wrote some twenty-five years earlier. Her situation is different, however. Firmly located in space, Helen is in Egypt, convinced of her own innocence, certain that a phantom of Helen made by Zeus caused the terrible war and that her real self has never been to Troy. But conviction of innocence does not allow her to dismiss others' perceptions of her. Like more contemporary heroes such as Edna Pontellier in *The Awakening*, Nora Helmer in *A Doll's House*, or Eva in *Tell Me a Riddle*, Helen cannot begin the process of authentic self-definition until she has come to terms with the identity created for her by the dominant culture. The self-discovery sought in "Leuké" and "Eidolon" rests upon the re-vision of tradition accomplished in "Pallinode." As she wanders through the Amen temple, Helen feels overwhelmed by hatred. To others, she is "Helena, Helen hated of all Greece"; as they fought, they were "cursing Helen through eternity" (*H.E.*, pp. 2, 4). She imagines the helmsman's "bitter oath" as he takes the soldiers to their death in war, ferries them to the underworld, or brings the few remaining home to bitter Pyrrhic victory:

> *O Helen, Helen, Daemon that thou art,*
>
> *we will be done forever*
> *with this charm, this evil philtre,*
> *this curse of Aphrodite;* (*H.E.*, p. 4)

The helmsman speaks with the voice of the dominant tradition: Helen's beauty covers her essential evil. She is the curse inherent in sexual love and passion, and her charm leads men to death. His "bitter oath" recalls Hesiod's description of how Aphrodite "endowed Pandora's face with charm and sensual appeal / Which cause black corrupting passion." Woman was created, according to Hesiod's tale, as the gods' revenge on mankind. Her natural beauty enhanced by a crown of flowers was a "snare" to induce men to welcome a gift that was the "ruin of mankind. / For both the earth and the sea are filled with evil."[20]

Helen's quest begins, then, in painful awareness of how negatively she has been defined. To others, she is a Pandora-figure, a Greek Eve whose association with the goddess of love and beauty brings sorrow, evil, and death to mankind. The weight of tradition, however, does not turn her to stone. H.D.'s prose reflections that open the epic remind us that she has precedents for revisionist mythmaking in Greek literature itself. Both Stesichorus and Euripides first *"reviled"* Helen and then were *"restored to sight"* for their second portraits. But H.D.'s pallinode is a far more fundamental critique of tradition than Euripides' and Stesichorus' revisions of the Helen myth. They both established Helen's innocence by seeing her as a virtuous and chaste wife who waits patiently in Egypt for her husband to reclaim her. H.D., on the other hand, bases her defense of Helen on a redefinition of innocence that squarely confronts the patriarchal mythos by which women were either chaste wife or illicit lover. H.D.'s "pallinode" is a "song against" the male-dominated system of values that victimized Helen as *both* wife and lover.

As the "Pallinode" unfolds, Helen slowly begins to realize that the weight of negative judgment led her to suppress all memory of going to Troy with Paris in a joyous act of springtime love. Her repression of past memories has been entirely successful until Achilles' sudden appearance in Egypt cracks the whole thrust of the traditional pallinodes. Helen believes Zeus sent a phantom to Troy and brought her, the chaste wife, to Egypt. But Achilles' anger and accusations of the beautiful woman who caused his death and that of his comrades force her to remember her joy in leaving the stern atmosphere of Sparta for the warm laughter of Troy. Her first response to Achilles' violent attack is overwhelming guilt: "How could I hide my eyes? / how could I veil my face? / with ash or charcoal from the embers?" (*H.E.*, p. 16). In short, she succumbs to the image of "Helen hated of all Greece." Her appeal to Thetis not only transforms Achilles' hatred into love, but more fundamentally begins the process by which Helen associates herself with the protean forms of the Goddess—particularly Isis, Aphrodite, and Astarte, as well as Thetis. Helen and Achilles meet occasionally in the "Pallinode" before he sails for Leuké, but the reflective action focuses mainly on Helen alone as she remembers earlier selves without shame.

Helen's recovery of the past and redefinition of her innocence take her ultimately back to the origins and meaning of the Trojan War, particularly as it is entangled in her family history. The myth of the golden apple marked "To the Fairest" that rolls into the midst of a wedding feast exists in the background of Helen's meditations. Paris chose Aphrodite, who then rewarded him with Helen. But Helen's primary focus is on the story of her twin sister Clytaemnestra and the king of the Greeks, Agamemnon. In their bitter tragedy, Helen sees parallels with her own life and with the myth of Isis and Osiris. As she translates the overlapping hieroglyphs of myth and history, she discovers that the opposing forces of Love ("L'Amour") and Death ("La Mort") structure human existence and explain the origins of the Trojan War. Within this context, neither she nor Aphrodite caused the war. Instead, the forces of Eros (Love) and Eris (Strife) clashed to produce a confrontation of worlds and world views.

Helen's L'Amour-La Mort, Eros-Eris, and Love-War are poetic expressions of Denis de Rougemont's interpretations of the Tristan myth and Freud's hypothesis about the two opposing instincts dominating the unconscious. "*Eros* and *Death*, those two were the chief subjects—in fact, the only subjects—of the Professor's eternal preoccupation," H.D. wrote (*T.F.*, p. 103). In *Civilization and Its Discontents*, Freud had argued that the warring instincts of bonding and aggression, Eros and death, rule the interior world of the unconscious and the exterior world of civilization itself.

> In all that follows I adopt the standpoint, therefore, that the inclination to aggression is an original, self-subsisting instinctual disposition in man, and . . . it constitutes the greatest impediment to civilization. . . . civilization is a process in the service of Eros, whose purpose is to combine single human individuals, and after that families, then races, peoples and nations, into one great unity, the unity of mankind. . . . But man's natural aggressive instinct, the hostility of each against all . . . opposes this programme of civilization. This aggressive instinct

is the derivative and the main representative of the death instinct which we have found alongside of Eros and which shares world-dominion with it. And now, I think, the meaning of the evolution of civilization is no longer obscure to us. It must present the struggle between Eros and Death, between the instinct of life and the instinct of destruction, as it works itself out in the human species.[21]

His later article "Analysis Terminable and Interminable" (1937) compared his theory of the two instincts with that of the Greek philosopher Empedocles. This ancient theory based on the two principles love (*philia*) and strife (*neikos*) conceived of the "world-process as a continuous, never-ceasing alternation of periods in which the one or the other of the two fundamental forces triumphs."[22]

This alternating process of Love and Death is the key to Helen's translation of her hieroglyphic moment on the desolate beach with Achilles when his assault turns to love. Her interpretation of this mystery leads her to see the same pattern structuring her family history, the Trojan War, and the myth of Isis and Osiris. The spiritual reality that manifests in the individual, familial, societal, and mythic level of existence is the interplay of opposing principles rooted in the unconscious. Departing radically from Freud's presentation, however, H.D. associated Eros with the woman's world and Thanatos with the man's world. Helen's reflections on her newly recovered memories center on the chasm and conflict between these worlds. Her "pallinode" rests finally on an understanding that she is a source of evil only from the perspective of the man's world which so continually distorts and devalues the woman's world.

H.D. relied upon her imagist craft to define the conflicting value systems which started the war. Helen, for example, contrasts the two worlds as she thinks of Achilles just after his arrival in Egypt:

does he dare remember
the unreality of war,
in this enchanted place?

his fortress and his tower
and his throne
were built for man, alone;

no echo or soft whisper
in those halls,
no iridescent sheen,

no iris-flower,
no sweep of strings,
no answering laughter,

but the trumpet's call; (H.E., pp. 30–31)

The imagist rendering of two worlds seems to be operating on the basis of traditional qualities associated with the "masculine" and the "feminine"—strength, power, war, heroism with the "masculine" and softness, flowers, gaiety, music, beauty, interiors with the "feminine." But throughout the epic H.D. carefully revised the conventional associations of "masculine" and "feminine" much as Virginia Woolf had done in To the Lighthouse. Never using the word "feminine" at all, H.D. portrayed the women's world as a powerful force for love, peace, order, and regeneration. Protean forms of the Goddess—Isis, Aphrodite, Astarte, Ishtar, Nepthys, Artemis, and Thetis—embody the powerful love force. Laughter, "shimmering" glances, flowers, softness, light, and music all represent the fertile joy of life. Carefully using the word "masculine," even the phrase *"the purely masculine 'iron-ring,'"* H.D. represented the "masculine" world as the negation of life and love (H.E., p. 55). Personified by the destructive "whirlwind" monster Typhon and the equivalent Egyptian god of desert winds (Set), the masculine world represents the equally powerful force of death, war, and chaos. Its character is imaged by the darkness, cold, metal, weapons, clanging sounds, and fortresses repeatedly associated with it. Hate, pride, tyranny, rape, and a "morality" based upon might are the emotions and behaviors validated by the masculine ethos.

Helen's defense begins to build as she sees the demonic images of war, the world that Achilles himself characterizes as an "iron-ring / whom Death made stronger" (H.E., p. 55):

the rasp of a several wheel

seemed to ring in the dark,
the spark of a sword on a shield,
the whirr of an arrow,

the crack of a broken lance,
then laughter mingled with fury,
as host encountered host; (H.E., p. 39)

This "laughter" is no "answering laughter" as in the halls of the women's world because it is the one-sided battle cry of the victor who feeds upon the destruction of others. Helen's Homeric images of war acquire a contemporary ring later in the "Pallinode," a shift that points to the underlying nature of her critique of masculine tradition. Modern words of World War II permeate her prose description of Achilles' power among the Greeks. Although he *"technically shares the Command,"* he is the *"indisputable dictator with his select body-guard."* A *"secret agreement"* and some *"counter-bargaining"* promised him *"Helen and world-leadership . . . contrary to the first agreement of the allies"* (*H.E.*, p. 51). Homeric references mingle with contemporary allusions as Achilles explains to Helen:

> I had broken the proud
> and re-moulded them to my whim;
> the elect, asleep in their tents,
>
> were my slaves, my servants;
> we were an iron-ring, unbreakable
>
> .   .   .   .
>
> into the ring of our Immortality,
> there came with a clamour of arms,
> as a roar of chargers, answering the trumpeter,
>
> the Command.   (*H.E.*, pp. 51–52)

Achilles recalls further how Odysseus unfolded his "plan of the iron-horse," questioned the significance of a "promise given," and told Achilles that "Helen will be your share / of the spoils of war," that "you should control the world" (*H.E.*, p. 52).

Terms such as "dictator," "allies," and "Command" are not Homeric, not even in translation. H.D.'s intent is not only to under-score the palimpsest of history, but also to broaden the base of her attack. Some of her contemporary words have distinctly fascist over-tones—particularly "elect," "dictator," and "High Command." During World War II, German chiefs of staff were called the "High Com-mand," and Odysseus' promise of "world leadership" is probably a direct reference to Hitler. H.D.'s contemporary allusions embedded in a recollection of the Trojan War extend her attack on the iron-ring of ancient Greece to include any social system founded on elitism, war, and tyranny. The dictator, whose will to command fulfills the mascu-line mystique of absolute power, personifies the "purely masculine" world view and thereby attempts to destroy the enchanted halls of the

Goddess. Directly influenced by an era characterized by the demonic rise of fascist states, H.D. identifies the most extreme forms of "masculine" values with fascism. Her "Cantos" recall Pound's *Cantos* in more ways than one: her attack on fascism as a "death-cult" is perhaps an answer to Pound's espousal of fascism in Italy and his celebration of the patriarchal, Confucian world view.

Helen's defense rests upon the connection H.D. made between the masculine mystique and hierarchical, terror-based, death-centered social systems. Even without the benefit of contemporary feminist theory, H.D. seemed to take their patriarchal nature as a defining characteristic of such social systems. In the prose reflection on A-chilles' speech to Helen, the poet says that *"the Command or the adamant rule of the inner circle of the warrior caste was 'bequest from the past.'"* The Achilleses, Agamemnons, Hitlers, and Mussolinis of the world are not freak accidents of history; they are part of a patriarchal chain structuring a social system. As Achilles explains to Helen:

> The Command was bequest from the past,
> from father to son,
> the Command bound past to the present
>
> and the present to aeons to come,
> the Command was my father, my brother,
> my lover [his male friend Patroklos], my God;   (*H.E.*, p. 61)

The fact that H.D.'s Achilles is based on Lord Dowding, Chief Marshal of the Royal Air Force, further suggests that she connected the origins of war with the "death-cult" motivating men on both sides of the conflict—Greece as well as Troy, England as well as Germany. Fascism and world dictatorship were an extreme version of the death-cult as patriarchal social system, but the potential for violence is inherent in any male-dominated system.

H.D. carefully delineated the position of women within this "warrior caste." As possessions prized for their beauty and sexual potential, the women are the "spoils of war"; the most beautiful—Helen—would go to the world leader, Achilles.[23] The theme of female sacrifice to the masculine "warrior cult" reappears many times throughout the epic. Helen explores the power structures of her world by examining the common pattern underlying the fates of other women: Cassandra, Polyxena, Briseis, Chryseis, and, most of all, the women in her own family. In reliving the story of her twin sister, Clytaemnestra, and her niece, Iphigenia, Helen comes to a full realization of the conflict between polarized worlds. When Helen is able to visualize *"her own fate in terms of that of her twin sister"* (*H.E.*, p. 74), she takes the first step in her inner quest to recover and accept her role at Troy.

The story of her sister clarifies for Helen the values of the woman's world as well as the patriarchal state and family which oppose it. Like Helen, Clytaemnestra was "hated by all Greece." Her name become synonymous with women's treachery and evil because she took a lover while her husband Agamemnon was in Troy and then killed him when he came home victorious with his concubine Cassandra. Deep in family history, however, Helen finds Clytaemnestra's motivations to be her defense of the woman's world. Clytaemnestra's wedding day defines that world for Helen. In contrast to the metallic world of war, it is characterized by the ascendance of peace and harmony. The Goddess rules through the Word, not the Sword, as humankind exists in organic relation to nature. Like the *komos* or wedding party with which all Greek comedy ends, the marriage is holy, incarnating the force of life in the real world. Helen recalls:

> She was a bride, my sister,
> with a bride's innocence,
> she was a lover of flowers
>
> and she wound in her hair,
> the same simple weeds
> that Iphigenia wore;
>
> she stepped forward,
> they stood together
> as one, before the altar;
>
> O Word of the Goddess,
> O Harmony and Grace,
> it was a moment
>
> of infinite beauty,
> but a war-Lord
> blighted that peace (*H.E.*, p. 74)

Agamemnon is the warlord who disrupts Harmony as he literally transforms the altar of marriage into the altar of sacrifice. Many years after his marriage, he is eager to lead the Greek troops to Troy to regain Menelaus' honor. But Apollo holds back the winds needed by the

Greek warships because the Greeks have violated the sacred hunting grounds of his sister Artemis. Calchas, the priest of Apollo, demands the sacrifice of a virgin to Artemis before the ships can leave Aulis for Troy. H.D.'s version of the familiar Homeric tale, however, highlights the dualism of Love and War. She considers Calchas to be *"a substitute or a double of the original Command,"* (*H.E.*, p. 87). He is the priest of the "warrior caste," a prophet for the "death-cult." His "dictate" sets in motion Agamemnon's betrayal of his marriage. The confrontation of two value systems becomes family history. The virgin he demands is Agamemnon's daughter Iphigenia, who is *"summoned to Aulis, on the pretext of a marriage to Achilles"* (*H.E.*, p. 72). Representative of the patriarchal family and state, Agamemnon sacrifices his daughter to the needs of the "elect." Representative of a matriarchal value system, Clytaemnestra murders Agamemnon in fury at the world of men. Helen's first step in her own defense is to create a "pallinode" for her sister:

> what did she care for the trumpet,
> the herald's cry at the gate,
> *war is over;*
>
> it is true she lay with her lover,
> but she could never forget
> the glint of steel at the throat
>
> of her child on the altar;
> Artemis snatched away
> the proffered sacrifice,
>
> but not even Artemis could veil
> that terrible moment,
> could make Clytaemnestra forget
>
> the lure, the deception, the lie
> that had brought her to Aulis;
> "we will pledge, forsooth, our dearest child
>
> to the greatest hero in Greece;
> bring her here
> to join hand with hand
>
> in the bridal pledge at the altar";
> but the pledge was a pledge to Death,
> to War and the armies of Greece. (*H.E.*, pp. 72–73)

Clytaemnestra's powerlessness in the face of Agamemnon's

treachery at this moment does not mean that H.D. associated passivity or helplessness with the Goddess or her human embodiments. The woman's world is at times defeated, but victimization is not the same as passive acceptance. *"Their* [Iphigenia, Clytaemnestra] *divinity is stronger than all the material forces gathered against them,"* H.D. wrote. The poem continues with a marvelous reversal on the image of Zeus as a swan who rapes Leda. Here Clytaemnestra and Iphigenia are the swans:

> Have you ever seen a swan,
> when you threaten its nest—
>
> .   .   .   .
>
> the wings of an angry swan
> can compass the earth,
>
> can drive the demons
> back to Tartarus,
> can measure heaven in their span;
>
> one swan and one cygnet
> were stronger than all the host,   (*H.E.,* p. 76)

The power of the Swan-mother is only one manifestation of a pervasive pattern. The power of the Goddess herself confronts the Command and ultimately wins Achilles' loyalty. Achilles explains the power of the Goddess to Helen:

> She is stronger than God, they say,
>
> She is stronger than Fate
> and a chaffing greave,
> loose at the ankle,   (*H.E.,* p. 61)

Achilles continues to tell Helen how the Goddess led him to renounce world leadership, the Command, and the masculine ring of war. The Goddess operated through Helen, her human counterpart, to defeat the Command. Achilles exchanged his magnetic, fatal glance with Helen just as he was about to fasten the loose greave partially covering his one mortal spot. Fastened instead in the "shimmering" light of their glance, he became "indifferent" to the battle (*H.E.,* p. 54). Paris killed him shortly thereafter and thus sealed the defeat of the Command. The power of the Goddess led the leader of the warrior caste to "barter the world / for a glance" (*H.E.,* p. 62). Achilles gains more

than he loses, however, for his appearance on the beach in Egypt signals his rebirth, as the "new Mortal," a hero whose status does not
depend upon tyranny. As the cause of his death, Helen only *seems*
to fulfill the role of the seductive, hated Helen. In reality, she provides the conditions necessary for his rebirth. This story of Achilles'
transformation is H.D.'s own, a change that underscores the polari-
zation of male and female worlds. Variants of the myth often place
Achilles on Leuké after death, but the fatal glance that signals his
absorption into the woman's world is entirely H.D.'s addition. To
Thomas Burnett Swann, Achilles appears weak and emasculated.[24]
But to H.D., the classical celebration of masculinity yields to Eros to
allow for the rebirth of the hero.

The voice of Thetis, Achilles' mother, speaks only once in the
"Pallinode" to help Helen define the nature of woman's power more
precisely. It is not violent or aggressive. Rather, it is invisible, intangible, and omniscient. Its agency is magic, not might:

Phoenix, the symbol of resurrection has vanquished indecision and doubt,
the eternal why *of the Sphinx. It is Thetis (Isis, Aphrodite) who tells us this,*
at last, in complete harmony with Helen.

Choragus (Image or Eidolon of Thetis):

> A woman's wiles are a net;
> they would take the stars
> or a grasshopper in its mesh;
>
> they would sweep the sea
> for a bubble's iridescence
> or a flying-fish;
>
> they would plunge beneath the surface,
> without fear of the treacherous deep
> or a monstrous octopus;
>
> what unexpected treasure,
> what talisman or magic ring
> may the net find?
>
> frailer than spider spins,
> or a worm for its bier,
> deep as a lion or a fox
>
> or a panther's lair,
> leaf upon leaf, hair upon hair
> as a bird's nest,

Phoenix
has vanquished
that ancient enemy, Sphinx. (*H.E.*, pp. 93–94)[25]

To some extent, H.D.'s use of the word "wiles" is ironic. It conjures up the familiar image of the deceitful woman who uses her "feminine wiles" to manipulate men, and it alludes to the net Clytaemnestra used to trap Agamemnon. In contrast, however, the "wiles" of the goddess weave a net of power that "catches" the earth, the stars, and the sea. Not the manipulations of a childish, powerless woman, these "wiles" ultimately "catch" the Phoenix, the vision of resurrection, and thereby express the regenerative powers of life which the goddess embodies. H.D.'s view is strongly pacifist as it offers a vision of power based on life instead of death. She rejects the notion that women should become like men or use the weapons of men in their fight against the death-cult. Helen decides that Clytaemnestra's fate was a dark one because she became her opposite in the defense of the woman's world:

Clytaemnestra struck with her mind,
with the Will-to-Power,
her Lord returned with Cassandra,

and she had a lover;
does it even the Balance
if a wife repeats a husband's folly?

never; the law is different;
if a woman fights,
she must fight by stealth,

with invisible gear;
no sword, no dagger, no spear
in a woman's hands

can make wrong, right; (*H.E.*, p. 97)

Linda Welshimer Wagner used this passage to argue that H.D. urged women to accept the dominance of men without rebellion.[26] But Helen's pallinode is fundamentally radical in its anticipation of contemporary feminism. Helen rejects the option of becoming "masculinized," adopting the values of hierarchical society, and defeating men with their own weapons. Instead, Helen learns in her own defense that the qualities of the woman's world are life-affirming. They must be restored and valued if civilization is to survive the destruction wrought by the masculine ethos. For H.D., who abhorred war, this change had to evolve through peaceful means, through the intangible net of the life force and the transforming power of love. Her poetic revaluation of a woman's world view represents her attempt to stop the cycle of violence.

The Goddess which H.D. invoked as the incarnation of Love represents a fusion of her reading in mysticism and mythology. The Love which overpowers Achilles is not simply the passion of a man for a woman. Helen's deification as Love on Melos is not a shrine to sexual beauty and desire (*H.E.*, p. 95). Love operates as the mystical life force that infuses all organic and spiritual things with the power of growth, synthesis, and resurrection. It is the Love of the Cathar heresy and the Moravian "love feasts" that H.D. associated with the Goddess. Like the Lady of the *Trilogy*, the Goddess in the epic is "Holy Wisdom, / *Santa Sophia*, the SS of the *Sanctus Spiritus*" (*T.*, p. 101). But the qualities H.D. gave the Goddess also echo those assigned to matriarchal societies in the established anthropological research of the nineteenth and early twentieth centuries. A number of writers H.D. read accepted J.J. Bachofen's theory that a matriarchal stage of human history everywhere preceded patriarchal social organization— most particularly, Arthur Weigall, Jane Harrison, Margaret Murray, Havelock Ellis, W.J. Perry, Sigmund Freud.

Bachofen argued that classical mythology encoded the uneasy transition from matriarchal to patriarchal societies and that the Great Goddesses of the Near East were vestiges of cultures whose primal deity was female and in which women were not dominated by men. But of greatest significance to H.D.'s epic, Bachofen did not envision matriarchal societies as the simple reversal of patriarchal societies. The Greek root (archos = rule) implies that patriarchy merely substituted the rule of men for the rule of women. But Bachofen and many of the writers who accepted his theory believed matriarchal societies to be different in *kind*, rather than in gender of the rulers. The alternative to patriarchy in his work and in H.D.'s epic is *not* rule by women, but rather an absence of all tyranny. Bachofen described matriarchal culture in terms strikingly parallel to the rule of the Goddess in H.D.'s epic: "it operates in a world of violence as the divine principle of love, of union, of peace."[27] Woman countered "violence with peace, enmity with conciliation, hate with love; and thus she guide[d] the wild, lawless existence of the earliest period toward a milder, friendlier culture, in whose center she sits enthroned as the embodiment of the higher principle." Religion, based in worship of the "mother principle," showed a "distinct leaning toward the mysterious, transcendent, supersensory element." Matriarchal peoples "feel the unity of all life, the harmony of the universal." Their societies were classless, based on cooperation and common ownership of material goods. In essential harmony with the environment, women in matriarchal societies contributed to civilization by ending nomadic existence, developing agriculture, and ensuring peace.

H.D.'s Goddess is the principle of Harmony established through Love. In a way similar to if not influenced by Bachofen's "mother principle," the Goddess counters violence with a gentle power stronger than death and implies a social order antithetical to the patriarchal Command. In her guise as Thetis, she taught the young Achilles "the laws and the arts of peace." Until he succumbed to the "lure of war," he was content with "the magic of little things" and the secret eidolon of Thetis that he kept in his cave (*H.E.*, pp. 284–87). As "Empress and lure of the sea . . . Regent of heaven and the star-zone," she teaches Helen to understand the "Mystery" embodied in the hieroglyphs of her family history, the Trojan War, and her meeting with Achilles (*H.E.*, pp. 253–54, 273–81, 303–04).

Helen's identification with the Goddess and her deification as Love in the "Pallinode" prepare her to remember her past by releasing her from guilt. Censorship of her trip to Troy was necessary only so long as she regarded herself as others saw her: the symbol of sexual beauty that leads men to ruin. Understood in the context of opposing matriarchal and patriarchal values, Helen's love for Paris becomes her rebellion against the iron-ring of the death-cult. Her flight from the family to whom she is nothing but a beautiful "stranger" is a revolt that parallels her sister's darker revenge. The defense of the "Pallinode" is complete. With innocence redefined, "Helena has withstood / the rancour of time and hate" (*H.E.*, p. 96). Helen is now ready to recapture the lost Helen of Troy. "Leuké" opens with her memory of sailing to Troy and a strong warning that the image is not the real Helen:

I am not nor mean to be
the Daemon they made of me;
going forward, my will was the wind,

(or the will of Aphrodite
filled the sail, as the story told
of my first rebellion;

the sail, they said,
was the veil of Aphrodite),

.   .   .   .

let them sing Helena for a thousand years,
let them name and re-name Helen,

I can not endure the weight of eternity,
they will never understand
how, a second time, I am free;   (H.E., pp. 109–10)

Helen recognizes that she bears the weight of patriarchal images, but now she no longer internalizes those images so that she is free to reflect fully on her past and future.

For H.D., women give birth to a new self by first destroying the false self created by the culture. The songs that "name and re-name Helen" have called her either virtuously chaste (Helen in Egypt) or destructively evil (Helen of Troy). As she greets Paris in Leuké to relive her Trojan experience, Helen has erased that traditional duality of woman as angel or demon. To be free of tradition, however, does not in itself accomplish the quest for self-definition. In "Leuké" and "Eidolon," her inner journey reveals a multiplicity of selves that bring pain and confusion. Once the censor of suppressed memories opens the door to past selves, Helen can at first find no pattern or certainty in the quicksand succession of identities: Helen, daughter of Zeus and child of worldly Sparta; Helen, the kidnapped child-bride of Theseus; Helen, the wife and mother in Sparta; Helen Dendritis in springtime love with Paris in Troy; Helen alone, in the timeless dimension of sacred Egypt; Helen, the older (perhaps even dead) lover of Achilles; Helen as Persephone, bride of death; Helen, seeking the healing of self-acceptance with Theseus; Helen of Leuké, alone, yet also together with Achilles and the child Euphorion. Helen's quest becomes the search to reconcile the seemingly contradictory selves of daughter, wife, mother, lover, and person alone.

In talking with Theseus, Helen realizes that if Achilles is Typhon through his association with the death-cult of men, then she must be Persephone, the bride of Hades and a goddess of death (H.E., p. 195). How, she asks, can her guise as Persephone be reconciled with herself as Thetis ("Pallinode") or her youthful identity with Paris ("Leuké")? Wholeness and the healing implicit in its discovery comes in part through Helen's identification with the Goddess in all her phases. H.D. directly used Robert Graves's *The White Goddess* as her source for the protean progression of the Goddess through the life cycle. Graves asserted that the Great Goddess appears in the three major phases of the moon. H.D. wrote in her notebook on Graves: "the New Moon is the white goddess of birth and growth; the Full Moon, the red goddess of love and battle; the old Moon, the black goddess of death and divination."[28] Helen sees the pattern structuring her shifting identities in these three phases of the moon. As the white goddess of birth and growth, Helen of Troy was Aphrodite with her young lover Paris-Adonis (*H.E.,* p. 159). As the red goddess of love and battle, Helen was identified with Thetis as mother in her relationship with Achilles that began in Troy and moved to Egypt. And finally, as the black goddess of death and divination, Helen became Persephone, the bride of Achilles-Dis, or Koré, the daughter of the goddess Demeter and seed of the rebirth to come.[29] The life process from youth, through maturity, to old age structures the fragments of Helen's life. The essence which infuses the parts with wholeness is the Goddess who can take many shapes. H.D. reflects in prose that she is called *"Thetis who (like Proteus) 'can change her shape'* " (*H.E.,* p. 193).

The resolution of Helen's quest for wholeness in the figure of the Goddess expresses what H.D. believed to be an essential component in woman's search for identity: the resurrection of the female divine spirit, the Goddess of matriarchal traditions. As the epic opens, Helen feels safe in a cocoon of forgetfulness under the guidance of the "all-father," the male Proteus who takes many shapes. In the process of quest, Helen discovers her identity as a woman in her recovery of the "Eidolon," the image of Thetis that dominates the final section of the epic. The essence of H.D.'s "pallinode" is the growing understanding and acceptance of the power and values of the woman's world view. This resurrection of the Goddess against the backdrop of conflicting male and female worlds is a later version of the alchemy in the *Trilogy* that restores the original potency and purity of the Goddess.

Just as the poet's alchemy had to purify cultural tradition of its misogyny in the *Trilogy,* however, so the poet in the later epic had to engage in a dialectical transformation of her source materials. H.D. did not invent the dualisms of Love and Death, matriarchy and patriarchy, that underlie the restoration of the Goddess; she found them eloquently expressed in esoteric tradition, mythological history, and psychoanalysis. But to make them serve her purpose, she had to "sublime" them, to purify them of their misogynist biases. Freud's controversial hypothesis that the unconscious contains the warring instincts, Eros and Thanatos, is fundamental to *Helen in Egypt*. But Freud never associated Eros with women or matriarchy; nor did he connect Thanatos with men or patriarchy. He asserted that women contributed nothing but weaving to the development of civilization and credited men, whose superegos are stronger, with all human progress.[30] Unlike Freud, Bachofen believed the contributions of the matriarchal period essential, but he considered matriarchal culture inferior to patriarchal culture. Harmony with nature was "tellurian," tantamount to "corporeal existence." The "triumph of paternity brings with it the liberation of the spirit from the manifestations of nature. . . . Maternity pertains to the physical side of man, the only thing he shares with the animals: the paternal-spiritual principle belongs to him alone."[31] In *Helen in Egypt*, the "mother principle" embodies the "liberation of the spirit" from the rule of war instituted by patriarchal society.

Robert Ambelain's description of Manichaean dualism abandons all notion of stages or progress, but his definitions of the "male principle" or "patriarchy" and the "female principle" or matriarchy were useless to H.D. The Goddess is not representative of darkness, passivity, and negation, but rather of light, life, and love. From H.D.'s perspective, the "feminine principle" that Ambelain and much esoteric tradition postulate is itself a reflection of a masculine ethos. In an act of revisionist mythmaking, H.D. made her "masculine principle" the "*absolute of negation*"—destructive, dark, and fiery in spite of its symbolic association with the sun (*H.E.*, pp. 195, 51). Her "feminine principle" is potent, life-giving, and never the embodiment of material existence or death. Similarly, H.D.'s Goddess never has the dual nature of the mother goddesses described in recent male mythologies. Joseph Campbell, Erich Neumann, and Robert Graves portray the Goddess as both devouring and life-giving. Jungians in particular would agree with H.D. that the "feminine principle" personified in the anima has been greatly undervalued in the rationalistic, technological west. But Jung's disciple Neumann sees the positive womb of the Great Mother balanced by the terrifying-toothed vagina of the castrating "Terrible Mother."[32] This balance of apocalyptic and demonic images of the Goddess in various cultures is in reality an intensified form of the dual image of woman that pervades Judeo-Christian religion and secular mass culture—woman is either a saint or a seductress, a loving wife or a castrating bitch, Mary or Eve. In contemporary advertising images or campaigns like the "Total Woman" phenomenon, the woman often tantalizingly combines the sexpot and saint images, but the category human does not exist as a real potential for women. What parades as restitution of women's value is in reality a constricting "feminine principle" that limits the growth of women and reflects a deep-seated ambivalence toward them. This androcentric ambivalence toward the goddesses of tradition is totally absent from H.D.'s work. The whole demonic aspect of the "feminine" image in fact never appears.

H.D.'s development of the Goddess as a symbol of woman's authentic self in *Helen in Egypt* represents the culmination of cultural transformation that began on a small scale in her imagist poems and grew to epic proportions in her later life. This progression from the early ode on the mute Helen, through the explosive anger in "Callypso Speaks," to the full-scale creation of a woman's mythology in the *Trilogy* and *Helen in Egypt* demonstrates a pattern of interaction with tradition that characterizes the nature of H.D.'s mythmaking. The rebirth of Psyche depends first upon a recognition of the androcentric roots of negative definition and then secondly upon a subversive transformation of existing traditions that ultimately destroys their patriarchal base. The metamorphosis of self from "otherness" to authenticity is not a uniquely personal act, H.D.'s heroes understood. Women's quest for selfhood involves direct confrontation with the dominant cultural norms shaping the nature and destiny of women in general. Yet hidden within those norms often lie the seeds of potential antithesis. H.D.'s work began immersed in patriarchal imagery: Freud's psychoanalysis and esoteric mysticism. She used these images to restore the bond with her mother, to resurrect the Goddess, to revise woman as a cultural symbol, and thus establish a valid dimension of women's quest.

In this process of cultural transformation, the role of the artist is crucial. The Goddess is a Muse, "mother" to art as well as vision. The artist's revisionist mythmaking is "revolutionary" in more ways than Gershom Scholem intended, for her art is a creative act that helps establish a new cultural tradition. H.D.'s image for the poet in the *Trilogy* centers on the "worm"—the caterpillar who becomes a butterfly and the resurrection serpent who sheds its skin. Condensing a complex dialectical process into image, she sees herself and her companions in art as the "carriers, the spinners"—"carriers" of the old and "spinners" of the new. Out of the cocoon of the old "husk of self," the poet spins a new mythos that contains both continuity and metamorphosis.

9

Poetics of Conflict and Transcendence

KABBALAH AND THE SEARCH FOR WHOLENESS

H.D.'s SEARCH for an authentic female voice in her art led her ever more inevitably into direct confrontation with patriarchal tradition. From a psychoanalytic perspective, H.D.'s creation of alternative, woman-centered mythologies demonstrates the escapist function of art, its basis in fantasy and wish fulfillment. But for H.D., art increasingly became the dimension in which she had the freedom to oppose existing realities and dominant, man-centered ideologies. Released from the limitations of an oppressive material world by the imagination, her art incorporated the radical potential of the dream, the vision that fulfills the wish for a different world. Not surprisingly for such an aesthetic, the structural center of many of H.D.'s epics is conflict, specifically a confrontation between man and woman which fundamentally motivates the plot. Callypso's opposition to Odysseus in "Callypso Speaks" served not only as a prototype of woman against the patriarchy, but also as archetype of conflict to which H.D. gave many forms in her later poetry: Mary Magdalene and Kaspar in the last volume of the *Trilogy*; Helen and Achilles in *Helen in Egypt*; Helen and Odysseus in *Winter Love*; H.D. herself and the rationalist, Germain, in *Sagesse*; H.D. and first Durand, then Perse, in *Hermetic Definition*.

These confrontations, however, are instances of a larger pattern, a poetic of conflict and polarity that permeates H.D.'s work. Poems like *Helen in Egypt* and *Hermetic Definition* are constructed on the framework of many interrelated dualisms whose poles exist in conflict. This poetic is firmly rooted in H.D.'s imagist work. The pervasive use of syntactically parallel negatives in her earliest work established an ambience of denial, as if the poet were debating with some un-named foe. Stylistic negatives frequently reinforced such imagistically rendered oppositions as sea and land, field and shore, harsh and lush beauty, or simply the poet and an unidentified "you."[1] Thematic, imagistic, and syntactical oppositions in her early work acquired a philosophic and spiritual base as her work developed, however. No doubt Freud's hypothesis of Eros and Thanatos as perpetually warring instincts combined with the strong Manichaean current in esoteric tradition to transform the oppositions in her early work to a philos-ophy of dualism.

In the *Trilogy*, for example, the search for "resurrection myth, resurrection reality" is frequently represented as the attempt to aban-don the "schisms in consciousness" for a discovery of the whole, the One. The poet's personae in several sections of *The Flowering of the Rod* are the wild geese who hover over the lost island of Atlantis. The difficulties of quest are represented in the two colors of the geese who personify the single mind of the poet. H.D. brought all the precision of her imagist craft to embody this spiritual schism in contrasting images of sand and sea, winter and summer, snow-shadow and palm-shadow, white and blue:

> Blue-geese, white-geese, you may say,
> yes, I know this duality, this double nostalgia;
>
> I know the insatiable longing
> in winter, for palm-shadow
>
> and sand and burnt sea-drift;
> but in the summer, as I watch
>
> the wave till its edge of foam
> touches the hot sand and instantly
>
> vanishes like snow on the equator,
> I would cry out, stay, stay;
>
> then I remember delicate enduring frost
> and its mid-winter dawn-pattern;
>
> .   .   .   .
>
> but it is also true that I pray,
> O, give me burning blue

and brittle burnt sea-weed
above the tide-line,

as I stand, still unsatisfied,
under the long shadow-on-snow of the pine. (*T.*, p. 118)

H.D. structured much of her work in the forties and fifties on
many versions of "this duality, this double nostalgia," or to quote another formulation, all the "two's and two's and two's in my life" (*T.F.*,
pp. 31–33). But she was not satisfied to record the polarities of the
universe in her work. "Chasm, schism in consciousness / must be
bridged over," she wrote (*T.*, p. 49). Like the wild geese in search of
the perfection symbolized by Atlantis, H.D. continually sought to
move beyond conflict to harmony, beyond dualism to unity. The poetics of polarity operated within the larger context of the search for
transcendence. The dynamics of her interactions with Freud demonstrate the pattern established in her work. First, the lines of opposition become evident: H.D. as woman, artist, spiritualist, and believer
establishes herself in conflict with Freud as man, scientist, materialist,
and Enlightenment rationalist. The conflict once delineated, H.D.'s
search for harmony begins. *Tribute to Freud* represents her synthesis
of science and art, reason and intuition, man and woman. H.D. regarded transcendence of dualism as essential to creativity; it parallels
the union of mother and father in the conception of the child who
combines elements of both parents in a new synthesis. As she wrote
in *The Gift*, "science and art must beget a new creative medium."[2]
The poem, the "child" of the poet, must paradoxically bridge the
"chasm" produced by polarity at the same time that it gives eloquent
expression to the "schisms" of material and spiritual existence. The
task of poetry is to:

recover the secret of Isis,
which is: there was One

in the beginning, Creator,
Fosterer, Begetter, the Same-forever

in the papyrus-swamp
in the Judean meadow   (*T.*, pp. 54–55)

The quest to recover the secret of Isis found rich resources within esoteric tradition. The Manichaean dualisms described by writers
like Denis de Rougemont and Robert Ambelain rested ultimately on

an affirmation of the Divine One which transcended the polarities and diversity of created forms. Ambelain, for example, wrote that an esoteric translation of Genesis uncovers "the three great hermetic principles: the unity of original substance; the original identity of the two seemingly contrary polarities—Light and Darkness; and finally the law of emanation as a generating process." The secret wisdom of the Gnostics was their knowledge of "Infinite Being, the source of all beings," the "incomprehensible Principle" out of which all that exists must emanate. A parallel esoteric tradition among the Egyptians, Ambelain wrote, affirmed the ultimate androgynous deity Atem, imaged in the *Book of the Dead* as a "bearded man with the breasts of a woman" and identified with "Phtah-Nou-le-Père" and "Phtah-Nou-la-Mère." In esoteric descendants of Egyptian, Greek, and Hebrew mysticism, the Seal of Solomon, a six-pointed star composed of two triangles, was a secret code concealing and revealing the "Mysterious Force that animates the Universe" through the principle of the "Two in One." The triangle that points up is the Luciferian symbol of Fire; "image of the phallus, it embodies the positive, masculine pole." The triangle that points down is the symbol of Water; "image of the clitoris, it embodies the negative, feminine pole." Taken together, the two triangles represent a Whole that incorporates all the dualisms of the universe.[3]

"Reintegration" into the Divine One can only be experienced through an alteration of rational modes of perception, according to H.D.'s sources. As Rodney Collin wrote, "the unity of things is not realisable by the ordinary mind, in an ordinary state of consciousness. The ordinary mind, refracted by the countless and contradictory promptings of different sides of human nature, must reflect the world as manifold and confused as is man himself. A unity, a pattern, an all-embracing meaning—if it exists—could only be discerned or experienced by a different kind of mind, in a different state of consciousness. It would only be realisable by a mind which had itself become unified."[4]

H.D.'s poetry records the transrational apprehension of the One through dream and religious vision conditioned by esoteric study. The "supernormal" states of mind she learned to decipher from the twin influences on her development confirmed in the *Trilogy* the "Presence" of "Spirit" that overtakes the poet as she regards the amber eyes of "the One, *Amen*, All-Father," the Goddess incarnated in the "half-

burnt-out apple-tree / blossoming," and the luminous face of the
Lady (*T.*, pp. 34, 87). Kaspar completes the sequence of religious experience when he glimpses Atlantis in the fleck of light in Mary
Magdalene's hair. In *Helen in Egypt*, Helen wonders how and when
"enlightenment comes" to the initiate:

> You may ask why I speak of Thoth-Amen,
> of Amen-Zeus or Zeus separately,
> you may think I invoke or recall
>
> a series of multiple gods,
>
> .   .   .   .
>
> how can you understand
>
> what few may acknowledge and live,
> what many acknowledge and die?
> He is One, yet the many
>
> manifest separately; He may manifest
> as a jackal and hound you to death?
> or is He changeable like air,
>
> and like air, invisible?
> God is beyond the manifest?
> He is ether and limitless space?   (*H.E.*, p. 78–79)

In *Sagesse*, the poet approaches the Divine One through studying
the seventy-two angels whose multiple attributes comprise the Whole.
The poet's revelation of Deity overtakes her as she looks at the photograph of the magnificent white-faced Scops owl. She imagines the owl
in a zoo and prays:

> May those who file before you feel
> something of what you are—that God is kept within
>
> the narrow confines of a cage, a pen;
> they will laugh and linger and some child may shudder,
>
> touched by the majesty, the lifted wings,
> the white mask and the eyes that seem to see,
>
> like God, everything and like God, see nothing;   (*S.*, p. 59)

The child who shudders at the incarnate God reappears in the poem
as the young girl who "took queer" during the Blitz. The bedridden
poet identifies with the child and weaves the story of the girl's strange
songs and her parents' sad concern during the war with her own nar-

rative, set in the late fifties. The young girl and the old woman form a palimpsest of superimposed eras. The child is a *"Christkind,"* whose fear of the bombs is tinged with religious awe and apprehension of the protective *"Father."* Like the poet, she endures "the ecstasy" engendered by the owl's "distant summons" (*S.*, pp. 61, 78–81). Knowledge of the divine comes to those who listen to the oracles of the unconsciousness: "laugh, they say, laugh, laugh, like children... / laugh, they say, like simpletons, like idiots, / fools and poets" (*S.*, p. 84).

While esoteric tradition provided H.D. with the ideal principle and imagery of the One, it did not fully reveal the process by which she could move from dualism to unity or from conflict to harmony—on either a personal or a universal level. The concept of psychic wholeness is implicit in Freud's descriptions of the alternating unconscious instincts, Eros and Thanatos, operating in every individual, everywhere. But Freud's belief in their perpetual conflict implies no notion of synthesis. Esoteric mysticism posits religious epiphany as the route to transcendence of dualism and diversity. But these experiences were not fully satisfactory to H.D. as a solution to the problem of duality. In fact, taken together, they posed the very polarity she sought to transcend. Like many mystical revelations, the divine "Presence" appeared in H.D.'s epiphanies either as God or Goddess, as divine father or mother. The imagery of revelation in the *Trilogy, Helen in Egypt*, and *Sagesse* is alternately male and female: Amen, Zeus, Ra, and the masculine Scops owl on the one hand and the Lady, Thetis, Isis, and the Grand Mer on the other. For H.D., the revelations of the Goddess had primacy because, on a personal level, union with the mother is the child's first love, and on a mythological level, worship of female deities preceded patriarchal monotheism. But did the primal Goddess, connected in H.D.'s mind with mystical Love, incorporate the God? In *Helen in Egypt*, H.D. associated peace with women and war with men, particularly masculine men. But then, she sought a vision of the whole that could include both God and Goddess, woman and man, war and peace, love and hate, life and death. The Goddess, as the representative of life and love in female form, could not serve fully as a symbol of the Whole. Her presence did not seem to incorporate the darker side of reality.

In her work, as in her life, the quest for wholeness took on a dialectical dimension to resolve the paradox of the Two in the One.

The logic of transcendence was evident in her interactions with Freud: first, he represented science, one pole of opposition; then she transformed him into the artist; ultimately, however, his scientific art and artistic science synthesized the duality of art and science. Similarly, Freud, the man who "felt so very masculine" became in the process of the transference a symbolic integration of mother and father. With the mother- and father-symbols of religious epiphany and poetic myth, H.D. applied the same logic of synthesis. Through reflection, she discovered the evolving processes of polarity, identity, and ultimately transcendence. Her emphasis on process reflected in part the Bergsonian dynamism that permeated much modernist search, and in part her own poetics of conflict and transcendence. As she wrote in reference to St.-John Perse in *Hermetic Definition*, "by antitheses [to Perse], I become ant or eel / . . . / I become small snake, / . . . / I float, swim and dart now, / straight to the antithetical centre" (*H.D.*, p. 37). Moving from thesis to antithesis, H.D.'s goal was a vision of the transcendent whole that incorporated all the complex dualisms of the universe.

It is difficult to pinpoint the source of H.D.'s dialectics—certainly there is no evidence that she immersed herself in the philosophy of Friedrich Hegel. But the Kabbalah, more than any specific mystical or philosophical source, offered H.D. a clearly dialectical model of transcendence that solved her dilemma of duality in the realm of symbol. As early as 1939, H.D. had encountered brief explanations of the creation myth in the Jewish mystical tradition filtered through Ambelain's syncretism. But the Kabbalah's influence as a paradigm of unity is most particularly evident in *Helen in Egypt*, the first long poem she wrote after reading Ambelain's *La Kabbale practique* (1951). The Kabbalah as defined in Ambelain's volumes was not inconsistent with other forms of esoteric tradition; indeed, in Ambelain's opinion, it was the supreme expression of the hermetic perspective.[5] Textual analysis of *Helen in Egypt* will demonstrate, however, that the specifics of the Kabbalah were especially suited to H.D.'s search for wholeness in both individual and universal dimensions of being.

The Kabbalah's great appeal to H.D. centered on three interrelated aspects of this centuries-old, evolving tradition: its concept of the Divine One and the nature of reality implicit in it; its doctrine of dialectical emanations; and its belief in the magic potency of the Word. The fundamental presupposition of the Kabbalah's creation myth is the prior reality of the nonmaterial spirit out of which the manifest world ultimately emanates. Before the beginnings of creation, the Supreme Deity, the En-Soph, existed, according to the Kabbalah, as the ultimate center of reality and the intangible source of the tangible world. The En-Soph (literally meaning "without end") is the infinite One, the pure potentiality that encompasses all possibility. As the perfect whole, it has no material existence, no attributes, no image, no words, no action. It is without will, without idea, without intention. In short, the En-Soph is the Void, Absolute Nothingness. Since the human mind cannot comprehend the Void in itself, the Kabbalah relies on imagery, even anthropomorphic imagery, to apprehend the En-Soph. Sometimes the seeker experiences the En-Soph as a blinding white flame, and sometimes as an endless dark night, black as ink. Or, relying even more on the known to describe the unknown, many have visualized the En-Soph as a "majestic Old Man" with snow-white hair, flowing beard, and sky-blue eyes.[6] But imagery of the En-Soph is recognized as the inadequacy of the human spirit to comprehend the One that exists beyond good and evil, light and dark, or male and female.

According to the Kabbalah, the process of creation began when potentiality became actuality, when the Supreme Void became manifest, when the Thought ("*Pensée*") became the Word ("*le Verbe*"). Paradoxically, the En-Soph, being complete, had the power to limit itself by entering the realm of being. As Ambelain recounted the myth, "the Infinite struck the Void with the sound of the Word" and a point of brilliant light appeared to begin the process of creation. This point of light, called the Kether or Crown, is the first of ten emanations known as the Sephiroth in the Kabbalah and as "eons" in related Gnostic mythology. Ambelain compared them to the "Ideas" of Plato, and Gershom Scholem called them "archetypes."[7] The ten Sephiroth, which taken together express all the latent potential of the En-Soph, are not themselves material. They are the "intermediaries" between the infinite and the finite, and each one manifests one of the ten potential attributes of the En-Soph as "idea." Each Sephira emanates from the one preceding it, moving further away from the perfection of the Void and closer to the imperfection that results finally in the material world. The Sephiroth appear frequently in the symbolic "garments" or "veils" of the Cosmic Tree or the Cosmic Man, Adam

Kadmon, whose head, arms, chest, genital area, and legs represent the succession of emanations (see Figures 4 and 5).

The emanations are based on the principles of polarity and synthesis with the overriding metaphor of dualism being the masculine and the feminine. The emanations on the right side of the body are designated masculine: Chokmah (Wisdom), Chesed (Mercy), and Netzach (Glory). Those on the left side are called feminine: Binah (Intelligence), Geburah (Justice), and Hod (Victory). And the four remaining Sephiroth combine the masculine and the feminine in a series of syntheses that go from the manifest perfection of the first emanation to the greater imperfection of the final emanation: Kether (Crown), the threshold to the En-Soph; Tiphereth (Beauty); Yesod (Foundation); and Malkuth (Kingdom), threshold to the world of material forms.

These ten "ideas" are not static principles, however. Central to the meditative mysticism of the Sephiroth, emanation is a dynamic, dialectical process in which the image of one Sephira yields to become its opposite. Creation begins with Kether, the androgynous One that incorporates the masculine and the feminine sides of the Cosmic Man. Out of Kether is born Chokmah, the archetypal father. Out of Chokmah comes Binah, the archetypal Mother. Together they form the perfect triad. But the middle triad begins to form as the masculine Chesed emerges from the feminine Binah. Chesed flows into the feminine Geburah, out of which emanates the androgynous Tiphereth to complete the second triad. The dialectical pattern in which masculine thesis becomes feminine antithesis repeats itself in the formation of the final triad. And the nine Sephiroth rest upon Malkuth, the "feet" of the Cosmic Man and gateway to the material world. To move backwards through the emanations in meditation is to pass through the dialectics of dualism toward synthesis and union with the Divine One. The Kabbalah therefore offers a model of transcendence based on the belief that every principle contains within it the seeds of its opposite.

The ten Sephiroth operate as magnetic forces in the universe through the magic of letters and numbers. The Word sets in motion the process of emanation. Kabbalists decode the myth of creation in Genesis as a celebration of the power of naming: "God said, Let there be light: and there was light" (Genesis 1:3). Christian Kabbalists quote John, whose myth of creation reads simply "In the beginning was the

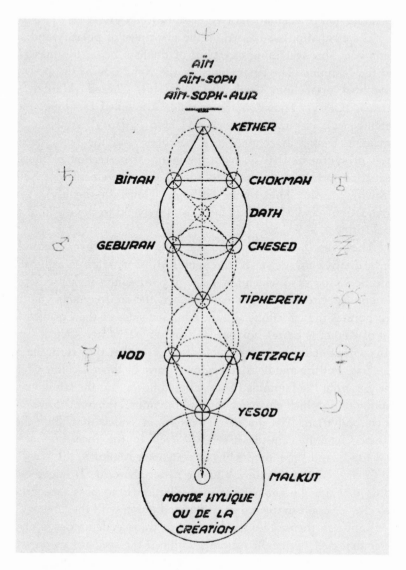

Figure 4. L'Arbre des Séphiroths, reproduced from
H.D.'s copy of Robert Ambelain's *Adam, dieu rouge* (astrological markings pencilled in by H.D.)

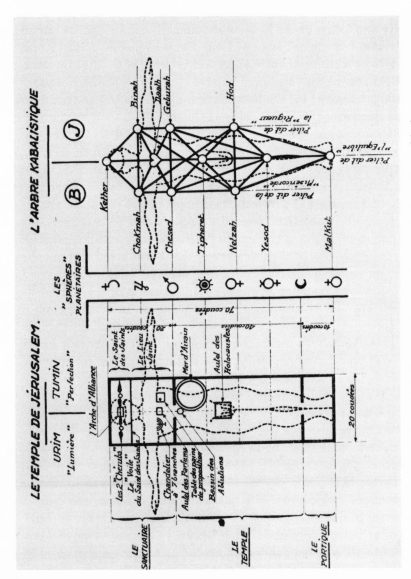

Figure 5. L'Arbre Kabbalistique, from Robert Ambelain, *La Kabbale practique*

Word" (John 1:1). The Zohar, the primary sacred text of the Kabbalah, says that the product of the first Word (Kether) incorporates the twenty-two letters of the Hebrew alphabet. Each letter begins one of the twenty-two divine names of God. The ten numbers of the Sephiroth also have the power of magic. Like the "ten" of the Pythagoreans, the Kabbalistic "ten" are "pure numbers" that incorporate all mathematical possibility.[8] For the Kabbalists, the sacred letters and numbers of the Sephiroth are vibrant, animate forces whose combination into words controls the creation of the world of physical forms. The potency of words and numbers, however, is so great that their meaning must be concealed. H.D. must surely have drawn parallels between the Kabbalah and Freud's concept of the dream as the symbolic language that conceals as it reveals the dangerous desires of the unconscious. For the Kabbalists believed that the sacred texts of orthodox tradition contained esoteric truths available only to the initiated. Those who understood the "alchemy of the Word" could root out the secret meanings which controlled the material world. Puns, word games, and manipulation of numbers are the tools of the Kabbalists in their creation of meaning. They rest not on trickery, but on a philosophy of language. Even before H.D. could read *La Kabbale practique*, Ambelain's earlier, brief synopses of the Kabbalah found their way into the development of her aesthetic and into the religious function of the poet's medium, language. In the *Trilogy*, the "alchemy of the Word" is H.D.'s central metaphor for recovering the Goddess, for decoding the esoteric "veneration" from the orthodox "venery." In the *Trilogy*, also, the poet seeks a vision of rebirth in the "anagrams, cryptograms" of the words which are "conditioned" to "hatch butterflies" (*T.*, p. 53).

Before H.D. could use the dialectics of the Kabbalah to resolve the dualisms that plagued the modern world, however, she had to revise this tradition so that its processes could offer authentic integration of archetypal mother-father symbols. In its specific mythology, the Kabbalah does not fulfill its potential as a myth of androgynous Wholeness. Mired in androcentric bias, its imagery continually reasserts the dualism of masculine and feminine which it seeks to transcend. Its goals of harmony, unity, and equilibrium are repeatedly thrown off balance by the weight of negative symbols for the feminine and positive symbols for the masculine. Although the very presence of the feminine in its concept of the Divine represents a liberation from the patriarchal monotheism of orthodox traditions, the Kabbalah unrevised could not offer H.D. a way to transcend the dualisms she found reflected throughout the universe. Ambelain's figures of the Sephiroth provide the first clue to androcentric bias: the Cosmic Man, or Adam Kadmon as he is frequently called, is not human, but male. The presence of male genitals in the Kabbalistic rendition of humanity is matched by the masculine imagery repeatedly associated with the supposedly androgynous En-Soph, Kether, and Tiphereth. When imagined, the En-Soph has a beard, Kether is the Yahweh of Genesis and Tiphereth is the Son of God, the Messiah, or the Christ of Christian Kabbalists. The only female imagery linked to the androgynous Sephiroth emerges with Malkuth, the last emanation, the one Ambelain called the "inferior mother," creator of material forms. The symbolism of the three triads similarly reinforces the religious ideology of female inferiority. Ambelain wrote that the first triad, the head of Adam Kadmon, was frequently known as the masculine triad because of its proximity to the pure spirituality and perfection of the En-Soph. The last triad, on the other hand, was perceived as the feminine triad because it was the triad of sexual generation, closest to the world of matter, and consequently the least spiritual of the three triads. The "practical" Kabbalah, Ambelain concluded, taught that the Angel of Light (Kether) on the right and the Angel of Darkness (Malkuth) on the left are the two forces that guard the soul. These two angels are "the two extreme poles of Divinity, his double aspect: creative and destructive, spiritual and material, benevolent and malevolent, positive and negative, etc." The list of dualisms continues: "The two universal forces—centripetal and centrifugal, attractive and repulsive, outward moving and inward moving, masculine and feminine, luminous and obscure, beneficent and maleficent—are expressed esoterically in the double symbol of Lucifer and Satan, of the related entities, the Good and the Bad."[9] Ambelain affirmed the concept of the En-Soph that incorporates all oppositions, but he regularly connected the forces of darkness, sexuality, evil, and matter with the feminine, and by extension with all women.

At least as Ambelain presented the creation mythology of the Kabbalah, the Cosmic Sephiroth provided H.D. with a vision of Wholeness based upon the assumptions of male superiority and female inferiority. To accept it unrevised would have involved H.D. in an inauthentic mythology whose foundation for women necessitated self-hatred. Just as she liberated the mother-symbol of psychoanalytic tradition from its misogynist framework, so she had to free the concept of Wholeness in the Kabbalah from its androcentric context so that its potential as a dialectical myth of transcendence could be fulfilled in her poetry. H.D.'s re-vision of the dialectics of the Kabbalah permeates all the major poems of the fifties. But *Helen in Egypt* demonstrates more clearly than any of the other poems how she first revised the Kabbalah and then used its dialectical model of transcendence to find the dynamic pattern of Wholeness structuring the confrontations of Love and Death.

H.D.'s fundamental re-vision of the Kabbalah's dualistic philosophy began with her revaluation of the poles. The protean forms of Amen, All-Father, and the Goddess are the archetypal Chokmah and Binah of the Kabbalah as well as the mother- and father-symbols of psychoanalytic theory. The personal quests of Helen and Achilles, the family history of the Greeks and Trojans, the forces that cause the war, and the mythic hieroglyph of Isis and Osiris all incarnate versions of the confrontation between archetypal mother and father figures. But the Goddess in H.D.'s epic does not embody the force of darkness, evil, and pure matter. As the force of Love, she stands powerfully on the threshold of regeneration and resurrection. The All-Father's role in the war is never clarified, but the archetypal masculine men incarnate the negative force of death and destruction. The confrontations between the men and women who represent the opposing forces of Love and Death reverse the misogynist triads of Solomon's Seal and the Kabbalah. The Kabbalistic En-Soph who incorporates the light and dark, however, stands behind the dualism of Love and Death. Like the meditations of the Kabbalists, the poet's central task is the search to understand the dialectical relationships between the opposing forces which reside in the One.

The paradigm of paradox in the epic is the confrontation between Helen and Achilles, the one incarnating Love and the other representing the "death-cult" that has destroyed victors and victims alike. Helen believes that the mystery of her identity and the meaning of war are contained in the hieroglyph of their meeting. Reflection reveals the stark pattern: first, she, as the human form of Isis, conjured the dead soul of Achilles through the magic of Love (Eros); then Achilles, on behalf of the warrior caste he led, attempts to strangle her (Eris); and finally, her appeal to the Goddess in her form as

Achilles' mother transforms his violence to love (Eros). Their meeting starkly encodes the confrontation of Eros and Eris, Love and Death. But to understand how Eros yields to Eris and Eris becomes Eros, Helen must understand not only the dualism but also the interrelationships between the polarities. She visualizes the interconnections in the tableau of death-become-love through the images associated with each pole: the shells of the Goddess and the motif for Achilles' violence, the "flash in the heaven at noon / that blinds the sun." "Their meeting" is:

> brighter than the sun at noon-day,
> yet whiter than frost,
> whiter than snow,
>
> whiter than the white drift of sand
> that lies like ground shells,
> dust of shells—
>
> —dust of skulls, I say;   (*H.E.*, pp. 160–61)

These images weave condensed details relating the sources of life (shells, sea) with death (skulls, war). The "dust of shells" differs from the "dust of skulls" by only a slight shift of sound. Imagist incarnation of the interrelated dualisms, however, does not provide Helen with a comprehension of the dialectics upon which final apprehension of the One depends. To unravel the mystery of her meeting with Achilles, she must reflect upon the underlying patterns that structured her family history and the war.

Decoding the myth of Isis and Osiris is the clue that allows her to understand how the forces of Love and Death operated dialectically in her own life. What she learns is that the poles of opposition relate to each other in a dynamic process through which one force literally becomes its opposite. Just as Chokmah, the father archetype, evolves into Binah, the mother archetype, in the Kabbalah, so Love contains within itself the seeds of its opposite, Death. As divinities of fertility, Isis and Osiris embody the power of the life force. Their love symbolizes the agency of Eros by which the earth returns to rich abundance each year. Set, the Egyptian god of death-dealing desert winds, corresponds to the monster Typhon, the "Whirlwind of War" (*H.E.*, p. 84). Representing the principle of death and aggression (Eris), Set dismembers his brother Osiris and scatters the pieces of his body all over the earth. The weeping Isis searches the world over for the limbs of Osiris, resurrects him briefly through the magic of her love, and later gives birth to their son Horus (Eros). Horus, the product of Eros, avenges the murder of his father by destroying Set, an act of violence that transforms Horus (Eros) into the agent of death (Eris). This alternating process of Eros and Eris clearly owes a great deal to Freud's description of unconscious instincts. But unlike Freud's theory of Eros and the death instinct, H.D.'s interplay of opposing forces is fundamentally dialectical. Horus, representative of the life principle, becomes his opposite when he destroys Set (*H.E.,* pp. 28–29, 32, 41, 46). Set, the victimizer, is himself victimized like the brother he killed. Helen finally understands that Set and Osiris "were not two but one, / Typhon-Osiris / to the initiate" (*H.E.,* p. 27). Within Eros resides the potential for death; within Eris lives the potential for life. The confrontation of Love and Death, therefore, is a dynamic process motivated by an inner identity between the opposites known only to the "initiate."[10]

Once she has grasped the dialectics of Egyptian myth, Helen can understand the interlocking pattern of Love and Death in her own family history. The marriage of Clytaemnestra and Agamemnon was a "moment of infinite beauty" that affirmed the power of Love through the "Word of the Goddess" (*H.E.,* p. 74). But Eris, the principle of strife, reasserts itself when Agamemnon treacherously brings his daughter Iphigenia to the altar of sacrifice. In retaliation, Clytaemnestra affirms the power of Eros over the warrior caste by taking a lover, Aigisthus. This resurgence of Eros, however, becomes Eris when Clytaemnestra kills Agamemnon for his betrayal of Iphigenia. Like Horus, Clytaemnestra murders on behalf of Eros and thereby becomes her opposite.

"It is as if Helen were re-living her own story and visualizing her own fate in terms of that of her twin-sister," H.D. reflected in the prose passage that precedes the story of Clytaemnestra (*H.E.,* p. 74). The twin sisters appear to be opposites—Helen is the daughter of Zeus, while Clytaemnestra's father is mortal; Helen serves Aphrodite, the Goddess of Love, while Clytaemnestra is a murderer. But in re-living the story of her sister, Helen realizes their common identity as agents of Eros whose Love becomes a force of Death during the Trojan War. Proteus, the principle of the One manifesting as the Many, "disclosed the mystery; *when they reach a certain degree / they are one, alike utterly"* (*H.E.,* p. 101). Helen's "pallinode" releases her from

the image of the Greek Eve, Helena hated of all Greece. But like Clytaemnestra, Helen's incarnation of Love contains a dialectical dimension of complexity that she is ready to discover in Leuké. Helen, the Goddess of Love, becomes a force for Death. Reflecting on the whole history of the war, Helen can now understand the role she played in the alternations of Love and Death. The origins of the war go back to the joyous wedding of Peleus and Thetis. Love begets War when the uninvited guest Eris casts a golden apple marked "To the Fairest" among the guests. Paris, designated the judge, selects Aphrodite, who rewards him with Helen. The wedding feast as a celebration of Eros must by definition leave out Eris. But this omission itself brings Eris to orchestrate strife among the goddesses. Their "petty strife" yields to the love of Paris and Helen, which in turn sets in motion the wheels of war (*H.E.*, p. 111). Helen uses this dialectical pattern to decipher the hieroglyphs of her meetings with Achilles. Their exchange of glances during battle was an epiphany of Love which in turn led to Achilles' unfastened greave and subsequent death. Paris was the *"agent, medium or intermediary of Love,"* for he shot the arrow that killed Achilles. Paradoxically, Love becomes a destroyer in the act of overpowering the forces of destruction. This dialectic which governed both Horus and Clytaemnestra clarifies the interlocking processes of Love and Death for Helen. Her discovery becomes a refrain repeated many times throughout her quest:

> . . . a bowman from the Walls

> let fly the dart;
> some said it was Apollo,
> but I, Helena, knew it was Love's arrow;

> it was Love, it was Apollo, it was Paris;   (*H.E.*, pp. 112–13)

Unlocking the mystery of the war allows Helen to see her confrontation on the beach with Achilles as a continuation of this dialectical interplay. Helen's magic as the incarnation of Eros draws the shade of Achilles to her. The power of Eros sets in motion the release of Eris when Achilles' recognition leads to attack. Eris in turn yields to Eros when the name of Thetis recalls Achilles to a gentler self. The power of Eros to transform Achilles' hatred is only possible, they both realize, because the capacity for love resides within the psyche of the man who embodies the masculine iron-ring of war. Achilles is the leader of the Command, and the agent of Death, but the power of his mother Thetis has lived on within his soul, to be awakened by the sight of Helen.

Helen and Achilles, both together and separately, unravel the process by which his dual nature has been forgotten and then restored. The pattern is strikingly reminiscent of Freud's concept of "normal" masculine development. Freud's theory of psychic bisexuality suggested that the boy who fulfills his masculine destiny repressed his love for his mother and his own capacity for androgyny as an adult. H.D. fused this developmental model with the dialectics of the Kabbalah by which each Sephira contained the seeds of antithetical emanation. Like Helen, Achilles must recapture and analyze the fragments of memory repressed in his unconscious. Over the burning embers of their fire on the beach, they realize that Achilles learned to suppress his love for the eidolon of Thetis, which he had treasured as a boy. Thetis had taught him "the trick, the magic of little things" and "the laws and the arts of peace" (H.E., p. 286). Gradually, he had abandoned the ways of his mother and "followed the lure of war." Although he had been the bravest of heroes, he "stared and stared / through the smoke and the glowing embers, / and wondered why he forgot / and why he just now remembered" (H.E., p. 287). With the eidolon of Thetis restored to consciousness, Achilles suddenly understands that his boyhood love led to the magnetic glance he exchanged with Helen in the midst of battle. As the leader of the warrior caste, he was the "purely masculine" man who had repressed the androgyny of his boyhood. Unlike the "normal" man of Freud's theory, however, Achilles suffered from the inadequacy and lifelessness of the masculine iron-ring of war. In Egypt, he tells Helen not to feel guilty for that glance, by explaining to her what she meant to him: " 'I can see you still, a mist / or a fountain of water / in that desert; we died of thirst' " (H.E., p. 48). Achilles' epiphany ends his life as a warrior, but opens up his regeneration as a "new Mortal." Death in battle became Love in a glance, which in turn caused the Death of the man. That Death, itself, however, destroyed only the rigid warrior. "Love's arrow" restores the Wholeness Achilles had lost in growing up to be the masculine hero of war:

> but I, Helena, know it was Love's arrow;
>
> the body honoured

by the Grecian host
was but an iron casement,

it was God's plan
to melt the icy fortress of the soul,
and free the man; (*H.E.*, pp. 9–10)

When Achilles appears limping on the sands of Egypt through the agency of Helen's magic, he is "the new Mortal, / shedding his glory" (*H.E.*, p. 10). His meeting with Helen embodies his new status, a fusion of the eidolon of Thetis (Eros) and the flash of a Star (Eris).[11]

Achilles' personal quest for transcendence of Love and Death ends in synthesis because the duality structures his own psyche as well as the forces of history and eternity. Similarly, Helen's search for Wholeness involves the union of her identification with the Goddess (Eros) and her comprehension of her role in the war (Eris). Like Achilles, she recovers fragments of childhood to reconstitute Helen of Sparta, a self that was lost as she became Helen of Troy with Paris and Helen of Egypt with Achilles. Theseus helps her to hear "*a voice within . . . an heroic voice, the voice of Helen of Sparta*" (*H.E.*, pp. 174, 176). The voice of Helen's origins is a voice of war:

O, the rage of the sea,

the thunder of battle,
shouting and the Walls
and the arrows; O, the beauty of arrows,

each bringing surcease, release;
do I love War?
is this Helena? (*H.E.*, p. 177)

Recovery of the young self who loved the "beauty of arrows" helps Helen understand how the Helen who embodied the Goddess of Love could share responsibility for the War with the warrior caste. Love's arrow killed Achilles in part because Helen Dendritis contained the "heroic voice" of Sparta within. Recognition of her own psychic duality clarifies the pattern by which Helen of Troy became Helen of Egypt. Helen's successive incarnations of the three phases of the Goddess express the dialectical alternations of Love and Death. As the love goddess Aphrodite, Helen's springtime love for Paris led to war. As the mother goddess Isis, Helen's magic drew Achilles' shade and helped him restore his mother to consciousness. As the death goddess

Persephone, Helen is the bride of Achilles in the afterworld (*H.E.*, p. 209). In Leuké, Paris attempts to bring Helen back to her identity as Helen Dendritis. But Helen must refuse because Helen Dendritis is only one phase of her whole identity, an aspect that does not incorporate the martial Helen of Sparta, the Helen whose love for Paris led to war, and the Helen whose marriage to Achilles reproduces the union of Persephone and Dis. Helen, it is true, shall be *"deified"* as "H-E-L-E-N-A" on the island of Melos where they shall "honour the name of Love" (*H.E.*, p. 95). But while Helen is Love, she can also become Death. Her healing identification with the protean forms of Aphrodite-Isis-Persephone occurs within the context of a recognition that the Goddess of mystical Love contains within the potential to become her opposite, the Goddess of Death and bride of Dis.

It is the pain engendered by this multiplicity of selves and the interlocking dualisms of Love and Death that brings Helen to Theseus. Achilles achieves his status as the "new Mortal" through the agency of Helen, who serves as a mother-symbol for him. But Helen's transcendence of duality emerges out of her conversations with Theseus, the old man she calls her "god-father" (*H.E.*, p. 176). His probing questions help her to "reconcile" all the parts of herself and all the oppositions interwoven into the dualism of Love and War. With Theseus, Helen will review the past *"picture by picture"* to find the pattern of integration: "I would renew the Quest, / I would bind myself with the Girdle, / the circlet, the starry Zone / . . . / I would read here / in my crystal, the Writing" (*H.E.*, p. 205). Helen reiterates her spherical talismans of wholeness—her Crystal and the Zodiacal Wheel —throughout the remainder of "Eidolon."[12]

As a woman who has recaptured her past without shame, understood her identity as the woman avatar of the Goddess, and perceived the dualities inherent in herself, Helen is ready for the final stage of the quest: understanding the transcendent Mystery of the One, the focus of "Eidolon." Like the Kabbalist who meditates on the dialectical interplay of the Sephiroth to reach the En-Soph, Helen's personal quest through "Pallinode" and "Leuké" leads her ultimately to an apprehension of the One that incorporates all the manifestations of the created world. While Helen has learned to "read" the *alternations* of Love and Death in the real world of chronological time, she has yet to apprehend the "single moment" of eternity that reveals the *fusion* of Love and Death in the nonexistent realm of the One. Unlike the traditional mystic, or even the poet of the *Trilogy*, Helen does not experience the One through epiphany. Instead, the reflective processes which H.D. learned from psychoanalysis gradually unravel the Mystery. In "Eidolon," Helen reviews once again all the events of personal and mythic history to understand the hermetic significance disguised in the punning opposites L'Amour and La Mort: that Love and War emanate from the same source. Now she struggles to answer the questions left unanswered in Leuké:

> did Ares bequeath his arrows
> alike to Eros, to Eris?
>
> O flame-tipped, O searing, O tearing
> burning, destructible fury
> of the challenge *to the fairest*;
>
> O flame-tipped, O searing,
> destroying arrow of Eros;
> O bliss of the end,
>
> Lethe, Death and forgetfulness,
> O bliss of the final
> unquestioned nuptial kiss.   (*H.E.*, p. 183)

Love is Death, Death is Love in the ecstasy of transcendence. From this perspective, Helen can review her past lovers and selves who had appeared like "broken arcs" as the half-circles which "complete the circle" when joined together (*H.E.*, pp. 189, 215). As she looks into her "white crystal" that relates the "out-of-time" to the "in-time," she sees the Whole that contains the individual "segments" of the "prismatic seven" (*H.E.*, p. 204). Now the *"preliminary tension"* between her lovers Paris and Achilles can be reconciled. In "Leuké," she had envisioned them as "god-like beasts" in the great Wheel of the Zodiac, frozen forever in the chase of opposites. But in "Eidolon," she can understand that the Zodiac is a "starry circle" that contains the arcs of opposition in a perfect sphere. *"La Mort, L'Amour will merge in the final illumination,"* H.D. explains, when Helen can "read" the hermetic mystery in the *"great 'frieze, the Zodiac hieroglyph'"* (*H.E.*, p. 271).[13]

Clusters of circle imagery lead to the *"final illumination,"* understanding the *"circle of the ever-recurring* 'eternal moment' " in Helen's archetypal meeting with Achilles when the "white shells" on the desolate beach fuse with the "white bones" of death (*H.E.*, pp. 277,

160–61). Once deciphered, the perfect circle of hate-become-love contains the final Mystery, the secret of the One. The power of the Word completed the circle of broken arcs. Love and Death fused to One when Helen uttered the "one secret, / unpronounceable name, / a whisper, a breath"—the name of Thetis (*H.E.*, pp. 277–79). As in the *Trilogy*, the secret of Isis reveals the One that transcends all the dualities of life.

The *"miraculous birth"* of the child Euphorion follows Helen's "translation" of the hieroglyphic meeting and signals her final initiation. As the name suggests, the child personifies the "euphoria" or mystic joy emerging from comprehension of the ultimate Mystery. As genealogical metaphor as well, Euphorion is also the symbol of each parent's individual transcendence. As H.D. reflects in prose: *"The promised Euphorion is not one child but two. It is 'the child in Chiron's cave'* [Achilles] *and the 'frail maiden,' stolen by Theseus from Sparta* [Helen]" (*H.E.*, p. 288). As the child of Helen and Achilles, Euphorion is the androgynous One that incorporates both the archetypal polarity of mother and father and the dualities within each of them.[14]

Helen's confusing circlings in the labyrinth of questions can now yield to comprehension of "L'Amour as La Mort" in the overlapping dimensions of the psyche, history and myth. She concludes in the final section of the epic:

> so the dart of Love
> is the dart of Death,
> and the secret is no secret;
>
> the simple path
> refutes at last
> the threat of the Labyrinth,
>
> the Sphinx is seen,
> the Beast is slain
> and the Phoenix-nest
>
> reveals the innermost
> key or the clue to the rest
> of the mystery;
>
> there is no before and no after,
> there is one finite moment
> that no infinite joy can disperse

or thought of past happiness
tempt from or dissipate;
now I know the best and the worst;

the seasons revolve around
a pause in the infinite rhythm
of the heart and of heaven. (*H.E.*, pp. 303–304)[15]

In the epic as well as in her life, the healing example of Theseus, ancient avatar of H.D.'s "blameless physician," is the symbol of the integration Helen seeks. H.D. wrote that Freud's "house in some indescribable way depends on father-mother. At the point of integration or regeneration, there is no conflict over rival loyalties" (*T.F.*, p. 146). In Theseus' warm shelter, Helen regards him as the "*alchemist si remarkable*" whose hermetic science unites the mother and father and serves as the "mid-wife to the soul" (*T.F.*, p. 116). In prose, H.D. reflected that Theseus was "*wholly intellectual and inspirational*" and fused the qualities of "*power and tenderness*": "The opposites have been reconciled, actually, in Theseus. 'The lyre or the sword? Theseus has both together' " (*H.E.*, pp. 206, 227, 297). By example, he embodies the healing synthesis of opposites. While he tells Helen the story of his heroic quest on the ship Argo, he exhibits the greatest care for her welfare. He offers her fleece-lined shoes before a warm fire and calms her "heart-storm." He is mother and father to Helen— traditional nurturer and hero fused into one. As androgynous parent, he oversees her rebirth into a new life and identity, one that parallels Achilles' transformation into the "new Mortal." He comforts her:

there is nothing to fear,
you are neither there nor here,

but wavering
like a Psyche
with half-dried wings. (*H.E.*, p. 166)

With Theseus, as with Freud, Psyche is reborn. As the "guardian of all beginnings," he watches over the wavering butterfly of Helen's newly released soul. "Before I leave, I fold the silver-grey rug. I have been caterpillar, worm, snug in the chrysalis," H.D. wrote of her sessions with Freud (*T.F.*, p. 177). In the memorial service that marked the end of her life on earth, Theseus' incantation of the Mystery guarded the passage of H.D.'s beginnings into the "eternal circle" of eternity:

Thus, thus, thus,
as day, night,
as wrong, right,

as dark, light,
as water, fire,
as earth, air,

as storm, calm,
as fruit, flower,
as life, death,

as death, life;
the rose deflowered,
the rose re-born;

Helen in Egypt,
Helen at home,
Helen in Hellas forever.   *(H.E.,* p. 190)[16]

NOTES

The repository for H.D.'s papers, including manuscripts of many unpublished as well as published works, is the Collection of American Literature, Beinecke Rare Book and Manuscript Library, Yale University, abbreviated below as "Beinecke." Abbreviations and publication information for frequently cited works by H.D. and Sigmund Freud are listed below. All citations from H.D.'s published works are to these editions and are identified in the text.

Abbreviations for Published Works by H.D.

B.M.L. — *Bid Me to Live (A Madrigal)*. New York: Grove Press, 1960.
E.T.T. — *End to Torment*. New York: New Directions, 1979.
H.E. — *Helen in Egypt*. 1961; rpt. New York: New Directions, 1974.
H.D. — *Hermetic Definition*. New York: New Directions, 1972.
P. — *Palimpsest*. 1926; rpt. Carbondale, Ill.: Southern Illinois University Press, 1968.
T.F. — *Tribute to Freud*. 1956; rpt. Boston: David R. Godine, 1974.
T. — *Trilogy*. New York: New Directions, 1973.
S. — *Sagesse*, in *Hermetic Definition*. New York: New Directions, 1972.
S.P. — *Selected Poems*. New York: Grove Press, 1957.

Abbreviations for Works by Sigmund Freud

C.D. — *Civilization and Its Discontents*, trans. James Strachey. 1930; rpt. New York: Norton, 1961.
F.I. — *The Future of an Illusion*, trans. W.D. Robson-Scott. 1928; rpt. New York: Doubleday, 1964.
G.I.P. — *A General Introduction to Psychoanalysis*, trans. Joan Riviere. 1916–1917; rpt. New York: Permabook, 1956.
I.D. — *The Interpretation of Dreams*, trans. James Strachey. 1930; rpt. New York: Avon, 1965.
N.I.L. — *New Introductory Lectures on Psychoanalysis*, trans. James Strachey. 1933; rpt. New York: Norton, 1964.
O.P. — *An Outline of Psychoanalysis*, trans. James Strachey. 1939; rpt. New York: Norton, 1949.
S.E. — *The Standard Edition of the Complete Psychological Works of Sigmund Freud*. London: Hogarth Press, 1950.
T.T. — *Therapy and Technique*, ed. Philip Rieff. New York: Collier, 1963.
T.C.S. — *Three Contributions to the Theory of Sex*, trans. A.A. Brill. 1905; rpt. New York: Dutton, 1962.

Introduction

1. For a literary history of imagism, see William Pratt, *The Imagist Poem* (New York: Dutton, 1963), pp. 11–39, and J.B. Harmer, *Victory in Limbo: Imagism, 1908–1917* (London: Secker & Warburg, 1975).

2. For information about H.D.'s early childhood, see particularly her *Tribute to Freud*; her largely unpublished memoir *The Gift* (1941–1943) and "Autobiographical Notes" at Beinecke; her memoir of Pound, *End to Torment*; and her cousin Francis Wolle's memoir, *A Moravian Heritage* (Boulder, Col.: Empire Reproductions, 1972).

3. Ezra Pound, "A Few Don'ts by an Imagiste," *Poetry*, 1 (March 1913), 200.

4. Cyrena N. Pondrom discovered H.D.'s important editorial and organizational contributions and detailed them in "Selected Letters from H.D. to F.S. Flint: A Commentary on the Imagist Period," *Contemporary Literature*, 10, No. 4 (Autumn 1969), 557–86.

5. H.D., "Advent" in *T.F.*, p. 149. "Advent," additional reflections on Freud, did not appear in the 1956 edition of *Tribute to Freud*. Norman Holmes Pearson included it in the 1974 edition, explaining that it had been written after World War II when she found the lost notebooks she had kept during her months in Vienna. The 1956 *Tribute to Freud* was written between September 19 and November 2, 1944.

6. "Poet Hilda Doolittle, on Yale Visit, Assails Imagist Label Used to Describe Her Work," *New Haven Register* (16 September 1956), p. 10.

7. H.D., *P.*, dedication page. Additional poems about Bryher appeared in *Heliodora* (New York: Houghton Mifflin, 1924) and *Red Roses for Bronze* (London: Chatto & Windus, 1931).

8. H.D. acted in and collaborated with Macpherson in the three films made by POOL production company: *Wing Beat* (1927); *Foothills* (1928–1930), and *Borderline* (1930). The latter is an ambitious film about interracial sex and violence, with Paul and Eslanda Robeson. I am indebted to Anne Friedberg's research on *Close-Up* for information about H.D.'s film involvement.

9. Letter dated March 29th to Viola Jordan, at Beinecke. The year was probably 1927 or 1928. H.D.'s letters to Jordan, who was also a good friend of Pound's, are an important source of information. They span the years between 1920–1951. Future references to this correspondence will be dated in the text.

10. The manuscripts for *Paint It Today* (1921), *Asphodel* (1921–1922), *Her* (1927), and *Pilate's Wife* (1924, 1929, 1934) are at Beinecke.

11. See Pearson's "Foreword" in *T.F.*, p. vii. In 1973, Pearson brought out a new edition of H.D.'s three war poems in a single volume entitled *Trilogy*.

12. H.D., "Notes on Recent Writing," p. 26, at Beinecke. This seventy-six-page manuscript written in 1949 contains important commentary on the shape and development of H.D.'s canon.

13. In addition to the works mentioned in the text, the collection at Beinecke includes five novels, two memoirs, and one epic-length poem, all still unpublished.

14. Some ten installments of Duncan's "H.D. Book" have appeared in such journals as *Coyote's Journal* (1966, 1967), *Origin* (1963), *Caterpillar* (1967, 1968, 1969), *Sumac* (1968), *Stony Brook Review* (1969), *TriQuarterly* (1968) and *Chicago Review* (1979). Duncan began his H.D. book in the late fifties when he wrote to Pearson to ask if he could schedule a series of conversations with H.D. They met and carried on a correspondence while H.D. was writing *Hermetic Definition* (1960–61). Their correspondence is at Beinecke.

15. H.D., *Her*, p. 296. See Susan Gubar's "The Echoing Spell of H.D.'s *Trilogy*," *Contemporary Literature*, 19, No. 2 (Spring 1978), 196–218, for discussion of the butterfly image in H.D.'s work.

16. Amy Lowell, "The Sisters," in *The Complete Poetical Works of Amy Lowell* (New York: Houghton Mifflin, 1955).

17. L.S. Dembo, "Norman Holmes Pearson on H.D.: An Interview," *Contemporary Literature*, 10, No. 4 (Autumn 1969), 438.

1. Freud as Guardian of Beginnings

1. *Her*, pp. 273–74. All subsequent references to *Her* will be identified within the text. Completed in 1927, *Her* is not a completely reliable source of factual information about H.D.'s life. H.D. pencilled in a name code on the manuscript cover for all the characters (except for Frances Gregg) in her roman à clef, but some of the events in the novel are not consistent with other memoirs.

2. Bryher, letter to author, 1 October 1971.

3. Ibid.; Bryher, *The Heart to Artemis* (New York: Harcourt, Brace & World, 1962), pp. 225, 253–54.

4. *T.F.*, p. 150; letter from H.D. to Macpherson, 31 March 1933; "Autobiographical Notes" indicate that H.D. saw Chadwick April 13–July 15, 1931, and Sachs on November 27, December 19–21, and December 22, 1931. H.D.'s and Bryher's letters to Macpherson, dating from 1930 to 1960, are at Beinecke. Subsequent letters to Macpherson are from this collection and will be dated in the text.

5. See also "Autobiographical Notes." None of the books to which H.D. referred appeared in the partial collection of her library that Pearson kept at Yale. He verified, however, that she had read a great quantity of the psychoanalytic literature in Bryher's collection. H.D. referred explicitly to the following in *Tribute to Freud: The Interpretation of Dreams, The Future of an Illusion, Totem and Taboo, Autobiographical Study, Delusion and Dream, Psychopathology of Everyday Life*. She also mentioned reading Otto Rank's *Der Mythus von der Geburt des Helden* (*T.F.*, p. 120).

6. Information comes from H.D.'s "Autobiographical Notes"; *Compassionate Friendship* (1955); *Magic Mirror* (1955); and the very important "Hirslanden Notebooks," four copybooks containing diary entries and dream records made during 1957–1959 (hereafter identified in the text as I, II, III, or IV). All manuscripts are at Beinecke.

7. For a discussion of the importance of free association in classical analysis, see Sigmund Freud, "Further Recommendations in the Technique of Psychoanalysis" (1923) in *T.T.*, p. 147. See also Norman Holland, "H.D.

and the 'Blameless Physician,'" *Contemporary Literature*, 10, No. 4 (Autumn 1969), 478, and Joseph Riddel, "H.D.'s Scene of Writing—Poetry As (And) Analysis," *Studies in the Literary Imagination*, 12, No. 1 (Spring 1979), 41–59.

8. See also H.D.'s letter to Jordan about her plans to use analysis, 15 February 1945; Bryher, *Heart to Artemis*, p. 254.

9. Like Thoreau, H.D. described her reasons for her psychoanalytic "retreat" many times; see *T.F.*, pp. 12–13, 39–41, 91, 93–94.

10. For Freud's discussion of water as a dream symbol, see *I.D.*, pp. 260, 435–37, 439. In analyzing the water dream of a woman patient, Freud himself connected the birth wish with her analysis (p. 436).

11. See for example theosophist Mabel Collins, *Light on the Path and Karma* (1885; rpt. London: Theosophical Publishing House, 1920). H.D. owned and marked two copies of Collins's book, one of which she kept inside a handtooled leather cover.

12. Merrill Moore, "Foreword," *Tribute to Freud* (New York: Pantheon, 1956), p. viii.

13. Joseph Riddel, "H.D. and the Poetics of 'Spiritual Realism,'" *Contemporary Literature*, 10, No. 4 (Autumn 1969), 448, 453–54; Holland, "H.D. and the 'Blameless Physician,'" pp. 485–93. See also my "Who Buried H.D.? A Poet, Her Critics, and Her Place in 'The Literary Tradition,'" *College English*, 36 No. 7 (March 1975), for a full discussion of the "phallic criticism" that Holland and Riddel represent.

14. H.D., "Dark Room" (chapter 1), p. 5 of *The Gift*; the manuscript of this mostly unpublished fictionalized memoir of her mother's youth and marriage and her own childhood is at Beinecke. Portions of *The Gift* were published in *Contemporary Literature*, 10, No. 4 (Autumn 1969). Written during 1941–1943, *The Gift* clearly paved the way for the *Trilogy*.

15. Hirslanden II and III contain information about her breakdowns; see also "Autobiographical Notes."

16. H.D., *E.T.T.*, p. 8. Later in the memoir, H.D. transformed the young pianist Van Cliburn into the son they might have had (p. 50). Her *Winter Love* (1959), published in *Hermetic Definition*, is a sequence of poems about her relationship with Pound, which was renewed during his stay in St. Elizabeths. It ends with the birth of "Espérance," the child who might have been.

17. Letter from H.D. to Pound, 20 February 1929 (?). H.D.'s existing letters to Pound are at Beinecke and cover the following periods, 1926–1939, 1951–1961. H.D.'s father burned all the early correspondence between Pound and H.D. (*E.T.T.*, pp. 37–38). Aldington's letters to H.D., which I read while this book was in production, confirm H.D.'s account of the events of 1916–1919 in her *Bid Me to Live* and in her letters to Pound. The father of her child was Cecil Gray, the music historian.

18. H.D., *The Sword Went Out to Sea*, p. 110. This unpublished autobiographical novel about her involvement in Spiritualism, her breakdown and recovery, was written in 1947. The manuscript is at Beinecke. H.D. may have had other nervous breakdowns that cannot be documented as yet with available materials.

19. See especially *T.*, pp. 6, 17, 42; *Magic Mirror*, pp. 7–8, 26–27; *The*

Sword Went Out to Sea (Part II). See also Riddel, "H.D. and the Poetics of 'Spiritual Realism'" for an excellent discussion of this image in her work (pp. 456–57).

20. *Magic Mirror*, pp. 7–8. Here and later in a repetition of this memory, H.D. added to the typed manuscript the pencilled words: "(But this never happened. Surely this was fantasy.)" This suggests that Aldington never actually burst in so angrily, but that her later fantasy connected him with psychological brutality and the death of their child. Her first "slight-breakdown" at college does not fit into this pattern. A possibly related link might be her father's ambitions for her and her failure to live up to them. Her breakdowns all involve a "breakdown" in relations with men and a sense that they have betrayed her in some way. She may have felt that her father rejected her because she could not be a Marie Curie.

21. Hirslanden II, pp. 7, 9, 28. In addition, H.D.'s "Autobiographical Notes" suggest that she was "stricken" and "very, very upset" at two different periods in 1931 and March 1932. These periods were connected with Macpherson and revelations about his relationships with two different men.

22. Letter from H.D. to Bryher, 21 April 1933. H.D.'s letters to Bryher cover the years 1918–1961 and are at Beinecke. This important and voluminous correspondence only became available to me after this book had gone to production. All future letters will be dated in the text.

23. In "Autobiographical Notes," H.D. indicated February 5–March 30 and July 27–November 8, 1939 as the composition periods for the novel. In 1948, she went over the manuscript again, as she did in the late fifties.

24. See *Tribute to Freud*, pp. xxxv–xxxviii for Fields's excellent discussion of the attitudes toward women that H.D. encountered. For feminist theorists and activists covering these issues, see Alice Rossi's *The Feminist Papers: From Adams to de Beauvoir* (New York: Bantam, 1973); Miriam Schneir's *Feminism: The Essential Historical Writings* (New York: Random House, 1972).

25. Ernest Jones, *The Life and Work of Sigmund Freud*, ed. and abridged by Lionel Trilling and Steven Marcus (New York: Anchor, 1963), pp. 35–36, 114. H.D. owned Jone's three volume biography. Volume I (1954) and Volume II (1955) are thoroughly marked. Volume III (1957) is unmarked.

26. Ibid., pp. 114–15. For a discussion of Freud and Mill, see also Betty Friedan, *The Feminine Mystique* (New York: Norton, 1963), pp. 103–25.

27. H.D., *Magic Mirror*, p. 49. For other references to tension between herself and her father over her math lessons, see T.F., pp. 143–44, and Hirslanden II, p. 27.

28. H.D., "The Suffragette," p. 3. The undated, unpublished seven-page manuscript is in a file of unpublished short stories at Beinecke.

29. Someone (Pearson?) noted on the manuscript of "The Suffragette," "sounds like Dora Marden [sic] but am not sure when Hilda met her." I am indebted to my research assistant Mary Frey for the information she gathered on Marsden from *The Freewoman* (1911–1912), *The New Free-*

woman (1913), *The Egoist* (1914–1919), and *Dear Miss Weaver: Harriet Shaw Weaver, 1876–1961*, by Jane Lidderdale and Mary Nicholson (New York: Viking, 1970).

30. Amy Lowell, "The Sisters" (1925) in *The Complete Poetical Works of Amy Lowell* (New York: Houghton Mifflin, 1955).

31. Bryher, *Two Selves* (Paris: Contact, 1923), p. 98. Bryher's *Development*, with its praiseworthy preface by Amy Lowell, records "Nancy's" earlier years and similarly contains many references to her anger at the constraints imposed on girls (London: Constable, 1920). See also *Heart to Artemis* for a record of Bryher's passionate concern for women's rights.

32. Bryher, *Two Selves*, p. 5.

33. Ibid., p. 96.

34. Suzanne Juhasz, *Naked and Fiery Forms: Modern American Poetry by Women, A New Tradition* (New York: Harper & Row, 1976), pp. 2–3.

35. See, for example, H.D.'s *P.*, pp. 15–33, and *B.M.L.*, pp. 70–71, 80–82, 97–103.

36. See H.D.'s *P.*, pp. 15–16, and Alfred Satterthwaite's informative article "John Cournos and 'H.D.,' " *Twentieth-Century Literature*, 22, No. 4 (December 1976), 394–410; it confirms H.D.'s account that Aldington told Yorke that H.D. "had no body." For other discussions of H.D. and Cournos, see Lucy Freibert, "Conflict and Creativity in the World of H.D.," *Journal of Women's Studies in Literature*, 1, No. 3 (Summer 1979), 258–71, and Peter E. Firchow, "Rico and Julia: The Hilda Doolittle–D.H. Lawrence Affair Reconsidered," *Journal of Modern Literature*, 8, No. 2 (1980), 51–76.

37. *B.M.L.*, pp. 25, 133. In "John Cournos and 'H.D.,' " Satterthwaite corroborated this fear of pregnancy. With incredible callousness to the feelings of women who faced death through pregnancies they could not control, he refers to H.D.'s "almost pathological fear of conception," p. 402.

38. *Paint It Today* seems to be an early draft for *Asphodel*. *Asphodel* begins with H.D.'s trip to Europe in 1911 and ends with the birth of her child in 1919. Its content therefore makes it a draft for *Bid Me to Live*, but the published novel left out the whole first part of *Asphodel*—the part incorporating H.D.'s relationship with Frances Gregg and her courtship with Aldington. All further references to these novels will be made in the text.

39. On the manuscript copy, H.D. crossed out "I am Her Gart, O.M., Old Maid precisely."

40. Rachel Blau DuPlessis, "Romantic Thralldom in H.D.," *Contemporary Literature*, 20, No. 2 (Summer 1979), 181. I am indebted to DuPlessis for directing me to *Her*. For extensive analysis of *Her*, see Friedman and DuPlessis, " 'I Had Two Loves Separate': H.D.'s Sexualities in *Her*," *Montemora*, 8 (Summer 1981).

41. See Adrienne Rich, "It Is the Lesbian in Us ..." (1976), in *On Lies, Secrets, and Silence: Selected Prose, 1966–1978* (New York: Norton, 1979), pp. 199–202, for an argument that the creative center of every woman is lesbian. H.D.'s letters to Bryher in 1933 and 1934 suggest however that Freud influenced her to associate her intellectual side with the masculine, much as Bryher herself had always done. By the forties and fifties, H.D. once again identified her muse as specifically female (see chapter 5).

42. Even in an autobiographical novel, the artist has license to change events to suit aesthetic or psychological needs. With *Asphodel* and *Her*, it is difficult to determine where biographical fact gives way to requirements of artistic narrative. For example, *Her* ends with Fayne's double betrayal of Hermione; Fayne seduces George Lowdnes and thereby ends both her relationship with Hermione and Hermione's engagement to George. Nowhere else does H.D. explain the end of her engagement to Pound in this way. Since H.D. was involved with both Bryher and Macpherson when she wrote *Her*, Fayne may represent a combination of Frances Gregg and Bryher. In addition, the ideal sister-love that Gregg represents in *Her* and *Asphodel* is well tempered by H.D.'s irritated references to her in her correspondence with Bryher and Macpherson.

43. Personal accounts suggest that inhibition was strong in both women. Pearson told me, for example, that H.D. loved many men and women with great passion, but always had difficulty with physical consummation of love. In a similar vein, Perdita Schaffner told me that H.D. and Bryher were "platonic lesbians." Satterthwaite's unsympathetic description of a nearly consummated sexual experience between H.D. and Cournos suggests as well that H.D. was a victim of the Victorian dichotomization of women into asexual ladies and sexual whores. Satterthwaite's source, however, is Cournos, his stepfather and a man who admittedly hated H.D.

44. See, for example, Jill Johnston, *Lesbian Nation: The Feminist Solution* (New York: Simon and Schuster, 1973), pp. 47–75. For other references to H.D.'s lesbianism, see Dolores Klaich, *Woman + Woman: Attitudes Toward Lesbianism* (New York: William Morrow, 1974), pp. 74–87; Beverly Lynch, "Love, Beyond Men and Women: H.D.," in *Lesbian Lives: Biographies of Women from The Ladder*, eds. Barbara Grier and Coletta Reid (Baltimore, Md.: Diana Press, 1976), pp. 258–72.

45. H.D., "The Master," an undated, unpublished poem written between 1933 and 1935. Robert Herring wanted to publish the poem in *Life and Letters Today*, but H.D. refused, writing to Bryher that she did not want her analysis "spoiled" by being made public (1 November 1935). I discovered this important poem while this book was in production. Rachel Blau DuPlessis and I have permission to publish this poem with commentary in a forthcoming issue of *Feminist Studies*.

46. Holland, "H.D. and the 'Blameless Physician,' " p. 493; see also pp. 485, 491. Holland's later book, *Poems in Persons: An Introduction to the Psychoanalysis of Literature* (New York: Norton, 1973), is more creative in some of its methodology. His approach to literature is phenomenological as he applies psychoanalytic analysis to the *readers* of literature. Nonetheless, he cannot resist psychoanalyzing H.D. as well in a chapter that is only slightly revised from his earlier article.

47. Riddel, "H.D. and the Poetics of 'Spiritual Realism,' " pp. 462, 453, 454, 455, 459. Although his article is riddled with his belief in H.D.'s "ambiguous role as woman poet," it contains some brilliant discussions of H.D.'s use of myth and concept of "spiritual realism." See also Kenneth Fields's brief but sharp critique of Riddel and Holland in his "Introduction" (*T.F.*, pp. xxxiv–xxxvi).

48. Hirslanden I, pp. 1–3. These nightmares began January 10, 1957, just at the time she was ordered to walk again after her hip injury. She commented: "The sediment of some past unresolved terror was revealed in a second nightmare."

2. Hieroglyphic Voices

1. Ernest Jones, *Psycho-Analysis* (1928; rpt. London: Ernest Benn, 1936), p. 77. H.D.'s copy of this pamphlet is heavily underlined throughout.

2. For spatial metaphors, see Freud, *G.I.P.*, p. 305; for archeological metaphors, which Freud frequently used, see, for example, his *C.D.*, pp. 16–18, and "Construction in Analysis" (1938) in *T.T.*, pp. 275–77.

3. Freud, *G.I.P.*, p. 222, and Jones, *Psycho-Analysis*, p. 58.

4. Freud, *O.P.*, p. 53.

5. For discussion of the analogous nature of these mental expressions, see Freud's *G.I.P.*, pp. 211, 251–52, 284–97, 381.

6. Freud, *G.I.P.*, pp. 241, 183, 181; see also *I.D.*, pp. 311–12.

7. For Freud's distinction between latent and manifest content, see *G.I.P.*, pp. 119–31, 183 and *I.D.*, pp. 311–12, 340–43. For his descriptions of the dream-work's techniques, see *I.D.*, pp. 311–546 and *G.I.P.*, pp. 156–92. For a discussion of over-determination, see *I.D.*, pp. 317–18.

8. Freud, *G.I.P.*, pp. 119–31, 183; *I.D.*, pp. 175–77, 508–509; see also "Revision of the Theory of Dreams" in *N.I.L.*, pp. 15–20. This theory of disguise was a major point of disagreement between Freud and Jung. See C.G. Jung, "Approaching the Unconscious," in *Man and His Symbols*, ed. C.G. Jung (New York: Dell, 1964), pp. 7–12, 30, 42. Pearson was mistaken, I believe, in referring to H.D. as a "quasi-Jungian." Although H.D. shared with Jung the belief in the dream as an important source of spiritual truth, she agreed fundamentally with Freud's theory of the dream as an obfuscating coded message, as enigmatic and confusing as the oracles of Delphi. See Pearson, "Foreword," in H.D.'s *H.D.*, p. vi.

9. Freud, "Recommendations for Physicians on the Psychoanalytic Method of Treatment" (1912) in *T.T.*, pp. 125–26 and "Further Recommendations in the Technique of Psychoanalysis" (1913) in *T.T.*, p. 147.

10. Lionel Trilling, "Freud and Literature," in Hendrik M. Ruitenbeek, ed., *Psychoanalysis and Literature* (New York: Dutton, 1964), pp. 266–67.

11. Philip Rieff, *Freud: The Mind of the Moralist* (New York: Doubleday, 1961), p. 140. For similar parallels, see Frederick Clarke Prescott, *The Poetic Mind* (New York: Macmillan, 1922), pp. 170–71; Jack J. Spector, *The Aesthetics of Freud* (New York: McGraw-Hill, 1972), pp. 88–94; Frederick J. Hoffman, *Freudianism and The Literary Mind* (Baton Rouge: Louisiana State University Press, 1957), pp. 42–43; Morton Kaplan and Robert Kloss, *The Unspoken Motive: A Guide to Psychoanalytic Literary Criticism* (New York: Free Press, 1973), p. 17; Kenneth Burke, "Freud and the Analysis of Poetry" (1939), in Ruitenbeek's *Psychoanalysis and Literature*, pp. 127–30.

12. Freud, *G.I.P.*, pp. 184, 127–28.

13. *Some Imagist Poets: An Anthology* (1915; rpt. New York: Kraus Reprint Co., 1969), pp. vi–vii.

14. Ezra Pound, "A Few Don'ts by an Imagiste," *Poetry*, 1 (March 1913), 200. In *The New Age Under Orange* (New York: Manchester University Press, 1967), Wallace Martin argued that while T.E. Hulme's concept of the Image was a philosophical derivation from Bergson, Pound's idea of the Image was psychological in origin (pp. 178–79). Martin stressed the role of *The New Age*, a widely read journal in literary London, in introducing psychoanalysis to England in the years between 1912–1920. If Martin is correct in assessing the indirect influence of Freud on Pound through Bernard Hart, H.D. may have been familiar with psychoanalytic theory as early as 1913.

15. F.S. Flint, "Imagisme," *Poetry*, 1 (March 1913), 198–200.

16. Freud, *G.I.P.*, pp. 179–82.

17. Robert Duncan, "Rites of Participation, Part II," *Caterpillar*, 2 (January 1968), 149–50.

18. See Freud, *I.D.*, pp. 340–43, and *G.I.P.*, pp. 182–83.

19. L.S. Dembo, "Norman Holmes Pearson on H.D.: An Interview," *Contemporary Literature*, 10, No. 4 (Autumn 1969), 441, 437.

20. "Poet Hilda Doolittle, on Yale Visit, Assails Imagist Label Used to Describe Her Work," *New Haven Register* (16 September 1956), p. 10.

21. *H.E.*, pp. 1–2. Euripides' *Helen in Egypt* was an important source for H.D.'s poem. She owned and marked Greek, French, and English editions of the play.

22. For discussion of the influence of film on H.D.'s technique in *Helen in Egypt*, see Charlotte Mandel, "Garbo/Helen: The Self-Projection of Beauty by H.D.," *Women's Studies*, 7, No. 1/2 (1980), 127–36, and her unpublished article, "The Redirected Image: Cinematic Dynamics in the Style of H.D.'s *Helen in Egypt*."

23. Letter from Bryher to Macpherson, 31 March 1933.

24. Pearson explained the origin of the prose passages in Dembo, "Norman Holmes Pearson on H.D.: An Interview," p. 440. Pearson had arranged for H.D. to make a recording of selected passages from the epic. H.D. introduced each selection of verse with a prose interpretation. Pearson encouraged her to write a "prose interlude" for every poetic sequence, and she did. The first edition of *Helen in Egypt* contained both the poetry and the prose.

25. Perdita Schaffner told me that H.D. owned many, if not all, of Woolf's books and read them avidly. The two women probably did not meet, however; Schaffner, Pearson, and Quentin Bell told me that the artistic circles of Bloomsbury and London bohemia rarely intersected. Additionally, Schaffner said, the women could not have been friends—"they were too much alike." The only reference to Woolf that I have seen in H.D.'s papers is in a letter to Brigit Patmore, with whom she frequently exchanged books in the twenties: "Ever so many thanks for 'Room' [*A Room of One's Own*?] + 'Lorm' [?] ... We are delighted with *all* the plunder. I myself have appropriated the Woolf + one or two others" (n.d.). This letter is one of ten undated letters to Patmore, at Beinecke.

Information on Joyce comes from Dembo, "Norman Holmes Pearson on H.D.: An Interview," p. 438.

26. See Bryher's *Heart to Artemis* (New York: Harcourt, Brace & World, 1962), pp. 28–29, 236–41. H.D. corresponded with Richardson from 1923–1950 and occasionally saw her. Twenty-seven letters from Richardson to H.D. are at Beinecke. They are informal, warm, admiring and supportive; she gave H.D. honest and critical readings of *Heliodora* and *Palimpsest.* H.D. also admired the work of two other women writing fiction in this period, Colette and Mary Butts.

27. L.S. Dembo, *Conceptions of Reality in Modern American Poetry* (Berkeley: University of California Press, 1965).

28. Virginia Woolf, "Mr. Bennett and Mrs. Brown" (1924) in *The Captain's Death Bed and Other Essays* (New York: Harcourt, Brace & World, 1950), pp. 94–119.

29. Virginia Woolf, *A Room of One's Own* (1929; rpt. New York: Harcourt, Brace & World, 1957); see especially pp. 83–118.

3. Delphi of the Mind

1. L.S. Dembo, "Norman Holmes Pearson on H.D.: An Interview," *Contemporary Literature,* 10, No. 4 (Autumn 1969), 438.

2. Sigmund Freud, *Delusion and Dream and Other Essays,* ed. Philip Rieff (Boston: Beacon Press, 1956), p. 123.

3. Freud, *G.I.P.,* p. 384.

4. Freud, *C.D.,* pp. 27–28.

5. Philip Rieff, *Freud: The Mind of the Moralist* (New York: Doubleday, 1961), p. 134. See also Jack J. Spector, *The Aesthetics of Freud* (New York: McGraw-Hill, 1972), for a discussion of Freud's theories on art.

6. See Sigmund Freud, *Leonardo da Vinci and a Memory of His Childhood,* trans. Alan Tyson (1910; rpt. New York: Norton, 1964) and "Delusion and Dream in Jensen's 'Gravida'" (1907) in *Delusion and Dream and Other Essays.*

7. Freud, *C.D.,* pp. 11–14.

8. Freud, *F.I.,* pp. 47–48; see also *C.D.,* pp. 19, 21.

9. Frederick Clarke Prescott's *The Poetic Mind* (New York: Macmillan, 1922) argued that in its origins poetry was prophecy which emerged out of the repressed, unresolved desires in the unconscious. The unconscious is the "visionary faculty" of the mind that produces dreams, hallucinations, mystic and poetic vision (p. 20): "The dreamer, the mystic, and the poet all go to the same source" (p. 27). The figure of Apollo, patron of prophecy and poetry, fuses all these functions that have since become separated. The parallels to H.D. are striking.

10. See Freud, *I.D.,* pp. 253–73.

11. H.D.'s Biblical sources are: (1) On Mary Magdalene: Matthew 28:10; Mark 16:9; Luke 8:1–12, 24:10; John 20:11–19. (2) On Mary and Martha of Bethany, sisters of Lazarus: Luke 10:38–42; John 11:1–45, 12:1–8. (3) On woman who washed Jesus' feet at Simon's house: Matthew 26:6–7; Mark 14:3; John 12:1–4; Luke 7:36–50. In linking all these women

as Mary Magdalene, H.D. followed a cult tradition beginning in 1279. See James Hastings, *A Dictionary of the Bible* (New York, 1902), II, pp. 284–86. I have not, however, been able to locate any source for H.D.'s meeting between Mary Magdalene and Kaspar. The story is most likely her own variant.

12. Freud, *G.I.P.*, p. 209; see also p. 30.

13. See also *T.F.*, pp. 37, 38; Ernest Jones, *Psycho-Analysis* (1928; rpt. London: Ernest Benn, 1936), pp. 17, 56, 60–61, for his description of Freud's evolutionary theory. H.D. heavily marked these passages. The Jones pamphlet includes discussion of *Totem and Taboo* and the work of Freud's anthropological disciple, Geza Roheim.

14. Freud, *G.I.P.*, pp. 157–66.

15. See ibid., pp. 210, 380, and Freud, "Analysis Terminable and Interminable" (1937) in *T.T.*, p. 259. While C.G. Jung is more known for his theory of inherited archetypes, the concept of hereditary transmission of universal symbols exists firmly in Freud's thought.

16. Norman Holland, "H.D. and the 'Blameless Physician,'" *Contemporary Literature*, 10, No. 4 (Autumn 1969), 485–87.

17. Joseph Riddel, "H.D. and the Poetics of 'Spiritual Realism.'" *Contemporary Literature*, 10, No. 4 (Autumn 1969), 464.

18. Jones, *Psycho-Analysis*, p. 15. H.D. heavily underlined this sentence and checked it in the margin.

19. See Paul A. Robinson, *The Freudian Left* (New York: Harper & Row, 1969), pp. 101ff. , on Geza Roheim's work. See also Jones, *Psycho-Analysis*, p. 61.

20. Jones, *Psycho-Analysis*, p. 61. Freud's theory of a universal unconscious should not be confused with C.G. Jung's concept of the "collective unconscious." Jung distinguished between a "personal unconscious" and a "collective unconscious." He basically accepted Freud's theories and judgments about the personal unconscious, which he believed was idiosyncratic in each individual. The collective unconscious is a deeper layer which is literally the same the world over. H.D. followed Freud in equating the personal dream with the tribal dream and the childhood of the individual with the childhood of the race. See Jung, *Two Essays on Analytical Psychology*, trans. R.F.C. Hull (New York: World, 1956), pp. 76, 87, 91, 136, 145–47, 277–78.

21. Dembo, "Norman Holmes Pearson on H.D.: An Interview," p. 438.

4. "Transcendental Issues"

1. See Freud's *G.I.P.*, pp. 105–107; *O.P.*, pp. 35–36; *F.I.*, pp. 39–41, 60; see also Ernest Jones, *Psycho-Analysis* (1928; rpt. London: Ernest Benn, 1936), pp. 8, 9, 10, 11, 13, 77. H.D. underlined many of these comparisons between psychoanalysis and other sciences, including the analogy to Darwin. For my basic idea in this chapter that Freud's conceptions of reality were significant to H.D.'s development, I am deeply indebted to my thesis adviser, L.S. Dembo. His book *Conceptions of Reality in Modern American Poetry* (Berkeley: University of California Press, 1965), places

modernist American poets in the philosophical context of epistemological and ontological issues. His work profoundly influenced my approach to H.D.

2. See, for example, Philip Rieff, *Freud: The Mind of the Moralist* (New York: Doubleday, 1961), pp. 23, 103–104, and throughout. Paul Roazen, *Freud: Political and Social Thought* (New York: Knopf, 1968), pp. 158–67; Richard Wollheim, *Sigmund Freud* (New York: Viking Press, 1971), pp. 272–73.

3. Freud, *F.I.*, p. 43, and "Dreams and Occultism" in *N.I.L.*, p. 33.

4. Freud, *F.I.*, pp. 37–38.

5. Ibid., pp. 19–35.

6. Freud, "Dreams and Occultism" in *N.I.L.*, pp. 31, 34; see also pp. 32–36.

7. Freud, *F.I.*, p. 50.

8. Freud, *G.I.P.*, pp. 377–78.

9. Ibid.

10. Ibid. This opposition of the reality principle and the pleasure principle is the cornerstone of Freud's psychoanalytic social contract theory in *Civilization and Its Discontents*, when he applied the theory of individual repression to the development of culture (pp. 21–32).

11. Freud, *G.I.P.*, pp. 380–81.

12. Ibid., p. 209.

13. Ibid., p. 221. See also *G.I.P.*, pp. 189, 209–23; *F.I.*, p. 53; and "Analysis Terminable and Interminable" (1937) in *T.T.*, p. 247. H.D. read many books expressing a linear view of progress; among the most important sources for her poetry were James Frazer, *The Golden Bough*, 3rd. ed. (London: Macmillan, 1914); Arthur Weigall, *The Paganism in Our Christianity* (London: Putnam, 1928); and Hans Schindler Bellamy, *The Book of Revelation as History* (London: Faber & Faber, 1942). To use the rich store of mythology, she had to abandon the Enlightenment lens of all these writers.

14. Freud, *G.I.P.*, pp. 241–45.

15. Freud, *C.D.*, p. 27. See also Lionel Trilling's "Freud and Literature" in Hendrik M. Ruitenbeek, ed., *Psychoanalysis and Literature* (New York: Dutton, 1964), pp. 259–60, for discussion of Freud's rationalist evaluation of art.

16. Rieff, *Freud: The Mind of the Moralist*, p. 134.

17. Freud, *C.D.*, p. 28; *F.I.*, pp. 37–45, 47–48, 88; see *F.I.*, pp. 48–49, for his distinction between delusion and illusion.

18. Freud, *F.I.*, pp. 86–92.

19. Freud, *C.D.*, pp. 28, 21.

20. See Rieff, *Freud: The Mind of the Moralist*, p. 359. Rieff argued that the implications for greater sexual freedom are in Freud's work, but that Freud himself would not have accepted them.

21. Freud, *G.I.P.*, pp. 154, 149, 221. I assume that the authorized translations have not tampered with the connotations of the original German. In any case, H.D. read Freud in English, and their sessions were in English as well.

22. Freud, *C.D.*, pp. 52, 42–45; *F.I.*, pp. 20–21.

23. See, for example, Stanley Edgar Hyman, "Psychoanalysis and the Climate of Tragedy" in *Freud and the Twentieth Century*, ed. Benjamin Nelson (New York: Meridian, 1957), pp. 170–81; see also Rieff, *Freud: The Mind of the Moralist*, pp. 59–61 on Freud's pessimism.

24. Freud, *O.P.*, pp. 14–17, 108–110, 42; see also Rieff, *Freud: The Mind of the Moralist*, p. 63.

25. Freud, *O.P.*, pp. 62–63. I have deliberately deemphasized Freud's idea of the superego's enmity to the ego because Freud's own concept of reality tends to collapse the distinctions between external reality and the superego. The ethics and customs of a culture, which the superego embodies, are part of the external world to which the healthy ego is joined, and so by helping the ego to reestablish strong ties with reality the Freudian analyst is also helping the superego maintain its powerful influence.

26. Rieff, *Freud: The Mind of the Moralist*, p. 69; see also pp. 76, 81, 103–107, 355.

27. Trilling, "Psychoanalysis and Literature," in Ruitenbeek, *Psychoanalysis and Literature*, pp. 256–57. For related arguments see Rieff, *Freud: The Mind of the Moralist*, pp. 76–77, 355; Richard Wolheim, *Sigmund Freud* (New York: Viking, 1971), p. 272. When Herbert Marcuse, in *Eros and Civilization* (1955; rpt. New York: Vintage Books, 1962), described Freud as a champion of the instincts, he ignored Freud's ethical and epistemological bias and explored the radical implications of Freud's theories. H.D. did the same.

28. Robert Duncan, "From the Day Book," *Origin* (July 10, 1963), pp. 10–12.

29. Cyrena N. Pondrom, *The Road from Paris: French Influence on English Poetry, 1900–1920* (New York: Cambridge University Press, 1973), p. 15.

30. Denis de Rougemont, *Love in the Western World*, trans. Montgomery Belgion (New York: Pantheon, 1956), pp. 61, 174. De Rougemont's study originally appeared as *L'Amour et l'occident* (Paris, 1939). Belgion's first English translation, *Passion and Society*, appeared in London in 1940. *Love in the Western World* is an expanded edition of *Passion and Society*. H.D. owned and thoroughly marked all three editions. She recommended the book to Jordan and said that she had read it several times —"THAT IS MY BIBLE, if you will" (30 July 1941 or 1944, year uncertain). H.D. may also have been familiar with Jung's denunciation of Freud's materialism in *Modern Man in Search of a Soul*, trans. W.S. Dell and Cary F. Baynes (New York: Harcourt, Brace & World, 1933), pp. 16, 41, 45, 116–18.

31. Most particularly, Douglas Bush has argued that "H.D. is a poet of escape" and that her use of myth attempts to re-create a serene Greek world that contrasts with "the ugliness and barbarism of modern life," in *Mythology and the Romantic Tradition in English Poetry* (Cambridge: Harvard University Press, 1973), pp. 502, 497. Linda Welshimer Wagner's generally useful discussion of *Helen in Egypt* nonetheless argued that myth was a "solace" or escape from the modern world, "*Helen in Egypt*: A Culmination," *Contemporary Literature*, 10, No. 4 (Autumn 1969), 523.

Vincent Quinn's useful introduction to the *Trilogy* as poetry of quest still sees the poetic search as escape from the "violent, vulgar, and trivial" actual world, *Hilda Doolittle* (New York: Twayne, 1968), p. 54. For a good critique of Bush, see E.B. Greenwood, "H.D. and the Problem of Escapism," *Essays in Criticism*, 21, No. 4 (1971), 365–76.

32. See also Bryher's memoir of their war experience together, *The Days of Mars: A Memoir, 1940–1946* (New York: Harcourt Brace Jovanovich, 1972).

33. See H.D.'s *Sagesse* in *H.D.*, pp. 67, 69 for another strong statement of psychic danger. The voice of Germain, mask for Erich Heydt, represents the perspective of reason and material reality; he attempts to draw the poet away from religious experience.

34. Pondrom, *The Road from Paris*, p. 15. See also Riddel's discussion of "spiritual realism" in his "H.D. and the Poetics of 'Spiritual Realism,'" pp. 466–71.

35. H.D., *Vale Ave*, p. 46. This long poem of seventy-four sections is as yet unpublished. The manuscript is at Beinecke. All quotations from the poem will hereafter be identified within the text as *V.A.*

36. Riddel, "H.D. and the Poetics of 'Spiritual Realism,'" pp. 457, 451, 466–67.

37. Edmund Leach, *Lévi-Strauss* (London: Collins, 1970), pp. 17, 27, 57.

38. Mircea Eliade, *Myth and Reality*, trans. Willard R. Trask (New York: Harper & Row, 1963), p. 5.

39. John Cournos, the "Ivan" in *Bid Me to Live*, has thoroughly marked a copy of H.D.'s roman à clef with bitter comments about H.D.'s cruelty, vicious inaccuracy, self-pity, and stupidity. See also ch. 1, n. 38.

40. Others have compared Freud to the artist as well. See especially Jack J. Spector, *The Aesthetics of Freud* (New York: McGraw-Hill, 1972), pp. ix, 34–37; Rieff, *Freud: The Mind of the Moralist*, pp. 20–27.

41. Both Marcuse in *Eros and Civilization* and Brown in *Life Against Death* (New York: Random House, 1959) base much of their reading of Freud on *Civilization and Its Discontents*. See also Paul Robinson's *The Freudian Left* (New York: Harper & Row, 1969) for a discussion of how writers like Marcuse, Reich, and Roheim used Freud's discoveries to develop social theories which the self-styled empiricist, Freud, could never have accepted.

42. Gregory Zilboorg, "Introduction," in Sigmund Freud's *Beyond the Pleasure Principle*, trans. James Strachey (1922; rpt. New York: Norton, 1961), pp. x–xi.

5. "The Professor Was Not Always Right"

1. H.D., "The Master," see ch. 1, n. 45.

2. Freud, "Femininity," in *N.I.L.*, p. 135. Freud's other significant expositions are referred to in following footnotes.

3. Freud, "Femininity," in *N.I.L.*, pp. 117–18. All phrases in quotation marks here and elsewhere are Freud's own.

4. Ibid., pp. 125, 129, and "The Passing of the Oedipus-Complex" (1924), in *S.E.*, II, p. 272.

5. Freud, "Femininity," in *N.I.L.*, pp. 118, 121–22, 128; *O.P.*, p. 97.

6. Freud, "The Psychogenesis of a Case of Homosexuality in a Woman" (1920), in *S.E.*, II, pp. 227–29.

7. Among the most significant are Juliet Mitchell, *Psychoanalysis and Feminism* (New York: Pantheon, 1974); Simone de Beauvoir, *The Second Sex*, trans. H.M. Parshley (1949; rpt. New York: Bantam, 1961): Karen Horney, *Feminine Psychology* (New York: Norton, 1967); Gregory Zilboorg, "Masculine and Feminine: Some Biological and Cultural Aspects," *Psychiatry*, 7 (1944), 257–96; Amy Guttmann, "Freud versus Feminism," *Dissent* (Spring 1979), 204–12; and Kate Millett, *Sexual Politics* (New York: Avon, 1969).

8. Mitchell, *Psychoanalysis and Feminism*, pp. 10–12, 16–17, 107, 353–54.

9. Ibid., pp. 31, 125–26, 129–31.

10. Freud, "Femininity," in *N.I.L.*, p. 124.

11. Freud, "The Passing of the Oedipus-Complex" (1924), in *S.E.*, II, p. 274.

12. Freud, "Femininity," in *N.I.L.*, p. 124.

13. Ibid., p. 119.

14. This point was first made by Dana Densmore in "Mr. Freud's Castration Fantasy," *No More Fun and Games*, 6 (May 1973), 114–15. See H.R. Hays, *The Dangerous Sex: The Myth of Feminine Evil* (New York: Pocket Books, 1964), for cross-cultural perspectives on myths of female castration; he records a number of creation myths in which women were first made by wounding males or neuters in the genital area.

15. Freud, "Some Psychical Consequences of the Anatomical Distinction Between the Sexes" (1925), *S.E.*, II, p. 47. See also Freud, *T.C.S.*, pp. 3–12; "Femininity," in *N.I.L.*, pp. 113–16, 131; *O.P.*, pp. 88–89; "Psychogenesis of a Case of Homosexuality in a Woman" (1920), in *S.E.*, II, pp. 210–11, 230–31; "Hysterical Phantasies and Their Relation to Bisexuality" (1908), in *Dora* (1905; rpt. New York: Collier, 1963).

16. For various feminist definitions of androgyny, see, for example, my "Androgyny: Feminist Definition and Debate," forthcoming in Susan Friedman and Nancy Topping Bazin, *Androgyny as Literary Vision*; the special issue on androgyny, *Women's Studies*, 2 (1974); Carolyn Heilbrun, *Toward a Recognition of Androgyny* (New York: Harper & Row, 1973); Mary Daly, *Beyond God the Father* (Boston: Beacon, 1973).

17. Freud, *T.C.S.*, pp. 5–9, 12; "Psychogenesis of a Case of Homosexuality in a Woman" (1920), *S.E.*, II, pp. 206–207. For an overview of theories on androgyny and homosexuality among Freud's contemporaries, see Barbara Fassler, "Theories of Homosexuality as Sources of Bloomsbury's Androgyny," *Signs*, 5, No. 5 (Winter 1979), 237–51. H.D. and Bryher were well aware of these theories; in 1919, for example, H.D. sent Bryher to Havelock Ellis and Bryher's letter to H.D. (20 March 1919) showed that Bryher accepted his theory that lesbians have a male soul

trapped in a female body. In the twenties and thirties, H.D.'s novels and letters about her own sexuality are more consistent with Freud's theories than with Ellis's.

18. Freud, "Some Psychical Consequences of the Anatomical Distinction Between the Sexes" (1924), *S.E.*, II; see also "Femininity," in *N.I.L.*, pp. 132–35.

19. For other connections between Bryher and H.D.'s mother, see *T.F.*, pp. 172–73, 182; Hirslanden III, pp. 26–27. H.D.'s letters to Bryher in the spring of 1933 indicate that Freud believed that H.D. also unconsciously connected Bryher with her younger brother.

20. Freud, "Psychogenesis of a Case of Homosexuality in a Woman" (1920), *S.E.*, II, pp. 208–209.

21. Letter from Bryher to Macpherson, 14 June 1933.

22. For the most important arguments on the revolutionary potential of the dream, see the works of Frantz Fanon, especially *The Wretched of the Earth*, trans. Constance Farrington (New York: Grove, 1963).

23. See also Hirslanden III, p. 27, and IV, p. 22.

24. H.D., "Dark Room," (chapter 1), p. 25 of *The Gift*.

25. See, for example, *Her*, pp. 38, 56, 106–109, 149, 164–75, and *Asphodel*, p. 97. In the *Her* manuscript, H.D. crossed out violent references to Her's desire at one point to hit and kill her Victorian mother (pp. 106ff).

26. See Freud, "Femininity," in *N.I.L.*, p. 126. Freud would probably have regarded the candle in H.D.'s dream as a phallic symbol, as he definitely did in another of H.D.'s memories (*T.F.*, p. 124).

27. H.D., *E.T.T.*, p. 41. This and subsequent discussions of H.D.'s mother are based on a paper I delivered at MLA in 1977 and "Psyche Reborn: Tradition, Re-Vision, and the Goddess as Mother-Symbol in H.D.'s Epic Poetry," *Women's Studies*, 6, No. 2 (1979), 147–60.

28. Kate Chopin's complete silence after the harsh reception of *The Awakening* and Virginia Woolf's extreme anxiety about critical reviews are only two of the many examples among women artists whose artistic voice has been dampened by the threat or reality of male condemnation. See Tillie Olsen's *Silences* (New York: Delta, 1978), for an extensive treatment of this issue.

29. "A Letter from William Carlos Williams to Norman Holmes Pearson Concerning Hilda Doolittle and Her Mother and Father (11 July 1955)," *William Carlos Williams Newsletter*, 2, No. 2 (1976), pp. 2–3. See also Emily Wallace's "Afterword: The House of the Father's Science and the Mother's Art" in the same issue (pp. 4–5).

30. H.D., "Dark Room" (chapter 1), p. 32 in *The Gift*.

31. Freud, "Femininity," in *N.I.L.*, p. 133. H.D.'s cousin Francis Wolle contradicted H.D. about her mother's preference in *A Moravian Heritage* (Boulder, Col.: Empire Reproductions, 1972), p. 59. Wolle's material provides valuable, if sometimes inaccurate, information, but he shows no comprehension of H.D.'s difficulties as a girl in a family of boys or a woman writer in a predominantly male tradition.

32. For separatist definitions of woman-identification, see Radicalesbians, "The Woman-Identified Woman" in *Radical Feminism*, ed. Anne

Koedt et al. (New York: Quadrangle, 1973), pp. 240–46; Mary Daly, *Gyn/Ecology* (Boston: Beacon, 1978).

33. In Hirslanden II, H.D. linked herself and her "favorite brother" Eric with Isis and Osiris (p. 41). *Compassionate Friendship* and *Magic Mirror* in particular associate a series of men in her life with Eric and/or her father as ideal father or brother symbols. Men most frequently linked by "superimposition" are Pound, Aldington, Gray and his "double" Macpherson, Van Eck, Schmideberg, Dowding, Lawrence, Cournos, and Heydt.

34. H.D., *Compassionate Friendship*, p. 83; *T.F.*, pp. 116, 124–25, 128, 131, 141; Hirslanden I, pp. 18–19.

35. H.D., *Winter Love* (1959) in *H.D.*, p. 108. I am indebted to Rachel Blau DuPlessis in "Romantic Thralldom in H.D.," *Contemporary Literature*, 20, No. 2 (Summer 1979), 178–203, for her insistence that male symbols form a crucial component in H.D.'s poetry and prose.

36. H.D., "Because One Is Happy" (chapter 4), p. 10 in *The Gift*.

37. The collection at Beinecke includes extensive materials on Lionel Durand and other sources for *Hermetic Definition*. H.D. quoted directly from Durand's review in *Newsweek*, 2 May 1960. Beginning four months after his death in January 1961, H.D. kept a diary (May 21–June 3, 1961) about Durand that attests to the strength of her obsession and the degree to which she transferred past loves onto a man who was respectful to her face, but condescending to her in print.

38. H.D.'s main source for the hermeticism that pervades the poem is Robert Ambelain's *Dans l'ombre des cathédrales* (Paris: Éditions Adyar, 1939). Ambelain claimed that Notre Dame rests upon the foundations of an ancient temple to Isis. The earliest settlers of Paris were known as the sons of Isis, or "Bar-Isis" ("bar," like "ben," meaning "son of") or "Parisis," later shortened to "Paris." Durand, the reporter from Paris, thus becomes the son of Isis in H.D.'s poem.

39. H.D. notes that "Judgement" is "masculine" in her diary on 30 May 1961. See Ambelain, *Dans l'ombre des cathédrales* for a discussion of the three doorways and the rosicrucian rose associated with Isis (pp. 12, 23–25, 51, 72–73).

40. Harold Bloom, *The Anxiety of Influence* (New York: Oxford University Press, 1973). See Annette Kolodny, "Dancing Through the Minefield," *Feminist Studies*, 6, No. 1 (Spring 1980), 1–25, for an analysis of how Bloom's Oedipal metaphors exclude women from the creative process.

41. For other discussions of the poet as mother in *Hermetic Definition*, see my "Who Buried H.D.? A Poet, Her Critics, and Her Place in 'The Literary Tradition,'" *College English*, 36, No. 7 (March 1975), 12–14; Vincent Quinn, "H.D.'s 'Hermetic Definition': The Poet as Archetypal Mother," *Contemporary Literature*, 18, No. 1 (Winter 1977), 51–61.

42. Durand diary (21 May 1961). However, the existence of the diary itself, written *after* Durand's death and the completion of the poem, demonstrates that the "tangles" perpetually renewed themselves—or, to use DuPlessis' phrase, the tangles of "romantic thralldom" were never finally unraveled in her life.

43. See Joseph N. Riddel's "H.D. and the Poetics of 'Spiritual Realism,'" *Contemporary Literature*, 10, No. 4 (Autumn 1969) for an opposing

argument that H.D.'s impulse to write originated in her recognition of the "incompleteness of the female" and a desire for the "hardness of male objectivity" (p. 449).

44. H.D., "Dark Room" (chapter 1), p. 32 in *The Gift*.

6. Initiations

1. See, for example, Freud, "Dreams and Occultism" in *N.I.L.*, pp. 31–56.

2. H.D., *Compassionate Friendship*, pp. 20, 31.

3. Peter Van Eck appears in a number of H.D.'s unpublished manuscripts as one of the many forms of "Le Prince Lointain." See especially *The Sword Went Out to Sea*. The Van Eck and "bell-jar" experiences stimulated H.D. to write "Notes on Thought and Vision," an unpublished essay on states of consciousness that is now at Beinecke. She showed the manuscript to her friend Havelock Ellis and was very disappointed in his disinterest (*T.F.*, p. 148).

4. Norman Holmes Pearson in interview with author (July 1972). Pearson said that H.D. was very impressed with Yeats's poetry. Robert Duncan disagreed with Pearson and claimed that H.D. was not close to Yeats and did not read his work: "Nights and Days," *Sumac* (Fall 1968), pp. 112, 131. H.D.'s copy of Yeats's *Letters on Poetry* (London: Oxford University Press, 1940) was in Pearson's collection of H.D.'s library.

5. H.D., "Narthex" in *The Second American Caravan: A Yearbook of American Literature*, Alfred Kreymborg et al., eds. (New York: Macaulay, 1928), pp. 225, 234, 235, 236. See "Autobiographical Notes," 1927, for H.D.'s statement that "Narthex" describes the trip H.D. took with Bryher and Macpherson shortly after their marriage. Entries in "Autobiographical Notes" indicate that this threesome was under great tension, especially when Macpherson's relations with two men in the early thirties became known to H.D. H.D.'s daughter confirmed this tension and explained that Macpherson and H.D. had been lovers (interview with author, May 1978).

6. These letters are extensively quoted in my "Mythology, Psychoanalysis and the Occult in the Late Poetry of H.D." (Ph.D. diss., University of Wisconsin, 1973), pp. 258–357; it also includes discussion of H.D.'s sources in numerology, astrology, Tarot, and Kabbalah as well as a list of H.D.'s books on the occult that Pearson kept at Yale.

7. H.D. sent two Tarot readings to Jordan in 1930, in letters dated 1 January and 10 March (year uncertain and dated by context). The first was based on the standard Celtic method described in one of her books, Paul-C. Jargot's *Les Cartes et les tarots* (Paris, n.d.). Her second reading was based on the more esoteric *Le Tarot astrologique* by Georges Muchery (Paris, 1927). Another book in her library, Oswald Wirth's *Introduction à l'étude du tarot* (Paris: Le Symbolisme, 1931), contains her pencilled calculations connected with readings she did for family and friends.

8. File entitled "Astronomy" at Beinecke. I am greatly indebted to Barbara Guest for telling me of this folder's existence. I would also like to thank Silvia Dobson for identifying the horoscope book as the work of herself and her sister, Molly Dobson.

9. Evangeline Adams, *Astrology: Your Place in the Sun* (New York: Dodd, Mead, 1927) and *Astrology: Your Place Among the Stars* (New York: Dodd, Mead, 1930).

10. The woman was Dr. Elizabeth Ashby. The "Astronomy" file at Beinecke includes a letter from Ashby to H.D. concerning Erich Heydt's chart.

11. Denis de Rougemont, *Love in the Western World*, trans. Montgomery Belgion (New York: Pantheon, 1956), pp. 61–108.

12. Ibid.

13. W.B. Crow, *Astronomical Religion* (London: Michael Houghton, 1942), pp. 4–6. This pamphlet, part of a series called *The Mysteries of the Ancients*, is an important source of symbols for the *Trilogy*. In *Tribute to Freud*, H.D. referred to this series and to another Crow essay (pp. 100–101).

14. Jean Chaboseau, *Le Tarot* (Paris: Éditions Niclaus, 1946), pp. 19–27. The translations are my own. H.D. kept her copy inside a beautifully tooled leather case. H.D. also owned Chaboseau's *La Voyance* (Paris: Éditions Niclaus, 1948).

15. Robert Ambelain, *Dans l'ombre des cathédrales* (Paris: Éditions Adyar, 1939). H.D.'s copy of this book is at Beinecke, along with several other books by Ambelain: *Adam, dieu rouge* (Paris: Éditions Niclaus, 1941); *Le Martinisme* (Paris: Éditions Niclaus, 1946); *La Kabbale practique* (Paris: Éditions Niclaus, 1951).

16. Ambelain, *Adam, dieu rouge*, pp. 3–60.

17. See Friedman, "Mythology, Psychoanalysis and the Occult in the Late Poetry of H.D." for an extensive discussion of H.D.'s important identification with Saint Theresa (pp. 339–44). H.D. regarded the second Saint Theresa as a kind of mother-symbol, who, like herself, affirmed the interconnections between art, religion, mystic love, and nonrational thought processes. See Ghéon's *Secret of the Saints* (New York: Sheed & Ward, 1944).

18. Hirslanden III, p. 4; *Magic Mirror*, p. 45; *The Sword Went Out to Sea*, pp. 3–4, 270. For descriptions of the Society, see *The Theosophical Movement, 1875–1950* (Los Angeles, Calif.: Cunningham Press, 1951), pp. 90–105, and Simeon Edmunds, *Spiritualism: A Critical Survey* (London: Aquarian Press, 1966), pp. 25–28, 108–12. William James, Henri Bergson, and Gilbert Murray were among the many well-known presidents of the Society.

19. Dorothy Cole bought the table for Bryher at the auction of Violet Hunt's possessions (Hirslanden III, p. 4).

20. Hugh Dowding, *Lynchgate* (London: Rider, 1945) and *Many Mansions* (London: Rider, 1943).

21. See also "Autobiographical Notes," in which a number of her meetings and important séances are dated.

22. See Rachel Blau DuPlessis' "Romantic Thralldom in H.D.," *Contemporary Literature*, 20, No. 2 (Summer 1979), 178–203 for an illuminating discussion of this pattern of enslavement and betrayal in H.D.'s art. DuPlessis' central argument is that H.D.'s narrative structures represent her attempts to define and transcend this "thralldom." H.D. also experienced Dowding's marriage in the fifties and Heydt's marriage in 1958 as betrayals

of sorts (Hirslanden I, IV). In *Her*, the young Hilda is similarly hurt by her half-brother Eric's marriage (*Her*, pp. 20–26).

23. Gustav Davidson, *A Dictionary of Angels* (New York: Free Press, 1967), p. xxxii.

24. See, for example, H.D.'s letters to Jordan, 1 May 1941 and 23 April 1945. *End to Torment* expresses her ambivalence toward Pound after the war—her compassion for his "confinement" and her anger at his support for the fascists: "There is no *reason* to accept, to condone, to forgive, to forget what Ezra has done" (p. 34). For a discussion of H.D. and Pound, see Rachel Blau DuPlessis, "Family, Sexes, Psyche: An Essay on H.D. and the Muse of the Woman Writer," *Montemora*, 6 (1979), 137–56.

25. Letter from H.D. to Jordan, 10 November 1941. Her correspondence from 1940–45 is filled with news of wartime London and thoroughly documents H.D.'s immersion in the war effort.

26. H.D.'s belief that significant change must begin within the individual parallels that of writers like D.H. Lawrence and Anaïs Nin. See, for example, Lawrence, "Study of Thomas Hardy" (1913) in *Phoenix*, ed. Edward McDonald (New York: Viking, 1964), pp. 404–10; Nin, *The Diary of Anaïs Nin, Volume II: 1934–1939* (New York: Harcourt, Brace & World, 1967), pp. 102–106, 140–45.

27. See, for example, Mary Daly, *Beyond God the Father: Toward a Philosophy of Women's Liberation* (Boston: Beacon Press, 1973) and *Religion and Sexism*, ed. Rosemary Ruether (New York: Simon & Schuster, 1974). For an earlier discussion of H.D.'s transformation of an androcentric heterodox tradition see my "Psyche Reborn: Tradition, Re-Vision, and the Goddess as Mother-Symbol in H.D.'s Epic Poetry," *Women's Studies*, 6, No. 2 (1979).

28. See, for example, de Rougemont, *Love in the Western World*, pp. 68–72; Ambelain, *Adam, dieu rouge*, pp. 198–205.

29. De Rougemont, *Love in the Western World*, pp. 116–18.

30. Gershom G. Scholem, *On the Kabbalah and Its Symbolism*, trans. Ralph Manheim (New York: Schocken, 1969), pp. 138–42. For Jewish-feminist critiques of Judaism, see Elizabeth Koltun, ed., *The Jewish Woman: New Perspectives* (New York: Schocken, 1976), and the journal *Lilith*.

31. H.D., *Asphodel*, p. 11.

32. H.D., *Pilate's Wife*, pp. 1–2. All further references to *Pilate's Wife* will be made within the text with the abbreviation *P.W.* H.D. compared *Pilate's Wife* to D.H. Lawrence's *The Man Who Died* when Stephen Guest told her that Lawrence used her as his model for Isis. She wrote that she liked the·Lawrence of this last novel, but the Lawrence of his other books (she mentioned specifically *Women in Love, Aaron's Rod, Fantasia*, and *Lady Chatterley's Lover*) was not the "*Man*" she had connected with in earlier years. She reflected that the Christ of *Pilate's Wife* was modeled somewhat after the Lawrence she had admired (*Compassionate Friendship*, pp. 45–54). For H.D.'s discussion of Lawrence, see *Tribute to Freud*, pp. 128, 131, 133–35, 139–42, 144, 149–50.

33. H.D., *The Mystery* (1951), unpublished historical novel at Beinecke.

34. H.D., "The Secret," (chapter 5), pp. 41, 44 of *The Gift*. H.D.'s footnotes to *The Gift* document her extensive reading in Moravian doctrine

and history. She also owned and marked several Moravian hymnals and liturgies. H.D. evaluated the Moravian Church partially on its treatment of women. Zinzendorf, she explained in her notes, was "an intimate friend of all carpenters, woodcutters, farmers, itinerant preachers, and all women" (p. 92).

35. For a complete reading of H.D.'s natal chart, see my "Mythology, Psychoanalysis and the Occult in the Late Poetry of H.D.," pp. 296–337. I am greatly indebted to Dr. Melinda Cummings for her generous assistance with my interpretation of what H.D. would have seen in her chart. In addition, I have relied largely on H.D.'s known astrology sources, especially the Adams and Muchery books.

36. Adams, *Astrology: Your Place in the Sun*, p. 60.

37. Adams, *Astrology: Your Place Among the Stars*, pp. 171–73. See also Muchery, *The Astrological Tarot*, trans. Marguerite Vallior (New York: Castle, n.d.), p. 56.

38. Ambelain, *Adam, dieu rouge*, pp. 189–90.

39. Adams, *Astrology: Your Place in the Sun*, pp. 104–13.

40. Ibid., p. 418. For Adams's descriptions of Jupiter and Uranus, see also pp. 338–39, 374–83, 418–42, 558–60, and *Astrology: Your Place in the Sun*, pp. 187–95. Counteracting the strong placement of Jupiter and Uranus in conjunction with Libra in H.D.'s chart was the less fortunate placement of Saturn in Cancer and Neptune in the House of Health. Muchery wrote that for people with Saturn in Cancer there is a "certain want of balance" (*The Astrological Tarot*, p. 109); Adams said that this placement leads to hypersensitivity and emotional vulnerability. H.D.'s Neptune in the sixth house (House of Health), Muchery wrote, would make her susceptible to illnesses, especially "peculiar ailments," which medical science "could not solve" (p. 128); Adams wrote that Neptune can cause nervous breakdown or hysteria. Since Virgo rules the "roots of the nervous system," "nervous disorders" in Virgo natives are not uncommon" (*Astrology: Your Place in the Sun*, p. 58).

41. H.D., *Compassionate Friendship*, p. 29.

42. In a letter to Jordan, H.D. wrote that she had "gone deep into the 1850 period in London, the pre-Raphaelites that is, the 'Victorian Romantics'" (9 January 1949). For William Morris, she had special associations. Pound had given her Morris' poems during their engagement (Hirslanden II, pp. 26–27), and her father had built bookcases and benches for her from Morris' designs (ibid.). Most importantly, H.D. regarded Morris an an ideal father-figure: "This 'William Morris' father might have sent me to an art school but the Professor of Astronomy and Mathematics insisted on my preparing for college" (ibid.).

43. Oswald Wirth, *Introduction à l'étude du tarot*, pp. 9 and 1–9. The translation is my own.

44. David Bakan, *Sigmund Freud and the Jewish Mystical Tradition* (1958; rpt. New York: Schocken, 1965).

45. Robert Ambelain in particular stressed this element of secrecy in all the esoteric traditions he discussed. His purpose was to give the reader the codes necessary to translate the complex and interlocking symbolism of a syncretist mystical tradition.

46. De Rougemont, *Love in the Western World*, pp. 26, 57.

47. Ibid., pp. 57 and 87–106.

48. See C.G. Jung, *Psychology and Religion* (1938; rpt. New York: Yale University Press, 1969), pp. 30–31; Jung, "Approaching the Unconscious," in *Man and His Symbols*, ed. Jung (New York: Dell, 1964), pp. 7–12, 30, 42.

49. H.D., *Compassionate Friendship*, p. 20.

50. Adams, *Astrology: Your Place Among the Stars*, p. 419.

51. Evangeline Adams, *The Bowl of Heaven* (New York: Dodd, Mead, 1926), p. 27.

52. Ibid., pp. 268–69.

53. See *E.T.T.*, pp. 11, 19, 23, 26, 33, 47, 50, 52. Pound also brought her volumes of Ibsen, Blake, Shaw, and Swedenborg (p. 23). See also Hirslanden II, p. 28, for a discussion of Pound, *Seraphita*, and Pound's introduction of Yogi philosophy.

54. Honoré de Balzac, *Seraphita*, trans. Katharine Prescott Wormeley (1889; rpt. Freeport, N.Y.: Books for Libraries Press, 1970), pp. 76–77.

55. Letter from H.D. to Jordan, 24 May 1929, and *The Sword Went Out to Sea*, p. 40.

56. Anaïs Nin, *The Diary of Anaïs Nin, Volume V: 1947–1955* (New York: Harcourt Brace Jovanovich, 1974), pp. 255–62.

57. Ambelain, *La Kabbale practique*, pp. 15–19. The translation is my own. See also another book owned by H.D., *Light on the Path and Karma* (1885; rpt. London: Theosophical Publishing House, 1920) by Mabel Collins, for a contrast between the "intuition" of the mystic with the "empirical measurement" of the scientist. The Tarot particularly relies upon a process of meditation and intuition. See an article H.D. read by Denis de Rougemont, "Presentation du tarot," *Hemispheres:: French-American Quarterly of Poetry*, 2 (Spring 1945), p. 36.

58. Harriette Augusta Curtiss and Frank Homer Curtiss, *The Key to the Universe* (New York: Dutton, 1919) and *Key to Destiny* (New York: Dutton, 1919); H.D. owned both books.

59. See H.D., "Narthex," for the most striking example of Bryher's associations with "intellect" and opposition to intuition and the occult, represented by both Venice and Macpherson. In her letter of 1 October 1971 to the author, Bryher denied any knowledge of H.D.'s collection of occult books or interest in the occult. Pearson told me that by 1971, Bryher also denied that any spiritualist séances occurred in her flat during the war. He explained that Bryher had either forgotten them or refused to admit that they happened, but he knew that the séances were in fact held at Lowndes Square and that Bryher was a part of the "circle."

60. H.D., "Dark Room" (chapter 1), p. 32 of *The Gift*.

61. Virginia Woolf, *A Room of One's Own* (1929; rpt. New York: Harcourt, Brace & World, 1957), p. 102.

7. "Companions of the Flame"

1. I have mentioned the twentieth-century mythmaking poets whose

work H.D. knew best. Some others who are part of this tradition are Hart Crane, Dylan Thomas, Wallace Stevens, Robert Graves, Robert Duncan, Anne Sexton, Charles Olson, and Gary Snyder. For some excellent critical discussions of mythmaking, see L.S. Dembo, *Conceptions of Reality in Modern American Poetry* (Berkeley: University of California Press, 1966), and Lillian Feder, *Ancient Myth in Modern Poetry* (Princeton: Princeton University Press, 1971).

2. T.S. Eliot, "Tradition and the Individual Talent," in *Selected Essays, 1917–1932* (New York: Harcourt Brace, 1932), p. 3.

3. Bernard Bergonzi, *T.S. Eliot* (New York: Collier, 1972), p. 64.

4. Many critiques of formalist criticism have often presumed the necessity for contextual criticism, but this presupposition is central to feminist criticism. For some discussion of this issue, see Annette Barnes, "Female Criticism: A Prologue," in *The Authority of Experience: Essays in Feminist Criticism,* ed. Arlyn Diamond and Lee R. Edwards (Amherst, Mass.: University of Massachusetts Press, 1977), pp. 1–15; *Feminist Criticism: Essays on Theory, Poetry, and Prose,* ed. Cheryl L. Brown and Karen Olson (Metuchen, N.J.: Scarecrow Press, 1978); Fraya Katz-Stoker, "The Other Criticism: Feminism vs. Formalism," in *Images of Women in Fiction,* ed. Susan Koppelman Cornillon (Bowling Green, Ohio: Bowling Green University Press, 1972), pp. 313–25.

5. See Florence Howe's analysis of Yeats's "Leda and the Swan" as reflective of a male, not universal, perspective on rape, in her *No More Masks! An Anthology of Poems by Women* (New York: Anchor, 1973), p. 15.

6. For an informative discussion of Williams's ties to Otto Weininger and his rebuttals to the feminist Dora Marsden in *The Egoist,* see *A Recognizable Image: William Carlos Williams on Art and Artists,* ed. Bram Dijkstra (New York: New Directions, 1978), pp. 45–46.

7. See, for example, Gershom G. Scholem, *On the Kabbalah and Its Symbolism,* trans. Ralph Manheim (New York: Schocken, 1969), p. 33; Robert Ambelain, *La Kabbale practique* (Paris: Éditions Niclaus, 1951), p. 15.

8. See, for example, Robert Ambelain, *Adam, dieu rouge* (Paris: Éditions Niclaus, 1941), pp. 80–100; Denis de Rougemont, *Love in the Western World,* trans. Montgomery Belgion (New York: Pantheon, 1956), pp. 67–68.

9. Ambelain, *Adam, dieu rouge,* pp. 75–76; the translation is my own.

10. See Susan Gubar's insightful analysis of female imagery in her valuable essay "The Echoing Spell of H.D.'s *Trilogy*," *Contemporary Literature,* 19, No. 2 (Spring 1978), 196–218. She argues that the "worm" image evokes the weaving and spinning characteristic of women's tasks while the shell imagery suggests not only Venus, but also female genitalia and pregnancy (pp. 201–205).

11. William Loftus Hare, *Mysticism of East and West* (London: J. Cape, 1923), p. 307. H.D. owned this book and thoroughly marked chapters 17–20 on Christian mysticism (pp. 302–52).

12. Ambelain, *Adam, dieu rouge,* p. 193.

13. Veronica, Pilate's wife, becomes convinced that Jesus is a follower of Zoroaster.

14. Ambelain based his claims on the work of two religious scholars, Drews and B. Smith (*Adam, dieu rouge*, pp. 69–75); Ambelain also drew parallels between Hermes and this "son of fire" worshipped by numerous middle eastern sects.

15. For other discussions of alchemy and modernist mythmaking, see my "Psyche Reborn: Tradition, Re-Vision, and the Goddess as Mother-Symbol in H.D.'s Epic Poetry," *Women's Studies*, 6, No. 2 (1979), 152–54 and " 'Re-Light the Flame': Alchemy as Modernist Mythmaking in H.D.'s *Trilogy*," paper delivered at MLA Special Session on Alchemy and Literature, December 1979.

16. In an otherwise groundbreaking discussion of the *Trilogy*, L.S. Dembo contrasted the "poet-devotée" of the *Trilogy* with the Eliot of *Four Quartets* and argued that "whereas Eliot seeks a Christian resolution, H.D. seeks one more generally aestheticistic," *Conceptions of Reality in Modern American Poetry*, p. 30. A more accurate contrast, I would argue, would stress Eliot's orthodox and H.D.'s heterodox leanings. Neither were "aestheticistic" poets; both were religious poets within a modernist framework.

17. Joseph L. Blau, "Magic and Kabbala," and Johannes Urzidil, "De la magie et de la science psychique chez Goethe," trans. Martin Jones, in *Hemispheres*, 2, No. 5 (Spring 1945), pp. 56, 23. Urzidil also related psychoanalysis to magic, mysticism, and poetry. H.D.'s copy of this special issue on magic and poetry is at Beinecke.

18. Dembo, *Conceptions of Reality in Modern American Poetry*, p. 4.

19. H.D.'s sources were Ambelain, *Adam, dieu rouge*, pp. 86–87, 106, 148–68, and Blau, "Magic and Kabbala," pp. 56–59.

20. See James Frazer, *The Golden Bough; a Study in Magic and Religion* (London: Macmillan, 1914), III, pp. 30–48. H.D. recorded the following in a red notebook now at Beinecke containing information culled from her reading: "*Sirius*—the brightest fixed star in sky—Isis or *Sirius. Sothis.*" The notebook is undated, but contains much material that H.D. adapted for *Helen in Egypt*.

21. Gershom G. Scholem, *On the Kabbalah and Its Symbolism*, pp. 7, 5–25.

8. "Born of One Mother"

1. Gillian Gollin, *Moravians in Two Worlds: A Study of Changing Communities* (New York: Columbia University Press, 1967), p. 11.

2. Adrienne Rich, "When We Dead Awaken: Writing as Re-Vision" (1971), reprinted in *Adrienne Rich's Poetry*, eds. Barbara Charlesworth Gelpi and Albert Gelpi (New York: Norton, 1975), pp. 90–91, 98.

3. Robert Ambelain, *Adam, dieu rouge*, pp. 127–28; the translation is my own. For a recent discussion of female divinity and feminism in Gnostic sects, see Elaine Pagels, "The Suppressed Gnostic Feminism," *New York Review of Books*, 26, No. 18 (22 November 1979), pp. 42–49.

4. For an earlier formulation of these ideas, see my "Psyche Reborn:

Tradition, Re-Vision, and the Goddess as Mother-Symbol in H.D.'s Epic Poetry," *Women's Studies*, 6, No. 2 (1979), 147–60. The Goddess in H.D.'s later poetry represents a significant shift from her aesthetic use of various goddesses as mythic masks in her imagist poetry to the theological function of the Goddess as an expression of divine spirit in her later poetry.

5. H.D. may have been familiar with many artistic portraits of Helen, but she certainly knew Edgar Allan Poe's "To Helen," quoted in *Tribute to Freud* (p. 97), and Yeats's "No Second Troy," "When Helen Lived," and "A Woman Homer Sung," in *The Collected Poems of W.B. Yeats* (New York: Macmillan, 1956), pp. 87–88, 89, 108.

6. See, for example, Nancy M. Henley, *Body Politics: Power, Sex, and Non-Verbal Communication* (Englewood Cliffs, N.J.: Prentice Hall, 1977), pp. 171–78.

7. Sigmund Freud, "Medusa's Head" (1922), in *S.E.*, XVIII, pp. 273–74.

8. For important exceptions to conventional portraits of Penelope, see James Joyce's *Ulysses* and H.D.'s "At Ithica" (*S.P.*, p. 49).

9. The manuscript of "Callypso Speaks" is at Beinecke, along with the other nine poems from the mid-thirties in the collection that H.D. entitled *The Dead Priestess Speaks*, but never published. In "Notes on Recent Writing," H.D. referred to these poems as "transitional," a necessary preparation for the *Trilogy* (pp. 60–61). H.D. published part of "Callypso Speaks" in *Poetry*, 52 (June 1938). What appears in *Selected Poems* is only one half of the entire poem in manuscript.

10. Rich, "When We Dead Awaken: Writing as Re-Vision," p. 91.

11. Ibid., p. 98.

12. See selections from the Church Fathers in *Not in God's Image*, eds. Julia O'Faolain and Lauro Martines (New York: Harper & Row, 1973), pp. 129–33.

13. For imagery and attributes of the Near Eastern goddesses, see Robert Graves, *The White Goddess* (1948; rpt. New York: Noonday, 1966), Erich Neumann, *The Great Mother* (New York: Pantheon, 1956), and Merlin Stone, *When God Was a Woman* (New York: Dial Press, 1976). This imagery appeared in the embroidery of the Cluny Unicorn tapestries which H.D. did during the war (letter to Jordan, 5 September 1947).

14. For discussions of the symbolic equation of woman with sexuality, mortality, and evil, see H.R. Hays, *The Dangerous Sex: The Myth of Feminine Evil* (New York: Putnam, 1964), and Eva Figes, *Patriarchal Attitudes* (New York: Fawcett, 1970).

15. H.D.'s etymology is supported by Robert Young's *Analytical Concordance to the Bible . . .* (New York: Funk & Wagnalls, 1955). H.D.'s source however was probably the Kabbalah. In Ambelain's *La Kabbale practique*, "marah," the Hebrew word for "bitter," is linked with the "Grand Mer" (p. 71). In her well-marked copy of Arthur Weigall's *The Paganism in Our Christianity* (London: Putnam, 1928), the comparativist argued further that when the cult of Mary supplanted worship of Isis and Aphrodite (associated with the Sea) and veneration of Artemis, Astarte, and Selene (associated with the Moon and/or Stars), Mary acquired the title "*Stella Maris*, Star of the Sea" (p. 132).

16. See L.S. Dembo, *Conceptions of Reality in Modern American*

Poetry (Berkeley: University of California Press, 1966), pp. 4–7 and throughout.

17. H.D. also departed from alchemical tradition in making her jewel wholly female instead of a symbolic representation of the marriage of king (sulphur) and queen (mercury).

18. The angels in John are unnamed, but esoteric tradition abounds with references to the "seven." H.D.'s "seven" appear to be her own combination since they do not match other lists of "seven" in her own or other source material. For a discussion that connects H.D.'s revision of John's Revelation with her book *The Hedgehog* (1936), see Susan Gubar's "The Echoing Spell of H.D.'s *Trilogy*," *Contemporary Literature*, 19, No. 2 (Spring 1978).

19. The process of cultural transformation must be repeated again in the final volume of the *Trilogy*. The "sinner" Mary Magdalene must be revealed through epiphany to represent not "unseemly" woman, but rather the human incarnation of the Goddess and the lost isle of Atlantis.

20. Hesiod, *Theogony* and *Works and Days* in *Collected Works* (Stuttgart: Carmina, recensuit, Aloisius Rzach, 1958).

21. Freud, *C.D.*, p. 69. See also Freud, *O.P.*, p. 20. H.D.'s use of the punning French opposites comes from Denis de Rougemont's *Love in the Western World*, trans. Montgomery Belgion (New York: Pantheon, 1956).

22. Freud, "Analysis Terminable and Interminable" (1937) in *T.T.*, p. 264.

23. Achilles' chance for world leadership represents a variant of Achilles mythology that is most probably H.D.'s own, one which emphasizes the contemporary reference of the poem.

24. Thomas Burnett Swann, *The Classical World of H.D.* (Lincoln: University of Nebraska Press, 1962), p. 177.

25. H.D.'s identification of the Sphinx as a masculine symbol and the Phoenix as a female resurrection symbol probably originates in Graves's *The White Goddess* (pp. 190, 413, 417). She took extensive notes on this book as well as other sources for the epic. Her notebook is at Beinecke.

26. Linda Welshimer Wagner, "Helen in Egypt: A Culmination," *Contemporary Literature*, 10, No. 4 (Autumn 1969), 527–30.

27. J.J. Bachofen, *Myths, Religion and Mother Right*, trans. Ralph Manheim (Princeton: Princeton University Press, 1967); this and the following quotations come from pp. 79–80, 86–87, 89, 91, 107. In "H.D.'s *Helen in Egypt*: A Recollection" (Ph.D. diss., Univ. of California-Santa Cruz, 1973), Janice Robinson argued, mistakenly I believe, that the epic represents H.D.'s realization "that the matriarchal state in her own mind must be put to an end" (pp. 87–88).

28. Graves, *The White Goddess*, p. 70, and H.D.'s notebook for *Helen in Egypt*, p. 15. For a prior discussion of Graves and the Goddess in H.D.'s epic, see my "Creating a Woman's Mythology: H.D.'s *Helen in Egypt*," *Women's Studies*, 5, No. 2 (1977), 163–98.

29. For different but illuminating analyses of the changing forms of Helen, see Rachel Blau DuPlessis' "Romantic Thralldom in H.D.," *Contemporary Literature*, 20, No. 2 (Summer 1979), and L.M. Freibert's "From

Semblance to Selfhood: The Evolution of Woman in H.D.'s Neo-Epic *Helen in Egypt*," *Arizona Quarterly*, in press, and "Conflict and Creativity in the World of H.D.," *Journal of Women's Studies and Literature*, 1, No. 3 (Summer 1979), 258–71.

30. Freud, "Femininity," in *N.I.L.*, p. 132.
31. Bachofen, *Myths, Religion and Mother Right*, pp. 109–10.
32. Neumann, *The Great Mother*, p. 168.

9. Poetics of Conflict and Transcendence

1. For some examples of repeated negatives, see "Adonis," "Never More Will the Wind," "Heat," "Orchard," "Pear Tree," "Lethe," "O Love Cease," and the translation of Sappho's Fragment 113 in H.D.'s *Selected Poems*. I am indebted to Suzanne Juhasz for bringing this stylistic pattern to my attention. For some poems centered on thematic opposition, see "The Helmsman," "Sea Rose," "Oread," "The Islands," "Helen," "Callypso Speaks," and "The Moon in Your Hands."

2. H.D., "Dark Room" (chapter 1), p. 32 in *The Gift*.

3. Robert Ambelain, *Adam, dieu rouge* (Paris: Éditions Niclaus, 1941), pp. 135, 85, 147–48, 173–74. All translations of Ambelain are my own. For useful discussions of androgyny in esoteric sects, see Wayne A. Meeks, "The Image of the Androgyne: Some Uses of a Symbol in Earliest Christianity," *History of Religions*, 13, No. 2 (February 1973), 165–208; Marilyn R. Farwell, "Virginia Woolf and Androgyny," *Contemporary Literature*, 16, No. 4 (Autumn 1975), 433–51; Mircea Eliade, *The Two and the One*, trans. J.M. Cohen (Chicago: University of Chicago Press, 1962).

4. Rodney Collin, *The Theory of Celestial Influence* (London: V. Stuart, 1954), p. xi. H.D. owned and marked this book.

5. Robert Ambelain, *La Kabbale practique* (Paris: Éditions Niclaus, 1951). H.D.'s immersion in the Kabbalah does not represent a conversion to Judaism even though the Kabbalah is overwhelmingly Jewish in origin and evolution. To my knowledge, H.D. did not read basic Kabbalistic texts such as the Zohar. What she learned came primarily through the syncretist filter of Ambelain. Although Ambelain's syncretist Kabbalah is uncharacteristic of most commentaries, his presentation of doctrine is basically consistent with what the leading Jewish authority on the Kabbalah, Gershom G. Scholem, has written.

6. Ambelain, *La Kabbale practique*, pp. 48–51, 68–69. Subsequent descriptions also come from the same book, pp. 15–109.

7. Ambelain, *La Kabbale practique*, p. 43; Gershom G. Scholem, *On the Kabbalah and Its Symbolism*, trans. Ralph Manheim (New York: Schocken, 1965), p. 103.

8. Ambelain, *La Kabbale practique*, pp. 58–61. In his *Kabbalah and Criticism* (New York: Seabury Press, 1975), Harold Bloom expanded even further on the significance of letters in the Kabbalah. He called it a "theory of rhetoric" and said that its "emphasis upon *interpretation* is finally what distinguishes Kabbalah from nearly every other variety of mysticism or theosophy, East or West" (pp. 18, 33). The emphasis on interpretation also

characterizes Freud's psychoanalysis, a similarity that no doubt greatly aided H.D.'s synthesis of the two traditions.

9. Robert Ambelain, *Adam, dieu rouge*, p. 174.

10. For the story of Set, Osiris, and Isis, H.D. followed her Egyptian sources closely—particularly E.A. Wallis Budge, *Egyptian Religion* (London: K. Paul, Trench, Trübner, 1908). H.D. owned and marked many of Budge's books on Egypt but her emphasis on dialectical patterns in Egyptian and Greek mythology is her own.

11. While H.D.'s story of Achilles' transformation is fully consistent with her adaptations of Freud's theory of bisexuality, her portrait of Achilles' quest has distinctly Jungian overtones. The "eidolon" is an "anima" image based on an important woman in Achilles' childhood.

12. H.D.'s notebook for *Helen in Egypt* includes a section on multiple associations linking the Grail, crystals, prisms, sacred vessels and boxes, the Phoenix egg, and the story of Psyche.

13. See ch. 8, n. 29 for references to other readings of "Leuké" and "Eidolon." My reading appeared in abbreviated form in "Creating a Woman's Mythology: H.D.'s *Helen in Egypt*," *Women's Studies*, 5, No. 2 (1977), 163–98.

14. The Child as a symbol of androgyny appeared elsewhere in H.D.'s writings. In *End to Torment* for example, the child she and Pound might have had becomes the Child or the perfect Seraphita-Seraphitus image, the "Being, he-her" who embodies the "perfection of the fiery moment" (pp. 11, 19, 23, 26, 33, 47, 50). See also "The Guest" (1946), H.D.'s short story set in Elizabethan times about "Hamnet and Judith twins, who are each other and are androgynous" (p. 8), at Beinecke. The patron of H.D.'s horoscope, Hermes, frequently appears as bisexual in mythology, and H.D. noted in her notebook for *Helen in Egypt* that Minerva was sometimes "male and female."

15. Even though "L'Amour" and "La Mort" are de Rougemont's terms, the dialectical interplay and fusion of L'Amour and La Mort are H.D.'s own. De Rougemont made a distinction between two kinds of love, *agape* and *eros*, a separation that H.D. never made. Eros, he believed, was the "passion" that contained a desire for death at the heart of mystical tradition.

16. A copy of *Helen in Egypt* at Beinecke contains a handwritten note [Pearson?] next to this passage stating that it was read at her memorial service.

Index

Aaron: rod of, 76, 217
Achilles, 60–67, 154, 255–269 *passim*,
273, 286–295 *passim*; Dowding as,
187, 260
Adam, 111, 172, 215
Adams, Evangeline, astrologer: books
of, read by H.D., 167, 170, 184,
185, 186, 192–193
"Advent" (H.D.), reflections on Freud,
39, 122, 134, 139. *See also*
Tribute to Freud
Agamemnon, 256, 261–262, 265, 288
Alcott, Louisa May, 138
Aldington, Richard, husband of H.D.,
1, 5, 6, 34, 36, 37, 143, 147–148,
187; affair with Dorothy Yorke, 3,
27, 29; dissolution of marriage,
3, 5, 31, 38, 39, 197, 243
Ambelain, Robert, 172, 214, 215, 219,
221, 222; on astrology, 185; on the
Kabbalah, 175, 176, 177 (ill.), 196,
279–286; on the male and the
female principle, 231–232, 270,
275–276; on mysticism, 173;
mentioned, 180, 192
Amen, 278, 286; temple of, 60, 254,
277
"Analysis Terminable and Interminable" (Freud), 257
Anne, Saint, 148, 172
Aphrodite, 181, 182, 248, 249; and
Helen in Egypt, 254, 255, 256, 258,
264, 268, 269, 288, 291, 292
Apollo, 76; and *Helen in Egypt*,
261–262, 289
Apuleius: and the myth of Psyche, 9
Artemis, 41, 258, 261–262
Asklepios: Caduceus and, 76; Freud
compared with, 26; mentioned, 215
Asphodel (H.D.), unpublished novel,
39, 44–46, 67; H.D.'s mother in,

139; on women and religion, 179–
180
Astarte, 248, 249, 250, 258
Astrology, 161, 166–170, 175, 184–
186, 192
Athena, 149, 181. *See also* Pallas
Athene
"Autobiographical Notes" (H.D.), 160
Autobiographical Study (Freud), 116

Bachofen, J.J.: on primeval matriar-
chy, 11, 145, 266–267, 270
Bakan, David: on Freud and Jewish
mysticism, 190
Balzac, Honoré de: *Seraphita* of,
H.D. reads, 193–194
Beckett, Samuel, 105
Beowulf, 10
Bergonzi, Bernard: on T.S. Eliot, 209
Bergson, Henri: and imagism, 1, 279
Beyond the Pleasure Principle (Freud),
120
Bhaduri, Arthur, psychic medium:
H.D. hears, 173–174, 186–187
Bid Me to Live (A Madrigal)
(H.D.), 3, 29, 31, 36, 38; and
Asphodel, 44; reviewed by Durand,
146
Blau, Joseph: on magic, 223
Blau du Plessis, Rachel: on *Her*,
41; on "romantic thralldom," 144
Blavatsky, Madame, 160
Bloom, Harold: on the anxiety of
influence, 12, 150
Boss, Medard, existential
psychoanalyst, 20
Bridge, The (Crane), 5, 11, 75
Brown, Norman O.: and Freud, 14,
119
Brown, Rita Mae: *Rubyfruit Jungle*
of, 141

Browning, Robert, 199; "My Last Duchess" of, 241

Bryher, pseudonym of Winifred Ellerman, lifelong friend of H.D.: *Development* of, 35–36; early life, 5–6; and H.D.'s interest in the occult, 201–202; interest in psychoanalylsis, 18, 19–20, 22, 67, 160; letters of, to H.D., 18, 19–20; letters of H.D. to, 30, 31, 46–47, 121, 131–132, 166–167; meets Bhaduri, 173; poems about, 5, 45; "refugee work," 176; relationship with H.D., 27, 38–39, 44, 132, 134; sexual duality of, 35–37, 43; travels with H.D., 131–132; *Two Selves* of, 35, 43, 129

Bunyan, John, 24

By Avon River (H.D.), 8, 197

"Callypso Speaks" (H.D.), 232, 236–243, 245, 271, 273

Cantos, The (Pound), 4, 5, 8, 10, 59, 64, 75, 208; and H.D., 148, 260; as "neo-epic," 67; and the rectification of the language, 243, 248–249

Cassandra: H.D. as, 187; and *Helen in Egypt*, 260–261, 265

Castle, The (Kafka), 105

Chaboseau, Jean: and hermeticism, 171–172, 175, 192, 214, 221

Chadwick, Mary, psychoanalyst: H.D.'s sessions with, 18, 19

Christ, 77, 244; Psyche compared with, 157. *See also* Jesus

Civilization and Its Discontents (Freud), 94–95; on art and religion, 71–72, 92–93; on Eros and Death, 256–257

Close-Up, film journal: H.D. writes for, 6, 18

Clytaemnestra, 83, 256, 261, 262, 263, 265, 288, 289

Coleridge, Samuel Taylor, 205

Collected Poems (H.D.), 7

Collin, Rodney: on celestial influence, 276

Compassionate Friendship (H.D.), unpublished memoir: Dowding in, 187–188; Freud in, 143, 158; Heydt in, 20

Copernicus: Freud compared with, 24

Cournos, John: his contempt for H.D., 115

Crane, Hart: *The Bridge* of, 5, 11, 75

Crow, W.B., 81; on religion, 171, 214

Curie, Marie, 26, 33, 200

Cybele, 148, 172

Darwin, Charles: Freud compared with, 24, 88

Davidson, Gustav: *Dictionary of Angels* of, 175

De Rougemont, Denis: *Love in the Western World* of, 101–102, 116, 170–171, 191, 214, 221, 222, 223, 256, 275–276

Dead Priestess Speaks, The (H.D.), unfinished collection of poems, 7

Dembo, L.S.: on H.D.'s use of Greek myth, 58–59, on the modernist view of language, 223; on "neo-epic" form, 67

Demeter, 10, 231; H.D.'s mother as, 139, 141, 142, 144

Development (Bryher); on the roles of the sexes, 35–36

Dobson, Molly: and H.D.'s horoscope, 166

Dobson, Silvia: and H.D.'s horoscope, 166

Doolittle, Charles Leander, father of H.D., astronomer, director of the Flower Observatory, 1, 140; ambitions for H.D., 26, 27, 33, 48, 200; death, 3, 27; H.D.'s feelings about, 73, 120, 131, 132, 133, 137–138, 141–146 *passim*, 186, 187, 188, 205–206; and H.D.'s interest in astrology, 161, 166–167; his sympathy with feminists, 33; mentioned, 157

Doolittle, Eric, half-brother of H.D., astronomer, 138; shares H.D.'s literary interests, 1

Doolittle, Gilbert, older brother of H.D., 26, 48, 141, 144, 148; death of, 3, 27, 29–30

Doolittle, Helen Wolle, mother of H.D., 1, 74, 110, 231; artistic talent of, 120, 137–140, 188, 205; described by William Carlos Williams, 140; favors son Gilbert over H.D., 26, 48, 173, 183; H.D.'s feelings about, 74, 131–135, 137–146, 148, 152–153; and the myth of Helen, 83, 140; mentioned, 157. *See also* Demeter

Dowding, Lord Hugh, lecturer on the occult, 173–175, 187, 188, 200–201; Achilles as, 260; *Many Mansions* of, 174; rejection of H.D., 27–28, 30, 37, 175, 197

"Dreams and Occultism" (Freud), 89

Duncan, Robert: "H.D. book" of, 8, 58, 99

Durand, Lionel, Haitian journalist, lover of H.D., 146–151; his review of *Bid Me to Live*, 146, 273

"Eidolon" (H.D.), third part of *Helen in Egypt*, 60, 61, 65, 254, 268–269, 292, 296

Eliade, Mircea: on myth as sacred history, 111

Eliot, George: *The Mill on the Floss* of, 48, 141

Eliot, T.S., 2, 10, 178, 208–210, 221, 223, 226, 228; *The Four Quartets* of, 4, 75, 209; H.D. reads works of, 67; "Prufrock" of, 3, 11; *The Waste Land* of, 75

Ellerman, Sir John, father, of Bryher, 5

Ellis, Havelock, 129, 266

Empedocles: Freud compared with, 257

End to Torment (H.D.), memoir of her relationship with Pound, 8, 27, 37, 38, 193; Heydt in, 21

Euphorion, child of Helen and Achilles, 61, 67, 268, 294

Euripides: *Helen* of, 60, 255; *Ion* of, translated by H.D., 7

Evans, Sir Arthur: at Knossos, 159

Eve, 111, 246; daughters of, 245, 271; and Helen, 255, 288–289; punished for seeking knowledge, 172, 215

Farnell, Lewis Richard: *Cults of the Greek States* of, 161

Fields, Kenneth: his introduction to *Tribute to Freud*, 68

Flowering of the Rod, The (H.D.), third volume of *Trilogy*, 78, 113–115, 274–275

Four Quartets, The (Eliot), 4, 75; as "neo-epic," 67

Frazer, Sir James, 111, 208, 225

Freud, Anna, 18

Freud, Sigmund: analysis of H.D., 9–14, 17–154 *passim*, 166, 176, 178, 182, 184, 188–190, 192, 194, 196, 204–206, 212, 223, 226, 247, 275; 279; on art and religion, 70–72, 88, 92–93, 97, 115, 119–120, 153, 222; on bisexuality and homosexuality, 128–130, 133–134; on civilization, 69, 79–80, 91–92, 212, 231, 247; correspondence with H.D., 7, 20; on dreams, 22, 23, 53–54, 66–67, 70–71, 77, 79, 80, 88, 89, 91, 92, 94, 189, 191, 212; empiricism of, 13, 88–89, 97, 108, 116; on Eros and death, 256–257, 270, 274, 278, 288; and H.D.'s interest in the occult, 157, 166–167, 188–196, 205–206; horoscope of, 166; as Janus, 51; materialism of, 13, 100, 115, 117, 119, 120, 126, 130, 136, 193; on matriarchy, 266; on the sexes, 13, 31–33, 49, 121–154 *passim*; as Theseus, 20, 66, 154, 295; works of, "Analysis Terminable and Interminable," 257, *Autobiographical Study*, 116, *Beyond the Pleasure Principle*, 120, *Civilization and Its Discontents*, 71–72, 92–93, 94–95, 256–257, "Dreams and Occultism," 89, *The Future of an Illusion*, 72, 92–93, 153, *A General Introduction to Psychoanalysis*, 52–53, 71, 94, *The Interpretation of Dreams*, 22, 52–53, 189, *Jokes and Their Relation to the Unconscious*, 189, *Moses and Monotheism*, 120, *New Introductory Lectures on Psychoanalysis*, 127–128, "The Psychogenesis of a Case of Homosexuality in a Woman," 124, 133, *The Psychopathology of Everyday Life*, 189, "The Relation of the Poet to Daydreaming," 71, "Some Psychical Consequences of the Anatomical Distinction Between the Sexes," 130, *Therapy and Technique*, 54, *Totem and Taboo*, 83. See also *Tribute to Freud, A*

Future of an Illusion, The (Freud), 72, 92–93, 153

Gabriel, 252, 253

General Introduction to Psychoanalysis, A (Freud), 52–53, 71, 94

Gift, The (H.D.), unpublished autobiographical novel, 8, 25, 153, 203, 275; on H.D.'s mother, 138, 139, 141, 145, 148; on H.D.'s grandmother, 183

Goethe, Johann Wolfgang von: "Kennst du das Land" of, 23–24, 25, 88

Graves, Robert: *The White Goddess* of, 269, 270

Gregg, Frances Josepha, friend of H.D., 1, 6, 38–39, 44, 45, 134; and *Her*, 40, 42, 43, 44, 180, 201; interest in the occult, 159, 160, 180, 201; interest in psychoanalysis, 17

"Grove of Academe" (H.D.), Volume two of *Hermetic Definition*, 146, 150

H.D. (Hilda Doolittle), 1–3, 25–28, 38–39, 110, 120, 137–138, 140–141, 183–184, 211; acts in films, 6; breakdowns, 20, 26–31, 175, 176; correspondence, 6, 7, 18, 19, 20, 30, 37, 46–47, 67, 121, 131–132, 137, 160–167, 170, 173, 174, 175, 182, 184–185, 192, 197, 199, 200, 201, 202, 203, 218, 249; daughter, 5, 27, 39, 134, 166; death of child, 20–21, 27, 29; disagreements with Freud, 12–14, 87–88, 97–100, 107, 108, 112–113, 115–154 *passim*; engagement to Pound, 1, 2, 6, 20–21, 37, 38, 40–41, 43, 143, 147–148, 187, 197, 201; horoscope of, 166, 167–170, 184–186, 192–193; marriage to Aldington, dissolution of marriage, 1, 3, 5, 6, 27, 29, 31, 34, 36, 37, 38, 39, 187, 197, 243; psychoanalyzed by Freud, 9–14, 17–154 *passim*, 157–159, 166, 176, 178, 182, 184, 188–190, 192, 194, 196, 197, 204–206, 223, 226, 247, 275, 279; sexuality of, 38–47 *passim*, 58, 180; travels with Bryher, 5–6, 131–132; visions at Corfu, 73–74, 100, 131, 132, 157, 159, 160, 166, 184, 186, 195, 203, 204; and war, 7–8, 20, 22–23, 27–30, 66, 102–105, 112, 139, 170, 176, 178, 187, 197, 207–215, 220–221, 259–262, 265–266, 277–278, 286–295; works of, "Advent," 39, 122, 134, 139, *Asphodel*, 39, 44–46, 67, 139, 179–180, "Autobiographical Notes," 160, *Bid Me to Live (A Madrigal)*, 3, 29, 31, 36, 38, 44, 146, *By Avon River*, 8, 197, "Callypso Speaks," 232, 236–243, 244, 245, 271, 273, *Collected Poems*, 7, *Compassionate Friendship*, 20, 143, 158, 187–188, *The Dead Priestess Speaks*, 7, "Eidolon," 60, 61, 65–66, 254, 268–269, 292–296, Euripides' *Ion*, translation of, 7; *The Flowering of the Rod*, 8, 78, 113–115, 274–275, *The Gift*, 8, 25, 138, 139, 141, 145, 148, 153, 183, 203, 275, "Heat," 2, *Hedylus*, 6, 67, "Helen," 232–236, 240–245, 271, *Helen in Egypt*, 8, 20, 21, 59–67, 76, 79, 83, 84, 109, 144, 146, 154, 187, 197, 229–230, 232, 243, 253–272, 273, 277, 278, 286–296, *Heliodora*, 7, *Her*, 9–10, 39–43, 44, 45, 46, 138, 139, 141, 147, 159, 179–180, 201, *Hermetic Definition*, 8, 37, 145–151, 230, 279, *Hippolytus Temporizes*, 7, *Hirslanden Notebooks*, 25–26, 26–27, 28, 144, 153, 173, 187–188, 197, 200, *Hymen*, 7, "Leuké," 60, 61, 65, 254, 255, 268, 269, 292, 293, *Magic Mirror*, 21, 29, 33, 187–188, 197, "The Master," 47, 121, "Moose Island," 6, *The Mystery*, 183, 187, "Narthex," 6, 30, 160, "Oread," 2, 56–59, 82, 98–99, *Paint It Today*, 39, 67, *Palimpsest*, 5, 6, 29, 30, 36, 38, 46, 67, 138; "Palinode," 60, 62, 65, 143, 254–256, 259, 264, 267, 269, 292, *Pilate's Wife*, 6, 180–192, 219, 231, "Red Rose and a Beggar," 146, 149, 150, *Red Roses for Bronze*, 7, 147, 243, "Rosemary in Avon," 4, *Sagesse*, 8, 21, 143, 146, 175–176, 228, 277, 278, *Sea Garden*, 2, 7, *Selected Poems of H.D.*, 56, "Star of Day," 146, 150, "The Suffragette," 33–34, *The Sword Went Out to Sea*, 28, 173, 174, 175, 178, 186–187, 199–200, 205, "Thorn Thicket," 187–188, *Tribute to Freud*, 7, 8, 9–11, 12, 14, 17, 20, 21, 22, 23, 24, 25, 26, 28, 29, 30, 31, 33, 37, 39, 46, 47, 48, 50, 51, 52, 53, 67, 68, 70, 73, 74, 75, 131, 132, 133, 134, 137, 138, 139, 140, 141, 153, 157, 158, 159, 160, 171, 175, 178, 185, 194, 195, 198, 199, 203–205, 256, 275, *Tribute to the Angels*, 8, 77, 219, 229, 232, 245, 246, 249, *Trilogy*, 8, 10, 29, 47, 75–78, 88, 98, 101–114 *passim*, 138, 143, 146, 153, 202, 266, 269, 273, 274, 276, 278, 284, 293, 294, *Vale Ave*, 45, 109, 111, 143–144, 187, 230, *The Walls Do Not Fall*, 8, 76–77, 104–105, 213, 215–221, *White Rose and the Red*, 187, *Winter Love*, 8, 144, 273, "Writing on the Wall," 120

Hall, Radclyffe: *Well of Loneliness* of, 44, 129

Harrison, Jane, 208, 266

Hart, Bernard, psychologist: and
Pound, 56, 98
Hathor, Egyptian deity, 217, 223
"Heat" (H.D.): and H.D.'s imagism, 2
Hedylus (H.D.): interior monologue
and, 6, 67
Helen, 60–67, 69, 79, 83, 144, 154, 187,
229–230, 233–235, 238, 253–272
passim, 273, 277, 286–296. *See also*
"Helen," *Helen in Egypt*, and
Winter Love
"Helen" (H.D.), 232–236, 240–245,
271
Helen in Egypt (H.D.), 8, 59–67, 76,
79, 83, 84, 109, 154, 187, 197, 243,
253–272, 273, 277, 278, 286–296; and
Dowding, 187; Freud as Theseus
in, 20, 66, 154, 295; Heydt as Paris
in, 21; mentioned, 45, 144, 146,
229–230, 232
Heliodora (H.D.), 7
Her (H.D.), unpublished autobiographical novel, 9–10, 39–43, 44,
45, 46, 138, 139, 141, 147, 159, 179–
180, 201
Hercules, 10, 68
Hermes, 185, 207, 217, 219–220, 223,
249; Trismegistus, 193, 247, 250
Hermetic Definition (H.D.), 8, 37,
145–151, 230, 279
Hermione, child of Helen, 62–64, 66
Hesiod: Pandora of, 246, 255
Hesperides, Paradise of the, 113–114
Heydt, Erich, psychoanalyst, 20–21,
175, 188
hieroglyphs, 50–69 *passim*, 98, 110,
117, 145, 154, 161, 191, 225–226, 251
Hippolytus Temporizes (H.D.), verse
drama, 7
Hirslanden Notebooks (H.D.), unpub-
lished journals, 25–26, 26–27, 28,
144, 153, 188, 197, 200; on
Bhaduri, 173; on Dowding, 187–188
Hitler, Adolf, 22, 93, 170, 176, 259
Holland, Norman: on H.D. and
Freud, 24–25, 47–49
Horney, Karen, 127, 153
Horus, Egyptian deity, 87
Hulme, T.E.: and imagism, 1
Huxley, Aldous, editor of D.H. Law-
rence's correspondence, 30
Hymen (H.D.), 7

Ibsen, Henrik, 210, 254
imagism, 1–5, 8, 10, 98, 107; and
H.D.'s early success, 1–3, 6, 7; and

Helen in Egypt, 61, 63, 257–258; and
psychoanalysis, 55–56, 59
Interpretation of Dreams, The (Freud),
22, 52–53, 189
Iphigenia, 261, 262, 263, 288
Ishtar, 244, 258
Isis, 10, 61–62, 83, 143, 147–150, 172,
180, 181, 224–225, 229, 230, 232,
244, 249, 256, 257, 264, 275, 278, 286,
287, 291, 292, 294

Jacob, ladder of: in Corfu visions, 73
James, Henry, 68
Janus, Roman guardian of doorways:
Freud compared with, 51, 83; reali-
ty compared with, 188–189
Jason, 10
Jehovah: as jealous god, 172, 215, 217
Jeremiah: Freud compared with, 118
Jesus, 19, 78, 249, 252, 253; cult of,
in *Pilate's Wife*, 180, 181–182, 231,
252, 253; name of, 219
Joan, Saint: in *Her* and *Asphodel*,
180, 235
John, Saint: *Gospel* of, 281, 284;
Revelation to, 106, 220–221, 244,
246, 247, 252–253
*Jokes and Their Relation to the
Unconscious* (Freud), 189
Jones, Ernest, biographer of Freud,
32–33, 50, 84, 88, 116
Jordan, Viola, friend and correspon-
dent of H.D., 6, 7, 19, 102–103, 137;
interest in the occult, 160–167, 173,
174, 182, 184–185, 192, 197, 199,
200–201, 202, 203, 218, 249
Joseph: and Freud, 24, 84
Joyce, James, 3, 34, 67, 198, 210, 236;
extends novel form, 4–5
Juhasz, Suzanne: on women poets,
36, 38
Jung, C.G.: and mysticism, 191–192,
270

Kabbalah, 12, 176–177 (ill.), 188, 224,
282–283 (ill.); and Ambelain, 175;
De Rougemont on, 171; and Freud,
190; myth of creation in, 279–286,
287, 290, 292
Kafka, Franz: *The Castle* of, 105
Keats, John, 199

Lancelot, 10
Lawrence, D.H., 132, 166, 198;
friendship with H.D., 3, 31, 36,
37; letters of, H.D. reads, 30; and

Pilate's Wife, 6; travels of, 4

Leach, Edmund: on Lévi-Strauss, 111

"Leuké" (H.D.), second part of *Helen in Egypt*, 60, 61, 65, 254, 255, 268, 269, 292, 293

Lilith, 111, 112, 143–144, 215, 230

Lowell, Amy, 2; "The Sisters" of, 35, 36, 43

Love in the Western World (De Rougemont), 101–102, 116, 170–171, 191, 214, 221, 222, 223, 256, 275–276

Lucifer, 111, 112, 143–144, 185, 215, 285

McAlmon, Robert, husband of Bryher, 5

Macpherson, Kenneth, friend and correspondent of H.D., 6, 18, 19, 37; married to Bryher, 5; and the occult, 160

Magic Mirror (H.D.), 197; Aldington in, 29; Dowding in, 187–188; and father's ambitions for H.D., 33; Heydt in, 21

Malinowski, Bronislaw, 111

Mammalie, H.D.'s grandmother: and H.D.'s psychic gifts, 183

Man Who Died, The (Lawrence), 6

Marcuse, Herbert, 14, 119

Marsden, Dora, British feminist: H.D.'s acquaintance with, 34, 35

Mary Magdalene, 78, 108, 273

Mary, 145, 148, 179, 247, 252–253, 271

"Master, The" (H.D.), poem about Freud, 47, 121

Medusa: and Helen, 235

Menelaus, husband of Helen, 60, 63–64, 262; and Proteus, 109

Mercury, 249; in Corfu visions, 73; Freud compared with, 24

Michelangelo: *Moses* of, 120

Mill, Harriet Taylor, 32

Mill, John Stuart, 32

Mitchell, Juliet: on Freud, 126–127

Mithra: cult of, in *Pilate's Wife*, 181–182

Moore, Merrill, 24

"Moose Island" (H.D.): interior monologue and , 6

Morris, William, 187; table made by, 173, 174

Moses, 73, 74, 76, 179, 219, 232, 247; Freud compared with, 24; H.D. compared with, 48, 185

Moses and Monotheism (Freud), 120

Mystery, The (H.D.), unpublished novel, 183, 187

"Narthex" (H.D.): interior monologue and, 6, 30, 160

New Introductory Lectures on Psychoanalysis (Freud), on feminity, 127–128

Newton, Isaac: Freud compared with, 24

Odysseus: in "Callypso Speaks," 236–243; in *Helen in Egypt*, 259, 273

Oedipus, 84; complex, 12, 123, 124, 125, 133, 135, 139

"Oread" (H.D.): and H.D.'s imagism, 2, 98–99; and psychoanalytic technique, 56–59, 82

Osiris, 83, 143, 224–225, 232, 256, 257, 286, 287, 288

Paint It Today (H.D.), unpublished novel, 39, 67

Palimpsest, 29, 30, 36, 38, 67, 138; dedicated to Bryher, 5; Freud reads, 46; interior monologue in, 6

Pallas Athene, 81–82. *See also* Athena

"Pallinode" (H.D.), first part of *Helen in Egypt*, 60, 62, 65, 143, 254–256, 259, 264, 267, 269, 292

Pandora, 238, 240, 246, 255

Paris, 61, 62–63, 65–66, 154; Durand as, 147–151, 255, 256, 267–269, 289; Heydt as, 21

Paterson (Williams), 4, 5, 10, 11, 75, 208, 209; as "neo-epic," 67, 201

Pearson, Norman Holmes, literary executor of H.D., 7, 11, 33, 85; compares H.D. with Stevens, 67; on H.D.'s use of Greek myth, 58

Percival, 10

Perse, St.-John: poetry of, 148–151, 273, 279

Persephone, daughter of Demeter: H.D. as, 139, 141, 142, 268, 269, 292

Perseus, 10; Freud compared with, 24; H.D. compared with, 25; and St.-John Perse, 149, 151

Pilate's Wife (H.D.), unpublished historical novel, 180–182, 219, 231; and D.H. Lawrence, 6

Plath, Sylvia, 242

Plato, 106, 107, 110, 280
Poe, Edgar Allan: *Helen* of, 233–235; tales of, 41
Pondrom, Cyrena, 99, 107
Pound, Ezra: *The Cantos* of, 4, 5, 8, 10, 59, 64, 67, 75, 148, 208, 243, 248–249, 260; engaged to H.D., 1, 2, 6, 20–21, 27, 37, 38, 143, 147–148, 187, 197; horoscope of, 166; and imagism, 56, 59, 98; and *Her*, 40–41, 43, 201; and language, 223, 243, 248–249; and politics, 34, 176, 208; mentioned, 193, 196, 210
Prometheus, 160, 215
Proteus, 109, 269, 288
Proust, Marcel, 68
Psyche: as persona of H.D., 9–11, 12, 13, 17, 25, 59, 79, 101, 115, 144, 145, 157, 214, 224, 228, 229, 232, 271, 295
"Psychogenesis of a Case of Homosexuality in a Woman, The" (Freud), 124, 133
Psychopathology of Everyday Life, The (Freud), 189

"Red Rose and a Beggar" (H.D.), Part One of *Hermetic Definition*, 149, 150
Red Roses for Bronze (H.D.) 7, 147, 243
"Relation of the Poet to Daydreaming, The" (Freud), 71
Rich, Adrienne, 230, 242, 243, 246
Richardson, Dorothy: *Pilgrimage* of, 6, 67
Riddel, Joseph: on H.D. and Freud, 24–25, 48–49; on H.D.'s "patterns," 110; on H.D.'s reading of Corfu visions, 83
Rieff, Philip: on Freud, 55, 71, 93, 96
Roheim, Geza, Freudian anthropologist, 84, 119
Rolland, Romain: Freud on, 72
"Rosemary in Avon" (H.D.), 4

Sachs, Hanns, psychoanalyst: sees Bryher, H.D., 18, 19, 31
Sagesse, 8, 146, 175–176, 228, 277, 278; H.D.'s parents in, 143; Heydt in, 21
Sappho, 10, 44
Schaffner, Perdita, daughter of H.D., 5, 27, 39, 166; Freud's friendship with, 134

Schmideberg, Walter, psychoanalyst, 20, 187
Scholem, Gershom G.: on Jewish mysticism, 226–228, 271–272, 280
Sea Garden (H.D.), 2, 7
Selected Poems of H.D., 56
Seraphita (Balzac), 193–194
Set, Egyptian deity, 83, 287–288
Sexton, Anne, 242
Shakespeare, William: Freud compared with, 118; *Winter's Tale* of, 40
Shaw, George Bernard: *Heartbreak House* of, 2, 37
Shelley, Percy Bysshe, 199, 208
"Some Psychical Consequences of the Anatomical Distinction Between the Sexes" (Freud), 130
Sophocles: Freud compared with, 118
"Star of Day" (H.D.), Part Three of *Hermetic Definition*, 146, 150
Stesichorus: and Helen, 60, 255
Stevens, Wallace, 75
Stowe, Harriet Beecher, 138
"Suffragette, The" (H.D.), 33–34
Swann, Thomas Burnett: on Achilles, 264
Swedenborg, Emanuel, 193
Swinburne, Algernon Charles: "Itylus" of, 43
Sword Went Out to Sea, The (H.D.), unpublished memoir, 28; on Bhaduri, 173; on the inner life, 178; on "Le Prince Lointain," 186–187; on a séance, 174, 175; on spiritualism, 199–200, 205

Tarot, 12, 74; H.D.'s interest in, 160–161, 176, 182, 184, 189–190, 197, 199, 201, 202; Chaboseau on, 171
Theocritus: translation of, by Pound, 2
Therapy and Technique (Freud), 54
Theresa, Saint: cult of, 172, 200, 201, 268
Theseus, 10; Freud as, 20, 66, 154, 291, 292, 294, 295
Thetis, mother of Achilles, 60, 230, 256, 258, 264, 267, 269, 278, 289, 290, 291, 294
Thoreau, Henry David: H.D. compared with, 23, 158
"Thorn Thicket" (H.D.): Dowding, 187–188

Thoth, Egyptian deity, 185; Freud as, 11; and language, 223, 249

Tighe, Mary: *Psyche* of, 10

Tiresias: in *The Waste Land*, 75

Totem and Taboo (Freud), 83

Tribute to Freud (H.D.), 7, 8, 9–11, 12, 14, 17, 20, 21, 22, 23, 24, 25, 26, 28, 29, 30, 31, 33, 37, 39, 46, 47, 48, 50, 51, 52, 53, 67, 68, 70, 73, 74, 75, 131, 132, 133, 134, 137, 138, 139, 140, 141, 153, 157, 158, 159, 160, 171, 175, 178, 185, 194, 195, 198, 199, 203–205, 256, 275

Tribute to the Angels (H.D.), Volume Two of *Trilogy*, 8, 77, 219, 229, 232, 245, 246, 249

Trilling, Lionel: on poetry and Freudian psychology, 55, 96

Trilogy (H.D.), 8, 10, 29, 47, 75–78, 88, 98, 101–114 *passim*, 138, 143, 146, 153, 202, 203–204, 229, 232, 243–253, 266, 269, 273, 274, 276, 278, 284, 293, 294

Tristan-Iseult myth: discussed by De Rougemont, 101–102, 191

Two Selves (Bryher), 35, 43, 129

Urzidil, Johannes: on poetry and magic, 223

Vale Ave, 45, 109, 111, 143–144, 187, 230

Van de Leeuw, J.J., doctor, patient of Freud, 19, 21–22; death of, 22, 27, 29–30

Van Eck, Peter, architect at Knossos, 131, 159, 166, 173, 187

Venus, 248–249

Victory, Wingless: in Corfu visions, 73; relation to Pallas Athena, 82

Wagner, Linda Welshimer, 265

Walls Do Not Fall, The (H.D.), Volume One of *Trilogy*, 76–77, 104–105, 213, 215–221, 246, 249

Waste Land, The (Eliot), 4, 10

Weigall, Arthur, writer on Christianity, 180, 266

White Rose and the Red (H.D.): and the Pre-Raphaelites, 187

Whitman, Walt, 208

Williams, William Carlos, 1, 140, 196; *Paterson* of, 4, 5, 10, 11, 67, 75, 201, 208, 209, 210, 211

Winter Love (H.D.), 8, 144, 273

Wirth, Oswald: on the Tarot, 189

Wolle, Helen. *See* Doolittle, Helen Wolle

Woolf, Virginia, 67, 141, 198; "Mr. Bennett and Mrs. Brown" of, 68; *A Room of One's Own* of, 68, 205; *To the Lighthouse* of, 68–69, 258

"Writing on the Wall" (H.D.), 20

Yeats, William Butler, 79; "Leda and the Swan" of, 210–211; and mysticism, 5, 160, 197, 200, 208, 210; and myth of Helen, 234

Yorke, Dorothy: affair with Aldington, 3, 27, 29, 37, 38

Zeus, 63, 145, 255, 277, 278; and the rape of Leda, 263, 268; transports Helen to Egypt, 60, 62

Zilboorg, Gregory: on Freud, 120

Zinzendorf, Count, 85; and the Moravian Church, 183; on love, 230

Zodiac, 161, 166, 168–169, 170, 184, 203–204, 246, 293